Psychology of Learner, Learning and Development

Psychology of Learner, Learning and Development

Ajaya Kumar Penthoi

SHIPRA

Rs. 995

ISBN: 978-81-7541-877-6

First Published in India in 2017

Psychology of Learner, Learning and Development

Published by:

SHIPRA PUBLICATIONS
LG 18-19, Pankaj Central Market,
I.P. Ext., Patparganj, Delhi 110092, India
Ph.:11- 47322068, 9650028065, 9810522367
info@shiprapublication.com
www.shiprapublication.com

the
of
s

Contents

1
Understanding Educational Psychology

Every individual is unique in his interest, attitude, thought and actions. He is a growing and development being. The needs and demands of an individual go on changing from time to time and from stage to stage. To have successful development of an individual keeping in pace with these changes, the teaching-learning process should be properly organized. In this direction, the knowledge of educational psychology provides immense help to the planners, educationists and teachers. Therefore it is essential to know the meaning, nature and scope of educational Psychology.

CONCEPT OF EDUCATIONAL PSYCHOLOGY

In order to understand the concept of Educational psychology, it is a need to understand both the meaning of education and psychology as Educational psychology is consisted of two words such as "Education" and "Psychology".

Meaning of Education

The derivative meaning of the term education explains that the word education has been derived from three different Latin words such as Educere, Educare and Educatum.

The word 'Educere' consists of two terms i.e. 'E' and 'Duco' E means out of and Duco means to lead or to develop. So Educere means leading the individual from the darkness to light or from ignorance to knowledge. Education is to develop the inner potentialities of an individual out of his body and mind.

The word 'Educare' means to take care of an individual of his education as he is a helpless, growing and developing being. So the elders and the experienced persons are to care or nourish the education of a child from his initial stage of life.

The word 'Educatum' means the act of teaching and training. A teacher or a trainer gives training to a child in order to develop his individuality.

The term education in its broad sense connotes, education is life and life is education and thus education is a life-long process. In narrower sense, education means school education and restricted to pupil-teacher relationship in the school.

Different individuals define the term education in different context. The philosophers have their unique definitions of education. After analysis of various definitions, it can be said that education means modification of or change of behaviour of an individual in a social desirable direction. This modification is the outcome of his experiences and learning. Through his education the individual changes his skills, attitudes, habits and adjust to his environment.

Meaning of Psychology

Initially, there was no separate subject as psychology. It was a part of the study of philosophy. Psychology was considered as mental philosophy. To acquire the present status it has undergone a conceptual evolution in course of time. Therefore to understand the meaning of psychology it is necessary to go through the history of the development of psychology.

Psychology as Science of Soul

The earliest definition of psychology was based on its etymological derivations. The word psychology is derived from two Greek words i.e. 'Psyche' and 'Logos'. Psyche means soul and logos means to study or science. So the word psychology means the science of soul or the study of soul. Such type of definition of the word psychology was supported by Descartes, Aristotle and Plato dating backs to 5th century B.C.

But this statement clarifying the meaning of the word psychology could not sustain for a long period of time due to the vague meaning of the term soul. Soul is something about which no particular meaning is found. It is an abstract idea and imaginary concept. No one has seen it, measured it and examined its nature and function.

Psychology as Science of Mind

Later psychology was defined as science of mind. Aristotle modified his former definition of psychology and emphasized on the study of mind.

Again, this statement "Psychology is a science of mind" could not clearly define the meaning of the term psychology because of the complex nature of mind. This meaning has been criticized that mind like soul is a complex phenomena and it is interpreted variedly by different psychologists. Mind is again invisible and abstract. Therefore scientific study of the mind is impossible.

Psychology as Science of Consciousness

Towards the last part of the 19th century, psychology was regarded as the study of consciousness. The school of structuralism supported it. The psychologists like William James and William Wundt defined psychology as a "Science of consciousness". Taking into the structure of mind the psychologists uphold the view that only conscious activities accounts for the function of an individual. But they neglected other structure of mind i.e. unconscious and subconscious structure of mid. The psychologists like Sigmund Freud opposed this meaning of the word psychology. Most of the activities are done by the individuals in his unconscious and subconscious conditions. Again, what is conscious activity for some body, it is unconscious for other. So this particular meaning about the term psychology becomes rejected.

Psychology as Science of Behaviour

This is the modern and widely accepted definition of psychology. In the beginning of the 20th century, psychology took a scientific shape. American psychologist Watson defined psychology as "Positive Science of behaviour". Compared to other meaning of the word Psychology stated earlier, it became more popular and accepted more till now.

A number of psychologists like Pillsbury, Mc Dougall, Munn and Woodworth popularized 'behaviour' as the subject matter of psychology.

Concept of Behaviour: The term behaviour is widely used in psychology. The term behaviour means the activities of an individual including both of his internal and external activities. Internal activities are the result of the functioning of one's mind which includes his thinking, reasoning, creativity, attitude, emotions, and intelligence. An individual before displaying his external activities, he does his internal activities in his mind. The bodily actions what are seen in an individual are called as external activities. So these external and internal activities constitute ones behaviour.

One's behaviour is seen to be changed and modified as per the time, need, situation and goals of the life. So behaviour is a dynamic concept. It is modifiable, changeable and controllable depending upon the individuals learning and his education.

Explaining the term behaviour Watson stated a formula that behaviour is the resultant effect of an individual's interaction in his environment. Symbolically he mentioned the formula as:

$$B = F(O \times E)$$

B Means Behaviour
F Means Function
O Means Organism and
E Means environment

So, behaviour is the product of the function of the organism in its environment

In winder sense, the term behaviour includes:

(a) All the activities of human life i.e., motor activities and cognitive activities
(b) Behaviour of all living organism i.e. human beings and animals. In psychology we study the behaviour of all human beings such as children, and adults—Normal and Abnormal

Definitions of Psychology

It is essential to study some of the definitions of the term psychology in order to understand its meaning.

Watson defines, "psychology as science of human as well as animal behaviour."

N.L. Munn states, "Psychology today concerns itself with the scientific investigation of behaviour"

Woodworth and Marquis say, "Psychology is the scientific study of activities of the individual in relation to his environment."

Bertrand Russell defines, "Psychology gives scientific analysis of the working of human mind."

Murphy defines, "Psychology is the Science that studies the responses which the living individuals make to their environment."

Ross says, "Psychology is the explanation of behaviour in mental psychical terms."

James Drever defines, "Psychology as a positive science which studies the behaviour of men and animals so for as that behaviour is regarded as an expression of that inner life of through and feelings which we call mental life."

Woods worth states, "Psychology is the study of mental life."

Crow and Crow define, "Psychology is the study of human behaviour and human relationship."

TYPES OF PSYCHOLOGY

In order to understand the meaning of psychology, it is also need to know about types of psychology. Broadly there are two types of psychology i.e. pure psychology and applied psychology.

Pure Psychology

Pure Psychology states about the laws and principles governing the behaviour of an organism. It deals with the theories of behaviour. It is called pure psychology because other branches of Psychology apply its major principles to understand the behaviour. This branch of psychology is studied for the sake of acquiring knowledge. Different branches of pure psychology are discussed below.

Child Psychology: Child psychology deals with the study of the behaviour of a child. The mind of a child is different from an adult individual. His intelligence, attitude, emotion stinking, reasoning, creativity etc. is not same as it is found in case of an adult individual. There in child psychology, children's behaviour is studied.

Adult Psychology: This branch of psychology deals with the behaviour of adults. Adults are different from children in their behaviour and adjustment. They are having higher mental developments than the children.

Social Psychology: This branch of psychology deals with individual's relationship with other individuals in the society. It studies how an individual's behaviour operates in the group and society.

Abnormal Psychology: Normal individuals behave normally. But there are some individuals who behave in a different way from the rest under similar conditions. Such individuals are referred as abnormal individuals. They require special treatment and special attention. Abnormal psychology studies mental disorders of all types, their causes and remedy.

Comparative Psychology: Comparative psychology is also called as Animal psychology. There the psychologists compare the behaviour of animals and derives some conclusion. In this branch, animal's behaviour is studied and then compared with the human behaviour.

Genetic Psychology: Genetic psychology is also called as developmental psychology. It studies the behaviour as it develops from birth through different stages of life such as infancy, childhood, adolescence and to an old age. In these branches, the influences of heredity are discussed in detail. Heredity is a biological process in which parental characteristics are transferred to their offspring's. Therefore it is necessary to know the ancestors in order to study the child's behaviour.

Experimental Psychology: In this branch of psychology, the psychologists conduct different experiments under controlled and scientific conditions to understand the functioning of mental process of human being. Learning, intelligence, attention, creativity, memory etc can be studies using the experimental psychology.

Para Psychology: This is a new branch of psychology. This branch of psychology studies the super conscious mind of the individual. It studies what happens to the soul after the death of the individual. It also studies, how a man perceives things in his closed eyes and how the soul of the individual operates.

Physiological Psychology: In this branch of psychology, the nerve systems, muscles, sense organs and the tissues are studied. Physiology of an individual has its effect on his mental process. So the physiological psychology studies the effect of the physiology of an individual on his behaviour. It describes how the physiological structure of an individual and his nerve system influences his behaviour

Applied Psychology

Applied psychology is a type of psychology which applies the major principles, theories and laws to the respective fields of studies. Knowledge of pure branches of psychology is applied in some practical fields.

Applied psychology can be of different types which are described below:

Criminal Psychology: Criminals are different from normal individuals in their behaviour. This branch of psychology deals with the criminal behaviour. It has strengthened the movement for establishing juvenile courts, reception homes, guidance clinics and training schools.

Clinical Psychology: Clinical psychology deals with the study of the behaviour of the client or patient. Psychologists generally use the knowledge of clinical psychology to diagnose the behaviour of their clients or patients. It is used by the medical practitioners for therapeutic purposes. This branch of psychology also deals with the problems of human adjustment. It studies the behaviour of problem children and tries to find out their solution.

Industrial Psychology: When psychology is applied to the field of industry to study the behaviour of the industrial workers then it is called as Industrial psychology. The workers working in the industries differ in their attitude, intelligence, personality, creativity, emotions thinking and reasoning etc. and thus their behaviour is different from others. So, Industrial psychology is used to study the behaviour of industrial workers. In this branch, the psychologists deal with the problems of personnel selection, training, and measurement of the efficiency of the industrial personnel's.

Educational Psychology: Educational psychology is called as an applied psychology because it applies the knowledge of psychology to the field of education. Education being a vast field involves various activities like teaching and learning. Educational psychology studies the behaviour of the learners in the field of education.

MEANING OF EDUCATIONAL PSYCHOLOGY

It is clear from the above discussions that education means the modification of behaviour of an individual and psychology means the study of the behaviour of individual. As the term educational psychology consists of these two words i.e. 'Education' and 'Psychology' so the term Educational Psychology means the study of the modification of behaviour in the field of education. It tells how children learn and what factors contribute to the effective learning of the learner.

The subject, educational psychology has a long history of its development. The then philosophers and psychologists like Aristotle, Plato, Rousseau, Pestalozzi, Herbert, Froebel, Galton, Ebbinghaus, Stanley Hall, William James, Alfred Binet, Sigmund Freud, Thorndike, Pavlov, Wechsler, G.W. Allport, L.M. Terman, Stern, B.F. Skinner, C.H. Judd, Watson, and Gestalt Psychologists' etc. have contributed a lot to the field of educational psychology for its development.

Definition of Educational Psychology

To have better understanding of the meaning of the term educational psychology the following definitions may be referred:

Crow & Crow defines, "Educational psychology describes and explains the learning experiences of an individual from birth through old age."

C.E. Skinner says, "Educational psychology is that branches of psychology which deals with teaching and learning."

Peel E.A. states, "Educational psychology is the science of education".

D.P. Ansubel describes, "Educational psychology is that branch, special branch of psychology, concerned with the nature, conditions outcomes, and evaluation of school learning and retention."

J.A. Stephen states, "Educational psychology is an organized study of educational enhancement.

Gates and other define, "Educational Psychology is the uses of principal and conclusions of psychology in the field of education."

Nature of Educational Psychology

The study of the nature of educational psychology also helps to know the meaning of the term educational psychology. Educational psychology has the following natures:

Educational Psychology is a Science: Educational psychology is treated as a science because it adopts scientific methods to deal with the educational problems. Like the subject of sciences, it employees the scientific steps such as formulation of hypothesis, collection of data, analysis and synthesis of data and interpretation of data in solving educational problems.

Educational Psychology is an Applied Science: Educational psychology is called as an applied science because the psychological principles and laws are applied to the field of education. The knowledge of psychology is applied to study the educational behaviour of the learners.

Educational Psychology is a growing and developing science: It is called as a growing and developing science because it is still in the process of development. Many new things are expected relating to the process of teaching and learning out of the researches in this field.

Educational Psychology is a social science: Educational psychology is called as a social science because it studies human behaviour in relation to the educational setup in the society. The behaviour of an individual in connection to the field of education in different stages i.e. primary, secondary and higher levels are studied within the frame work of the society.

Educational Psychology as a positive science: Educational psychology is called as a positive science but not a normative science because it studies the behaviour of the individual and deals the educational problems as they are. It does not state what ought to be like philosophical studies.

SCOPE OF EDUCATIONAL PSYCHOLOGY

It is discussed earlier that educational psychology applies principles of psychology to the field of education. The field of education is very vast. It includes the entire process of teaching and learning both in formal, informal and no-formal settings including primary, secondary and higher education run through school, colleges and universities. Hence the scope of educational psychology is very wide pervasive. But for the sake of convenience we can delimit the study of educational psychology into five major areas, where educational psychology plays its significant role. The areas are mentioned below.

The Learner

In the whole process of education, the learner occupies the central position. Learner means the child who learns. Today, the entire process of education has been child entered which means that before going to discuss about different aspects of education like aims of education, curriculum, methods of teaching and instruction and the evaluation procedure etc. it is necessary to study the condition or background of the learners. Studying the conditions or background of the learner means knowing his age, intelligence, attitude, interest, ability, efficiencies etc. Learners differ from one to another in the matter of their growth and development of their abilities and interests. While considering about the planning of different aspects of education such as aims of education, curriculum, methods of teaching and learning, evaluation procedure etc. for different stages of education, it is need to know the learner. Educational psychology helps a lot in this direction. That is why; the study of the learner contributes a major area of educational psychology.

The Learning Experiences

After knowing the learner, it is next to set the learning experiences for the education of the learner. Learning experiences means the body of knowledge required for the education and learning of the learner. It requires framing curriculum. As learners differ from one to another in their abilities and efficiencies as per their age, and growth and development, the planning of the curriculum should also differ at different stages of education. The study of educational psychology also covers this area and provides necessary guidance about the determination of learning experiences.

The Learning Process

After deciding the learner and learning experiences, it is next to decide about the learning process. It is an important area of educational psychology. In this area, the major principles and theories of learning, memory, thinking, and reasoning problem solving etc. are discussed. This area of educational psychology mainly deals with how learning takes place, what is the nature of learning? And what are the conditions for the effective learning?

The Learning Situation

Learning situation means the aids and environment where the learner learns. This area of educational psychology discusses about the pupil-teacher interaction, class room climate, school environment, group dynamics, guidance and counseling, evaluation process and various aids which facilitate learning of the learners. This area of educational psychology specifically describes the contents, quality and the structure of the educational situations—formal, informal and non-formal.

The Teacher

It is one of the important areas of educational psychology. Teacher is one who guides, teaches, facilitates and counsells the learners to learn in an effective way. Teacher training has its direct link with the learner's learning. Therefore a teacher occupies an important place in the whole process of education. A teacher should know about himself before going to teach. It means that a teacher should know his limitations, ability, intelligence, aspirations, conflicts, and adjustment etc. this area of educational psychology tries to make a teacher successful and effective.

APPLICATIONS OF EDUCATIONAL PSYCHOLOGY IN THE FIELD OF EDUCATION

The study of educational psychology has a lot of contributions to the field of education. A teacher benefits himself and applies the knowledge of educational psychology in the following under mention purposes.

Understanding the Learner: Educational psychology helps a teacher to understand the developmental features of the learner like his intelligence, attitude, aptitude, interest, emotions, motivation, age, creativity and thanking etc at different stage of growth and development. Such knowledge helps a teacher to plan for the education and learning of the learner.

Understanding the Learning Process: Educational psychology helps a teacher to understand the processes of learning and accordingly plans for the effective learning of the learners.

Understanding Individual Difference: Every individual is unique in his body, mind and spirit. So individuals differ from one to another in different aspects. The study of educational psychology helps a teacher to understand it and advise separate learning strategies for their development.

Preparing Curriculum: The study of educational psychology helps a teacher to prepare curriculum for the learners. Curriculum means organized learning experiences to be set for the purpose of teaching and learning. It requires systematic organization of the syllabus and study materials keeping in view of the levels of growth and development of the learner. Children differ from class to class in their physical and mental dimension, so the curriculum should differ accordingly. Educational psychology provides guidance in the direction of planning and construction of curriculum.

Understanding Group Dynamics: The individual is not at all complete in himself. He has to share with his fellow beings as he is a social being. He interacts with the group for the fulfillment of his needs and desires. In the classroom context, learners part among themselves in learning and share their view in the group. The study of educational psychology helps a teacher to understand the nature of group dynamics and profitably use it for classroom learning.

Providing Guidance and Counseling: In the pace of learning, all learners do not learn at the same rate. Some feel difficulties in their learning and some feel easy. It is the duty of a teacher to help all the learners in their learning and development. Hence, the study of educational psychology helps a teacher to provide guidance and counseling to the needy students in the path of their development and learning.

Helping in Evaluation and Assessment: After providing instruction a teacher wants to measure his learner's performances. Measuring the performance of the learners is not an easy task. It requires understanding of the evaluation and assessment procedures. Educational psychology also helps a teacher in this direction.

Dealing the Special Learners: Intellectually, all learners do not possess the same quantity of intelligence. Accordingly, they differ in their development and learning. In the pace of learning some are found gifted and some are found backward and slow. A teacher has to deal all these learners and aim for their maximum development. The study of educational psychology helps a teacher to handle these children effectively.

Understanding the Mental Health and Adjustment: As has been discussed earlier, individuals differ from one to another in many ways. In the process of learning it is found that some children posses good mental health and well adjust to the learning situations and some are found deviated and do not get adjusted the same. The study of educational psychology helps a teacher to acquire the knowledge of mental hygiene and preventing maladjustment problems in the learners.

Selecting Methodology of Teaching and Instruction: Effective learning depends on effective teaching of the teacher. A teacher should have aim of helping the learners to learn effectively. It needs the selection of appropriate methods of teaching and instruction. Educational psychology helps a teacher in this matter.

Helping in Research: Educational psychology also helps a teacher in conducting researches in the field of education. Burning classroom problems relating to the teaching and learning are studied and generalizations are made on the basis of the researches.

Selecting Goals of Learning: The aim of education is to bring all round development of the learners in the social desirable manner. Therefore teaching objectives are set at different levels of education. A teacher should have to select these goals of learning depending on the growth and developmental characteristics of the learners and accordingly provide instruction for the achievement of the same.

Knowing the Teacher himself: Educational psychology helps a teacher to know himself, his abilities and disabilities, his limitations and possibilities, and prepare him to be an effective teacher and beneficial for the learners.

2
Methods Used in Educational Psychology

The main objective of educational psychology is to develop skills and competencies in the prospective teachers to understand, control and predict the behaviour of the learners in the process of teaching and learning. While dealing with the teaching-learning process, the teacher encounters certain behavioural problem of the learners. In order to study the behavioural problem of the learners, the teacher requires collecting data by employing various methods. Therefore it is essential to discuss about the methods used in educational psychology.

CLASSIFICATION OF METHODS

Methods used in the field of educational psychology can be classified into the following two categories such as the Subjective methods and Objective methods.

Methods of Education Psychology

1. Subjective Methods   2. Objective Methods

Subjective Methods

Subjective methods are those in which the subject under study plays a prime role. The role of external force is secondary and unimportant. Statistical analysis is not possible in case of subjective methods.

The following two types of methods are used in subjective methods.

Introspection Method: Introspection method is one of the oldest method and dating back to Vedic period. Indian Rishis and philosophers used this method for discovery of truth.

The word introspection is composed of two words such as 'intro' and 'spection'. 'Intro' means within and 'spection' means looking. Thus the word introspection means looking within one self. It also means self-observation, i.e. observation by an individual of his own inner actions of mind through imagination, feelings, mediations and memories. In this method, the subject/individual observes, analyses and reports his own inner state of mind. To have this method, the individual require developing higher state of mind.

Advantages

- Introspection method is readily available and can be used by anybody at any time.
- It is does not require any laboratory, so it is economical.
- It develops concentration power of an individual.

Disadvantages

- This method can't be used by ordinary individuals. The individual having higher mental development can use it.
- Children and abnormal persons can't use this method.
- It suffers from subjectivity. It can't be verified by others.
- Mind is dynamic. Hence it is difficult to introspect it properly.
- The psycho-analysts reject this method because it fails to study the conscious and unconscious part of the mind.

***Anecdotal Method*:** In anecdotal method, the subject narrates his significant event of his life and the psychologist notes down every details being narrated by the individual and finally comes to his conclusion on the basis of the analysis chart.

Advantages

- This method is economical.
- This method is easy to use.

Disadvantage

- This method lacks validity and reliability.
- Empirical analysis of data is not possible in this method.
- In this method, the subject may add or hide something according to his own wish.

Objective Methods

Objective methods are those in which the subject under study plays secondary role and the internal force plays a prime role. Statistical analysis of data is possible in case of objective methods.

The following are the different categories of Objective methods.

***Observation Method*:** Observation method is one of the important methods of educational psychology. It is also a popular method of collecting data. In this method, the behaviour of an individual is observed by another one. The behaviour observed may be expressed in the form of speech, gestures and bodily changes. Through observation, the overt behaviour of an individual is observed in an appropriate situation which provides a clue to know his covert behaviour.

Depending on the nature or purpose of the study, observation may be the following types:

Natural observation: Natural observation is also called as uncontrolled observation. This method is used to observe the specific behavioural characteristics of children or adult in a natural setting. The subject under study is not aware that he is being observed by somebody else. For example, a teacher can have natural observation of the behaviour of the learners in the playground, library, classrooms etc.

Controlled observation: This type of observation is well planned and controlled. This type of observation is done under controlled. This type of observation is done under controlled conditions by the observer. The artificial situation is created by an observer to observe the specific behaviour of the learners. This is generally made by trained psychologists; various devices are used to make this observation objective, and reliable.

Participant observation: In participant observation, the observer becomes more or less a member of the group under observation and shares the situation as a stranger, an attentive listener, or a complete participant observer. He keeps perfect rapport with the group of children or adults so that they may not become conscious of his presence and behave in a natural manner.

Non-participant observation: Non-participant observation is used for infants and abnormal persons. In the method, the observer does not participate in the group and takes a position at a place where his presence is least disturbing to the group and observes the behaviour of subjects under study. It helps to record large quantities.

Advantages

- Observation method is simple to use and it requires less training.
- It is purposive
- It helps in studying the behaviour of children, adults, animals and abnormal persons.
- It helps in studying a large number of people at a time.
- Statistical analysis of data is possible.

Disadvantages

- It is subjective in nature. The result of the observation may vary from time to time. Observation method of individual characteristics may differ from place to place, person to person and from time to time.
- Observation method does not directly help to know the covert behaviour of the individuals it is used only to observe overt behaviours'.
- Sometime the subjects under study inhibit their natural behaviour and plays artificial behaviour when they become aware of the fact that they are being observed.
- Subjectivity of the interpretation: the observer may be biased in his interpretation by his liking, disliking and values, impressions, and prejudices.
- It is labourious and time consuming.

Interview Method: In interview method, the interviewer comes to a face to face contact with the subject. He asks a number of questions during the interview and records them carefully. Data being collected through interview method can be statistically analyzed and interpreted.

Advantages

- It helps to establish a good rapport with the interviewee.
- It helps to know a great deal about the subject.
- It enables the psychologists to give proper guidance to the child.

Disadvantages

- This method is time consuming and labourious.
- It also suffers from the subjectivity of the data interpretation.

Questionnaire Method: Questionnaire consists of a series of questions printed on a sheet with a proper sequence so as to be asked to the individuals under study and collect the required data. Most of the questions relates to the personality problem of children, general problems of the children and some specific problems to which children face.

Advantages

- It can be applied on a large sample at a time.
- It is objective.
- It helps in statistically analysis of data

Disadvantage

- It can't be applied to all, only the literates can answer the questionnaire.
- Sometimes the respondent gives the wrong answer intentionally which influence the purpose of the study.
- Some respondents misunderstand the equation and fail to give right answer to the question.

Case History Method: Case history method is also called as clinical method. It is primarily used to collect the details information on the behaviour problem of maladjusted and deviant classes. The main purpose of this method is to study individual case a cases of group to detect and diagnose their specific problems and to suggest therapeutic measures to rehabilitate them in their environment. This method is popularly used by psychiatrists, Psychologists and guidance workers in child guidance clinics and mental hygiene centers. This method is used to understand the causes and sources of individuals fear, anxiety, worries, obsessions and his personal, social, educational and vocational maladjustments.

In this method, all possible details about the case are collected from different sources like the case himself, parents, family members, friends, his teachers, classmates, pear groups and neighbours.

This method utilizes various techniques to compile relevant information which has direct or indirect bearing on the specific problem of the case such as observation, interviews, medical examination, sociometry, questionnaire, checklists and some testing techniques such as test of intelligence personality, aptitude, interest, and attitude.

In case of studying the cases of the group having some common problem there can be use of two approaches such as; longitudinal approach and cross-sectional approach to collect the data.

Longitudinal Approach: In this method, the group is studied by the same investigator for a long period of time to study the developmental characteristics of the problem. This technique is much beneficial to study the physical, mental, language, interest, emotional and social developmental characteristics of children. But this method is labourious and time consuming.

Cross-sectional Approach: In this method, a cross section of the sample (the group) is studied simultaneously by the investigator; a number of children of similar age having common problems are studied at a time to draw a generalization about the group.

Advantages

- It helps in getting the detailed information about the case.
- It helps in rehabilitating the maladjusted individuals.
- It helps generalization of the problem.

Disadvantages

- It is expensive and time consuming.
- It is labourious.
- It depends on other methods to collect required data and it is not sufficient itself.
- The interpretation of the result may be biased and subjective.
- Information's collected from different sources may not be true and thus influences the motive of this method.

Experimental Method: Experimental method is the most reliable and scientific method of educational psychology. It is a special form of observation. In this method the subject under study is controlled in a psychological laboratory to study the problem.

The development of this method in psychology is of very recent origin. Wilhelm Wundt, a German psychologists opened the first psychological laboratory at Leipzig in 1879 and thus led the foundation of experimental method in psychology.

Experimental method helps the experimenter to study a psychological problem under the desired condition which can be altered according to his requirements. In this method all conditions or variables affecting the behaviour under study are kept constant or controlled. Only one single specific condition is changed deliberately to observe its effect on the behaviour. This specific condition or variable is called as 'independent' variable. Any change in the independent variable causes a change in the second variable which is called as dependent variable. For example we are interested to study the influence of sounds on the learning and achievement of a group of students. Thus there are two variables like sounds and learning and achievement. Therefore sounds will be the independent variable and learning and achievement will be the dependent variable. All other conditions like sitting arrangements, ventilation and lighting will be kept constant in the classroom. Only the gravity of the sound would be varied from time to time.

In an experiment, both the subjects (Students) and the experimenter work with close two groups, i.e. one control group and an experimental group if there is only one independent variable. In case of more than one independent variable, there may be one control group and as many experimental groups as the independent variables. The performance of the experimental groups is compared with that of the control group to see the effect of independent variable on the dependent variable. Subject in the control group do not get any extra treatment form the experimenter. But the experimental group receives extra treatment from the experimenter according to his requirement.

Experimental method follows all the steps of scientific method. The steps followed in the experimental method are:

1. Selecting a problem.
2. Formulating hypothesis.
3. Selecting a design.
4. Conducting the experiment.
5. Analyzing the result and verifying the hypothesis.

Experimental Design: Experimental design depends on the number of groups involved in an experiment. The number of groups may be varying from one to many depending on the nature of the problem and the number of variables. The followings are some designs commonly used in researches.

Single Group Design: In this design the experimenter tests or studies on some particular aspect of behaviour and then gives special treatment to the same group according to his set objectives. Then he gives special treatment to the same group and tests them after some time. He statistically analyses the data and calculates the difference between the pre-test and post-test results of the group. For example, the experimenter wants to study the effect of use of Audio-Visual aids in teaching. Then before teaching with Audio-Visual aids, we have to test the group and record their achievement/ result. Then the group will be taught with Audio-Visual aids for one month besides the normal teaching. After this again we will test the same group. It the performance or achievement in the second test is better; we can conclude that teaching with Audio-Visual aids has some positive effect on teaching.

(Group) ———	(Pretest) -	(Treatment) -	(Post Test)
	T1	(Teaching with AV aids)	T2

Equivalent Groups Design: Equivalent group design also called as two group design where the investigator uses two parallel groups or equivalent groups to study the effect of an independent variable on some dependent variable.

One group is called as control group and another is called as experimental group. The experimental group is given special treatment (independent variable) where as the control group is not given any sort of special treatment. Then both the groups are tested finally and their results are compared to study the effect of the special treatment (independent variable) and accordingly conclusions are drawn.

Diagrammatically the equivalent group design can be expressed as:

Group	Pre-test	Treatment (Independent Variable)	Post-Test
Control	T1	Not-Given	T2
Experimental	T1	Given	T2

Multi Group Design: Sometimes the experimenter wants to study the effect of one variable on a number of groups or the effect of many variables on many groups. In such situations, he adopts this multi groups design. To compare the result, higher order of statistics like ANOVA (Analysis of variance) is used. In this design, there can be one control group and as many as experimental groups according to the number of independent variables used in the study. It is also called as factorial design.

Diagrammatically this design is expressed as—

Groups	X	Ind. Variables	X	Dep. Variables
3	X	2	X	2
4	X	2	X	2

Advantages

- Findings of the experimental method are verifiable
- It gives objective, precise and reliable information about the problem.
- It is systematic and scientific one.
- It helps in better prediction of the result.

Disadvantages

- It can't be used in all circumstances
- It is labourious and time consuming.
- It is not economical as it needs a good deal of apparatus.
- Untrained teachers can't use this method.
- Experimental data can't provide insight into the covert behaviour of children.
- This method fails to study the entire drives and feelings of the children.
- All problems of educational psychology can't be studied by this method.

Psycho-Analytic Method: This method was developed by Sigmund Freud. According to this method, the psychologists try to probe into the unconscious level of the mind of the subject. Efforts are made to locate the repressed wishes and impulses of the individuals mind which stay at the unconscious level. After locating them, the psychologist prescribes measures and re-educate the subject to bring him to his normal life. Different types of psycho-analysis method are:

Hypnotism: In this method, the subject is induced to an artificial sleep with comfortable way. After sometimes, the subject feels comfortable and forgets the present. In this stage the psycho-analyst asks some simple questions about his emotional life and the subject discloses some unfulfilled desires at his unconscious level. Then the psychologist tries to cure the subject by providing right type of remedial measures.

Free Association Method: In this method the subject / patient is asked to sit in a comfortable chair. A piece of cloth is tied around his eyes. Thus he is kept away from the objects of the world. Then the subject is asked to tell about his emotional problems. All the responses are noted down and later on analyzed. This analysis reveals hidden events connected with the emotional life of the subject. Then the subject is given education to be cured and leads a normal life.

Analysis of Dreams: The unsatisfied desires are suppressed by the subject at his conscious level and go to the unconscious level. The subject finds these desires fulfilled in his dreams. These dreams are recorded, analyzed, interpreted and the cause of mental disorder is located and then treatment is provided to the subject to become normal.

Word Association Method: There are some important words like love, hate etc. which are closely connected to our emotional life. Jung on the basis of the above approach prepared a list of one hundred words which are connected with our emotional life and problems.

The psycho-analyst mentions these words one by one and the subject is allowed to give one response only for each word. All the responses are noted down and analyzed by comparing them with the key prepared by Jung. It helps to locate the specific mental disorder o the subject and then possible remedies are provided to bring the subject into normal life.

Advantage

- It is helpful for the treatment of abnormal individuals.
- It is individualistic in its approach and thus gives good result.
- It is clinical and
- It is useful to rehabilitate the mentally disorder individuals.

Disadvantage

- It is time consuming and labourious.
- It is not economical.
- It is not applicable for the normal individuals.

Socio-metric Method: The socio-metric method has gained its popularity because of the structure of the group is studied and the status of each individual in the group is measured. It covers all the members of the group. Each member describes his personal acceptance or rejection of the various members of the group for some particular activity.

Socio-metric method is of great value in school situations. It helps to locate the most social and the socially isolated children in the school. It helps to develop better social cohesion among the children. Therefore the teacher should carefully. Handle this method.

Survey Method: It is the most common method used in educational psychology. It is useful to study the local, national, and international aspect of education. It help in solving significant educational and psychological problems. Survey method involves all the activities of collection of data, comparison, measurement, classification, Evaluation and generalization. It makes use of various techniques in the collection of data such as tests, questionnaire, observation, interview and statistical analysis of data. Quantitative and qualitative analysis of data is possible in case of survey method.

There are three broad types of survey method which share common features of carrying out their observation on samples of individuals which are regarded as representative of the larger population to which they belong.

The Field Study: It is conducted in natural classroom teaching-learning situations spread over a wide area. For developing Programmed material for a particular class in a particular subject, this field method of survey can be used.

The programmed material at its initial stage is tested on individual and small group of students for whom it is developed after two try-outs it may be tried out in actual classroom situation for final validation. This is called as the field try-out. Experiments on micro-teaching and interaction analysis are the examples of field studies.

Developmental Survey: Development studies may be longitudinal or cross-sectional. In developmental surveys the typical pattern of change in the growth and decline of behaviour over a specific period of life span of a group or whole population is studied for example, the development of intelligence in culturally disadvantaged children from birth to five years may be studied using the longitudinal or cross sectional method of study.

Differential Survey: In this method, attempt is made to establish a typical difference between the groups of individuals for example; we can study the difference in intelligence between boys and girls. In this method the difference or similarities in two sets of variable are obtained.

Advantages

- Its scope is very wide. A large number of individuals can be studies at a particular time.
- Statistical analysis can be employed.
- It helps to do both the quantitative and qualitative analysis of data.
- The results of this method are more reliable and valid.

Disadvantages

- It is labourious and expensive.
- It is time consuming.
- Improper selection of sample lead to invalid results.
- This method requires trained and experienced investigators. Everybody cannot handle this method.

Comparative Method: A comparative study of the individual in relation to other individual helps in understanding them better. In this method the behaviour of two individuals are compared to see any differences or similarities on some particular problem.

This method is of great value to understand the instinctive behaviour of children.

Statistical Method: Statistical method is not an independent method. It is treated as a co-method helping to other methods. Statistical method helps in precision of the data and drawing valid conclusion about the problem. Statistical analysis includes various techniques i.e., calculation of mean, percentage, standard deviation, t test and correlation etc. to determine the inter-relationship and clarifying their meaning. Statistical method makes the study reliable and valid and also it increases authenticity of the problem.

Advantages

- It increases accuracy of the study.
- It makes the study more valid.
- It makes the interpretation easy.

Disadvantages

- All can't use this method. Only those having mathematical knowledge can use this method.
- It does not help in qualitative analysis of the data.

3
Schools of Psychology

The study of psychology has not developed into its present status all of a sudden. It has passed through different ages and gradually it has become now a science. The evolution of the study of psychology experiences different systems which defined psychology in different ways. Study of these systems will contribute to know various aspects of psychology.

Since the inception of the subject of psychology, different psychologists interpreted their studies in different ways having no common agreement. Therefore there was an attempt to organise these isolated bits into a group of similar studies. Such an attempt leads to function of the different schools of psychology. However, all schools are inter-related and have an impact on each other.

From the development point of view all the schools of psychology should be studied as follows.

STRUCTURALISM

Structuralism as a school of psychology came into existence with the establishment of the psychological labouratory in Leipzig of Germany in the year 1879. The psychologist Wundt was its founder. Wundt tried to understand the structure of the mind and developed his own system of psychology.

E.B. Titchener of U.S.A. the student of Wundt supported this school and emphasized the importance of consciousness as the subject matter of psychology. This school analyzed the mental components like sensation, imagery, feelings etc. just as a matter is divided into its different component in chemistry.

The school of structuralism adopted Experimental method, and Introspection method to study the mind. The sensation, images, feelings constituted the subject matter of the study of this school.

Contributions: Structuralism school has contributed to the field of psychology a lot. It gave a scientific approach to psychology and influenced educational psychology. It highlighted the experimental method in educational psychology.

Criticism: In spite of its valuable contributions, this school of psychology 'structuralism' was severely criticized as it laid too much stress on the introspection method. It neglected other aspects.

FUNCTIONALISM

Functionalism as a school of psychology took its birth in America opposed to the structuralism. The main protagonists of this school were the pragmatic philosopher John Dewey and James R. Angle. The supporters of this school are William James, H.A. Carr, E.L. Thorndike and R.S. Woodworth.

Functionalists stated that psychology should study human abilities and capacities. The existing process o the mind is not important rather its function is more important. So they stress on the dynamism of consciousness. Their attention was on the functions of consciousness.

John Dewey established functional psychology at Chicago University in 1896 and contributed a lot to the field of educational psychology and education. His book "How we think" is a landmark in the field of educational psychology. His analysis of thinking process is a great contribution to the field of education. John Dewey tried to establish an adjustment between the psychological activities and the atmosphere.

James R Angle being considered as the profounder of the school of functionalism tried to investigate the working of the mental process and stated that mental processes enable the individual to solve their future problems as well.

A.A. Carr supporting the school of functionalism said that functionalism examines the content of a situation from all angles. The individual tries to adjust himself according to them. The individual becomes mentally prepared to mentally solve his problems. In this way Carr emphasized conformation of behaviour. This conformation is not structural but a functional aspect of mental activity. Carr described mental activity as psycho-physical.

E.L. Thorndike and R.S. Woodworth supporting the school of functionalism emphasized the role of motivation in learning and behaviour.

Functionalists adopted the method of experiment in their studies. The present schools of psychology support more and less the principle of functional psychology

Contributions: Functionalism contributed to the field of education in the following ways:

1. Creating a healthy atmosphere in the school.
2. Stressed on learning by doing method in education and child contrived curriculum.
3. Creating utility-centered curriculum and community centered curium.
4. Emphasis on democracy in education.
5. Emphasis on the worth of the individual.
6. Realized the importance of mental testing.
7. Use of project method of teaching.
8. Importance of scientific enquiry in education.

BEHAVIOURISM

Behaviourism as a school of psychology dominated the school of structuralism and functionalism. J.B. Watson, (John Broadus Watson) an American Psychologist is known as the founder of this school. In 1914 he wrote a book" Behaviour, An introduction to comparative psychology" which envisages his behaviouristic ideas and thoughts.

The other psychologists who supported the school of behaviourism were William James, Evan Pavlov, B.F. Skinner, Tollman, C.L. Hull, E.L. Thorndike, E.R. Guthrie and Bechtervene.

William James emphasized the physical activities of the individual and the resultant human behaviour.

Evan Pavlov highlighted the natural reflexes resulting natural reflexes actions and the effect of external stimulus resulting in conditioned reflex action.

B.F. Skinner gave importance to operant conditioning in learning and led to the development of teaching machines and programmed learning.

Tollman emphasized on purposive and goal learning.

C.L. Hall viewed about the quantitative natural learning and emphasized on three types of variables-independent, dependent and intervening variables.

E.L. Thorndike experimented on the principle of "Trial and error" in learning and emphasized the law of motivation, Law of exercise and law of effect in learning.

E.R. Guthrie advocated an extreme form of connectionism between a stimulus and the resultant behaviour. When that stimulus is presented, the same type of behaviour takes place.

Bachtervene, the Russian psychologist carrying experiments on motor reflexes both of human being and animals located some causes of mental diseases.

All these behaviourists contributed a lot to the field of education and learning and greatly influenced the field of educational psychology.

Metnod Adopted

Behaviourism adopted observation method, testing, conditioned reflex Techniques and experimental method in item studies. The main subject matter o the study of the school of behaviourism was to know the effect of environment on the behaviour.

Contributions: The school of behaviourism contributed to the field of educational psychology and education in the following aspects:

1. Developing the psychology of learning and motivation.
2. Developing programmed learning as a new methodology of teaching.
3. Highlighting the importance of environment in learning and growth and development o a chilled.
4. Solving the problems of education of maladjusted children by suggesting remedial measures.
5. Giving stress to the study of mental processes in place of the study of emotions and mental structures.
6. Stressing on the use of experiment methods in researches and education.

PSYCHOANALYSIS

The school of psychoanalysis is considered as a New Approach to psychology and education. The Austrian Medical Practitioner, Sigmund Friend (1856-1939) is called as the father of this school. His followers like Alfred Adler (1872-1937) and Carl Jung (1875) renamed this psychology as "individual psychology" and "Analytical Psychology" respectively.

The school of psychoanalysis revolts against structuralism, functionalism and Gestalt school on the ground that these schools are abstract and intellectualistic dealing with surface mental phenomena like perception, sensation, thinking and learning. But psychoanalytic school deals mostly with motives and their conflicts in the shape of urges, instincts, desires, repressions and resistance. Freud gave the concept of unconsciousness which has significant influence on thoughts, feelings and actins of human beings.

The subject matter of the study of this school is human motive and instincts. Psychoanalysis school adopted clinical and case study method in its study.

Topography of Mind

Sigmund Freud stated that there are three topographical levels of the mind i.e. conscious level, pre-conscious level and unconscious level.

The conscious level represents the immediate awareness. It comprises all our thoughts, and feelings which we are aware of at a given moment.

The pre-conscious level comprises thoughts that can become conscious in appropriate situation or circumstances. It is that aspect of the mind that is recallable either through an effort of will or through association. But there is a continuous intercourse between the conscious and the pre-conscious aspects.

The unconscious level comprises thoughts and feelings which an individual can not ordinarily recall at all. It is a vast and store house of unsatisfied desires and motives, infantile wishes and feelings. All urges of an individual originate from this source of unconscious level of the mind. Freud mentions following means to prove the existence of unconscious mind.

I. Inability to recall all the experiences
II. Sleep-violating (Somnambulism)
III. Post-hypnotic suggestions
IV. Solution of problem during step
V. Formation of dreams
VI. Morbid forgetfulness
VII. Step of tongue
VIII. Sneers of psycho-analytical therapy

Dynamic Aspect of Mind

Fred also recognized the three dynamic aspects of the mind i.e. Id, Ego and super Ego. According Freud, behaviour is the resultant of the interaction of these three forces called Id, Ego and Super Ego operating at the conscious, sub-conscious and unconscious level of mind.

"Id" represents the primitive basis of mind and it is the main reservoir of both the life and death instincts. It is completely unconscious and is characterized by "hedonism" or the pleasure principle. It comprises primarily of instants, impulses, urges and drives. These are not at rest but continuously striving to express themselves in primitive and original form of behaviour, but these impulses do not get direct access to the environment as they are unorganized, unstructured destructive libido seeking an outlet. They get their expression through Ego.

"Ego" represents the logical and reality aspect of the mind operating mostly at the conscious level of mind. Ego maintains a balance between the wishes of the Id at one hand the demands of the external reality on the other. Ego is conscious externally and unconscious internally. It always tries to manage and control the Id which is instinctive by nature.

The "Super Ego" represents the social and moral aspect of our mind fully operating at the conscious level of the mind. It always tries to socialize the individual. It consists of the forces of repression, self-observation and self-criticism.

When instinctive behaviour of an individual (Id based) becomes out of control of Ego and Super Ego, it is called as abnormal behaviour and when it becomes controlled by Ego and Super Ego, then it is called as normal behaviour.

Resistance and Repression

The unconscious motives do not lie dormant. They become urgent and seek to be satisfied and when denied, they awaken anxiety, shame and a guilty feeling in the conscious self which therefore resists and tries to hold them down. The conscious self represses these unpleasant motives down and inward. But during sleep, the conscious self relaxes its vigilance and allows the unconscious motives emerge to a certain extent.

Conflicts and Complexes

To Freud, all behaviour is the resultant effect of the dynamic conflicts between the forces of Id, Ego and super-Ego. Such conflicts may be conscious and unconscious.

The Id impulse is largely sexual and aggressive in nature and wants to be immediately satisfied. But these come in conflicts with Ego and Super Ego. Such conflicts operate in conscious and unconscious levels of mind. When an individual becomes aware of the conflict and the source of causing it, then the conflict results at the conscious level, on contrary, when the individual is not aware of the conflict and its source then it is at unconscious level. Here the individual experiences feelings of pain, stress and anxiety. Due to social apposition, the Id impulses are not satisfied and are repressed down in the unconscious level. This is called as repression.

The repressed wishes, desires and motive remain active in the unconscious mind though they are repressed down by the Ego and super-Ego. They gradually acquire strength by moving alliance with other allied repressed experiences and form an active group. This group of repressed desires or motives working with a common goal coming back to the conscious level of the mind is called as "Complex". When such complexes are formed, they give rise to conflicts.

The complexes tries to come back in the conscious level but the forces of Ego and super Ego do not permit this. But when the complexes come back and at the conscious level, they give rise to tension and conflicts. More often, the complexes express themselves in the dreams, step of tongue and forgetfulness, mannerism of speech. Sometimes they may manifest themselves in mental mechanisms i.e. transference, projection, identification, rationalization and others. The complexes may also cause neurotic disturbances or psychotic disorder of various types.

Life and Death Instincts

Freud states that there are two main forces acting in opposition directions. These two urges are called "Eros" or life instincts and "Thanatos' or death instincts.

Life instincts includes the principles of self preservation, growth, propagation of own species, love and contraction. On the other hand the death instincts include the principles of decay, death, destruction, hatred and aggression. All living beings try to avoid these death instincts and want to live as long as possible and want that all should love them.

Freud says that Eros tend to bind man to together in families, classes and even a larger groups with love and justice within the group but with hostility and aggression for outsiders. Therefore Eros and Thanatoes instincts are not opposed but mutually independent forces, the intermixture of these two instincts lead to the Freudian principle of ambivalence loving and hating the same person.

Libido and Narcissism

Libido is the energy that works throughout the whole psychic system. It is the energy of the instincts and source of sexual love, self love, parental love, friendship and love of humanity. When libido flows outward, it causes self-love and when the libido flows inward it causes narcissism.

Sex-instincts

Freud said that man's whole life revolves around sex; sex has a great influence in the life of a man. The methods of sexual activities keep changing with age. Freud states, sexuality commence from infancy and not from adolescence. Freud held the view that "Sex" constitutes the life energy and its meaning is very extensive.

Sexuality embraces many activities which have no connection with genitals. Freud included all pleasurable activities of the child under the general head of sexuality.

Sexuality has three distinct phases depending on the pleasure derived from different zones of the body i.e. oral, anal and phallic.

(i) Oral Phase: The infant derives libidinal satisfaction from the mouth by shocking the thumb.

(ii) Anal Phase: Libidinal satisfaction is derived by the child from the movement of the anus when he passes his stools.

(iii) Phallic Phase: During this phase the child tries to have his libidinal satisfaction through his sex organs or genitals

The later stage of the phallic phase, the individual wants to have his libidinal satisfaction either through homo sexuality or hetro-sexuality, at this stage, boy's keeps interest in girls and vice-versa to fulfill their sex instincts.

Sexual development takes a turn after latency period (05-12 years). The super-Ego resists the infantile urges and the child learns to repress his sex desired.

Contributions: The psychoanalytic school has contributed a lot to the field of psychology and education in the following aspects:

1. It revolted against the study of mind and soul and forwarded the meaning of psychology as the "Science of consciousness.

2. It determined the aim of education as the development of the whole personality and development of emotions for socially desirable purposes.
3. It stressed the importance of play in the education of children.
4. It gave impetus to 'Child-guidance' freedom of the child' and 'mental hygiene in the field of education.
5. It stressed on the provision of healthy environment both at home and school for the better education of the children.
6. It helped to understand the mal-adjusted and delinquent children and solving their problems.
7. It gave the concept of individual psychology and social psychology which is a significant contribution to the field of psychology.
8. It helped to have treatment of mental diseases and mental problems.
9. It gave the knowledge about the basis of human behaviour.

GESTALT SCHOOL

The Gestalt school of psychology originated from the Germany. The main advocates of this school are Max Wertheimer, Kurt Koffka and Wolfgang Kohler.

The Gestalt psychology opposed the ancient psychology and put for warded the fact that a new form takes place on coming together of several factor which is beyond the factors used. Gestalt psychology keeps the whole form in view and not a part of it.

Gestalt psychologist defines that, learning or behavioural changes takes place as a whole but not in part. Gestalt is a Germany word which means" an organized pattern" or "Configuration" or simply an organized whole in contrast to collection of parts. The Gestalt psychology is holistic in nature.

Gestalt psychologists used introspection, Demonstration and Experiment methods in their studies. The subject matter of the study in this school is "organization of consciousness".

Max Wertheimer and Gestalt Psychology

The main propagator of Gestalt psychology is Max Wertheimer. Gestalt psychology took its origin when Wertheimer published his classical papers about the basis of this school during 1912.

Wertheimer and his followers made several experiments about direct knowledge and perception and formulated a series of "Law of Perception" which constitute a significant contribution to the study of psychology.

Laws of Perception

The law of perception is also called as the law of "Pragnanz", which suggests the direction of events. The following factors are responsible for a good Gestalt of Pragnanz.

Similarity: Similarity means, similar items tend to form groups in perception which help in learning. For example, the aggregation of lines or dots will form a group when they are perceived.

------------------	....
------------------	....
------------------	....
Group-I	Group-II

Proximity: Proximity means, nearness of parts. Nearness of parts to each other help in a good perceptual organization, for example, dots placed very near to each other can form a line.

.... A line

Closureness: This factor states that closed areas form a stable perception in comparison to unclosed areas. And thus closureness is an essential base for a good perceptual organization. Thus, an incomplete circle will be viewed as a circle and an incomplete triangle as a triangle because of closureness.

Good Continuation: This factor is closely related to the law of closures. It means that, in perception one tend to continue straight lines as straight lines and curves as curves. That means, the objects retain their original perceptual characteristics through continuity.

A Straight Line

A Curve

Familiarity: Familiarity means the organization resembles some familiar figure or object. It becomes easy to perceive that figure. For example, the collection and organization of dots make an outline of a triangle and then it is perceived as a triangle and so also in case of a circle.

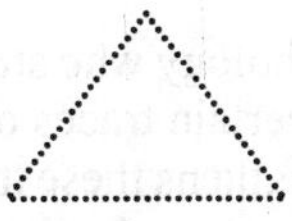
A Triangle

A Circle

Mind Set or Attitude: This factor of mind set or attitude states that if the observer is truly and actively looks for a certain figure, then he/she more likely to finds it.

Woodworth classifies Wertheimer's facts of organization into the following groups

i) Peripheral Factors: Woodworth restates proximity, similarity and continuity as peripheral factors which remain present in the given collection of stimuli.

ii) Central Factor: Central factor originates in the organism and imposed on the stimuli such factors are familiarity and set an attitude.

iii) Reinforcing Factors: Reinforcing factors are similar to the reinforcement of a conditioned reflex or to the law of effect. These factors are factors of permanence, good figure and closure.

Gestalts and Learning

Gestalts are of view that, the creative learning occurs when a particular organism comes across a problem which can't be solved by habitual means. According to Gestalts, Learning takes place in the shape of perceptual organization of the cognitive field through a series of hierarchically related solutions that tend to become increasingly most specific. The perceptual organization directs "focusing", "centering", feeling gaps and better gestalt.

Kohler's ape, Wertheimer's children and Donkan's College students, all demonstrated behaviour which suggested increased focus on the missing link or parts of the problem. The factors applied to the field of perception are again applied to the field of learning.

Gestalts viewed that, the readiness with which the solution is found is related with the motivational factors of the organism, and its previous training. The final solution tends to occur in a sudden reorganization of the perceptual field i.e. the sudden flash of insight; Learning is not explorative, imaginative, purposive and creative.

Insight in Learning

The solution of a problem or learning takes place with the sudden flash of insight. Gestalists believed in insightful learning. The essential characteristics of insightful learning are:

i) It depends on mental maturity and previous experience of the learner.
ii) It follows a period of practice of "Trail and error. "This is called as behavioural hypotheses.
iii) It is explorative, imaginative, creative and purposive.
iv) It can be transferred to identical or similar situations.

Trace Theory of Learning

Koffka is one of the propagators of Gestalt psychology who stressed on Trace learning. He states that past experiences leave certain traces on our memory. It is the function of learning to identity and strengthens these traces. It creates new traces. The trace is the result of past experience and unit persistence, the conservation of past experience provides a base for the new experiences.

Contributions: The main contribution of this school is:

i) It helped to organize effective teaching which requires interaction of the entire topics of each subject as a whole.
ii) It developed concept of mind to make it extensive.
iii) It helped a lot to curriculum construction.
iv) It helped to understand dynamism of human behaviour.
v) It highlighted the concept of perception, imagination and insight in the process o learning.
vi) It gave importance to memory in learning.

HORMIC SCHOOL

Mc Dougall, a British psychologist is called as the father of Hormic School of psychology. It his book "Introduction to social psychology" (1908), he attempted to provide a psychological foundation for the social sciences".

Hormic psychologists' studied motives, purposes or urges in human behaviour and stated that motives". Or urges influences human behaviour. The motives or urges from the basis of human behaviour.

Mc Dougall was the first person to define psychology as science of behaviour. According to him, "The striving to achieve an end" is the mark of behaviour and the behaviour is the characteristic of living beings. Purposive behaviour is the same as goal seeking. In a fully fledged purposive act, two factors combine to elicit behaviour i.e. desire and foresight. An individual foresee the goal and then desires to attain it. Mc Dougall, by analysis proved that behaviour is always purposive.

Objective Criteria of Purposive Behaviour

In 1912, Mc Dougall formulated the following objective criteria of a purposive behaviour:

i) Persistence: An activity may start in response to stimulus but continues after the stimulus is ceased.
ii) Variation: With all the persistence, there is considerable variation of the activity. An obstacle is over and the same goal is attained as if there has been no obstacle.
iii) Termination: The activity terminates, when the goal is reached and some other activity takes its place.
iv) Repetition: Repetition improves the activity. Mc Dougall said that, there must be a number of fundamental motives which are nature and hereditary and all other motives must be derived from these primaries in the course of individual's experience.

Instincts

Mc Dougall called primary motives as instincts. To him these instincts are innate and are got by a child at birth. These are given by nature. The style of expression of these basis or primary motives depends on the environment and education of the child. The instincts are found in all creatures of a class. An emotion goes with each instinct and there does not come a change in it. Mc Dougall has listed the following important instincts and the related emotional expressions:

Instincts	-	**Related Emotions**
Food seeking	-	Hunger
Flight	-	Fear
Pugnacity	-	Anger
Curiosity	-	Wonder
Construction	-	Joy for creation
Submission	-	Accepting inferiority
Distress	-	To Appeal
Gregariousness	-	To seek company
Parental	-	To care the children
Mating	-	To have sex desire
Laughter	-	Amusement
Acquisition	-	Amusement
Self-assertion	-	To seek to dominate
Disjust	-	To reject certain substance

All these instincts are inborn and do not change and these are hereditary by nature. Taking into consideration of all the aspects of an instinct, Mc Dougall gave a comprehensive definition of instincts as: "An instinct is an inherited psycho physical disposition which determines its possessor to perceive, and to pay attention to objects of a certain class, to experience emotional excitement of a particular quality upon perceiving such an object and to act in regard to it in a particular manner or at least to experience an impulse to such action" Therefore, instinct are innate tendencies which the following aspects:

Cognitive aspect: The instincts of this aspect make an individual interested in certain object or situation.

Emotive aspect: The instincts of emotive aspect makes an individual feel certain emotions toward certain objects.

Conative aspect: The instincts of conative aspect make an individual act towards certain object in a particular manner.

Mc Dougall recognizes another modification of instincts. Sometimes instinctive tendencies become combined into sentiments. They become combined by being attached to the same object. A man's love for a certain woman includes sex desire and also source of tender, propensity, these two natural tendencies and probably others as well are attached to that one love object and are thus combined into the sentiment of love, which is a powerful adult motive.

Mc. Dougall said that — human behaviour is directly motivated by sentiments derived from their instincts.

Contributions: The main contributions of Hormic School of psychology are:

i) It highlights that emotion as the source of mental energy.
ii) Hormic psychology provided the concepts of sentiment, born attitude, emotions, feelings, inclination, mental energy, aptitude, anger, repulsion, etc. to psychology and education.
iii) It gave importance to instincts as the potential factors of behaviour.
iv) It highlights three tendencies/aspects of instincts i.e. cognitive, emotive and conative which have a great social significance.
v) It provided the base for the socialization of indicates.
vi) It helped in the development of will and character.

4
Human Body System and Psychology

In the previous chapter, it has been discussed that, Psychology means the science of behaviour. Human behaviour is consisted of both of his internal and external activities. The internal activities are the expression of the function of mind and the external activities are result of the function of body. These internal and external activities are correlated and interdependent on each other. Human body system includes mind and nervous systems which has a close association with the behaviour of human being. Therefore it is essential to know the relationship between human body system and psychology.

MEANING OF HUMAN BODY

Human body is a complex phenomenon. It is consisted of so many elements such as nervous system, brain, bones, fleshes, water and air organized in a delicate and systematic manner. The entire body system operates with the functioning of the nervous system. The nervous are thread-like substances/ fibers which are spread over the whole body. They are linked with spinal cord and it is through spinal cord, they are connected with the brain and other parts of body.

The brain and nervous system of an individual constitute the internal part of the body which has great bearing upon his psychology; thinking, reasoning, feeling, intelligence, emotion, imagination and creativity etc.

The head, nose, ears, eyes, skin, hands and legs constitute the outer part of the body system. The nervous systems are connected with all these outer parts of body. The functioning of these internal and outer parts of the body in a coordinated manner determines the behaviour of human beings. Whenever we see something or touch something, the message is conveyed to the brains them to act in a particular manner. So, the nervous systems acts like the messenger in the body system. Human body fed sensation due to these nervous systems.

MEANING OF MIND

The mind represents the total mental processes. The mental process includes sentiments, perception, attention, thinking, reasoning, decision making, emotions, feelings, attitude etc. All these mental processes put together are called as the mind. Mind is something internal and unseen but it is felt by the individuals. It is an abstract entity about which no particular definition can be given.

Relationship of Mind with Body

The body and mind are closely inter-related with each other. Mind is not separated from body. It is related with body. Every link of the body is controlled by the mind. Mind relates to brain. Developed brain lead to developed mind for example the brain of a bird is more developed than that of a fish, man's brain is more developed than that of a monkey's brain and their mind is found to be developed in this order.

Modern Psychologists consider that mind does not exist beyond body. If body is destroyed, then mind is also destroyed. Mind is the developed form of body and mind is called as the executive in the body system.

Philosophers like Aristotle says that sound mind exists in sound body from this definition it becomes clear that, the healthy body lead to develop a healthy or sound mind. Thus body and mind are inter-linked. The body performs its different activities as per the direction of the mind. So body and mind are mutually related.

Aspect of Mind

It has been discussed above that, mind means mental processes. These mental processes constitute three aspects of mind i.e. cognitive aspect of mind, affective aspect of mind and conative aspects of mind.

Cognitive Aspects of Mind: It represents the knowledge aspect of the mind. Cognitive aspect of the mind begets knowledge in the man. This aspect helps a man to respond to the different stimulus mentally. It includes thinking, reasoning, attitude, creativity, perception etc.

Affective aspect of Mind: This aspect of mind relates to the emotions of an individual. It represents the feeling aspects. Due to this aspect of mind an individual mentally feels pain and pleasure, fear and anger etc.

Conative aspect of Mind: This aspect of mind performs all short of physical activities or bodily activities by the direction of the cognitive aspect of the mind. It relates to the movement of body: hands and legs. It also refers to the doing aspect of the mind. It includes habits, character, instincts, reflexes etc.

However, these three aspects of mind are interlinked and dependent on each other. They function in an organized manner. Normal functioning of these three aspects of mind results into the normal behaviour of an individual and vice-versa. If one aspect is found weak and another is found more active, then there can be some flaws in personality of the individual.

Body and mind influence each other. A healthy body with smooth functioning of its nervous system and balanced secretion of glands lead to a good mental process and a developed mind on the other hand, any short of mental disorders like tensions, frustration, and conflicts etc. lead to affect the body of an individual resulting into physical ailments.

NERVOUS SYSTEM AND MIND

There exists a close link between our nervous system and mind. The interaction of these results the behaviour of an individual at cognitive, affective and psycho-motor or conative levels.

Human nervous system is made up of millions of nerve cells. These nerves are the thread like fibers spread over the entire body. They are linked with the brain by the help of spinal cord. They are also connected with other parts of body. Nerves carry all types of sensations to the brain and brain orders. The nerves are to act accordingly. So, nerves do the activities like messenger.

There are two types of nerves i.e. sensory nerves and motor nerves. The sensory nerves carry the message of the different parts of body to the brain and motor nerves run from the brain to other parts of the body and make them act.

Aspect of the Nervous System

There are two aspects of nervous system i.e. central nervous system and peripheral nervous system.

Central Nervous System

Central Nervous System exists in the bony case formed by the skill and spinal cord. Both the **brain** and **spinal cord** are considered as the important elements of the nervous system.

The Brain: The brain is composed of following five main elements,

1 Cerebrum: Cerebrum is the upper and largest part of the brain. It controls all higher mental activities like thinking, reasoning, learning, judging and remembering etc.
2. Mid Brain: Mid brain connects to the brain and the hind brain. It controls various movements from one place to the other.
3. Cerebellum: Cerebellum is the hind element of the brain located behind and beneath cerebellum. It helps in standing in a state of balance condition and standing treat.
4. Thalamus: Thalamus is located above the mind brain and serves as a special connecting center. All the sensory impulses pass through it to the brain.
5. Medulla Oblongata: Medulla oblongata joins the brain with the spinal cord. It regulates the digestion, respiration and circulation of blood in the body. It helps in preserving our life.

The Spinal Cord: The spinal cord lies within the back bone of our body. It is composed of two types of matters i.e. gray and the white matter. The spinal cord acts like a channel of communication from the brain to the body. All the mechanical actions are controlled by the spinal cord. It conveys sense impression caught by the sensory organs to the brain and the brain decides the manner of action to be taken. Spinal cord directs the motor nerves for action.

Peripheral Nervous System

The Peripheral nervous System also plays an important role. The nerve tissues of this system lie outside the region of peripheral nervous system. These set of nerves act on the sense impressions to the control nervous system and also convey the order of the control nervous system to the muscles for action.

There are two parts in the peripheral nervous system, i.e. the somatic system and the Autonomic system.

Somatic System: In somatic system, the motor and sensory nerves operate side by side and in close cooperation with each other.

Autonomic System: The Autonomic System serves the blood vessels to heart, glands and other internal organs of the body. It has two parts such as Sympathetic system and Para-sympathetic System.

The Sympathetic System relates to the emotions of an individual. Increase of heart beat, and blood pressure and other bodily changes due to the sympathetic system of the Autonomic system.

The Para-sympathetic System tries to conserve the energy of the body and becomes active when the individual is seen to be calm and quiet.

Both the sympathetic and Para-sympathetic system of the Autonomic system works in harmony with each other and helps in adjusting under various situations.

Human behaviour to a great extent is influenced by the functions of the nervous systems. Individual's emotional development upon his nervous system. Learning of an individual depends on the nervous system. Any defect of this system retards intellectual development. The receptors like eye, ear, nose and tongue which carry impressions become meaningful with the help of the nervous system. Malfunctioning of the nervous system cause nervousness, epilepsy, Hysteria, and many psychological disorders in the individual and affect the behaviours.

THE GLANDS AND HUMAN BEHAVIOUR

There are many glands in a human body. There glands are cell structures located in different parts of body. The glands help in physical and mental development of the human being. Glands secret different substances mixed in the blood stream. Some of these secretions help in digestive process and some of them pull out the waste matter.

The glands are of two kinds such as Duct Glands and Duct less Glands.

The Duct Glands

The duct glands secret their fluids/substances through ducts or channels. Tear glands, street glands are duct glands in our body.

The Ductless Glands

The ductless glands are also called as Endocrine glands which have no channels but their internal secretions affect the behaviour of the human beings. They influence the emotional behaviour. The most important ductless glands are thyroid glands, adrenal glands, gonads and pituitary glands.

Thyroid Glands: The thyroid glands are situated under the base of the neck in front of the wind pipe. It secrets a chemical like substance known as thyroxin. The secretion of this gland helps in the physical development of an individual. It gives alertness and smartness to the individual. Under active of this gland makes the individual sluggish, dull, slow, forgetful and stupid. Over active of the glands makes the individual instability and develops anger, fear and other excitements. The individual becomes restless and irritable. The balanced secretion of this gland helps in good physical development and emotional stability.

Adrenal Glands: The adrenal glands are small glands lying on the surface of each kidney. They secret a chemical substance called as adrenalin which stimulates the nervous system. These glands are very active in the emotional state of the individual. It helps in increasing the strength of the body and stimulates the muscles. It makes the individual ready to fight or meet any emergency. Its under-active makes individual emotionally weak.

Pituitary Glands: The Pituitary glands are located at the base of the brain and in the middle of the head. The fluids produced by these glands helps in physical growth of the body. Therefore it is called as a growth gland. It helps in uniform growth of body i.e. bones, muscles and limbs. Its over-activity leads to abnormal growth of the body and it's under activity produces dwarfs with normal intelligence.

Gonads: The Gonads are called as the sex glands. These glands are situated at the primary sex organs in female ovary and male testis. They exercise a great influence on the sexual behaviour of the individuals. They affect the emotional stability and also help in general development of the individuals. Their over-activity makes the individual over sexed and their under-activity makes the individual weak in sexual urges.

The ductless glands play a vital role in human body influencing their behaviours. Smooth and balanced functioning of the ductless gland leads to develop a good physique and results in good personality in the man and vice-versa. These glands stimulate the nervous system and exercise a great control on the emotional development of the human beings.

EDUCATIONAL IMPLICATIONS

The study of human body system and their psychology has a great value to the field of education. It has helped to devise individualized teaching learning methods. It has implications for the development of objectives of learning, curriculum planning and devising teaching learning strategies. It has helped to teachers to understand about the growth and developmental pattern of human beings and accordingly setting the educational activities for their development.

5
Human Growth and Development

The basic aim of education is to bring all-round development of the learner. It requires understanding the process of growth and development of the learner in order to organize different aspects of education: Aims of education, curriculum, and methods of Teaching and evaluation strategy to meet the goal of education. Therefore it is essential to know in detail the nature of human growth and development.

MEANING OF GROWTH AND DEVELOPMENT

Growth refers to the physical change of the body. The increase in size, height and weight of the body is called as growth. It also includes the changes in the body proportions of the individual. Growth is a process of change. A child grows in weight, height in body proportions etc. starting from his birth up to the attainment of maturity. Growth can be measured quantitatively and it is observable contrary to development. At different stages of growth, a number of physical changes take place in the child. Growth of an Individual has its impact upon his behaviour and personality.

Development refers to change in bodily functions. The qualitative change in various aspects of body is known as development. It implies over all changes in the individual that takes place throughout his life. Development is a progressive series of functional changes in the child and such changes lead the child towards maturity.

Crow and crow (1962) defines growth and development that; "Growth refers to structural and physiological changes and development is concerned with growth as well as those changes is behaviour which result from environment situations".

E.B. Hurlock (1959) defines development as a progressive series of changes that occur in an orderly predictable pattern as a result of maturation and experience.

J.F. Anderson (1950) defined; development is a complex process of integrating many structures and functions.

Thus growth and development are mutually dependent on each other development is more inclusive term than growth and it includes maturation.

DIFFERENCE BETWEEN GROWTH AND DEVELOPMENT

Though growth and development are used interchangeably to denote the changes, these two terms are same and can be used differently.

	Growth	*Development*
1.	Growth refers to structural change of the body	Development refers to functional change of the body
2.	Growth denotes to physical changes.	Development denotes to overall changes including physical changes.
3.	Growth is a part of Development process.	Development includes growth and it is a whole process.
4.	Growth is quantitatively measured.	Development is qualitatively measured.
5.	Growth is not a cóntinuous process.	Development is a continuous process.
6.	Growth continuous up to maturation stage and then it stops.	Development includes maturation and continuous even after maturation.
7.	Changes in body i.e. height, weight and size etc. is called as growth	Qualitative changes in social, physical, mental and emotional aspect of body is called as development.
8.	Growth is always additive in nature. It always adds something to the existing structure of the body.	Development is both additive and subtractive in nature. It may add new features and may eliminate some old features to improve upon the quality of bodily functions.
9.	Growth refers to changes in the particular aspects of the body.	Development implies the organization of the body as a whole.

PRINCIPLES OF DEVELOPMENT

Followings are the important principles of development.

Development Follows a Pattern: Development follows definite sequence or pattern. In case of physical development, we can see that the development proceeds from head to toe. The upper parts of the body grows earlier than the lower parts. At birth, the head is much larger as compared to adult head. Similarly, the development of movement is seen earlier in upper parts of the body. A child can raise his head first with better control before he can move his chest or hand or leg.

Development Proceeds from General to Specific: The development proceeds from general to specific direction. It is found that the general activities precede specific activity in all actions of an individual. The movement of the child is of a general nature in the initial stage of life but later on they become specific.

A Continuous Process: The process of development continues from the conception through birth to lifelong i.e. from womb to tomb. All dimensions of development continue to grow gradually until they reach their maximum for example a child does not speak all on a sudden. He develops a speech habit by continuous efforts.

Individual Difference in Growth and Development: In human growth and development, there are seen individual differences. Each individual grows in his own unique. No two individuals grow and develop in the same rate. Some grow taller and some grow dwarf, some get biological maturity earlier and some get it late. Some develop good intelligence and some develop less intelligence. So the principle of individual difference operates in the process of growth and development.

Predictable: It is seen that every child grows and develops in his own way and nearly constantly with this about presumption it can be predicted about the other range of development of an individual keeping view of his preset rate of development. The prediction about the development is possible in case of the children of average or normal development but not in case of abnormal children.

A Product of Heredity and Environment: Both heredity and environment determine the growth and development of a child. Heredity is mainly responsible for the physical development and intellectual development where as environment is responsible for intellectual, social and temperamental developments of the child. The mutual role of heredity and environment facilitates a child's growth and development.

Principal of Inter-relation: Most of the traits of growth and development are positively correlated. This means one is superior in one respect, he is also found superior in other respects. A child having superior intelligence is seen to be good in sociability but this may not be always true. Sometimes a Lin and thin individual is found to have good intelligence but not sociable.

Principal of Integration: Development proceeds from general responses to specific responses and back. The specific responses are integrated to form the whole. In the process of development, movement takes place from whole to part and again from part to whole.

Spiral and not Linear: Development does not occur in linear manner, but takes a break during which development is consolidated so, there is a back and forth movement giving a spiral form one type of development takes its origin or base from other developmental characteristics for example, mental development has its root of base with physical development.

Rate of Development not Uniform: Through development is a continuous process, the rate of development is not uniform at all stages of life. At infancy, the rate of development is high and in childhood stage the rate of development is low. Again at the stage of puberty, there is sudden rise in the growth and development and at the adulthood stage; the rate of development becomes slow.

Principle of Developmental Direction: Development follows the direction of cephalo-cadal as well as proximo-distal. Development from head to limbs i.e. longitudinal axis is called as cephalo-cadal and the development from the center to the periphery direction is called as proximo-distal. Child gains control over its head first and then arms and legs last. So also, child learns to control large muscles first and then learns to control smaller muscles later for example, the child controls over his arms and the hand and then control his fingers.

FACTORS DETERMINING GROWTH AND DEVELOPMENT

There are certain factors which affect human growth and development. These factors are mainly categorized as "Heredity" and "Environment". But other factors like maturation, learning, nutrition and sex also influence the growth and development.

Heredity

Heredity contributes to human growth and development. Heredity is a biological process through which genetic characteristic are transmitted from parents to offspring. Through heredity, we inherit the traits not only from our immediate parents but also from our fore parents. Hereditarily we own to seven generations.

Mechanism of Heredity: Heredity is called as a biological process. This process depends on the union of sperm cells from the father and the egg cell from the mother. This united cell is called as fertilized ovum or the zygote. Life begins with the formation of zygote in the womb of the mother.

Father Child Mother

↓ ↑ ↓

(Sperm) → (Zygote) ← (Egg)

[Sperm + Egg = Zygote]

(Formation of Zygote and Beginning of Life of the Child)

The male and female reproductive organs produce germ cells. The male germ cells called as spermatozoa are produced by their testis and female germ cell called as ova are produced by their ovaries. Union of these male and female germ cells creates life with the formation of zygote.

Heredity is fixed in the zygote. Each cell contains 23 (Twenty Three) pairs chromosomes such chromosomes are consisted of number of minute particles called genes. These genes are really the bearers of hereditary characters. Different gene combinations which are chance factors are responsible for different physical and mental characteristics. That is why we find individual differences in height, size or colour of body, type of blood and mental abilities.

Through numerous cell divisions, the hereditary characteristics from zygote spread throughout the body. The zygote develops into an embryo inside the mother's womb. Therefore, heredity is fixed before the birth of the baby.

Theories of Heredity: To understand the meaning of Heredity, it is essential to have study about the theories of heredity. Some of the theories of heredity are:

Weisman's Theory of Heredity: Weisman's theory of heredity is also called as the continuity of the germ plasma that is transmitted from generation to generation. These germ cells of each parent are responsible for the new human body.

Weisman's theory of heredity based on two generations, i.e. the parents are only a trustee of the germ plasma rather than the producer of the child, and the heredity of the child is ancestral as the germ plasma of the parents are transmitted to the child and the same continues to the next generations.

Basing on this theory, Weisman come into the following conclusion that, (1) heredity of the child is ancestral (2) The child does not inherit the acquired traits of his parents (3) Like begets like i.e. intelligent parents mostly have intelligent children.

Galton's Theory of Heredity: According to Sir Francis Galton, one half of the traits come from immediate parents, one fourth from the grandparents, both maternal and parental, one eight from great grandparents and so on. So the sum of the series can described as 1/2 + ¼ + ¼ + 1/16 .... is equal to the total inheritance of the organism. This is also called the principle of convergence. Galton's theory highlights the fact that, heredity of the child does not go mainly to immediate parents but to his remote ancestors as well.

Mendel's Theory of Heredity: Experimenting on peas in his garden Gregor Mendel stated out the theory that Heredity is the sum total of all the traits present in the form of endowments right at the term of conception, in the fertilized ovum. Therefore, he defined heredity that "Heredity means the biological potential passed on through the genes from the parents to the children at the term of conception".

Lamarck's Theory of Heredity: As an environmentalist, Lamarck has contributed a lot to the explanation of variations among the series. According to Lamarck, a living organism adapts itself to the environment and modifies itself in-order to fulfill his need and make changes in the environment. These modifications are passed on to the next generation.

Darwin's Theory of Heredity: Sir Charles Darwin an English scientist (1809-1882) in his book "Origin of the Species" explained his theory of heredity that struggle for existence goes on in all the species. Leading or natural selection based on the principle of survival of the fittest. During this struggle for existence, structural modifications take place and they are passed on from generation to generation.

***Laws of Heredity*:** There are certain laws or principles that govern the process of heredity. These laws are:

Law of Resemblance: This law implies that "Like begets like". It means the offspring resemble the parents in many respects. The parents in average cases produce their own type. A Child takes after his parents in size, colour, and height and to some extend mental abilities.

Law of Variation: Offspring vary from their parents due to variation in gene combinations. Tall parents even produce dwarf children. Parents with fair complexion also produce children with back complexion. A bright parent may have dull child. Thus heredity operates in such a way that offspring's are never exact replicas of their parents.

Law of Regression: Law of regression states that, in successive generations variations tend to move towards the average or the normal of the species to which they belong by regression, it means to tend towards average, but not to progress towards the extremes heredity operates in such a way that off springs, in case of extreme characteristics of their parents usually tend to more towards the normal rather than towards the extremes.

For example, if the parents are extremely intelligent, their offspring may have less intelligence. If the parents are extremely dull, the off-springs may tend towards average. This happens due to the fact that, heredity of a child is determined by his immediate parents by 50 per cent and the remaining is determined by ancestral parents.

Law of Dominance and Segregation: Mendel while explaining the cause of variation in the offspring of some parents stated that, parents may carry genes of opposite traits. There are two degrees of the same trait: dominant and recessive. And the traits which are not dominant in the parents may be dominant in their offspring. For example, the parents may carry the genes of tallness and dwarfness, fair skin and black skin etc. The Traits which is dominant can be seen with the parents but such genes may be recessive in the offspring, so, the parents may be tall but their offspring will have a short stature. The genes for tallness become dominant in parents, where as the genes for dwarfness become dominant in the offspring.

Law of Non-Transmission of Acquired Traits: The traits acquired by parents through learning or living in the environment are not transmitted to their offspring through heredity. The personality traits and social characteristics like leadership, honesty, simplicity etc. are not transmitted to the offspring.

Impact of Heredity: Heredity impacts the following aspects of growth and development like physical growth of the child such as height, size of the body, stature of the body, colour of the body, hair and eye composition, structure of the face. Individual's intelligence, aptitude, and instincts are also greatly influenced by hereditary characters.

Environment

Oxford dictionary defines the term" Environment" as surroundings. It implies that all that as surrounds the child from the time of his/her birth onwards till his/her death.

Environment in wider sense includes a number of situations and experiences that influence the development of the child's various stimulations, experiences that the child gets from the physical, social and psychological world constitute his environment.

According to Woodworth, Environment covers all the outside factors that have acted on the individual since he began life."

Environment is psychological sense is very wide and complex other than geographical environment as is used in popular sense. Environment of a child not only post natal but also pre-natal. That means environment of a child starts functioning from the very conception of the child inside his mother's womb and continues till his death. Two individuals may have same physical environment but very and can never be same.

Kinds of Environment

We may categories the environment into following three kinds:

1. Physical Environment: Physical Environment is otherwise known as geographical environment or natural environment. It includes various physical forces and geographical conditions like climate, topography, plants and vegetation that effect the physical growth of the child. For example, the people of high and up lands are seen to be fair complexion than the people of coastal areas. Food, clothing and shelter which constitute the main living condition of the individual come in the scope of physical environment.

2. Social Environment: Different social agencies constitute the social environment of man. Man is called as a social animal who likes to live in group. The scope of social environment is very vast starting from the individual himself to his family, community, society, school, religious places, state, nation and the world at large. It consists of different world of people, social institutions, social event and activities, culture of the society, social experiences, interpersonal relationships and societal interaction etc. It too includes religion, politics and economic conditions. Social environment greatly influences the growth and development of a child.

3. Psychological Environment: Psychological environment is also called as mental environment. It is very complex in nature. One's psychological environment greatly influences his/her growth and development. It includes the psychological world of the child such as his interest, attitude, motives emotional states, intelligence and thoughts etc.

Relative Significance of Heredity and Environment

Controversy arises among the psychologists regarding the importance of heredity and environment for the growth and development of the individual. Some place more importance to heredity and some others attach more importance to environment.

Hereditarians, Francis Galton, the English psychologist out of his study stated that, heredity is all important for the growth and development of the child. Environment has nothing to do with it.

On the other hand, the environmentalists stated that, it is only environment that help the growth and development of the individual they ignored heredity of the child and said that environment can change the heredity of an individual. J.B. Watson, the American psychologist strongly supported environment for the growth and development of the child.

However, the controversy between the hereditarians and environmentalists regarding the importance of heredity and environment for growth and development of the child is now days disregarded. It is now commonly agreed that both the heredity and environment acts upon the growth and development of the child. As Page has rightly remarked "Every phenomenon of life is the product of both heredity and environment." Each determines the development of the individual and neither of them can be ignored or under rated. Both heredity and environment are complementary to each other. Heredity provides the base on which environment builds the personality of the individual. It is the product of heredity and environment (H x E) but not the addition of heredity and environment (H + E) that determine the development of the individual.

There are certain characteristics like physical characteristics such as height, size of the body, structure of the body, shape of the body etc. are mostly determined by heredity but the social moral and temperamental characteristics are mainly determined by environment. So, equal importance should be given to heredity and environment of an individual in the process of an individual's growth and development.

Maturation

Maturation as factor of growth and development plays a vital role in the process of growth and development of an individual. Maturation means the level of optimum physiological growth at which the child is able to develop some abilities. If proper maturation is not attained, it becomes difficult on the part of the child to develop mentally, emotionally and socially. Inner potentialities come into action after maturation is attained.

Maturation is a development process within which an individual from time to time manifests different traits — physical, mental, intellectual, social and emotional, maturation accelerates the process of development of an individual and makes him/her productive.

Learning

Learning is also a factor of growth and development. Development is the interaction between maturation and learning. Maturation is the growth from within but learning is the outward growth. Learning maximizes one's development. One may have potentialities but he fails to develop without learning. So learning helps in development. Proper learning assists in intellectual, emotional, social and moral aspects of development of the child. We can easily find out the development differences between learning and non-learning being.

Nutrition

Nutrition as a factor also affects physical growth and development. Nutrition helps in building sound physique of an individual. Adequate physical growth result is good intellectual and emotional growth. Nutrition provides the energy for physical, mental and emotional growth of the child.

Sex

Sex also plays an important role in the growth and development. Developmental differences are found in boys and girls due to the factor of sex in respect of physical, mental, emotional and social aspects.

Thus there are a number of factors of growth and development which are to be understood by the teachers to harness these factors in positive direction and provide the base or the maximum development of the learners.

6
Dimensions of Human Development

Human growth and development takes place through different stages. Different dimensions of development develop through these stages of life. From the very beginning of life of a child, his behaviour continuously changes as a result of the development of different dimensions of developments in him. Again different child develop differently with respect to these developmental characteristics. Therefore the teacher has to acquire the knowledge of the different dimensions of human development and their characteristics so that he can help his students to develop successfully.

STAGES OF HUMAN DEVELOPMENT

According to Dr. Ernest Jones, human development takes place in the following four defined stages,

1. **Infancy**—From birth to 5 years of age
2. **Childhood**—From 6 to 12 years of age
3. **Adolescence**—From 13 to 19 years of age
4. **Adulthood**—from 20 years to onwards

There are different views regarding the ages up to which infancy and childhood lasts and maturity begins. Some psychologists state that, the infancy lasts up to 7 years and the late adolescence continue up to 21 years. However the psychologists have classified the stages of infancy and childhood into different sub-stages like,

- **Infancy**—from birth to 2 years
- **Pre-childhood**—From 3 to 6 years
- **Early childhood**—From 6 to 9 years
- **Late childhood**—From 10 to 12 years

As there are individual differences with respect to gender, environment and hereditary factors, there is no rigidity in theses classifications.

DIMENSIONS OF HUMAN DEVELOPMENT

Following are the dimensions of development which go through and develop in different stages of life and different developmental characteristics are developed in these stages of life.

Physical Development

Physical growth and development is the root of all changes in human life. Improper physical growth and development of a child leads to affect his mental and social development and creates his adjustment problem. Physical growth influences the behavioural development of an individual. Adequate physical growth and development of the child determines his physical wellbeing.

Principles of Physical Growth and Development

Physical growth and development takes place according to certain biological principles. Cole and Morgan state that, the human body shows an orderly series of changes in size, proportion and function from cradle to the grave. The skeleton, internal organs, muscles, nervous system and the glands go through a series of development that inevitably influence an individual's intellectual and emotional reactions. Followings are the principles of physical growth and development,

- Physical development is rhythmic but not a regular process. Rapid growth is followed by slow growth and then rapid growth is resumed at a stipulated period.
- Each part of the body follows its own pattern of development.
- Different parts of the body of the child grow faster in winter months than the summer.
- Rapid growth of the body takes place in infancy. Growth becomes steady during the childhood period. Again physical growth becomes rapid in the adolescence period.

Characteristics of Physical Growth and Development

Physical growth and development is characterized in the following aspects,

- Changes in the height of the body
- Changes in the weight of the body
- Changes in the proportions of the body
- Increase of the strength of the bones and joints of the body
- Increase of the size and shape of the body
- Changes in the functioning of the Nervous systems and glands
- Changes in the functioning of the Internal Organs

Physical Development at different Stages

Physical Development of human beings occurring at different stages of his life is discussed below.

Infancy (0-5 years) Stage: During Infancy, physical growth and development takes place rapidly. This period is called as the root of the development of many of the future traits and characteristics. The Educationists and psychologists attach great importance to this stage of life. The height and weight of the baby increase rapidly during his/her period of infancy. The average height and weight of a baby remains only about 50 cm and 3.5 kg at the time of birth. Length does not change as rapidly as its weight. For the infant's length at birth is already 75 per cent of what it will be at two years of age. Changes in length and weight are accompanied by transformations in the infant's body proportions. The head grows the fastest and the infant's physical structure and central nervous system undergo dramatic and rapid change during the first two years of life. The infant's weight doubles by five months of age, triples by twelve months of age, and quadruples by the age of twenty-four months. The rapid changes in infants' body proportions affect other domains of development such as perceptual, motor, cognitive, and emotional development.

Developmental milestones in physical growth and development during the infancy are the following types.

- Birth to 2 months: Infants become able to move his/her arm and leg in uncoordinatedly along with weak neck muscles.
- 3 to 4 months: Infants become able to control his/her neck and control his/her head movement.
- 4 to 5 months: Infants become able to roll from side to back and reverse.
- 6 to 7 months: Infants become able to turn completely from back to front and reverse.
- 7 to 8 months: Infants become able to sit up steadily with the support of their arms.
- 9 to 10 months: Infants become able to creep on their stomachs and begin to crawl on their hands and knees.
- 10 to 11 months: Infants become able to walk by holding the hand of others.
- 12 to 15 months: Infants become able to stand without holding anything and walk.
- 16 to 18 months: Infants become able to walk well, hold and throw a ball.
- 19 to 24 months: Infants become able to run and climb.
- 25 to 36 months: Infant's motor skills become more refined. They can alternate feet while climbing stairs, ride a tricycle, jump and balance on one foot. They can throw a ball overhand.
- 36 to 48 months: Infants become able to run and skip well, play simple ball games, and are skilled in riding tricycle.
- 48 to 60 months: Infants become able to skip, run, play with a ball, and climb

Childhood Stage (6-12 years): This period ranges from 5 to 12 years of age. From the point of view of physical growth and development, this period is called as the period of consolidation. The health of the child generally remains better during this period. Internally, the child acquires strength of his body. His bones, joints and nervous system become stronger. During this period the child engages himself in different types of play-activities which strengthen his limbs.

Adolescence Stage (13-19 years): The period of adolescence continues from 13 to 19 years of age. It is also known as teen age. During this period, physical growth and development again takes place rapidly as like as the infancy stage. The child reaches at the maximum limit of his physical growth and development. During this period, a lot of physiological changes are marked in the body of girls and boys and we can mark a great difference in the growth of boys and girls.

Adolescence is characterized by dramatic physical changes moving the individual from childhood into physical maturity. Early, prepubescent changes are noted with the appearance of secondary sexual characteristics.

Girls may begin to develop breast buds as early as 8 years old, with full breast development achieved anywhere from 12 to 18 years. Pubic hair growth as well as armpit and leg hair typically begins at about age 9 or 10, and reaches adult distribution patterns at about 13 to 14 years.

Menarche (the beginning of menstrual periods) typically occurs about 2 years after initial pubescent changes are noted. It may occur as early as 10 years, or as late as 15 years, with the average in the United States being about 12.5 years. A rapid growth in height occurs for girls between the ages of about 9.5 and 14.5 years, peaking somewhere around 12 years.

Boys may begin to notice enlargement of the testicles and scrotum as early as 9 years of age, followed closely by lengthening of the penis. Adult size and shape of the genitals is typically reached by age 16 to 17 years. Pubic hair growth as well as armpit, leg, chest, and facial hair begins in boys at about age 12, and reaches adult distribution patterns at about 15 to 16 years.

A rapid growth in height occurs for boys between the ages of about 10.5 to 11 and 16 to 18, peaking around age 14. Puberty is not marked with a sudden incident in boys, as it is with the onset of menstruation in girls. The appearance of regular nocturnal emissions (wet dreams) marks the onset of puberty in boys and typically occurs between the ages of 13 and 17 years, with the average about 14.5 years.

A remarkable growth of height of the body of both boys and girls are attained during this period. However, the average growth of girls remains better than the boys in respect of their weight and height. The body proportions get its mature size during this period. All parts of body acquire adult proportions by the end of 18 years of age. The muscles, bones and joints become more strengthened.

During adolescence period, the internal organs also get their maturity. The skeleton becomes longer day by day. Glandular changes also take place during physical growth. Different gland like, thyroid, pituitary, thymus and sex glands develop to the maximum extent. The changes in the glands affect the behaviour of the adolescents-boys and girls. The masculine and feminine characteristics are developed in the boys and girls during this period.

Secondary sex characteristics appear in different parts of the body of adolescents. Genital organs in the adolescents get their maturity and increase in size. Both girls and boys develop interest in opposite sexes. The reproductive organs of adolescents-boys and girls become active. The boys and girls acquire more ability, skills and strength of their body. Girls seem to mature earlier than the boys in physical activity. Both boys and girls develop athletic abilities during this period of adolescence.

Adulthood Stage (20-onward till end of life): Adulthood stage begins at the age of 20 years and lasts until the end of the life of an individual. During this period the weight of the body increases but the height of the body remain constant. The body proportions remain unchanged as like as the adolescence period. This is also known as the period of consolidation and decay so far as the physical growth and development is concerned.

Mental Development

Mental means pertaining to mind. Mental also refers to the collective aspects of intellect and consciousness. Mental development refers to the development of mind. Explaining the mental or cognitive development James Drever remarks, it implies, "Progressive appearance and organization of mental abilities and functions in the course of the individual's passage from birth to maturity."

Characteristics of Mental Development

Mental development is characterized in the following aspects,

- Development of power of thinking
- Development of Reasoning
- Development of Problem solving ability
- Development of conceptualization and Understanding.
- Information processing
- Overall intelligence.
- Development of Perception power
- Development of Imagination
- Imitation
- Development of Memory
- Use of languages
- Development of Creativity
- Development of Curiosity

Mental Development at Different Stages

Mental Development of human beings occurring at different stages of his life is discussed below.

Infancy Stage: During infancy, the baby develops the power of reasoning, memory, and recognition. He begins to recognize and memorize many things. A child experiences many kinds of sensations like coldness, hot, hardness, pain, pleasure, sounds, lights etc. the child becomes able to compare and generalize in rudimentary form. The child starts imitating others. He develops curiosity to know various things around him. His/her questioning attitude develops. Creative impulses develop in infants during the period of infancy. Perception power develops with the increase of age with use of signs and symbols. Attention span also increases.

According to Piaget, **The sensory-motor stage** is the first of the four stages of cognitive development revealed in the stage of infancy. In this stage, infants construct an understanding of the world by coordinating sensory experiences (such as seeing and hearing) with physical and motoric actions. Infants gain knowledge of the world from the physical actions they perform on it. An infant progresses from reflexive, instinctual action at birth to the beginning of symbolic thought toward the end of the stage. Infants become able to internalize schemes.

Childhood Stage: This period ranges from 5 to 12 years of age. During this period, the imitation power of the child becomes more active. He becomes able to do many things as imitating his elders. This is also called as the period of intellectual advancement. The rate of cognitive development is rapid at this stage. The child learns to solve his simple problems. The power of reasoning, thinking, perception, observation and attention are developed in this stage. During the period of childhood, intellectual development takes place following the two stages i.e., Preoperational stage, Concrete Operational stage.

The **Preoperational** stage is the second of four stages of cognitive development. During this stage, the child learns to use and to represent objects by images, words, and drawings. The child is able to form stable concepts as well as mental reasoning and magical beliefs. Logical thinking is not developed in children during this stage rather symbolic and intuitive thoughts develop in children. Piaget considered that children primarily learn through imitation and play throughout these first two stages, as they build up symbolic images through internalized activity.

The **Concrete operational** stage is the third of four stages of cognitive development in Piaget's theory. This stage, which follows the Preoperational stage, occurs during the childhood period ranging between the ages of 7 to 11 years and is characterized by the appropriate use of logic. During this stage, children develop the ability to arrange the objects according their size, shape and other characteristics, develop ability to recognize logical relationships among elements in a serial order, and perform 'transitive inferences' (ability to transit), develop ability to name and identify sets of objects according to appearance, size or other characteristic, including the idea that one set of objects can include another (ability to classify), develop ability to take account multiple elements to solve a problem (ability to decenter), develop ability to understand the position of numbers or objects which can be changed and returned to their original state (ability to reverse), develop ability to understand the quantity, length and number of objects/items (ability to conserve) and develop ability to view things from another's perspective. During childhood stage, children fail to carry hypothetical thinking or logical thinking.

Adolescence Stage: During adolescence period, the individual starts understanding, memorizing, thinking and reasoning. Mental development is greatly influenced by maturation and learning. During the stage of adolescence the cognitive development of the individual is characterized by attending, perceiving, observing, remembering, imagining, thinking, problem solving as well as developing language habits. The individual becomes able to take decisions.

According to Piaget, adolescence period is called as the period of **Formal Operational stage** in intellectual development of an individual The formal operational period is the fourth and final periods of cognitive development in Piaget's theory. This stage, which follows the Concrete Operational stage, commences at around 11 years of age (puberty) and continues into adulthood. In this stage, individuals move beyond concrete experiences and begin to think abstractly, reason logically and draw conclusions from the information available, as well as apply all these processes to hypothetical situations. The adolescent's thought at the formal operational level is evident in the adolescent's verbal problem solving ability. Adolescents begin to think scientifically, devise plans to solve problems and systematically test solutions. They use hypothetical-deductive reasoning, which means that they develop hypotheses or best guesses, and systematically deduce, or conclude, which is the best path to follow in solving the problem. During this stage the young adult is able to understand such things as love, "shades of gray", logical proofs and values. During this stage the young adult begins to entertain possibilities for the future and is fascinated with what they can be.

Adulthood Stage: During this period, the intellectual development is consolidated. Individual enriches his experiences through learning. But the rate of intellectual development becomes steady. All the characteristics of mental development developed during the stage of adolescence are consolidated.

Social Development

Human being is a social being and he can't live alone. Social existence and progress of human beings require the help of a social group. The process of socialization helps an individual to become a social being. To Aristotle, a man is a social animal because his being and progress depend on his social living. From the very beginning of life of an individual, social qualities are present but they manifest themselves and develop through out of his life according to his progress in age by the effect of the process of socialization. Socialization is a process of development of social qualities which brings desirable changes in the social behaviour of the individual.

Hurlock states, Social development means the attainment of maturity in social relationship.

Garrett states, Socialization or social development is the process whereby the biological individual is converted into human person.

The process of socialization starts just after the birth of a new born child and the process of socialization continues throughout the life.

Parental care is important from the initial life of an individual for the development of positive social qualities. A sound environment can be helpful for the individual to integrate social values and positive social qualities and vice versa.

Characteristics of Social Development

Social development is characterized in the following aspects,

- Development of dependability.
- Development of relationship.
- Development of trust and belief.
- Development of friendship.
- Development of power of interaction.
- Development of sense of group life.
- Development of sense of belongingness.
- Development of sense of cooperativeness.
- Development of sense of kindness and piety.
- Development of sense of submissiveness.
- Development of sense of sharing.
- Development of power of understanding.
- Development of helping attitude.
- Development of leadership.

Social Development at different Stages

Social Development of human beings occurring at different stages of his life is discussed below.

Infancy (0-5 years) Stage: Infancy stage is considered as the vital stage in view of social development of an individual. It may be called as the foundation stage for all types of development including social development of an individual. During this stage, an infant is expected to have his social qualities like dependability, trust, identity, sharing, cooperation, friendship etc. This happens when the new born baby become aware of his parents (father-mother), cousins and other adult members around him and attending him to fulfill his needs. Here the infant tries to imitate others of his social behaviour and tries to integrate them in him. Sometimes, if proper environment is not availed, the infant develops shyness, timidity and selfish attitudes.

Childhood (6-12 years) Stage: From the point of view of the development of social behaviours, the childhood period is very important. The sense of group life, helpfulness and friendship consolidates in the child at this stage of development. Children want to play with their groups of own age. Children become acquainted with the rules and regulation of the schools and act accordingly in order to adjust themselves. Children imitate and learn from their groups and group life impacts the childhood behaviour of children. A sense of belongingness is installed during this stage of development in the children.

Adolescence (13-19 years) Stage: Adolescence state is very crucial stage of development of social qualities in the life of an individual. During this stage, an individual is expected to develop the social qualities like power of understanding and adjustment, group life, submissiveness, helpfulness, cooperativeness, trust, kindness, piety, leadership etc. If sound environment is not availed, then the negative social qualities like hostility and enmity may develop in adolescents. Adolescents want to keep relationship with heterogeneous groups and their gregarious attitude is more developed. However, the adolescence stage is called as the period of consolidation and restoration stage of development of social behaviour of an individual.

Adulthood (20 years–onwards Stag) Stage: During this period, the social development is consolidated. Individual enriches his experiences through learning. But the rate of social development becomes more solid. All the characteristics of social development developed during the stage of adolescence are consolidated. The prime social qualities that develop during this stage are leadership, interaction, adjustment, decision making, cooperativeness, trust, kindness etc.

Emotional Development

Along with physical and cognitive development, every child proceeds through the phases of emotional development. Emotions are not as easy to study or recognize as cognition. Emotional development is the emergence of a child's experience, expression, understanding, and regulation of emotions from birth through late adolescence. Emotional development does not occur in isolation but cognitive and behavioural development interact with emotional development and social and cultural influences, and context also play a role. Individual's extra ordinary achievement and success depends on his emotional development. Emotions are the conditions or type of feelings that make changes in the body and cognitive aspect of an individual as a result an individual become favourable or against of some situation. Individuals differ in their emotional development. Some are found to be emotionally stable and some are found to be emotionally unstable. Some are able to control their emotions and some are found unable to control their emotions. One's success or failure depends on his emotional development. In order to have proper emotional development in the children, the role of environment and parental care is more important.

The word 'emotion' has been derived from the Latin word 'Emovere' which means to stir up, to agitate or to excite. Woodworth defines emotions as a moved or stirred up state of an organism. It is a stirred state of feelings that is the way it appears to the individual himself. It is a disturbed muscular and glandular activity that is the way it appears to an external observer. Crow and crow defines emotions as a dynamic internal adjustment that appears for the satisfaction, protection and welfare of the individual. T. Jersild stated that the term emotion denotes a state of being moved, stirred up or aroused in some way. Erkinson states that, when psychological crisis arises in somebody, then his/her emotional characteristics are displayed. So it becomes clear that, emotion is a state of feelings that bring bodily changes in the individual himself which is observable to others. Emotions involve feelings, impulses, physical and psychological reactions.

Characteristics of Emotional Development

Emotional development is characterized in the following aspects,

- Changes in normal behaviour.
- Changes in bodily actions.
- Changes in mental actions.
- Internal changes of body.(Increase in heart beats, increase in blood pressure)
- Visibility of external changes in the body. (Crying, trembling, laughing, smiling etc.)
- Development of sense of fear and braveness.
- Development of sense of pain and pleasure.
- Development of intensity of feelings.
- Development sense of individuality.
- Development of self-concept.
- Development of self-esteem.
- Development of egocentrism.
- Development of sense of autonomy and shame.
- Development of sense of intimacy and isolation.
- Development of sense of competence and inferiority
- Development of sense of anger.
- Development of feelings of distress.
- Development of feeling of disgust
- Development of feelings of curiosity.
- Development of feelings of creativeness.

Nature of Emotional Development

The followings are the natures of emotional development:

1. Emotions are universally found in everybody but the intensity of a particular emotion varies from one to another: Every individual is found to have emotional behaviours like crying, smiling, laughing, trusting, shame, autonomy, self-esteem, fear, braveness etc. but some are found to control a particular emotion and some fail to control the same. The intensity of a particular emotion (higher or lower) makes the individual feel his emotion in a distinct way.

2. The Root of emotion is one's psychological crisis: Erkinson says the root of emotional development is one's own psychological crisis. When someone fail to reach his goals and his needs, motives, desires are blocked then his emotions abrupt and take distinct shape.

3. Emotional development is influenced by one's heredity and environment: One's heredity and environment has its positive impact on his emotional development. Some are found shy by birth and some are found brave. So also some are found to keep intimacy with others and some are found to keep him isolated. On the same way if positive and sound environment is provided to someone, he/she may become stable in his emotions and vice versa.

4. Emotions are displayed in one's psychological and physiological changes: When some one's emotion is found disturbed, his/her psychological and physical appearances changes and become observable to others. Psychologically someone may feel pain or pleasure, depressed or relaxed, fear or fearless etc. and physiologically someone may be fond crying or laughing, trembling or relaxing etc.

5. Emotions are persistent at all stages of life: Emotional characteristics are found to be persistent at all stages of life. But the intensity of a particular emotion may differ at all stages. As someone grow and attain maturity, he/she become able to control his/her emotions.

6. Emotions are varying in types: There are different types of emotions and thereby different types of emotional expressions. For example, someone shows his/her emotional expression of crying and someone shows his/her emotional expression of laughing at a moment.

7. Emotions are related to one's basic instincts: Basic instincts are called as the root of the development of emotions. When someone's basic instinct is not fulfilled then, his/her emotional state becomes disturbed and he/she displays reactions. Individuals who can control his/her instinctual needs become rational in his/her emotions and vice versa.

8. Individual difference found in emotional development: The law of individual difference operates in the field of emotional development. Though all types of emotions are normally distributed in all, the individuals differ in their emotions in respect of their intensity. Some individuals are found to have well control capacity on their emotions and some are found to have less control capacity on their emotions.

9. Emotions are time bound: Emotional expressions are time bound. Some of the emotional expressions are persistent for a long period of time and some are persistent for a short period of time. When the individual become emotional at moment, after some time he/she becomes normal in his/her behaviour. For example, an individual may show anger for moment, but after some time he is found to be normal.

Kinds of Emotions

T. Jersild is of opinion that there are of two types emotions such as positive emotions and negative emotions.

Positive Emotions: positive emotions are those which assist the individual to have an optimistic approach in his life. Individuals having positive emotions are seem to feel joy, happiness, love, affection, curious, creative, brave, gregarious, stable etc.

Negative Emotion: Negative emotions are those which assist the individual to have a pessimistic approach in his life. Individuals having negative emotions are seem to be unhappy, painful, fearing, angry, coward, isolated, unstable, hostile, etc.

Conditions of Arousal of Emotions

The following conditions may arouse certain type of emotions in an individual

1. When the needs, demands, desires, motives and goals of an individual are threatened and blocked and the individual fails to reach them.
2. When the personal pride and self-esteem of an individual is damaged, then he/she expresses his/her negative emotions like fear, anger, anxiety hostility etc.
3. When the inner state of mind of the individual is disturbed, the individual expresses his/her emotions. When an individual feels mentally imbalanced, depressed and abnormal, his/her emotional reactions outburst.
4. When the interest of an individual changes, his/her emotional reactions takes birth.
5. When social situations compels or goes against the interest of an individual, then the individual shows his emotional reactions.

Emotional Development at different Stages

Emotional Development of human beings occurring at different stages of his life is discussed below.

Infancy (0-5 years) Stage: So far the emotional development is concerned; the period of infancy is of great important. The root of emotional development is installed during this infancy stage. Psychologists are of opinion that, emotional experiences start from birth. *Rank* states that, a newborn baby experiences an emotion of anxiety. *Sussan Issancs* held the view that, infants shows his emotions like fear, anger, love, hate. *Watson* stated that emotional expressions like love, anger, fear is seen to be developed during the infancy stage. The new born baby shows displeasure if someone misdeals with his/ her nearer like father, mother, brother and sister.

Childhood (6-12 years) Stage: Childhood stage is an important stage from the point of view of emotional development. During this stage, children acquire a fair amount of stability and control over their emotions of anger, jealousy, fear, and joy. When the child is teased, threatened and betrayed, hi s/her negative emotions reactions like anger, hostility, loneliness etc come to happen. During childhood stage, children become more egocentric. When the child get positive situation, he/she smiles and displays love and affection. Emotional expression of children are found sudden, brief and for short period of time. Their emotional expressions do not persist for a long time. Children do not show one type of emotion, but they show different types of emotion at a time.

Adolescence (13-19 years) Stage: It is an important stage of emotional development. Adolescence period is called as the period of stress and strain. During this stage, the emotional characteristics like love, hate, fear, jealousy reaches at the extreme level. Adolescents are found to have fluctuated moods. Ross therefore said the adolescents live an intensely emotional life. Both positive and negative emotional behaviours arise in the adolescents with a constant alternation between intense excitement and deep depression. Thwarted adolescent's/teenager's love may end in suicide and appreciated teenagers may show creativeness. During this stage, adolescent's extreme emotionality of hate may lead to aggression, extreme fear may lead to nervousness, extreme jealousy may lead to revengeful actions. When adolescents fail to control their emotions, they are found to display the behaviours like nose-picking, nail biting, constantly quarrelling with his/her class mates and members of his family and may show pugnacity too. Adolescent's emotions are found complex. Their varied experiences from different environments add to the complexity of their emotional development. Adolescents become able to hide their true emotional experiences. Therefore it is difficult to understand the emotions of adolescents. Further, adolescent's emotional feelings are widened. Adolescents begin to appreciate others and emotionally form friendship, form groups and take leadership in the group. Adolescents need recognition before others and want to act and behave independently having freedom. During this stage, there develops capacity of tolerance in the adolescents and they become able to tolerate or bear up tensions, troubles, frustrations and failures. During this stage, adolescents begin to love their neighbours, friends, members of his group, fellow beings. They begin to sympathies the persons in trouble. During adolescents the common emotional expressions like love and affection, pleasure and delight, worries and anxieties are caused in adolescents. During childhood love of children centers around the object of interest which satisfy the immediate needs of the child. But in the adolescence stage, love of adolescents centers on near relatives, pets, opposite sex. During this period, love takes a sexual colour and becomes a source of pleasure.

Adulthood (20 years-onwards) Stage: During adulthood period, an adult person supposes to have more understanding power and more matured in all aspect of his life. He/she possesses sufficient knowledge about his/her surroundings, followings and therefore tries to adjust himself/herself accordingly. In this stage all the emotional expressions like anger, fear, anxiety, love, affection, hate, etc are consolidated. An adult tries to control his emotions keeping in view of the situations and becomes more adjusted. All the emotional qualities which are seen to be expressed during the childhood and adolescence stage become evident during the adulthood period but they are found to be stabled and controllable conditions.

Factors influencing Emotional Development

The following factors influence the emotional development of children

Physiological Factors: If the physiological condition of children remains sound then their emotional development become sound and healthy and vice versa. Physically weak children are porn to emotional disturbances in comparison to healthy children. In a healthy child, glandular secretions are found to be normal and thus his/her emotional development is found positive. But in case of physically weak children, malfunctioning of his/her gland tends to create problems in his/her emotional development.

Cognitive Factors: Cognitive factors include intelligence, thinking, reasoning, imagination, memory and other mental make-ups. Sound mental development helps an individual to have better understanding and better adjustment and vice versa. Children having poor mental or cognitive development are found to be less adjusted and possess less control over his emotions. But in other hand children having better mental development possess more controlling capacity on their emotions.

Societal and Family Factors: Children generally follow and imitate the behaviour of their immediate kins, elders and relatives. Relationship is a great factor that influences the emotional development of children. A healthy relationship in the family and society helps children to imbibe healthy and positive emotions and vice versa.

Schooling Factors: School environment, teacher's attitude, class mate's relationship in the life of children has positive impact on their emotional development. Children during schooling stage imitate teacher's behaviour, friend's behaviour and accordingly they express their emotions. So a sound school environment helps to build sound and positive emotions and vice versa.

- *Methods of training Emotions*: Emotions in original form are primitive by nature. All creative, extraordinary and unusual activities human beings are the result of emotional expressions. So, there is a need to channelize and harness the emotion of children from the very beginning of their life. Possible care should be taken to train the emotions towards better cause and negative emotions need to be channelized. In this direction the following methods may be taken to train the emotions of children,
  - *Repression*: Sometimes children express undesirable emotions which are not acceptable by the society and others. At this situation restriction is imposed and punishment is laid on the children. Children are enforced to sublimit their emotions in the threat of punishment and strict rules and regulations. It causes an adverse effect on the emotional development of children. Therefore repression of emotions should not be done rather steps to be taken to motivate children to channelize their negative emotions into positive one appreciable by others.
  - *Expression*: Children should get ample opportunity and freedom to express their positive emotions. Children should be warned about the evil consequences of their undesirable emotions.
  - *Engagement*: Children should be kept busy and engaged in some activities so that they will get little time to express their evil emotions.

- *Redirection*: This method implies that, attempt should be made to redirect the primitive emotions of children into healthier and socially desirable emotions. Here scope is to be given to children to redirect their emotions with proper guidance.
- *Substitution*: This method implies that, lower order of emotions is to be substituted by the higher and noble order of emotions.
- *Channelization*: Channelization means providing desirable channels to outlet the undesirable emotions into socially desirable emotions. Ample opportunity is to be provided in the name of provision of extra-curricular or co-curricular activities in the schools, creative activities, problem solving activities, cultural and religious activities in the schools and communities etc.

Educational Implications

The study of Emotional Development has a great value in the field of education and educational psychology. The educational implications of the study of emotional development are as follows,

1. Both parents and teachers are to cordially deal with their children. They should not tease, ridicule and underestimate them and their activities before others rather they should appreciate and help them to understand the reality.
2. Sometimes the unusual emotions become creative actions. Therefore strict rules and regulations should not be imposed on children to suppress their emotions. Rather, children should be made aware of the evil effect of their odd and undesirable emotions and helped to express their positive and socially desirable emotions.
3. Ample opportunity is to be provided by teachers at their schools and parents at their homes for their children to express their desirable and healthy emotions. They should encourage them and provide wide scope to express their emotions.
4. Steps to be taken by the parents and the teachers at their respective places to keep their children mentally engaged in some activities.
5. Teachers in the schools should provide opportunity to their students to participate in the co-curricular activities like debate, discussion, drama. Seminars, conferences, games and sports etc which will help to channelize the evil emotions of the children in creative fields.
6. Parents are to take care in order to keep their children physically healthy so that positive emotions may develop in their children.
7. Parents should try to maintain sound and healthy relationship among the family members which will develop healthy emotions in their children.
8. Teachers and parents should train their children to live a cooperative life which will install sound and positive emotions in their children.
9. Both the teachers and parents should try to fulfill the desirable needs and demands of their children on priority basis and pay individual attention towards them.
10. Parents and teachers should try to eliminate the negative emotions from their children and help to form healthy emotions.

Moral Development

A new born baby initially is born with his primitive instincts. Gradually he imitates his relatives, parents, teachers, friends and others and learns to socially interact with them gradually along with the increase of his age. His primitive behaviour becomes polished and he becomes social animal by shaping his instinctive behaviour. Gradually, the character of a child is formed in the line of social needs. Child become capable of distinguishing between right and wrong, good and bad, just and unjust etc keeping in view of the social norms. This is called as the morality of the child. Moral development does not happen all of a sudden in the children. It takes a long time in its development in the child. The education, language development, development of intelligence and imagination etc, help a child's moral development. The role of society, parents, and elder members has positive impact on the moral development of children. Therefore a healthy environment supports more for the moral development of children and vice versa. The study of the process of moral and character development of children has a great value in the field of education and for the teachers because character plays a vital role in the life of an individual. The formation of character starts from the very beginning of life. The psychologist Sigmund Freud told that, whatever the child has to become, becomes within early four or five years. Therefore, teachers and parents should take care for the formation of good character in their children. As because, it has been told that, when wealth is lost nothing is lost, when health is lost something is lost, when character is lost everything is lost.

Moral development takes place from infancy to adulthood with the emergence, change, and understanding of morality. In the field of moral development, morality is defined as principles for how individuals ought to treat one another with respect to justice and others' welfare and rights. Moral development is a process through which a child develops proper attitudes towards the other people in the society based on various things such social and cultural norms, laws and rules. Moral development is also called as character development. Children possessing good moral character get respectable position in the society.

Defining character or morality, Peck and others stated that, character is a persisting pattern of attitude and motives which produces a rather predictable kind and quality of moral behaviour.

Mc dougall stated that, character is thus the sum total of acquired dispositions, a mental structure which is lasting, enduring and ever influencing conduct. It is definitely a product of social interaction. Good character is made and does not innately exist.

James Drever defined character that, it is that integration of habits, sentiments and ideals which renders an individual's action relatively stable and predictable.

Out of these definitions it becomes clear that, character or morality of a child is a type of predictable behaviour including his habits, sentiments and ideals ought to be shown towards others for respect and welfare according to social norms and values. This moral and character development is rooted out of his social interaction. Moral character or character is an evaluation of a particular individual's stable moral qualities. The concept of character implies to a variety of attributes including the existence or lack of virtues such as empathy, courage, fortitude, integrity, reliance, respect, humility, honesty, sincerity, and loyalty or of good behaviours or habits, Moral character primarily refers to the assemblage of qualities that distinguish one individual from another wit on a reference to a cultural. One's moral character comprises of his virtues and vices.

Characteristics of Moral Development

The moral development is characterized by the development of the following qualities.

- Truthfulness
- Honesty
- Loyalty
- Integrity
- Reliance
- Courage
- Empathy
- Respect
- Humility
- Sincerity
- Good habits
- Tolerance
- Obedience
- Self-control
- Power of consciousness
- Reliability
- Positive will-power

Factors Influencing Moral and Character Development of Individuals

The following factors influence the moral and character development of an individual,

Physical factors: Physical factors include the health and health related issues like nutrition, diet, illness etc. A physically healthy individual is expected to have sound moral character than the physically unhealthy individual. Therefore a healthy body implies a healthy character.

Cognitive factors: Cognitive factors include one's intelligence, memory, interest, thinking and reasoning powers etc. An individual having sound mentality and good intelligence is expected to have good moral character. Psychologist, Lewis Madison Terman held the view that; children having good and more intelligence are found to be more truthful, tolerant, honest and obedient and vice versa

Social factors: social factors include home, school, neighbour and religion related factors. The conducive and healthy environment of home, school, society, religious places and neighbourhood help children to imbibe positive moral values and develop good character and vice versa.

Mass-Media Factors: Children can learn moral lessons by reading value based books, magazines, newspapers etc. Sometimes, children can learn moral lessons by means of recreation by watching good cinemas and movies. Children imitate and follow the moral character of the characters displayed in books and cinemas and like to be in their life.

Moral Development at Different Stages

Infancy (0-5 years) Stage: Infancy stage is very important stage for development. Here in this stage, infants imitate their parents and other relatives and internalize in them. Infants observe their parents and family members sitting in prayer at their home and religious places like temples, mosques, gurudwara, church etc. and they sit with them to take part in prayer. This helps the children to inculcate moral values in them. Therefore family or home environment should be healthy for the children. Parents should try to maintain right relationship among the family members and always practice right things before their children. During this stage infants are expected to develop the moral qualities like respect, truthfulness, humility, nobleness, obedience and courage etc.

Childhood (6-12 Years) Stage: Childhood stage is a stage of consolidation in respect of moral development. Here children get new environment of school and peers and imitate their friends, classmates, teachers. So the school environment should be healthy for the moral development of children. Here children acquire the power of discriminating between rights and wrong, children build courage to express their temperaments. The chief moral values expected to be developed during this stage are nobility, humility, self-respect, obedience, punctuality, sincerity, empathy etc.

Adolescence (13-19 Years) Stage: Adolescence period is very important in view of the moral and character development of adolescents. It is period of stress and strain. Here in this stage, adolescents want to prove their self-identity before other and satisfy their motives. Along with their physical and mental development moral development becomes solid too. They display their actions in conformity with the social and cultural values. Moral values like integrity, self-respect, honesty, kindness, humility, tolerance, reliability, courage, empathy, self-control, truthfulness etc are expected to develop in the adolescents. During this stage, adolescents become more aware of the values of right and wrong, justice and injustice etc. Adolescent's behaviour is governed by group and social morals. Adolescence stage is called as the real stage of moral development. Religious integrity greatly influences the moral development of adolescents.

Adulthood (20 years-onwards) Stage: This is a period of consolidation from the point of view of the moral and character development of individuals. During this stage no unique moral quality develops rather the developed moral values at the previous stage are refined and get solidarity. An adult individual is expected to bear upon moral character keeping in the mind of existing social and cultural norms and stands. An adult individual is capable of applying his judgment on right and wrong, justice and injustice actions basing on his self-perception and social norms.

Theories of Moral Development

Some of the theories explaining the moral development of individuals are described below.

Theory of James Drever: According to the psychologist James Drever, the character of an individual develops as his feelings develop from a simple stage to a more complex stage. James Drever stated that character or moral development passes through certain stages like Perceptual stage, Ideational stage and rational stage.

1. *Perceptual Stage*: At this stage (Infancy-Childhood) a child is found guided by his crude emotions. Here he/she imitates and perceives other's behaviour and try to learn the same. So a child's primitive emotion does not guide him in developing his character.
2. *Ideational Stage*: Ideational stage (Adolescence stage) is a stage where the emotions and feelings become mature than the first stage. The feelings of individuals at this stage centers around object and persons coming in contact with them. During this period, individuals are found to be sentimental in different fields-social, intellectual, aesthetic, religious, political etc. But, development of sentiments centers around some objects or persons
3. *Rational Stage*: This is a stage (Adulthood) where individuals develop Self-Regarding sentiments. Which is a higher order of sentiment? Self-Regarding sentiment are also known as master sentiment. During this period, an individual is expected to be rational in his thought and action, respectful towards others, honest, decisive.

Theory of Mc Dougal: According to MacDougal, character development of individuals are seen through four stages such as feeling of pleasure and pain stage, reward and punishment stage, praise and blame stage and Self-Regarding sentiment stage.

1. *Pleasure and Pain stage*: This stage of MacDougal is same as the Perceptual stage being suggested by James Drever. During this period, crude emotions are developed in children. The behaviour of children is governed by their instincts. Children during this period fail to judge the future or result but want to fulfill their immediate need and become interested in immediate pain and pleasure. The activities which give pleasure are repeated and the activities which give pain are avoided by the children. Therefore the character of children during this stage is determined by their feeling of pain and pleasure.
2. *Reward and Punishment stage*: Reward and punishment stage is also equals to the Ideational stage of Drever. During this stage, different sentiments are developed and this sentimental and instinctual behaviour of children are sublimated and shaped by the influence of their teachers, parents and peers. Parents and teachers restrict the child from wrong actions and explain the merits and demerits of the same. Thus by the pressure of punishment from the parents and teachers, children check their wrong and instinctive behaviour. The pressure of rewards from the teachers and parents promote the behaviour of children in right direction.

3. *Praise and Blame stage*: During adolescence stage, adolescents become more sentimental in almost all of their actions. They want freedom and autonomy but social restriction compels them to modify their behaviour and channelize them into socially desirable behaviours. Social praise and blame has their positive impact on the character development of individuals. Social praise increase the feeling of confidence and courage in the individuals to do something but on the other hand blame creates a feeling of demoralized. But in some cases, social blame becomes beneficial for the individuals to improve their character. Therefore, the character of individuals are determined by praise or blame
4. *Self-regarding stage*: As the individual become older and matured, their sentiments become controlled. During this stage, individuals develop ideals of their own which remains above the control of praise and blame. Individuals build their own philosophy of life and master sentiment; this is called as the Self-regarding. It is called as the final and last stage of character development of individuals. During this stage, characters of individuals are determined by their self-regarding.

Theory of Cronbach: Cronbach suggested following five stages of character development.

1. *The Amoral stage*: Amoral stage continues from birth to 2 years of age. During this period infants are found active. Their emotions are governed by instincts and they are unable to control their instincts. Therefore, infants fail to discriminate between good and bad, right and wrong actions.
2. *The Self-Centered stage*: This stage continues from 2 years to 6 years of age. During this period children shows their interest on different objects of their own interest and they try to satisfy their needs and desires immediately. Children are found little concern about the social values and norms. They center their activities on their needs only. During this stage, children sometimes develop anti-social trends. The socialization of children is not mature in this stage. So parental guidance plays a vital role in the development of good character in the children during this stage.
3. *The conventional Stage*: This stage continues from 6 years to 8 years of age. This is also called as the later childhood stage. During this stage, children learn from their parents, peers and teachers. During this period, children follow elder in participating different ceremonies, prayers, and worships and become aware of the social norms and like to be.
4. *The Irrational Conscientious stage*: This stage continues from 8 years to 12 years of age. During this period, children start to integrate a mental makeup and develop a conscience in them. Children become able to examine their behaviour in accordance to the social needs and norms. Children also develop certain sentiments in them, their thoughts are found to irrational.
5. *The Rational Conscientious stage*: This stage continues from 13 to 18 years of age. During this stage, children reach the stage of adolescence. The adolescents want to satisfy their needs and interests in conformity to the social needs. Here they need autonomy and freedom. Extreme autonomy

and freedom sometimes develop negative characters in the adolescents. The adolescents develop their self-esteem. Their irrational thoughts and feelings become rational therefore; adolescents critically analyze the value and result of certain actions basing upon his conscience. Their sentiments are controlled and master sentiment is developed and adolescents become capable of channelizing their emotions towards better cause. This is called as the highest stage of moral/character development in the life of an individual.

Theory of Piaget: Piaget is well known for his theory of cognitive development of children. He has also proposed his own theory about children's moral development. Piaget recognized that cognitive development is closely tied to moral development. Cognitive theories of Piaget and Kohlberg assume that cognitive development underpins moral development. A child can only develop its moral thinking as its ability to think improves and develops. In his book 'The Moral Judgment of the Child' (1932), Piaget states that all morality consists in a system of rules.

Piaget suggested three stages of Moral development such as Pre-moral stage, Heteronomous—morality stage and Autonomous Morality stage.

1. *Pre-Moral Stage:* This stage continues from birth to 3 years of age. During this period, a child possesses little concept of morality and rules. This stage is also compares to the Freud's oral stage. During this period, child become more concerned with his own activities and fails to care others and gratify his own motives. He is not aware of social norms and others self. Here, children fail to distinguish what is wrong and what is right. Their conception about right and wrong is guided by their parents and elders.
2. *Hetronomous-Morality Stage:* This stage continues from 4 to 10 years of age. This is also called as moral realism stage. During this stage, child's moral reasoning is governed by external rules laid down by others. At this stage children become more socio-centric and try to abide the social norms. He starts to feel about other's self and act/ behave accordingly. During this period, children are tending to apply logic and hypotheses at this stage.
3. *Autonomous Morality Stage:* This stage continues from 10 years to onwards. Piaget address this stage as matured adult thinking stage, this is also called as moral relativism stage. During this period, the child develops a more flexible view of rules and morality. In this stage, the ethics of cooperation and complexity of moral issues are better understood. During this stage, individuals become have the concept of social justice in their mind and act accordingly. Individuals become fully aware of the result of criminal actions.

Theory of Kohlberg: Stages of the development of morality proposed by Lawrence Kohlberg constitute an adaptation of Jean Piaget's theory of moral development. Kohlberg viewed that moral reasoning, the basis for ethical behaviour, proceeds through six identifiable developmental stages coming under three major stages such as Pre-conventional morality stage, Conventional morality stage and Post-conventional morality stage which are discussed below:

1. *Pre-conventional Morality Stage:* The pre-conventional level of morality is commonly found in children, although adults can also exhibit this. The pre-conventional Morality consists of two stages such as the first and second stages of moral development. These two stages of moral development are fully concerned with the self of the children and children are found to be egocentric. Children with pre-conventional morality fail to adopt or internalize society's conventions regarding what is right or what is wrong.

   Obedience and punishment driven Stage (Stage-I): During this stage, children are found to be fully ego-centric. In this period, children focus on the direct consequences of their actions on themselves. In the afraid of punishment, children forcibly abide the rules.

   Self-interest driven stage (Stage-II): At this stage children remain more concerned with the gratification of their own self. But at the same time, they remain alerts about the rights of others. This type of feelings of moral sense forces children to make a compromise on the efforts for satisfying his needs and others.
2. *Conventional Stage Morality stage:* The conventional stage of morality is seen to be developed in the adolescents and adults. The conventional stage consists of the third and fourth stages of moral development. Conventional morality is characterized by an acceptance of society's conventions concerning right and wrong. At this level an individual obeys rules and follows norms of the society even when there are no consequences for obedience or disobedience.

   Interpersonal accord and conformity driven stage (Stage-III): During this stage, the self of individual enters the society by filling social roles. Individuals play perceived roles and become receptive to approval or disapproval from others. They try to be a "good boy" or "good girl" and live up to the expectations of others. Individuals accept the approved social norms and become conscious of other's intentions.

   Authority and social rules obedience driven stag (Stage-IV): During this stage individuals obey the social conventions, social rules and feel the importance of maintaining a functioning society. Moral reasoning in stage four is thus beyond the need for individual approval exhibited in stage three. A central ideal or ideals often prescribe what is right and wrong. In this stage individuals become capable of understanding the social norms, social rules, social justice, social laws and social system.
3. *Post-Conventional Morality stage:* The post-conventional Morality level is also known as the principled level of morality. It is marked by a growing realization that individuals are separate entities from society, and that the individual's own perspective may take precedence over society's view. Individuals may disobey rules inconsistent with their own principles. Post-conventional moralists live by their own ethical principles. People who exhibit post-conventional morality view rules as useful but changeable. Rules are not absolute dictates that must be obeyed without question. Because post-conventional individuals elevate their own moral evaluation

of a situation over social conventions The conventional morality stage include stage five and stage six of the development of morality.

Social contract driven stage (Stage-V): In this stage, individuals understands the values of the society and accepts the established norms of the society, respects the social needs and rights of others. Individuals perform right actions. Individuals' conceive that, Laws are social contracts rather than rigid edicts and it can be changed to promote the general welfare at the time of necessity to meet the greatest good for the greatest number of people. In this stage, democratic feelings develop in the individuals.

Universal ethical principles driven stage (Stage-VI): This stage of moral development is based on the abstract reasoning using universal ethical principles. At this stage, individuals do not hesitate to sacrifice their life for the cause of greater interest. Individuals elevate their self to the social and universal self. This is called as the highest level of moral development in the life of individuals.

Carol Gilligan's Theory of Ethics of Care and Moral Development: Carol Gilligan a student of developmental Psychologist, Lawrence Kohlberg, who introduced the theory of stages of moral development. Gilligan revealed the gender differences of moral development and included the caring perspective in her theory. Gilligan stated that males and females are socialized differently, and females are more apt than males to stress interpersonal relationships and take responsibility for the well-being of others. Gilligan suggested this difference is due to the child's relationship with the mother and that females are traditionally taught a moral perspective that focuses on community and caring about personal relationships.

Gilligan proposed the Stages of the Ethics of Care theory, which addresses what makes actions 'right' or 'wrong'. Gilligan's theory focused on both care-based morality and justice-based morality. Care based morality is found more common in girls. It develops in girls due to their interconnectedness with their mothers through whom they learn to avoid violence and help those in need. Girls remain less inclined to worry about issues of fairness. On the other hand, Justice based morality is universally found and developed in boys. It develops in boys due to their autonomous nature and their interaction with others through whom they learn to avoid inequality. Boys remain inclined to the concept of inequality as they are least connected with their mothers.

Gilligan's Stages of Ethics of Care: Like Kohlberg, Gilligan proposed three stages in her Ethics of Care theory such as pre-conventional, conventional and post-conventional stages. Within each stage there are goals and specific transition points that move the individual through these stages. Gilligan suggests that these transitions are fueled by changes in the sense of self rather than in changes in cognitive capability.

The following table displays the stages of development of ethical acre and morality.

Gilligan's Stages of the Ethic of Care	
Stage of Development of Morality	**Goal of Individual**
Pre-Conventional stage (Stage-I)	Self Survival
Transition is from selfishness—to—responsibility to others	
Conventional stage (Stage-II)	Self-sacrifice is goodness
Transition is from goodness—to—truth that she/he is a person too	
Post Conventional stage (Stage-III)	Respect to other's self and Non-violence

Though Gilligan did not mentioned any specific age of the development of ethics and morality, he viewed that, an individual is seen to proceed through three different stages of his moral development equivalent to Kohlberg' stages of moral development such as Pre-conventional, conventional and post-conventional stage. Each stage of moral development tries to fulfill certain goals. During pre-conventional stage, one's ethical and moral values center around his self and goal is self-survival. Here one does not get worry about others. During Conventional stage, one's ethical and moral values center round the self of others. During this stage, someone is found worry about others and he becomes ready to sacrifice his self for the goodness of others. In between there is a transition stage, where one's moral development get shifted from his selfishness to self-sacrifice for others and performing responsibility for the fulfillment of the need of others. During post-conventional stage, one's ethical and moral development center round the universal truth and respect to other's self. During this stage, someone is found to bear the moral values of nonviolênce and respect to others and not hurting to anyone. In between conventional and post-conventional stage, there is a transition stage, where one's moral development get shifted from goodness to truth and the individual become aware of her/his self.

Educational Implications

Study of moral development has a great educational value. The highest goal of education is to develop a good moral character in the children. Therefore, it is the responsibility of parents and teachers to build the character of their children both at their homes and schools. The curriculum at schools should be reformed in the light of development of moral values in the children. Parents and teachers should encourage their children to inculcate good habits and encourage them to do right actions. Teacher should emphasize the ethical and moral aspect of the subjects they teach to their students. Both parents and teachers should try to understand the sentiments of their children and accordingly deal with them. At the time of necessity, parents and teachers should apply the technique of rewards and punishment judiciously for their children in order to control their emotions. Teachers and parents should exhibit the pictures of the great men and their deeds, heroic actions etc in the schools and homes. Teachers and parents should encourage their children to study the biography of the great men, great leaders and religious persons.

Language Development

Man is a social being who wants to interact with his fellow beings. This interaction process needs language. Language is a way of communication and social control. Language and human life is closely related. All human beings make use of language since their birth to death. Language helps the individual in the process of his development. Language is required for effective communication. Languages help to express one's inner feelings to others. Mental development of an individual cannot be studied properly without his/her language development. Someone's language developments indicate his/her level of mental development. Someone's language developments go along with his mental development. One's language development positively influences to his personality development and exerts its impact on his/her adjustment process. Successful language developments of an individual help him to flourish in his life. Therefore, it is need to understand the pattern of language development of children in their life.

The term language has been derived from the Latin word 'Lingua' which implies tongue. Language includes whole process of phenomena associated with human vocal and auditory communication of emotions and ideas. Language is the sum total of an individual's verbal and non-verbal expression related to his communication process. Language development refers to development of ability of an individual to express his thoughts and feelings by the use of symbols, words and sentences. It is the acquisition of a power of expression, interaction and communication of thoughts and feelings through adopting the means of symbols, words and sentences. Language is a social phenomenon. The evolution of language finds is root from the very existence of human being in the society. The use of language is as old as human civilization. There are several languages all over the world. The accuracy of language depends on the knowledge of grammar and correct pronunciation, correct spelling, correct reading and correct listening. Phonemes and morphemes are two important aspect languages.

Encyclopedia Britannica defines language as an arbitrary system of vocal symbols by means of which human being, as member of a social group and participants, in culture, interact and communicate.

Allen defines; Language is a means of communicating thoughts.

Plato says, Ideas and feelings are the realizations but when these are revealed through mouth, it is known as language.

Characteristics of Language Development

Language development is characterized as follows,

- Development of ability to use symbolical expression
- Development of the ability to use words for expression of feelings and thoughts
- Development of the ability to communicate with others
- Development of the ability to understand other's expression

- Development of the ability to read
- Development of the ability to write
- Development of the ability to speak

Types of Language

Language is of two types such as non-Verbal and Verbal.

1. *Non-Verbal/Symbolic Language:* It is a type of language which involves different symbolical expressions. An individual expresses his ideas and feelings through some symbols.
2. *Verbal Language:* Verbal language is a type of language which involves different sounds, words and sentences for expression of ideas and feelings of an individual. It may involve the activities like reading, writing and speaking.

Nature of Language

The followings are the nature of language.

1. *Language is a system*: Language is a system of complex whole just as human body where different parts of body are inter connected and operate in coordination. Language also represents as a system which involve the coordinated functions of words, structures, sounds,
2. *Language is learnt:* Language does not automatically come to an individual rather it is learnt by the individual through continuous practice and imitation.
3. *Language is social artifacts:* Language finds its root in the society and culture. Language is a divine gift for individuals which is cultured from their social life. One's linguistic power gets enriched through his interaction and effective communication with his fellow beings.
4. *Language is evolutionary*: language has developed from the origin of the human civilization and still it is in the process of evolution. Different sounds, words, sentences, structures etc. are coming out day by day. Human speech and dialects have been modified into the form of language in the due course of time, day by day, man is trying to find out innovative usage of language.
5. *Language is a dynamic phenomenon:* Language is a dynamic but not a static phenomenon. Language is in a continuous process of change just like social change. Primitive man's language has been changed and modified to modern languages with the impact of culture and science.
6. *Language is climatically influenced:* It is called that, language is a speech. Climatic condition of a particular society or nation has it's positive impact/influence on speech pattern of its inhabitants. That is why different styles of pronunciation or sounds are found in case of peoples of different countries.
7. *Language is a cultural product:* Every language is a product of a particular culture or society. Language has its meaning in relation a culture. Therefore there are no similar or equal words in any two languages.
8. *Language is a means but not an end:* Language is a means of communication. Man shares his ideas and feelings with his fellow beings

by means of language either verbally or no-verbally. All the literatures are the expressions of languages in its different forms. Language help to proceed on communication so, it is a means but not an end itself.

9. *Language is a science:* language is a science because; the mechanism of language is built upon the systematic coordination of sounds, alphabets, words and structures. Scientific organization of words, sounds and structures breeds language,
10. *Language is psycho-operated:* The systematic expression of language depends on one's psychology. While taking on the activities of reading, writing and listening, an individual has to employ his psychological processes of reasoning, thinking, intelligence, motives, emotions, feelings etc.

Functions of Language

Use of language serves the following functions for an individual such as,

1. *Communicative function*: In communicative function, language is used by an individual to communicate his ideas or feelings to others either by symbolic way or by verbal way.
2. *Interactive function*: In interactive function, language is used by an individual to interact with others, to have conversation with others in a social process.
3. *Expressive function*: In expressive function, language is used by an individual to express his own ideas and feelings either through symbolical or verbal manner.
4. *Informative function*: Human civilization has developed by advancement of the informative process. Today's globalization requires mutual sharing of information. In this regard language helps in disseminating information through books, literatures, newspapers, magazine; journals etc. people use language of their own to convey messages to others.
5. *Preservative function*: Man is fortunate to have his divine gift of language. From the very inception of human civilization, man has built a long culture in the field of science, commerce, trade and arts. The past experiences of human society have been converted into human culture. Development of language ahs helped the man to preserve his culture in the form of literature found expressed in books and journals.

Components of Language Development

Language development in children incorporate the following four components such as,

1. *Phonology:* Phonology involves the rules about the structure and sequence of speech sounds of the individual.
2. *Semantics:* Semantics consists of vocabulary and expression of concepts through words.
3. *Grammar:* Grammar involves two parts such as Syntax and Morphology. The part, Syntax refers to the rules in which words are arranges into sentences. The second part, Morphology refers to the use of grammatical rules to frame sentences indicating tense, active or passive voice etc.

4. *Pragmatics:* Pragmatics involves the rules for appropriate and effective communication skills. There are three pragmatic rules such as a) using language for greeting, demanding etc, b) changing language for talking differently and c) turn taking while using language, staying on topic etc.

Language Development at Different Stages

Infancy (0-5 Years) Stage: Piaget considers this stage as sensory motor and pre-operational stage of in view of cognitive and language development of children. During infancy stage, children learn and acquire language through imitation and association method. Children practice to repeat the sounds they imitate from their parents, elders and caregivers. Positive reinforcement at this time helps children to build sound language development. After birth to around one year, the baby starts to make speech sounds. From 12 to 24 months, babies recognize the correct pronunciation of familiar words. Babies can use phonological strategies to simplify word pronunciation At the initial stage of life of children until the last 2 years of age, infants language development is found to be physical. Infants imitate the sounds from their caregivers and repeat the same. Children completing 24 to 30 months develop awareness of rhyme as well as rising intonation, use and understand why question and basic spatial terms such as in, on or under. Children completing age of 36 to 60 months, phonological awareness continues to improve as well as their pronunciation, understand basic colour words and kinship terms and comprehend When and how questions as well as basic shape words such as circle, square and triangle, recognize, names and sounds letters and numbers and children start using telegraphic speech, which are two word combinations. Up to the end of their 5 years of age, children learn to speak but their speaking is self centered and object oriented. During this stage, children continue to add grammatical morphemes and gradually produce complex grammatical structures.

Childhood (6-12 years) Stage: Piaget considers this stage as concrete operational stage in view of the cognitive and language development of children. During childhood stage, sense of hearing plays a crucial role, providing the basis for speech and communication skills. At this stage, children become capable of using logic and solving problems in the form of stories dealing only with facts rather than abstract ideas. Language at this stage is used to refer to specific and concrete facts, not mental concepts. By the age of 6 to 10 years, children master syllable stress patterns which help to distinguish slight differences between similar words. Children can understand meanings of words based on their definitions and appreciate and grasp the multiple meanings of words and use words precisely through metaphors and puns and children become able to acquire new information from written texts and can explain relationships between multiple meaning words. During this period, children's writing skill develops. Children now become able to write complete sentences on some topic and able to have simple form of conversation.

Adolescence (13-19 Years) Stage: Piaget considers this stage as formal operational period in view of cognitive and language development of individuals. During adolescence stage, individuals start to use their abstract reasoning and make a mental distinction between their self and an idea they consider. Children at this stage use language to express and debate abstract theoretical concepts such as those found in mathematics, philosophy or logic. At this stage, an individual become able to comprehend abstract ideas, turn his/her speech on different topics, write essays artistically and converse adequately with his/her fellow beings. At this stage, vocabulary stock and power is enormously developed. Individuals can write complex texts applying grammatical rules. During this stage, individuals become able to read perfectly books and literatures following rules of grammar.

Adulthood (20 years-onwards) Stage: During this stage, language development of individuals reaches full maturation. At this stage, individuals are found perfect in all the linguistic skills like reading, writing, listening and understanding correct language. Individuals become able to carry abstract and imaginary thinking by using language in his mind and individuals can frame varied mental concepts and define the meaning of words and sentences in their coexistence. Individuals can read, write and understand complex type of literatures. This period also can be said as the consolidation in view of language development.

Theories of Language Development

Following theories explain the process of language development in human beings.

B.F. Skinner's Learned Theory

Learned theory of language development given by B.F. Skinner is also known as Behaviourist theory of language development. B.F. Skinner (1957) in his book "Verbal Behaviour" stated that like other behaviours, language behaviour is learned through conditioning. Language is learned through association, imitation and reinforcement. Thus, the language behaviour of children is controlled through reinforcement from an external source like parents and other care takers. According to Skinner, children learn words by associating sounds with objects, actions, and events. They also learn words and syntax by imitating others. Adults enable children to learn words and syntax by reinforcing correct speech. Practice and reinforcement strengthens the language development of children. Skinner's theory stresses environmental influence on language development. During this stage, children fail to write but it is initial stage of writing begins.

Noam Chomsky's Innate Theory

Noam Chomsky (1969) gave a new perspective on language development after Skinner's theory basing upon his own observation called innate theory or psychologist theory of language development. Chomsky pointed out that children raised in environments, some children get better reinforcement and some children do not get it. But it is found that, children learn their language at same step and same pace though their environment and reinforcement differs. The rate of language development may vary but almost all children learn language naturally. This was true even for children raised in families where parents did not explicitly teach the dominant language. Chomsky also pointed out that, Language acquisition is uniform across languages and children learn the rules of grammar universally. Noam Chomsky held the view that, inborn/innate biological ability help children to learn and generate complex language. According to Chomsky, language is innately human and acquired through biological maturation rather than learned over time. Thus, he replaced the term language learning with language acquisition. Chomsky stated that all children have a built-in cognitive system in their brains similar to a language organ that explains their ability to store highly complex language structures. He referred to this system as a language acquisition device (LAD).

According to Chomsky, LAD is common in all humans which allow them to develop language naturally. This LAD enables humans to acquire and process language by interpreting language, developing grammatical rules, and generating language responses.

Later on Chomsky replaced LAD with Universal Grammar (UG) with the proposition that, on the surface, all dialects and languages look and sound different but there are some basic principles shared by most dialects and languages. According to Chomsky, humans are born with the UG rules already built in, and this is what gives us the ability to learn any language. According to Chowmsky, UG contains two components such as Structure dependency and Set of parameters.

A. *Structure dependency:* The structure dependency refers to all grammatical operations within sentences defined in terms of the structure of phrases rather than words. Each phrase contains a main word called 'Head' and all phrases in a particular language have the head in the same position. However, the head position is different across different languages.
B. *Set of parameters:* The set of parameters refers to the placement of the head in the phrase structure. For example, English is a head-initial language. Consider the options for word order when using an object in a sentence. In an English environment, the correct grammar structure would be a subject-verb-object series ("The boy hit the ball."). However in other languages such as Japanese, which is a head-final language, the correct word order would be subject-object-verb. As children are raised in their native language environment, they unconsciously set their grammar structure to match their surroundings, thus setting their parameters.

Lev Vygotsky's Transactional Theory

Opposed to B.F. Skinner's learned theory and Chomsky's innate theory of language development, Soviet Psychologist, Lev Vygotsky highlighted transactional theory of language development which was made prominent in the western world by James Brunner. Transactional theory is also known as interactional theory of language development. This theory held the view that, language development of children are seen to happen through social interaction. Interactional theory is largely based on Socio-Cultural theories of Soviet Psychologist Lev Vygotsky. Unlike other approaches, it emphasizes the role of feedback and reinforcement in language acquisition. Specifically, it states that much of a child's linguistic growth stems from modeling of and interaction with parents and other adults, who very frequently provide instructive correction. This theory affirms that language development as a product of both nature (innate/biological) and nurture (environment/reinforcement). In other words, a child´s language is developed through the interaction of his/her biological make-up and the impact of his/her environment. More specifically, this theory emphasizes the social function of language development. According to supporters of the social interaction theory, infants begin to develop language through social interactions with their caregivers. In fact, purposes for learning language by individuals are socially related. Infants influence the behaviours of their caretakers with their crying, body gestures, and facial expressions from day of their birth. Parents and caretakers in turn respond to these communicative actions with verbal language, establishing the roots for future language development of their children. When the child begins to produce verbal language sounds, the adult responds with more complex forms. Then the child imitates the more complex form, and so on.

The Empiricist Theory

The supporters of Empiricist theory of language development are Plato, Hobbes and Locke. According empiricists, language emerge in children from their abstracted sense impressions and sensory experiences. The empiricist theory of language development states that children have their own general brain processes which are sufficient enough for their language acquisition. During this process, it is necessary for the child to be actively engaged with their environment. The parents or caregivers should adopt appropriately a particular way of communicating with their children in order to help then to learn languages. This is known as child-directed speech (CDS). CDS is used so that children are given the necessary linguistic information needed for their language. Empiricism is a general approach and sometimes goes along with the interactionist approach.

Piaget's Theory of Language Development

According to Jean Piaget, language development of children goes along with their cognitive development. Language development of children is a continuation of their general cognitive development. From his research into children's language and thinking, Jean Piaget gave the idea that children do not think like adults. Piaget's cognitive theory describes the mental structures or "schemas" of children as they develop from infants to adults. Piaget stated that, children actively construct their own understanding of the world through their interactions with their environment. Piaget's theory purports that children's language reflects the development of their logical thinking and reasoning skills in "periods" or stages, Piaget pointed out four stages of children's cognitive development such as sensory motor stage, Pre-operational stage, concrete operational stage and formal operational stage. Piaget believed that these four stages of cognitive and linguistic development were universal and that no children ever skipped over one of the four steps

1. *Sensory-motor Stage:* During Sensory-motor period which last until 2 years of age of infant's language development is basically physical. During this period they imitate the sounds from their parents and caregivers and practice the same sounds. They deal with the symbolical expression of language and begin to use a limited number of heard words.

2. *Preoperational Stage*: During Pre-operational stage which starts at 2 years and last until 6 or 7 years of age, children learn to talk. During this stage, children may describe what they do. Children become able to acquire some vocabulary stocks and start to use them.
3. *Concrete operational Stage*: During concrete operational period which starts at 7 years and last until 12 years of age, children become capable of using logic and solving problems in the form of stories as long as the story deals only with facts rather than abstract ideas. Language at this stage is used to refer to specific and concrete facts, not mental concepts.
4. *Formal operational Stage*: During formal operational stage which starts at 12 years and onwards, children start to use their abstract reasoning and make a mental distinction between their self and an idea they consider. Children at this stage use language to express and debate abstract theoretical concepts such as those found in mathematics, philosophy or logic.

Relational Frame Theory

The relational frame theory (RFT) was the contribution of Hayes, Barnes-Holmes, Roche (2001). Based upon the principles of Skinnerian Behaviourism, RFT states that children acquire language purely through interacting with their environment. Empirical studies supporting the predictions of RFT suggest that children learn language via a system of inherent reinforcements, challenging the view that language acquisition is based upon innate, language-specific cognitive capacities.

Emergenist Theory

Emergenist theories proposed by Mac Whinny's competition model state that language acquisition is a cognitive process that emerges from the interaction of biological pressures and the environment. According to these theories, neither nature nor nurture alone is sufficient for language learning but both the nature and nurture must work together in order to help children to learn and acquire a language. The proponents of these theories argue that general cognitive processes subserve language acquisition and that the end result of these processes is language learning such as word learning and grammar learning. Most of the empirical studies support the predictions of these theories and argue that that language acquisition is a more complex process.

7
Adolescence Growth and Development

Adolescence is a stage of human growth and development. Every individual passes through this stage of growth and development in his life. This stage is seen to be attained within the age range of 13 to 19 years of age of an individual. This stage is said to be a vital stage in the development of an individual. During this period, children tend toward maturity of their physical organs which exerts a great impact on his other aspect of developments like mental, moral, social and emotional aspects. So this stage is called as a period of stress and strain in the life of an individual. Therefore, it is essential to understand the characteristics of adolescence development which will help in devising educational strategies for the fullest development and adjustment of the adolescents. Parents and teachers are to carefully deal with the adolescents keeping in view of their needs and interests.

MEANING AND DEFINITIONS OF ADOLESCENCE

The term adolescence means to grow to maturity. Adolescence period is a transitional period between childhood and adulthood stage. It emerges from the childhood stage and ends in the adulthood stage. Adolescence is a period of expansion after childhood. Therefore children attain maturity of their physical, mental, moral, emotional and social aspects.

Jersild defines that, Adolescence is that span of years during which boys and girls move from childhood to adulthood-mentally, emotionally, socially and physically.

Hall defines that, Adolescence is a period of stress and strain, storm and strife.

Kullen states that, Adolescence is a period which is characterized by sexual, social, occupational and ideological adjustment and striving for independence from parents.

Baron pointed out that, Adolescence is a period beginning with the onset of puberty and ending when individuals assume adult roles and responsibilities.

Out of the above definitions it become clear that, adolescence stage which is a transitional phase in between childhood and adulthood stage ranging from 13 to 19 years of age called as' teen age' is a critical point in the life of an individual in view of his physical, mental emotional, social and moral development putting a stress and strain on the individual. Different sentiments develop during this stage in the individuals.

CHARACTERISTICS OF PHYSICAL GROWTH AND DEVELOPMENT DURING ADOLESCENCE PERIOD

During adolescence period, physical growth and development again takes place rapidly as like as the infancy stage. The child reaches at the maximum limit of his physical growth and development. During this period, a lot of physiological changes are marked in the body of girls and boys and we can mark a great difference in the growth of boys and girls.

Adolescence is characterized by dramatic physical changes moving the individual from childhood into physical maturity. Early, prepubescent changes are noted with the appearance of secondary sexual characteristics.

Girls may begin to develop breast buds as early as 8 years old, with full breast development achieved anywhere from 12 to 18 years. Pubic hairs growth in armpit and other private parts typically begins at about age 9 or 10, and reaches adult distribution patterns at about 13 to 14 years.

Menarche (the beginning of menstrual periods) typically occurs about 2 years after initial pubescent changes are noted. It may occur as early as 10 years, or as late as 15 years. A rapid growth in height occurs for girls between the ages of about 9.5 and 14.5 years, peaking somewhere around 12 years.

Boys may begin to notice enlargement of the testicles and scrotum as early as 9 years of age, followed closely by lengthening of the penis. Adult size and shape of the genitals is typically reached by age 16 to 17 years. Pubic hair growth—as well as armpit, leg, chest, and facial hair—begins in boys at about age 12, and reaches adult distribution patterns at about 15 to 16 years.

A rapid growth in height occurs for boys between the ages of about 10 to 11 and 16 to 18, peaking around age 14. Puberty is not marked with a sudden incident in boys, as it is with the onset of menstruation in girls. The appearance of regular nocturnal emissions (wet dreams) marks the onset of puberty in boys and typically occurs between the ages of 13 and 17 years, with the average about 14.5 years.

A remarkable growth of height of the body of both boys and girls are attained during this period. However, the average growth of girls remains better than the boys in respect of their weight and height. The body proportions get its mature size during this period. All parts of body acquire adult proportions by the end of 18 years of age. The muscles, bones and joints become more strengthened.

During adolescence period, the internal organs also get their maturity. The skeleton becomes longer day by day. Glandular changes also take place during physical growth. Different gland like, thyroid, pituitary, thymus and sex glands develop to the maximum extent. The changes in the glands affect the behaviour of the adolescents-boys and girls. The masculine and feminine characteristics are developed in the boys and girls during this period.

Secondary sex characteristics appear in different parts of the body of adolescents. Genital organs in the adolescents get their maturity and increase in size. Both girls and boys develop interest in opposite sexes. The reproductive organs of adolescents-boys and girls become active. The boys and girls acquire more ability, skills and strength of their body. Girls seem to mature earlier than the boys in physical activity. Both boys and girls develop athletic abilities during this period of adolescence.

The adolescent individuals both boys and girls become physically active and develop ability, skills, strength and sped in doing various physical activities. Girls seem to get maturity earlier than the boys in physical activity. Bothe boys and girls develop athletic ability at this stage.

CHARACTERISTICS OF MENTAL DEVELOPMENT DURING ADOLESCENCE PERIOD

During adolescence period, the individual starts understanding, memorizing, thinking and reasoning. Mental development is greatly influenced by maturation and learning. During the stage of adolescence the cognitive development of the individual is characterized by attending, perceiving, observing, remembering, imagining, thinking, problem solving as well as developing language habits. The individual becomes able to take decisions. The sensation and perception power, imagination and thinking power of individuals are more vigorously developed in the stage of adolescence.

According to Piaget, adolescence period is called as the period of Formal Operational stage in intellectual development of an individual. The formal operational period is the fourth and final of the periods of cognitive development in Piaget's theory. This stage, which follows the Concrete Operational stage, commences at around 11 years of age (puberty) and continues into adulthood. In this stage, individuals move beyond concrete experiences and begin to think abstractly, reason logically and draw conclusions from the information available, as well as apply all these processes to hypothetical situations. Adolescents begin to think more as a scientist thinks, devising plans to solve problems and systematically testing solutions They use hypothetical-deductive reasoning, which means that they develop hypotheses or best guesses, and systematically deduce, or conclude, which is the best path to follow in solving the problem. During this stage the young adult is able to understand such things as love, "shades of gray", logical proofs and values. During this stage the young adult begins to entertain possibilities for the future and is fascinated with what they can be.

CHARACTERISTICS OF EMOTIONAL DEVELOPMENT DURING ADOLESCENCE PERIOD

Adolescence stage is an important stage of emotional development. Adolescence period is called as the period of stress and strain. During this stage, the emotional characteristics like love, hate, fear, jealousy reaches at the extreme level. Adolescents are found to have fluctuated moods. *Ross* therefore said the adolescents live an intensely emotional life. Both positive and negative emotional behaviours arise in the adolescents with a constant alternation between intense excitement and deep depression. Thwarted adolescents/teenager's love may end in suicide and appreciated teen agers may show creativeness. During this stage, adolescent's extreme emotionality of hate may lead to aggression, extreme fear may lead to nervousness, extreme jealousy may lead to revengeful actions. When adolescents fail to control their emotions, they are found to display the behaviours like nose-picking, nail biting, constantly quarrelling with his/her class mates and members of his family and may show pugnacity too. Adolescent's emotions are found complex. Their varied experiences from different environments add to the complexity of their emotional development. Adolescents become able to hide their true emotional experiences. Therefore it is difficult to understand the emotions of adolescents. Further, adolescent's emotional feelings are widened. Adolescents begin to appreciate others and emotionally form friendship, form groups and take leadership in the group. Adolescents need recognition before others and want to act and behave independently having freedom. During this stage, there develops capacity of tolerance in the adolescents and they become able to tolerate or bear up tensions, troubles, frustrations and failures. During this stage, adolescents begin to love their neighbours, friends and members of his group, individuals of opposite sex and fellow beings. They begin to sympathies the persons in trouble. During adolescents the common emotional expressions like love and affection, pleasure and delight, worries and anxieties are caused in adolescents. During childhood love of children centers around the object of interest which satisfy the immediate needs of the child. But in the adolescence stage, love of adolescents centers on near relatives, pets, opposite sex. During this period, love takes a sexual colour and becomes a source of pleasure.

CHARACTERISTICS OF SOCIAL DEVELOPMENT DURING ADOLESCENCE PERIOD

Adolescence state is very crucial stage of development of social qualities in the life of an individual. During this stage, an individual is expected to develop the social qualities like power of understanding and adjustment, group life, submissiveness, helpfulness, cooperativeness, trust, kindness, piety, leadership etc. If sound environment is not availed, then the negative social qualities like hostility and enmity may develop in adolescents. Adolescents want to keep relationship with heterogeneous groups and their gregarious attitude is more developed. However, the adolescence stage is called as the period of consolidation and restoration stage of development of social behaviour of an individual. During this period adolescents become more socially conscious, understands the self of others, develop sense of social responsibilities, develop sense of group loyalties, become more responsive towards their social and community needs, develop social maturity and adopt with gangs and other social groups. One of the major social qualities that are the leadership quality is found to develop in the adolescents during the stage of adolescence. At this stage, social, cultural, recreational and vocational interests also develop in the adolescents.

CHARACTERISTICS OF MORAL DEVELOPMENT DURING ADOLESCENCE PERIOD

Adolescence period is very important in view of the moral and character development of adolescents. Here in this stage, adolescents want to prove their self identity before other and satisfy their motives. Along with their physical and mental development, moral development becomes solid too. They display their actions in conformity with the social and cultural values. Moral values like, integrity, self respect, honesty, kindness, humility, tolerance, reliability, courage, empathy, self control, truthfulness are expected to develop in the adolescents. During this stage, adolescents become more aware of the values of right and wrong, justice and injustice. Adolescent's behaviour is governed by group and social morals. Adolescence stage is called as the real stage of moral development. Religious integrity greatly influences the moral development of adolescents.

NEEDS OF ADOLESCENTS

According to Hall, adolescence period is a period of stress and strain in adolescent's life. Therefore varied interests develop in them. It is need to understand the needs of the adolescents while framing the aims and objectives and curriculum in the system of education. Broadly needs are of two types such as primary needs and secondary needs. Primary needs are physiological needs felt by the individuals and secondary needs are the social and psychological needs felt by the individuals. In the absence of fulfillment of needs, individuals feel maladjusted. Adolescence experiences a good number of needs owing to their maturity and development both of primary and secondary in nature. Primary needs include the needs of sex, needs of basic things like food, clothing and shelter, and rest. Secondary needs include the needs of wealth, love, prestige, independence, freedom, leadership, recognition etc. However during adolescence stage, the following needs are commonly felt by the adolescents.

Sexual Need: Adolescence period is a remarkable period of sexual development in the adolescents. Sexual development takes auto-eroticism during infancy stage, homo-sexualism during childhood stage but during adolescence stage, it takes the form of hetro-sexuality. So, the adolescents start to love the individuals of opposite sex. Individuals become more conscious of their physical changes of their body and found to be more curious about sex. When social pressure and social conscience check the sexual need of infants and then, it is channelized into different awkward behaviour in them. In this stage better sex education is to be provided to adolescents.

Gregarious Need: During adolescence period, the gregarious need come in front and play a vital role in the life of adolescents. Adolescents want to become a part of their gang/group, want freedom from their parents and take part in the group activities. So, during this period, if the adolescents are not properly educated and misdirected then there may develop anti-social tendencies in the adolescents. Therefore adolescents should be encouraged to participate in the healthy and good social/community activities such as NCC, Scouts and Social services etc.

Adventurous Need: During adolescence stage, emotions of adolescent peak the maximum development. Therefore different sentiments develop in the adolescents at this stage. Adventurous need develops in the adolescents at the time of adolescence in the individuals. Adolescents found to be whimsical and challenging to take part in the different activities without conceiving fear and danger. It takes the form of aimless wandering.

Social Recognition Need: Adolescents want to become recognized for their deeds. They want praise, gift and awards for their all acts. Adolescents become ambitious to have success and getting social status. Therefore parents and teachers should help their children to participate in social and group activities, cultural activities, seminars, debate and competitions.

Freedom/Independence Need: Adolescents need freedom and independence of their activities. They become intolerance of over strictness and interference of others in their activities. Even the children do not like their parental interference in their activities and become reactive. They want freedom of self-expression; want to overcome the social restrictions, social conventions in order to achieve their goals. Sometimes adolescents also show the dependency nature. They need inspiration from heroes and the persons whom they like and need to be secured and fruitful.

PROBLEMS OF ADOLESCENTS

Depending on the developmental characteristics and needs, the problems of the adolescents can easily be guessed. As the needs of the adolescents are found diverse, their problems are also found different types. Peculiar type of physical, mental, emotional and social developments of adolescents give rise to different type of needs and in turn when these needs are not fulfilled, it creates a number of problems in them. Major problems found in the adolescence stage are given below.

Sexual Problem: During adolescence period, the urge of sex heightens in the individuals. Heterosexuality tendency develops in the adolescents so that, boys become interested in girls and vice versa. But parental pressure and social restrictions does not satisfy the sex need of adolescents and thereby they face the problem of sex and become maladjusted.

Sentimental/Emotional Problem: During adolescence period physiological changes occurs in the individual and become mature. Different internal organs start functioning inside the body of the individuals. Abnormal functioning of the endocrine glands gives rise to a number of emotional problems like superiority and inferiority complexes, excess anger and fear, frustration etc. There develops different types of sentiments and emotions in the individual at the adolescence stage.

Social Adjustment Problem: During adolescence period, adolescents desire to participate in the group activities, show their leadership and want to be recognized before others. But sometimes their parents and teachers put rigid restrictions and do not allow them to do so. This leads to develop maladjustment problem in the adolescents.

Moral Problems: During adolescence period, adolescents face the moral problem. Due to attainment of biological maturity, sex feeling remains in the core of all conducts of an adolescent. But the emotional maturity still is not attained at the stage of adolescence. Therefore, adolescents fail to have judicious judgment. This leads to create a problem of morality and self-control in the adolescents.

Career Problem: During adolescence period, career need surmounts in adolescents. Adolescence is a time for making decision for future careers and future vocations. Adolescents want economic freedom and do not want to depend on their parents. But, they are ignorant of the world of occupations and careers. Therefore, adolescents fail to take appropriate decisions of their own which place a career problem for them.

DEVELOPMENT OF SELF-CONCEPT AND SELF-IDENTITY IN ADOLESCENTS

Adolescence period starts after the childhood stage. It may be called as teen age period. It is probably lasts up to 20 years of age. During this period, adolescent's physique, mental, emotional, social and moral aspects maximize their development. This period is called as the period of stress and train for the adolescents. They more float in the unconscious minds sparing to the social needs and social customs. They need more autonomy and want to expose their self-identity. All of their activities are dominated by unconscious motives and emotionality. More of the adolescents are found to be whimsical in their actions without considering the social and moral values. They develop their own self concept. Therefore proper training and guidance is required for the adolescents in respect of their education and learning.

Self-Concept: Adolescence is a unique stage of life seen between childhood and adulthood. It's a time when adolescent desire to have more responsibility than kids, but at the same time they do not feel ready for the duties of being an adult. This is stage when they feel about who they are?

The part of the natural process of teenager's development is the development of their self-concept. Self-concept refers to a set of abilities, opinions and thoughts by which we define and categorize ourselves. For adolescents, their self-concept begins being much more complex and tangible than it was when they were children. A child may not realize how he can be nice and not nice but at the same time an adolescent can.

A teen may point to their values and morals as part of who they are. They may talk about careers or goals, schools they want to attend, awards they have received or activities in which they excel. Other teens may point out they don't know yet who they are, or that they're still getting to know themselves. Teens are much more focused on what is expected of them and how they compare to others than they were as children.

Self-Identity: Identity refers to our sense of who we are as individuals and as members of social groups. Our identities are not simply our own creation. Identities grow in response to both internal and external factors. To some extent, each of us chooses an identity, but identities are also formed by environmental forces out of our control. Identity is dynamic and complex, and changes over time.

Erikson's theory explains stage of identity development shaping through one's lifespan. Psychologist James Marcia focused on teen identity development and expanded on Erikson's concepts of identity crisis and identity confusion during adolescence. He explained that teens go through four unique stages in their quest toward forming an identity and called each stage an identity status. Each status describes where an adolescent is in the process of exploring values, beliefs and goals that will make up their self-concept.

Adolescent Identity Development: The development of a strong and stable sense of self is widely considered to be one of the central tasks of adolescence.

Despite the fact that identity development occurs throughout one's lifetime, adolescence is the first time that individuals begin to think about how our identity may affect our lives. During adolescence, we are much more self-conscious about our changing identities than at any other stage in our lives.

In the 1960s, psychologist Erikson argued that, adolescents face a major identity crisis, "Identity vs. Identity Diffusicn," which he considered one of the stages of psycho-social development. Successful resolution leads to a secure identity; failure leads to role confusion and a weak sense of self. The key to resolving this crisis lies within the adolescent's interaction with others.

SELF-IDENTITY AND SOCIAL IDENTITY

Self-identity: It refers to how someone defines himself. Self-identity forms the basis of some one's self-esteem. In adolescence, the way we see ourselves changes in response to peers, family, and school, among other social environments.

Social Identity: It refers to how others see and label someone and it is constructed by others, and may differ from self-identity. Typically, people categorize individuals according to broad, socially-defined labels. For example, if you have dark skin, you may be labeled "black" by others even though you may not have adopted that identity for yourself.

A positive self-identity is correlated with positive self-esteem. All identities are not equally valued by society, so some adolescents may especially need reinforcement to help them construct a positive sense of self.

Dimensions of Identity: Many dimensions of our identity intersect to form our sense of self and cannot be separated from one another. Visible dimensions of identity, such as race and gender, tend to be more important for individuals since they are significant to the individual in every social context and carry more serious consequences in society. For example, race may be important in all social interactions, but political identity, which is not ordinarily visible, may be relevant for some individuals only during election time

Identity Diffusion: It is the status of adolescents who have not made a commitment to a particular identity. A youth who has not yet considered college or job prospects, for example, could be said to be in the "identity diffusion" status with respect to his professional identity (although in other dimensions his self-identity may be strong). This status may not be resolved unless some experience forces a crisis.

EDUCATIONAL IMPLICATIONS OF THE STUDY OF ADOLESCENCE DEVELOPMENT

Adolescence period is a landmark phase in the life of an individual. It creates havoc in the life. Hall therefore called this stage as the stage of stress and strain in the life of an individual. All type of sentiments grows and develops in this period and attains maturity. This period is important in view of physical, mental, social, moral and emotional development of the adolescent individuals.

- Adolescents feeling, needs and problems are to be properly addressed so that their problems can be minimized and make them adjusted.
- Both teachers and parents should realize the importance of this stage of

development of their children and provide necessary guidance for their development. Parents should judiciously deal with their children; motivate them to be social and good in their activities. Parents should not impose strict rules and extreme discipline on their adolescent children rather should motivate and try to channelize their sentiments in the positive direction.

- Teachers should understand the need of their adolescent students/children and organize different extra-curricular and co-curricular activities in their schools. Curriculum should be graded in the schools to suit the physical maturity of the students. Manual works like games, sports, gardening, carpentry and wood work etc. should be a part of school activities which will promote the physical strength of the students.
- Teachers should assign and promote cooperative group work in the schools so that, it will minimize the problem of complexes in the adolescents. Teachers should psychologically handle the adolescent boys and girls while dealing with them.
- Teachers should organize guidance clinics to help the students suffering from physical problems and parents too should consult with the doctors to promote the physical growth of their children suffering from the physical problems.
- Both teachers and parents should engage their children in the creative activities like dance, music, crafts, and arts.
- Both teachers and parents should affectionately deal with their adolescent children understanding their emotions.
- Both parents and teachers should not unnecessarily interfere in the free activities of their adolescent children but should provide guided freedom to them.
- Teachers should give adolescence and sex education to their adolescent children in their schools and teach moral values.
- The school libraries should have sufficient books on the biographies of national heroes, patriotic, religious personalities, spiritual leaders and social reformers and children should be encouraged to read them.

8
Theories of Human Development

Individual is a growing and developing being. From the womb of her mother up to the death of an individual, a number of changes are reflected in the individual in respect of his physique and psychic aspects. It is through a biological process called Heredity, a Zygote is formed at the initial stage inside the womb of the mother and gradually it grows in shape, gets with different parts of the body and finally with a passage of stipulated time that is approximately about nine months and ten days an individual takes birth in the form of a new born child either a girl or boy depending upon interaction of the X and Y chromosomes received from his parents. And then, the life of a new born child starts to experience/pass through different stages of life like, Infancy, child hood, Adolescence and Adulthood stage in his environment where he get nourished about his care, education, learning, training, food and nutrition and accordingly he/she gets his/her growth and development in different areas like, physical, mental, emotional, social and linguistic characteristics. The study of the theories of human development has a great implication in the field of learning and education which is to be known by the every prospective teachers and teacher educators who deal with the children about their learning.

CONCEPT OF DEVELOPMENT

While growth refers to the change in the shape, size and structure of the body, development refers to the qualitative or functional change of the body of an individual. Development is a continuous process beginning from the time of birth to death of an individual. E.B. Hurlock (1959) defines development as a progressive series of changes that occur in an orderly predictable pattern as a result of maturation and experience.

Both growth and development go hand in hand. But sometimes, miss matching is seen, in some cases, even after sufficient growth of the body is achieved, development is delayed or not exhibited in some areas/qualities which result into abnormality.

THEORIES OF HUMAN DEVELOPMENT

Different psychologists have given different theories on human development displaying different principles, characteristics and explain about the process of human developmental pattern which are discussed below.

Sigmund Freud's Psychoanalytic Theory of Development

One of the most influential theories of human development is psychoanalytic theory suggested by Sigmund Freud. Many modern theories of counseling or psychotherapy are extensions, modifications, or reactions against psychoanalytic theory. Psychoanalytic theory examines the factors that motivate behaviour by focusing on the role of the unconscious. Sigmund Freud and Erik Erikson are examples of theorists who support this approach. Freud was a pioneer with his psychoanalytic theory of personality and his theory of psychosexual development. Erikson expanded Freud's theories in many ways and developed his own theory of **psychosocial development**.

Psychoanalytic theory highlights about the role of unconscious motivation and the importance of early experiences on development. Freud was the first to think of the presence of the unconscious mind and its role in human behaviour.

Three Levels of Consciousness

Freud believed that there are three levels of consciousness. First is the **unconsciousness** mind, which exists outside of an individual's awareness. Next is the **preconscious** mind, which includes all information that an individual is not currently aware of but that can be recalled. Finally, the **conscious** mind, which state individual's current state of awareness.

Id, Ego, Superego

Freud stated that, there are three parts of the personality in his psychoanalytic theory. These are the **id**, **superego**, and **ego**. The id is the first to develop, the ego is second, and the superego is the last to develop.

The id is the biological component of the personality and includes human instincts. The id operates in unconscious mind of an individual operating on the pleasure principles demanding all wishes and needs should be met immediately.

The ego operates in preconscious and conscious mind of an individual. The ego is the part of the personality that makes decisions and faces the consequences operating on the **reality principle**. It adopts the reality principle to fulfill the desires of the id in a method that is both socially appropriate and realistic. Ego mediates in between the id and the superego.

The superego represents an individual's conscience. It is always concerned with what is socially acceptable. The superego pushes an individual to obtain the **ego ideal** that means thinking about what is right and what is wrong.

Erikson's Theory of Psychosocial Development

Erik Erikson is known for his theory of psychosocial development which displays eight stages of identity formation that revolve around conflict and resolution. It tells, how do we develop an identity, or a sense of self? Erikson believed that individuals work on constructing psychosocial identities throughout their whole lives. By 'psychosocial,' he meant interplay between one's inner lives called 'psycho' and his/her outer and social lives called 'social'. Erikson stated that as someone grows he/she passes through eight distinct stages of development. He thought that each stage is defined by a specific conflict between a pair of opposing behaviours. The ability or inability to resolve these conflicts affects one's personality and identity.

Erikson defines four childhood stages and three adult stages, bridging together by one stage called adolescence. In each stage an individual will have to get a resolution of certain conflicts which shape the pattern of his behaviour.

The first stage called as infancy (oral-sensory) stage, encompassing the first year of life is defined by a conflict between trust and mistrust. Infants during this time learn to trust their parents. If they are reliably cared then they will develop trust in opposite, if they are neglected or abused, they will develop mistrust.

The second stage, called as toddler (muscular-anal) stage is defined by the conflict between autonomy and shame and doubt. Parents, who allow their toddlers between the ages of 1 to 3 years to explore their surroundings and develop interests of their own, help to foster a sense of autonomy. But parents who are too restrictive or cautious with their children can instead leave them with doubt about their abilities.

A related conflict between initiative and guilt defines the next stage, the pre-school (loco-motor) stage. Children in this stage, between the ages of three to six years, need to develop initiative, or independent decision-making, about planning and doing various activities. If they are not encouraged to do this, or if their efforts are dismissed, they may learn to feel guilt instead about their desire for independence.

The last childhood stage is called latency is defined by a conflict between industry and inferiority. Children in this stage are between the ages of six to twelve years, and during this time are starting to gain real adult skills like reading, writing and logic. If they are encouraged, they will develop industriousness or motivation to keep learning and practicing. Children who aren't encouraged to work hard at learning new skills will instead feel inferior and unmotivated.

The stage of adolescence is defined as a conflict resolution between identity and role confusion. At this stage between 12 to 19 years of age, an adolescent wants to perform heroic actions and want to be recognized by fellow beings. When desirable conditions provided an adolescent develops his self-identity in different fields. Here at this stage, he becomes confused about the area where he could establish his identity.

The stage of adulthood is defined as a conflict between intimacy and isolation. Here at this stage between the age of 19 to 40 years of age, an individual either is seen to be intimately or closely related to someone or identifies himself as an isolated one. At this time he wants to be loved by others. If healthy conditions permits then someone develop intimacy otherwise he develops an isolated personality.

The stage of middle adulthood covering the age of 40 to 65 years is considered as the period of conflict resolution between generative and stagnation. This is the period when an individual seek care from his nearest ones and becomes dependent on others.

The stage of seniors covering the ages from 65 years to above is considered as the period of conflict resolution between ego integrity and despair. The virtues an individual develop is wisdom. At this time someone views himself as man of wisdom and source of inspiration for others.

Erikson's stages of the psychosocial development is displays in the below mentioned table.

Erikson's Stages of Psychosocial development Presented in Tabular Form

Gropup	*Age*	*Virtue*	*Crisis*
Infants	0 to 18 Months	Hope	Trust Vs. Mistrust
Toddlers	18 to 3 years	Will	Autonomy Vs. Shame and Doubt
Pre-School	3 to 6 Years	Purpose	Initiative Vs. Guilt
Childhood	6 to 12 Years	Competence	Industry Vs. Inferiority
Adolescence	12 to 18 Years	Fidelity	Identity Vs. Role Confusion
Young Adults	19 to 40 Years	Love	Intimacy Vs. Isolation
Middle Adult-hood	40 to 65 Years	Care	Generative Vs. Stagnation
Seniors	65+ Years	Wisdom	Ego Integrity Vs. Despair

Learning Theories of Development

Skinner says, Learning is the modification of behaviour through experiences. All types of learning are purposive and goal directed. Learning is said to be a life-long process as like as education which never ends. Learning means acquisition of skills, knowledge, experiences, habits and abilities in the individuals/learners. It helps to solve problems and achieve goals of life. Someone learns to adjust to his environment.

Many factors become helpful for learning like, sound environment, good teaching, adequate parental as well as teacher's feedback and reinforcement, sound physical facilities, good health, nutrition, guidance, economic support, good intelligence, self-interest, motivation, attention etc. Learning begins when an individual encounters some problem in his path to achieve the goals. The method through which he overcomes his problems (searching possible solutions) become take the shape of his learning and it becomes habitual or a practice. One's past experiences may help to have newer learning. Searching the source of solution of problem and achieving the goals is called as learning. Passive learning does not become pervasive but one's active learning becomes more result oriented, success based and durable as well as sustainable too.

To explain about the nature and characteristics of learning many theories of learning have been presents by different psychologists. These learning theories explain the way of behaviour modification and development of individuality. Some of the theories of learning are discussed below which provide empirical evidence of behaviour modifications in a scientific approach.

Learning theories focus on how behaviour is learned. Some individuals who developed theories that focus on how people learn new behaviours. Ivan Pavlov studied learning through association in his theory of classical conditioning. B.F. Skinner examined the effects of reinforcement and punishment in his theory of operant conditioning. Albert Bandura considered the effects of behaviour modeling in his social learning theory.

Classical Conditioning Theory

Evan Pavlov is the profounder of **classical conditioning theory of learning**. It is otherwise referred to as respondent conditioning. Classical conditioning is a process where an artificial stimulus being paired with natural stimulus possess the ability of a natural stimulus.

Classical conditioning occurs when an individual learn to associate the original response with a secondary or substituted stimulus. A natural stimulus i.e. unconditioned stimulus produces a response without any previous learning. This response is called an unconditioned response. For an example 'food' creates involuntary responses and causes someone to experience salivation, which is a natural response that is not learned, and happens automatically. But gradually the respondent become habitual and experience to learn to elicit the same response 'salivation' to an neutral/artificial stimulus acquiring the power of an unconditioned stimuli in its continuous association 'for example ringing of bell' when he becomes conditioned. This learning theory tells that children learn to associate desirable responses with different stimuli by conditioning. It is helpful in building desirable attitudes, eliminating bad habits and forming healthy habits for the learning and development of the children. This theory highlighted the impact of reward and punishment in the process of learning and development.

Operant Conditioning Theory

B.F Skinner is the profounder of the **operant conditioning theory of learning.** It is also referred to as instrumental conditioning. In operant conditioning, learning refers to changes in behaviour as a result of experiences that occur after a response. Operant conditioning involves changing voluntary behaviours. A behaviour response is followed by either reinforcement or punishment. Reinforcement following a behaviour will cause the behaviour to increase, but if behaviour is followed by punishment the behaviour will decrease.

There are two types of reinforcement such as positive reinforcement and Negative reinforcement. Positive reinforcement refers to the addition of something positive. Examples would be offering praise/prize when a desired behaviour is displayed. Negative reinforcement occurs when something undesirable is removed when a behaviour is displayed. Because of its name, negative reinforcement is often confused with punishment. The key difference is that negative reinforcement involves the removal of a negative consequence to increase the likelihood of a response. Reinforcement always increases the occurrence of a response, while punishment always decreases the occurrence of a response.

There are also two types of punishment that occur in operant conditioning such as positive punishment and negative punishment. Positive punishment means the addition of something undesirable. Negative punishment is the removal of something pleasing.

Reinforcement has a great force in shaping the behaviour of an individual and his development. If children will be given adequate and proper reinforcement then their behaviour will be modified in better way.

Piaget's Theory of Cognitive Development

Another way to look at human development is through the process of **cognitive development**. Cognitive development theories are concerned with the development of thought processes influencing insight and understanding of the world around us. A major proponent in cognitive development theory is **Jean Piaget**. He contributed the fact about child development by proposing the idea that children think differently than adults. Piaget's **stages of cognitive development** propose the sequential steps that take place in children's intellectual development.

According to psychologist Jean Piaget, children progress through a series of four critical stages of cognitive development. Each stage is marked by shifts in how kids understand the world. Piaget believed that children are like "little scientists" who actively try to explore and make sense of the world around them. Through his observations of his children, Piaget suggested four distinct stages involved in the process of intellectual/cognitive development of children.

- The Sensory motor stage covering from birth to age 2 (cognitive ability to form schemes and reflex actions developed at this stage)
- The Pre-operational stage covering from age 2 to about age 7 (Cognitive ability to assimilate and accommodate experiences, knowledge developed at this stage)
- The Concrete operational stage covering from age 7 to 11 (cognitive ability to deal with concrete situation developed at this stage)
- The formal operational stage, which begins in adolescence and spans into adulthood (Cognitive ability to deal with abstract situations, imaginative and problematic situations developed at this stage)

The Swiss psychologist, Jean Piaget, introduced a developmental epistemology that focused on the growth of intelligence from infancy to adulthood. Piaget's theory is influenced by the ideas that intelligence, like a biological system, constructs the structures it needs to function, knowledge is the interaction between the individual and the environment and the growth of intelligence is influenced by four factors such as physical environment, social environment, maturation and equilibration.

The following basic assumptions were the guiding factors in the theory of cognitive development suggested by Piaget.

1. Children are active and motivated learners making use of their sense to explore and seek information about the world around them by different reflex actions.
2. Children construct knowledge from their experiences and observation in the process of interaction and learning. They continually add to their knowledge in order to create understanding and beliefs in them about the world organized into a scheme or groupings of similar actions or thoughts. Later on this scheme may change but it provides bases for formation of new knowledge.
3. Children learn through two processes such as assimilation and accommodation operating hand in hand. Assimilation is defined as dealing

with a new event in a way that is consistent with an existing scheme. For example, a child may assimilate a new animal seen at the zoo into their existing animal 'mammals' scheme. Accommodation is the process of dealing with new information or events by either modifying an existing scheme or forming a new one. For example, a child may think of the animal seen at zoo flying and thus create a new scheme of animals.

4. Child's cognitive development is the result of interaction with his physical and social environments. This interaction helps children to construct new knowledge and new thoughts, new approach to deal with the situation around the children.
6. Children/adolescents develop increasingly complex thoughts by the process of equilibration. Paiget states equilibrium is a state when learners' becomes able to explain new events and new ideas with existing schemes. Out of their cognitive conflicts (true or false, or two contradicting position) called disequilibrium state experienced by a child or adolescent, their higher order of thoughts or complex level of thoughts develops.

Albert Bandura's Theory of Social Cognitive Development

The psychologist, Albert Bandura discovered the importance of behavioural models while working with patients having snake phobias. Albert Bandura's social learning theory stresses the importance of observational learning, imitation and modeling. His theory integrates a continuous interaction between behaviours, personal factors including cognition and the environment referred to as reciprocal causation model. However, Bandura does not suggest that the three factors in the triadic model make equal contributions to behaviour. The influence of behaviour, environment and person depends on which factor is strongest at any particular moment.

Bandura in his triadic model states that 'B' or behaviour, refers to response, skill, etc., The 'E' or environment refers to the situation, roles, models and relationships and 'P', or person refers to the cognition and personal factors such as self-efficacy, motives and personality. These three factors interactively help someone to learn and develop. Bandura signifies the role of models in the following manners.

1. Modeled behaviours serve as cues to initiate similar behaviours in others.
2. Modeled behaviour serves to strengthen or weaken the learner's existing restraints against the performance of a modeled behaviour.
3. Models can be used to demonstrate new patterns of behaviour.

Bronfenbrenner's Ecological Systems Theory of Development

Urie Bronfenbrenner's ecological systems theory explores the five levels of the environment that influence human development. This theory explains about how the ecological system leaves an impact on a child's development as a result of his social relationships with the world around him.

Bronfenbrenner believed that a person's development is affected by everything present in their environment. He divided the person's environment into five different levels: the microsystem, the mesosystem, the exosystem, the macrosystem, and the chronosystem.

Microsystem: The microsystem is the system closest to the person and the one in which they have direct contact. Some examples would be home, school, daycare, or work place. A microsystem typically includes family, peers, or caregivers. Relationships in a microsystem are bi-directional. In other words, your reactions to the people in your microsystem will affect how they treat you in return. This is the most influential level of the ecological systems theory.

Mesosystem: The next level of ecological systems theory is the mesosystem. The mesosystem consists of the interactions between the different parts of a person's microsystem. The mesosystem is where a person's individual Microsystems do not function independently, but are interconnected and assert influence upon one another. These interactions have an indirect impact on the individual.

Exosystem: The third level, exosystem refers to a setting that does not involve the person as an active participant, but still affects them. This includes decisions that have bearing on the person, but in which they have no participation in the decision-making process. An example would be a child being affected by a parent receiving a promotion at work or losing their job.

Macrosystem: The fourth level, macrosystem encompasses the cultural environment in which the person lives and all other systems that affect them. Examples could include the economy, cultural values, and political systems. The macrosystem can have either a positive or a negative effect on a person's development.

Chronosystem: The fifth level, chronosystem includes the environmental events and transitions taking place throughout the life span of an individual involving the socio-historical contexts that influence his life.

Charles Darwin's Evolutionary Theory of Development

Darwin's evolutionary theory states about instinctual learning and human development through natural selection. Natural selection is a process through which a species adapts to its environment by changing its genetic makeup from one generation to the next. The concept of natural selection can also be applied to human learning.

When evolutionary theory is applied to human learning, it is referred to as evolutionary developmental psychology. Evolutionary developmental psychology is the application of Charles Darwin's theory of evolution to human development. It involves both the genetic and environmental conditions that have formed the processes that take place during development. Evolutionary theory assumes that our behaviours have developed through the process of natural selection. These selected behaviours are not only the end products of our development as adults, but also include the characteristic behaviours that occur during different developmental periods.

Gilbert Gottlieb's Epigenetic Psychobiological Systems Theory of Development

Epigenetic psychobiological systems perspective is an emergent theory that views development as a product of interaction between biological and environmental forces. It includes both the genetic forces and the direct influence of the environmental forces on the expression of these genes. The theory highlights the effect of the dynamic interaction between these two forces influences the process of development. Each person's genetic potential is present at birth, but the expression of that potential is dependent upon how they are nurtured by their environment. Gottlieb believed that the influences occur over the course of evolution taking place throughout an individual's lifespan. Gottlieb describes four different interacting dynamics such as behaviour, neural activity; genetic activity and environment which interact with one another and shapes individual development.

Associated Terms

The associated terms Gottlieb used in the theory of epigenetic psychobiological systems perspective were **ethnology** and **epigenesist**. The term 'Ethnology' is the study of behaviour as it relates to evolution and the survival of a species. Psychobiological epigenetic systems perspective builds on the idea of ethnology. An example of this would be a behaviour, such as a nomadic life style, developing as a result of adaption to a specific environment, such as food scarcity. The term 'epigenesis' refers to a process through which one's genetics and environment play a role in development. Because of the complex interactions that take place, developmental outcomes are difficult to predict.

Carl Roger's Humanistic Theory of Personality Development

Carl Rogers was a prominent psychologist and one of the founding members of the humanist movement. Along with Abraham Maslow, he focused on the growth potential of healthy individuals and greatly contributed to our understanding of the self and personality. Both Rogers' and Maslow's theories focus on individual choices and do not hold that biology is deterministic. They emphasized free will and self-determination, with each individual desiring to become the best person they can become.

Humanistic psychologists emphasized the active role of the individual in shaping their internal and external worlds. Rogers advanced the field by stressing that the human person is an active, creative, experiencing being who lives in the present and subjectively responds to current perception, relationships, and encounters. He coined the term ***actualizing tendency,*** which refers to a person's basic instinct to succeed at his or her highest possible capacity. Through person-centered counseling and scientific therapy research, Rogers formed his theory of personality development, which highlighted free will and the great reservoir of human potential for goodness.

Personality Development and the Self-Concept: Rogers based his theories of personality development on humanistic psychology and theories of subjective experience. He believed that everyone exists in a constantly changing world of experiences where he is at the center. A person reacts to changes in their phenomenal field, which includes external objects and people as well as internal thoughts and emotion.

Phenomenal Field: Individual's subjective reality, all that they are aware of, including objects and people as well as their behaviours, thoughts, images, and ideas come under the Phenomenal Field suggested by Rogers.

Carl Roger's Phenomenal Field

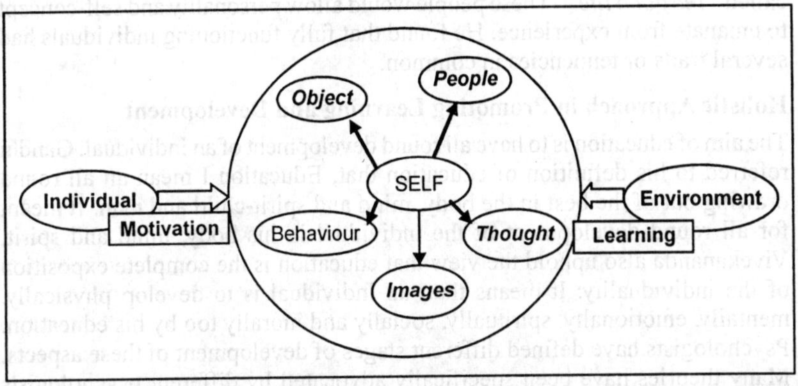

Rogers believed that all behaviour is motivated by self-actualizing tendencies, which drive a person to achieve at their highest level. As a result of their interactions with the environment and others, an individual forms a structure of the self or self-concept—an organized, fluid, conceptual pattern of concepts and values related to the self. If a person has a positive self-concept, they tend to feel good about which they are and often see the world as a safe and positive place. If they have a negative self-concept, they may feel unhappy with who they are.

Ideal Self vs. Real Self: Rogers further divided the self into two categories such as the ideal self and the real self. The ideal self is the person that someone would like to be and the real self is the person that someone actually is. Rogers focused on the idea that there is need to achieve consistency between these two selves. There one can experience congruence when his thoughts about his real self and ideal self are very similar and accurate. High congruence leads to a greater sense of self-worth and a healthy, productive life. But when there is a great discrepancy between someone's ideal and actual selves, at that moment he/she experience a state of incongruence, which can lead to maladjustment.

Unconditional Positive Regard: In the development of the self-concept, Rogers remarked the importance of unconditional positive regard, or unconditional love. People rose in an environment of unconditional positive regard, in which no preconceived conditions of worth are present, have the opportunity to fully actualize. When people are raised in an environment of conditional positive regard, in which worth and love are only given under certain conditions, they must match or achieve those conditions in order to receive the love or positive regard they yearn for. Their ideal self is thereby determined by others based on these conditions, and they are forced to develop outside of their own true actualizing tendency; this contributes to incongruence and a greater gap between the real self and the ideal self.

The Good Life: Rogers described life in terms of principles rather than stages of development. These principles exist in fluid processes rather than static states. He claimed that a fully functioning person would continually aim to fulfill his or her potential in each of these processes, achieving what he called *"the good life."* These people would allow personality and self-concept to emanate from experience. He found that fully functioning individuals had several traits or tendencies in common.

Holistic Approach in Promoting Learning and Development

The aim of education is to have all round development of an individual. Gandhi referred to his definition of education that, Education I mean an all round drawing out of the best in the body, mind and spirit-child and man. It meant for all round development of the individual in his body, mind and spirit. Vivekananda also uphold the view that education is the complete exposition of the individuality. It means that, an individual is to develop physically, mentally, emotionally, spiritually, socially and morally too by his education. Psychologists have defined different stages of development of these aspects. Many theories have been specifically advocated by different psychologists for development of personality, learning and behaviour of individuals that have been discussed above.

As per above discussions, some psychologists stressed on the classical conditioning methods of behaviour modification and learning and some others stressed on the cognitive methods of behaviour modification, learning and development. However, an individual is not a compartmental but a complete entity where his physical, mental, emotional and social qualities develop in an integrative method/way. All these aspects are co-related. We can't imagine the development of one's mental traits without the development of physical aspects. Similarly one's social development depends and correlated with his mental development-thinking, reasoning, language, intelligence, imagination, creativity etc. Therefore, there is need to adopt the holistic approach for promoting learning and development.

In our educational practice related to teaching and learning strategies, equal stress should be laid on cognitive development and physical development of the learners. The curriculum should integrate and re organize the learning activities both for physical, mental, moral, social and emotional development of the learners. All the theories of learning are to be suitably practiced in the learning environments/schools in an integrative and holistic approach resulting all round development of the learners-physically, mentally, morally, emotionally and socially.

GENDER DIFFERENCE AND DEVELOPMENT

Gender stereotypes are abundantly seen in the society. There is a common conception for most of the people that boys are better in math than the girls and similarly girls are better in art and crafts than boys. This type of notion leads to develop the gender differences. The growth and developmental pattern of boys and girls is found different in many aspects and it has attracted the field of research and has become an area of debate. What constitute a base for these differences? Whether the nature or the nurture conditions account for gender differences?

Nature and Gender Differences in Development

Nature refers to heredity, or traits that are genetic. Researchers agree that heredity determines physiological differences in males and females. Some of these differences are present at birth, and some differences don't present themselves until the child reaches puberty. Heredity causes girls to reach puberty earlier than boys. It also causes boys (once they have reached puberty) to have more muscle composition and be taller than girls in general. Heredity, or specifically different hormones, accounts for gender differences as well. Boys are more physically aggressive, a trait that has been linked to the increased levels of testosterone in boys. Researchers have also argued that hormones may play a role in the differences observed in visual-spatial and verbal abilities among children. A small difference has been found among researchers indicating boys have slightly higher visual-spatial abilities while girls have slightly higher verbal abilities.

Nurture and Gender Differences in Development

Nurture or the environment refers to all environmental influences on development after conception. Level of attachment, beliefs, values and how much attention one is given are all examples of environmental influences. In almost every culture we see practices that promote gender-specific behaviours. The environment and specific cultures foster the idea that behaviours are more appropriate for males and others are more appropriate for females. Gender stereotypes are prevalent and perpetuated by parents, peers, teachers and even the child themselves.

Environmental Influences on Gender Differences

Parents are seen treating their sons and daughters differently. They typically respond more frequently to requests for help from daughters, while sons are usually encouraged to solve problems independently. In addition, many parents encourage gender-typical behaviours by offering gender-specific toys such as dolls for girls and Cycles for boys.

9
Individual Differences

No two individuals are alike. Individuals differ from each other in different aspects. Each one has his own qualities which differentiates him from other. Even twins having their physical resemblance also differ in many respects. Individuals may have similar characteristics but they differ from each other in degree and quantitatively. The individual difference put a great problem in education. The main aim of education is to bring all round development of learners. It needs to understand the needs, interest, abilities and intelligence of the learners and accordingly provide them instruction and facilities to develop. But in the same classroom, children having their same age level found differing in their interest, attitude, needs, capabilities and level of intelligence. So there is a need to address the needs of the individual learner and fulfill his needs and help him to develop. The present days trend of child centered education mean to understand needs, interest, abilities and intelligence of each child and centered the educational process in order to help him to learn and develop. Therefore, it is essential to have a study on the issues of individual difference in the field of education which will help teachers and educational planners in developing specific programme of instruction. The study of individual difference has helped to the growth of a new branch of study in the field of psychology that is" Differential psychology" being supported by the psychologists named as Wunndt, Cattle, Jastrow, Ebbibg Hause and Kraepelin. The study of individual difference has promoted the programme of Individualized Instruction in the field of education.

MEANING OF INDIVIDUAL DIFFERENCE

Individual difference means variability of an individual from another in respect to their specific trait or traits quantitatively. It is assumed that, all the human characteristics are universally distributed in all individuals. But when one individual is compared to another with respect to a particular human characteristic say' intelligence' then it is found that there is quantitative difference in the these two individuals in their intelligence. All individuals have their own sense organs, muscles and glands, but in there functioning there are individual differences.

Defining Individual difference, Tyler said that, variability of individuals from one to another is law of nature. Tyler states, measurable difference, have been shown to exist in physical, size and shape, psychological functions, motor capacities, intelligence, achievement and knowledge, interest, attitude and personality traits.

Dictionary of education defines that individual difference stand for variation or deviations among individuals in regard to a single characteristic or number of characteristics.

TYPES OF INDIVIDUAL DIFFERENCES

Individual difference is of two types such as inter individual difference and intra individual difference.

1. *Inter Individual Difference:* Inter individual difference means, two individuals differ from one to another in respect of a particular trait though the same trait/quality exists within them. For example, one individual may have good intelligence, but another individual may not have good intelligence.
2. *Intra Individual Difference:* Intra individual difference means, the same individual differ within himself with respect to his different traits/qualities. For example, an individual may have good intelligence but he may not have good physique.

AREAS/FIELDS OF INDIVIDUAL DIFFERENCES

The followings are the major areas of individual differences.

Physical difference: Every individual has his own physique: size, shape, height and weight of his body. Therefore physically one individual is found to be different from other in respect of their height, weight, appearance, size, complex of the body, etc. It is because of physical differences, one individual is found to be of white complex and another one is of black complex, one individual is found to be fatty and another one is lean and thin, one individual is found to be of more height and another one is of short height. So individuals differ both in structurally and functionally. No two individuals are found to have equal physical strengths.

Mental difference: There is individual difference in mental aspects. No two individuals are found to have same level of reasoning capacity, intelligence, interests, feelings, thinking power, creativity capacity, imagination and perception power, memory etc. Individuals differ from one another in their mental makeup according to the principle of degree. Therefore if someone is found to be more intelligent, then another one is found to be less intelligent, if someone is found to have more thinking power, then another one is found to have less thinking power. No two individual think at the equal rate and equal thing at a time. No two individuals have equal level of intelligence and interest on some subject.

Social difference: Individuals also differ socially. The social qualities are distributed normally in all individuals like cooperation, friendship, leadership, sacrifice etc. But, individuals differ from one to another in their respective social qualities. Some individual is found to have more leadership quality and another do not have the same or less leadership quality. Someone wants to lead a group life and another one want to lead a lonely life. Some like to have friendship with others but another one do not like the same. So socially individuals differ from one to another.

Emotional difference: There is also emotional difference among the individuals. Though individuals do not differ in kind, they greatly differ in degree as regards to their emotional qualities like fear, anger, self-esteem, sentiments, feelings, ego, tolerance capacity etc. Some people are found to have great control over their emotional expressions and some do not have the same. Thus there are emotional differences among individuals.

Attitudinal difference: Individuals differ in their attitudes towards peoples, institutions, objects, principles, rules and regulations. Therefore some people are found to have good and positive attitude towards the social customs and some people are found to have negative and bad attitude towards the same.

Interest difference: Individuals also differ in their interests. Interest difference is found in man to man, man to woman, adolescents to adults and society to society. Each individual has his own interest. Therefore we remark interest difference in boys and girls in a particular activity. Boys and girls differ in their interest while selecting books, courses, games etc.

Personality difference: Individuals differ in their personality factors. Some individuals are found to be extroverts and some are found to be introverts and some are found to be ambiverts.

Sex difference: Individual difference is also found in men and women on ground of their sex. Biologically functional differences are found in men and women. Men and women differ in their interest, emotions, attitudes, strength of their body, feelings etc.

Moral difference: Individuals also morally differ from one to another. It is because of moral differences, someone is found to be more courageous and others are not found so, some are found to have good character and others are not found so, some are found sympathetic towards others and others are not found sympathetic towards others, etc.

Racial and Cultural difference: On the basis of race and culture, individuals differ among themselves. Race and culture of the individuals make them different in their physical makeup, mind makeup, interest, attitude, emotions etc. It is because of cultural differences, Indian people are found to be peace loving and Chinese people are found to be cruel and war loving. American people are found to be white complexion while the people of West Indies are of black complexion.

Intelligence difference: Intelligence is both a factor and cause of individual difference. Individuals differ in their level of intelligence. That is why someone is found more intelligent and another is found less intelligent.

Aptitude difference: Aptitude means a special ability of an individual to do something. Individuals differ in their special abilities. Someone is found better in singing while another one is found better in playing. No two individuals play at the same rate and same manner. So also no two individual can climb the mountain at the same race.

CAUSES OF INDIVIDUAL DIFFERENCES

Individual difference is found on the basis of the following causes:

Heredity: Individual differences occur due to their genetic factors. Every individual inherits certain characteristics from his parents through genetic codes. But the phenotype or the expressed forms of his characteristics depend on contributions their socio-cultural environment. This is the reason why someone is not become exactly like his parents and his parents do not become exactly like his grandparents. Individuals do share similarities with his parents in respect of many physical attributes like height, colour of eyes, shape of nose etc. Individuals inherit certain cognitive, emotional and other characteristics from their parents like intellectual competence, love for sport, creativity etc. However, the own characteristics of an individual develop largely by the support from the environment which he inhabit. All physical differences among the individuals are caused by their heredity. Every individual has his own genetic characteristics which differentiate him from others.

Environment: Due to environment, individual difference occurs. Each individual is born and brought up in a different environment from other. Every individual learn some traits and acquire the same from his own environment during his life time. These acquired traits differentiate him from others. The nature of the individual is shaped by his society, culture, physical surroundings, facilities etc. As the living pattern and environmental setup of the individuals varies, their acquired traits also vary which make them different from each other.

Education: In breeding individual difference, the factor of education also play the role. Education is said to be a means of modification of one's behaviour. Education makes someone enriched in his personality, behaviour, actions, manners, skills, language in the positive way. All the social, emotional and intellectual traits are modified through one's proper education. Education brings about differences in the interest, attitude, adjustment and personality of an individual. Therefore it is seen that highly educated people is different from the low educated people and educated people are different from the uneducated people in many respects.

Nutrition: Rich nutrition helps to build good and healthy physique in an individual and poor nutrition affect the physical health of an individual. So the individuals availing nutritious food are seen to have more physical strength, healthier, and thereby possess sound mentality. But individuals not able to have nutritious food are seen to be physically weak, ill healthy, and mentally not sound. Therefore the factor of nutrition also plays a role in making individual differences among the individuals.

Sex: Sex is a cause of individual difference. It is due sex variation, we find differences in men and women in respect of their physical appearance, structure of their body, physical strength, attitude, interest, emotions, feelings and abilities.

Intelligence: Intelligence is an important cause of individual difference. Intelligence has positive impact on one's thinking, reasoning, feelings, emotions, perception, and imagination power. One's intelligence is supported and developed by own genetic as well as environment. As, there exist genetic and environmental variations for each and every individual, this leads to variation in their quantum or level of intelligence. Therefore variation in the level intelligence of the individuals makes them differ from one to another.

Race and Culture: Race and culture is influenced and developed by the geographical and environmental conditions. Due to geo-physical differences, there happen the racial and cultural differences. Again this racial and cultural impact is seen on their natives. Therefore it is seen that, African people are found different from the American people in respect of their food habit, hair style, body complexion, eye-composition, pronunciation and personality etc.

Indian people are found different from the British people in respect of their personality, speech, pronunciation, body pattern etc. So race and culture of individuals make them different from one to another.

Age: One's growth and development of mentality, emotions and temperaments, social behaviours, physique and moral pattern proceeds according to his increase of age. Therefore, a child can't be like an adolescent in respect of his mental development, physical development etc. The behavioural patter of individuals is modified according to their age. There is difference in the individuals on the grounds of their age. So age is also a cause of individual difference.

MEASUREMENT OF INDIVIDUAL DIFFERENCES

From our discussion, it became clear that, individuals differ from one to another in many respects such as their physical, mental, moral, social, intelligence, attitude, interest, emotions and personality etc. To measure each variable, a number of techniques are available and that can be used to measure their variations among the individuals. In order to measure individual differences the following tools may be used.

- Intelligence tests
- Personality tests
- Interest inventories
- Attitude sales
- Aptitude Tests
- Achievement tests
- Rating Scales
- Socio metric devices
- Check lists etc.

Individual difference can be studied/ measured by following two approaches such as Cross-Sectional approach and longitudinal approach. By cross sectional approach, different individuals or different groups are tested at the same time. By longitudinal approach, an individual or a group is tested over a long period of time in respect of each of their traits.

EDUCATIONAL IMPLICATIONS

Study of individual difference has a great educational value for the teachers and parents. It has helped to revolutionize the field of education by introducing the new branch of study i.e. differential psychology. The study of individual difference has enabled the teachers to practice individualized instruction in their class room situations. It has helped to understand the individual learner and their abilities. Study of individual differences put forth the following educational implications for teachers.

- *Selecting Aims of Education:* The sole aim of education is to bring all round development of the learner. So the abilities of the learners should be developed. It needs to orient the aim of education to develop the ability of the individual learner.
- *Constructing Curriculum:* As we know, the learners differ in their interest,

attitude, intelligence, motivation, learning and aptitudes. Therefore, the curriculum should be according to the needs, interest and capabilities of the learners. The learner's age and level of intelligence should be taken into consideration while planning for their curriculum. Curriculum should be diversified allowing the learners to select their subject as per their interest and capability.

- *Deciding Methods of Teaching:* Children vary in their interest. A single method of teaching can't suit the interest of the learner. Therefore a teacher will have to adopt various method of teaching keeping in view of the individual difference of the learners. The method of teaching to be adopted for 10th class students can't be helpful for the students of class 2. Hence teacher will have to decide about the appropriateness of the method of teaching deciding upon the individual difference of learners.
- *Planning Co-curricular Activities:* While planning co-curricular activities in the schools, learner's abilities and interest should be addressed individually. Various co-curricular activities like games, sports, drama, dance, competitions, debate, literary activities should find their place to provide choice for the learners according to their interest.
- *Selecting Teaching Aids:* Teaching aids help to teach meaningfully and in a better way and helping the learner to learn easily. As we have discussed that, teacher should use appropriate method of teaching suiting the need, interest and level of understanding of the individual learners. Therefore, the teaching aids should be psychologically prepared and applied keeping in view of the individual differences in the class room. For example, a teacher will have to use separate teaching aids for nursery learner and other teaching aids for 10th grade learners. In the same line, a teacher will have to use separate teaching aids for physically challenged learners and other teaching aids for the normal learners.
- *Providing Individualized Instruction:* No two learners are equal in the rate of their learning as because there is difference in their level of understanding, intelligence, attitudes, interests etc. Therefore same method of instruction can't be beneficial for them for their learning and development. Therefore, it needs to provide special help, extra time teaching, coaching facilities to the needy and slow learners. On the same line talented and intelligent learners are to be given special provisions apart from their normal class room provisions for their development. Thus the study of individual differences has helped the teacher to provide individualized instruction for the learners.
- *Making Homogenous Grouping:* It is understood that, individuals differ from one to another in many respects. The learners are also found differing among themselves in their level of intelligence and rate of learning. Therefore it will not be judicious for the teacher to adopt same type of teaching learning practices for all. He will have to group his learners into different groups according to their level of understanding, intelligence and then provide certain type of educational incentives.
- *Providing Guidance and Counseling:* Study of individual difference can help the teacher to provide educational and vocational guidance for the learners. Schools should recruit the counselor to plan the guidance techniques keeping in view of needs and requirements of the learners.

10
Personality

We often hear to someone speaking that, his/her personality is not good or his /her personality is good. Then what does personality mean? Every individual is unique in his personality. Personality of an individual determines his success and failure of his life. One of the major objectives of our education system is to develop the personality of children. The Indian Education Commission popularly known as the Kothari Commission (1964-66) also stressed this objective of education out of the four objectives of education such as Developing Democratic Citizenship, Developing Leadership, and Developing Productivity. Personality plays a key role in the life of an individual. Therefore it is need to understand about the meaning, types, theories and strategies of promoting personality.

MEANING OF PERSONALITY

The term personality is derived from the Latin word 'persona' which means mask. By using the mask, an actor hides his own identity and plays the role of some other personality and leaves an impression on the audiences. Gradually, the meaning of the word persona shifted from the mask to the person himself who acted on the stage.

In psychological sense, the meaning of the term personality is wide. It includes the physical, mental, emotional make-up of an individual. The word personality is associated with the synonyms like character, nature, disposition etc.

Defining the term personality, Muir said, Personality is the whole individual considered as whole. It may be defined as most characteristics integration of an individual's structure, modes of interest, attitudes, behaviour, capacities, abilities and attitudes.

G.W. Allpoert defined that, personality is the dynamic organization within the individual of those psychophysical systems that determine his unique adjustment within the environment.

H.J Eysneck in his book the "Structure of Human Personality" gave a comprehensive definition about personality and said that, Personality is the more or less stable and enduring organization of a person's character, temperament, intellect, and physique which determine his unique adjustment to the environment.

Modern Psychologist adopting perceptual Approach to behaviour added a dimension called self-concept to personality which comes through learning. From infancy to adolescence period, the individual grows and gradually become aware of his self and thinks to be different from others in view of his physical, mental, social and emotional characteristics. During adolescence stage, an adolescent when he starts advancing feels that he has a personality and an identity of his own which is different from others and thereby he develops his self-concept. Another factor which contributes to the development of personality is one's self-actualization or the concept of becoming. It is dependent on his learning and motivation.

Therefore, out of the above definitions, it becomes clear that, personality of an individual is a sum total of his physical, mental, emotional, temperamental characteristics organized and integrated as whole which determine his unique way of adjustment to his environment. Every individual is unique in his personality. Personality of an individual is not a static or fixed characteristic rather it is dynamic and can be developed or improved by his motivation, training and education.

FACTORS INFLUENCING PERSONALITY

The following factors influence the growth of personality of an individual.

Physiological Factors: Physiological factors include the heredity, chemique (functioning of glands and body secretions), physique, body, size, structure, shape, strength, looks and constitution of the individual. Individuals found normal in their chemique and body pattern without any physical deformity possess sound personality and vice versa.

Psychological Factors: Psychological factors that influence personality of an individual include motives, interest, emotions, temperaments, and attitude, will and intellectual capacities. Strong and positive psychological conditions contribute to develop sound personality of an individual and vice versa.

Environmental Factors: Environmental factors include family, society, school, community, culture, mass media, education, training and nutrition of an individual. Adequate and proper environmental conditions promote sound personality of an individual and vice versa.

THEORIES OF PERSONALITY

Theories of personality can be classified into the following categories.

Type Theory of Personality

These theories or approaches lay stress on the classification of persons into different types on the basis of their personality characteristics.

Temperamental Types

Hippocrates (400BC) was the first to categorize human personality on the basis of body humours. He believed that, body fluids or juices tend to develop different types of personality. Out of his study, he found four different body fluids like blood, black bile, yellow bile and flegms which resulted in four types of temperaments. All individuals possess these four body fluids but in varying degree. The dominance of a particular type of body fluid determines the personality of a person.

	Type of Body Humours	*Personality Types Developed*	*Characteristics Manifested*
1	Blood	Sanguine personality	Active, optimistic, quick, and unstable
2	Black Bile	Melancholic personality type	Slow, Sad and pessimistic
3	Yellow Bile	Choleric personality	Irritable, unstable and short-tempered
4	Phlegm	Phlegmatic personality	Slow, week and unexcitable

Constitutional Types

E. Kretschmer (1925) a German Psychologist categorized human beings into following four types of personality on the basis of their physical structure.

1. *Asthenic Types*: These persons are found lean and thin, tall, self-centered, idealistic, intellectual, dreamy, bookish, peaceful, lonely and withdrawing.
2. *Pyknic Types*: These persons are found fat, round faced, short, sociable, happy, realistic, bulging stomach and objective.
3. *Athletic Type:* These persons are found Muscular, strong, bony, active, and energetic, less thinking and action oriented.
4. *Dysplastic Type*: These persons are like abnormal built, abnormal characteristics and nervous.

Soma Type

William H. Scheldon (1940) an American Psychologist classified persons into following three types of personality on the basis of their physical characteristics or morphology.

1. *Endomorphic Type*: These persons are found soft and round shaped in their physique and fond of eating more, deep sleep and sociable.
2. *Ectomorphic Types*: These persons are found thin and tall shaped in their physique and withdrawing, artistic, lonely and speaking slow in nature.
3. *Mesomorphic Types*: These persons are found strong and muscular in their physique and daring, powerful, competitive, authoritarian, loud speaking in nature.

Psychological Types

Carl Jung (1933) a Swiss Psychologist attempted to classify human beings into the following three types of personalities on the basis of their sociability.

1. *Extrovert types:* These persons are found highly sociable, realistic and prompt in action, optimistic, action oriented, quick in taking decision, flexible, adaptable, egoistic, friendly, optimistic, objective outlook, fluent and progressive in nature.
2. *Introverts Types:* These persons are found self-centered, lonely, shy, short tempered, pessimistic, subjective, slow in taking decision, unsociable, inflexible, conservative, not friendly, idealistic, and not adaptable in nature.
3. *Ambivert Types:* These persons are found possessing both the extrovert

and introvert personality characteristics and a mixture of both. Some persons show extrovert tendencies in one situation and introvert characteristics in some other situations. It is also seen that, children found introvert in child hood stage grow and found extrovert in their adolescence period. Therefore modern Psychologists categorized these persons as ambiverts.

Spranger's Types of Personality

Spranger has classified personalities into the following six types on the basis of their area of interests.

1. *Theoretical*: All philosophers, scientists, inventors fall into this category.
2. *Economic:* This type of personality attaches more importance to money and they are money minded.
3. *Aesthetic:* This type of persons takes interest in art and literature.
4. *Political*: This type of persons takes interest in political activities and seeks leadership and administration.
5. *Religious*: This type of persons keeps interest in religious activities. They keep firm faith on God. All saints, priests and devotees fall into this category.
6. *Social*: People of this category keep interest in social activity

Limitations of Typological Approach to Study Personality

Typological approach to study personality suffers from the limitations that, compartmentalization of persons into different personality types is very difficult. Individuals who show one symptoms of personality in one situation may show another and contrasting symptoms in another situation as human characteristics are dynamic in nature. A few characteristics are found as fixed characteristics but all other characteristics of human being are changeable and dynamic.

Trait Theory of Personality

These theories lay stress on the different traits of personality as the basis of classification of personality.

Some of the Psychologist apart from typological approach has adopted trait approach for understanding personality. These psychologists mean trait as a mode of behaviour. Psychologist, *Woodworth* defined trait as some particular quality of behaviour such as cheerfulness or self-reliance which characterize the individual in a wide range of his activities and is fairly consistent over a period of time. He considered, personality is a sum total of these traits. *Gordon Allport* assumed traits as dynamic and flexible dispositions resulting from integration of specific habits, expressing characteristic modes of adaptation to one's surroundings. Trait approach of personality states about variety of traits that a person depicts in a variety of situations. Different personality traits grow and develop in a person at different time of his life span.

Characteristics of Personality Traits

- *Scalability*: Traits can be quantitatively measured or scaled.
- *Flexibility*: Traits are not static but flexible and become stable with maturation.

- *Universality:* Traits are universally distributed in all human beings but in varying degree.
- *Traits are mental sets*: Trait is a readiness to respond to any variety of situations.
- *Traits are higher order of habits*: Traits are recurrent in the habitual way in the behaviour of human beings.
- *Traits are frame of reference*: Traits are organized frame of reference which includes all of the beliefs, feelings, attitudes, emotions about the situation.
- *Traits are inquisitional and learned*: All social traits are inquisitional and learned from the environment.

Types of Personality Traits

Following types of personality traits have been proposed by different psychologists.

Cattell's Types of Personality Traits

Cattell a British born American Psychologist (1973) developed a theory of personality traits as a hierarchy of traits. He studied personality traits by means of correlation and factor analysis. He defined a trait as a structure of the personality inferred from behaviour in different situations. According to Cattell, personality traits are of the following types.

- *Common traits*: Common traits are found widely distributed in general population like honesty, aggression, cooperation etc.
- *Unique traits*: Unique traits are found scarcely distributed among the general population. These traits are like emotional reactions, temperamental traits etc.
- *Surface traits*: Surface traits are easily manifested in the persons and are seen outwardly in their overt behaviour. These traits are like curiosity, interests, dependability etc.
- *Source trait:* Source traits are the under laying traits that determine the behaviour of the individual. These traits are like emotional traits, motives urges etc.

Out of his method of factor analysis, Cattell propagated the following 16 pairs of personality traits generally found distribute in the people.

Factors (+)	*Vs.*	*Factors (-)*
A. Cyclothamia (warm and sociable).		Schizothymia (aloof and stiff)
B. General Intelligence (Bright).		Mental defects (dull)
C. Emotional stability.		Emotionally unstable
E. Dominance (aggressive, competitive)		Submission (mild)
F. Surgency (enthusiastic, happy, lucky).		Disurgency (sober, serious)
G. Character (super ego strength).		Lack of rigid (internal standards)
H. Parmia (adventurous, thick-skinned)		Threctia (shy, timid)
I. Premsia (sensitive).		Harria (realistic)

(Contd.)

Factors (+)	*Vs.*	*Factors (-)*
L. Protension (suspecting, jealous).		Relaxed security (accepting, adapting)
M. Autia (introverted, absent minded).		Praxerma (practical, objective minded)
N. Shrewdness (sophisticated, polished)		Naivele (simple, unpretentious)
Q. Guilt proneness (timid, insecure).		Confident (self secured)
Q1. Radicalism, dynamic, experimenting		Conservatism
Q2. Self sufficiency.		Group dependency
Q3. High self-sentiment.		Poor self-sentiment
Q4. High excitability.		Low tension

Source: Cattell (1973).

Thus Cattell attempted to describe and predict the behaviour of persons on the basis of their personality traits. Cattell equally stressed on the genetic and environmental factors for the development of personality. cattell's theory accounted the motivational variables like urges, sentiments and attitude of the persons situationally play the role in developing one' personality.

Cattell's personality theory was criticized on account that, this theory stressed more on the overt behaviour apart from the internal conditions. It laid importance to the projected picture of human functioning only. On the other hand Cattell did not apply full use of factor analytical approach to develop more and higher order factors to identify dimensions of personality.

Eysenck's Types of Personality Traits

Like Cattell, Eysenck (1947) developed a hierarchy of personality traits basing on the factor analysis. He suggested following four levels of personality traits arranged in a hierarchical order.

- *Specific response level*: It is the lowest level of personality traits. Specific traits grow out of a particular response to a single act.
- *Habitual response level:* This is the second level of the development of personality trait. Here the individual habitually responds in a similar manner to same situations. In case of an Introvert person, he does not like to talk with others frankly and he also loves loneliness.
- *Trait level*: At this level, an individual exhibits different similar personality traits of certain types. If he is an introvert, then all characteristics of an introvert personality like persistence, shyness, rigidity and irritability qualities are seen
- *Type level*: This is the highest level where we can recognize someone as a distinct personality type taking into consideration of his all similar personality traits. Taking into account of all these characteristics like persistence, rigidity, shyness and irritability we can now say that someone is of Introvert type of personality.

Integrating personality traits, Eysenck has suggested four types of personality such as Introvert type, Extrovert type, Neurotic type and psychotic types.

Gordon Allport's Types of Personality Traits

Allport recognized and classified the following three traits of personality. Allport opined that, personality consists of certain kind of traits on the

- *Cardinal trait:* Cardinal traits are broad in nature and form the human behaviour in widest range of situations.
- *Central traits*: Central traits are not as broad as cardinal traits but fairly general.
- *Secondary traits*: Secondary traits are found in an individual when he faces a particular problem. These traits are manifested in all individuals to some extent.

Shortcomings of Trait Theory of Personality:

Shortcomings of Trait Theory of Personality

- Traits are not fixed or permanent characteristics but are changeable from situation to situation
- It is difficult to measure the trait objectively. Difficulties lie in quantifying human personality traits. There is no availability of proper and standard units to measure the human personality traits.
- It is very difficult to assess the human personality taking into reference of a single or particular trait. Most of the human traits are correlated and inter related to each other. Personality of an individual is the result of the integration of traits.
- It suffers from subjectivity. Individuals differ on their assessment of traits.

Humanistic and Developmental Theories of Personality

These theories lay stress on the instincts, motivation, learning and self of the individual as the basis of the development of personality

Developmental and Humanistic approaches to study personality were supported by Sigmund Freud, Alfred Adler, Carl Rogers, and Abram Maslow.

Freud's Psychoanalytic Approach

Psychoanalytic approach to study personality was advocated by Sigmund Freud (1856-1939). He applied psychoanalysis method for understanding human behaviour and treating mental illness. Psychoanalytic approach is also known as developmental and dynamic approach of personality. Psychoanalytic theory is based on the importance of instincts which determine all human activities. To Freud, there are two instincts which influence and determine human behaviour that is Eros and Thanatos. Eros is the life instinct that seeks love and preservation and Thantos is the death instinct. These two are the basis of the cause of all human activities and personality.

Freud's psychoanalytic approach of personality is built on the premise of mind which is topographical and dynamic. Freud advocated that mind is consisted of three layers covering certain provinces such as conscious, sub-conscious and unconscious mind.

These three levels of mind is always seen to be engaged in clash and compromise to develop certain type of behavioural characteristics resulting again to a certain type of personality. Freud stated that most of the human behaviours are erupted from the unconscious mind. The conscious mind makes a compromise and tries to develop a socially acceptable personality trait in the individual and make him adjusted in the environment.

Further Freud advocated that mind is consisted of three dynamic aspects such as Id, ego and super ego interrelated to each other. Id is the immoral, raw and savage basis of human personality that is hidden at the deepest level of his unconscious mind. It is more pleasure seeking and does not obey the moral principles and rules. It always seeks satisfaction. All the desires, aspirations, motives and tendencies of an individual are restored in Id. It is animalistic in nature.

Ego on the other hand does not allow the id to dominate and rule on the individual and therefore intermediate and check the activities of id. Ego follows the principle of reality and act with intelligence to guide, control and select the motive to be satisfied.

Super ego, the third level of personality operates on the ethical and moral principles. It is idealistic. It acts as decision making unit in the individual and passes the socially acceptable behaviour on the part of an individual. It adopts social norms.

Freud advocated that individuals having powerful ego are found having strong and balanced personality. Here ego is capable of maintaining a balance between the id and super ego. If the ego is found week in the individual, then he is seen to have maladjusted personality. An individual may be both unlawful and immoral in his personality because if his dominant characteristic of id or may be neurotic type if his super ego dominates the ego which does not allow to satisfy of his desirable repressed wishes.

Freud also stated that, sex is vital in the life of an individual to develop personality. Sex is life energy. Sexual needs as the basic needs to be fulfilled to develop a balanced personality. A person found to be adjusted or maladjusted to the extent to which his sexual needs are satisfied. Freud developed the theory of personality considering his psychosexual development of the individual passing through five different stages like.

- *Oral stage*: During this stage, sexual needs are gratified through mouth orally by sucking. Children feel pleasure in putting objects in mouth and sucking.
- *Anal stage*: During this stage, sexual pleasure is derived from the annal activity. Children feel pleasure from their annus or urethra by letting waste materials.
- *Pre-Latency Stage*: During this stage, probably in the childhood stage, children derive sexual pleasure by playing with genetically organs. They become aware of the differences of sexes. Parental guidance at this stage either develops deprivation complexes in the girls or castration complex in the boys. Similarly there may develop either Electra tendencies in the girls or Oedipus tendencies in the boys because of their parental control.
- *The Latency stage*: This stage is evident at six years of age in case of girls and eight years of age in case of boys and continues up to their puberty. At this stage, boys and girls prefer the company of their own sex and neglect opposite sex.

- *The genital stage*: Genital stage begins with the unset of puberty in the life of adolescents. At this stage, male and female adolescents feel strong sensation in their genitals and seek satisfaction out of their opposite sex. They want to derive sexual pleasure from self-stimulation of their genitals. During this stage, boys and girls fall in love with their opposite sex.

Adler's Theory of Personality

Alfred Adler did not agree with the views of Freud on the structure of personality and proposed another comprehensive theory of personality on the assumption that, child is helpless baby at his initial life and depends on others for his nourishment. He feels small before elders and feels inferiority. In the course of time, he struggles for superiority. On the other hand Adler stressed on the will for power as the basic desire motivate the human activities. All individuals strive to be powerful and achieve their goals but they act in different way. Adler called this as style of life. So each individual has his own style of life and thus distinct type of personality. Adler therefore gave an individual approach in the study of personality.

Carl Roger's Self Theory of Personality

Carl Roger's self-theory of personality states that, each individual is unique in his self that include emotional feelings, strivings and ideas that value and interprets as his own. Rogers in his theory of personality highlighted the importance of motivation in the development of personality. According to Rogers, the self of the in individual bears four characteristics as follows.

A. Self-strive for self-consistency
B. Efforts to seek independence spontaneity and integration of life forces act upon the self.
C. Learning and perception bring changes in the self and behaviour.
D. Self-examination brings modification in self.

Rogers also added another following three themes to the self.

I. *Self-actualization theme*: It helps the individual to understand and appreciate the developmental possibilities of his own from infancy to adulthood.
II. *Self-maintenance theme*: It helps the individual to differentiate him from others and making plan for progress of his own.
III. *Self-enhancement theme*: It help the individual to modify his self to be better and thus he has to struggle and feel pleasure and pain for enhancing of his self.

Abram Maslow's Theory of Personality

Abraham H. Maslow an American psychologist adopting humanistic approach attempted to study human personality. He stated that, every individual has some impulses that induces him to act, grow and fulfill of his potentialities. By birth every individual is good and neutral rather than evil during his course of life in the way of fulfillment of his goals as his impulses motivates. The manners through which an individual achieve his goals and respond to his environment determine his personality. The behaviour and personality depends on his style of striving toward the ultimate goal of self-realization. In the way of self-actualization of goals, there may be some sub-goals or lower-order needs for satisfaction. Maslow has arranged these needs in a hierarchical order called as hierarchy of needs most often looked as pyramid of needs. Human needs proceed through simple to complex needs and these needs play a major role in motivating human behaviour and personality.

Maslow in his hierarchy of needs mentioned that, every individual strives for his self-actualization from lowest level of needs to highest level of needs passing through the following five levels of needs.

1. *Physiological needs*: These needed are basic needs and treated as lowest level of needs like need for food, sleep, warmth, air, water, sex etc. After actualizing these needs, one proceeds to next level.
2. *Security needs:* These needs include the needs for safety and security. These needs are important for survival but not as demanding as physiological needs. Security needs are comparatively higher needs than the basic needs. Health care, physical safety, financial security etc. are felt by the individual after fulfillment of his basic needs.
3. *Social needs*: Needs for belonging, love, affection, friendship etc. are included in Social needs. Man is a social being and ultimately strives to fulfill these social needs for his growth and development. These needs are still complex compared to security and basic needs.
4. *Self-esteem needs*: After fulfillment of above three needs, this self-esteem needs becomes increasingly more important. These needs include social recognition, personal worth and accomplishments.
5. *Self-actualization needs*: This is the highest level of needs in the Maslow's hierarchy of needs and more complex to be realized. At this level, individuals become aware of his self, potentialities, relied on his self and don't influenced by the opinion of others. They remain interested in fulfillment of their potentialities.

Learning Theory of Personality

These theories propose that learning and personality development go hand in hand. Learning helps in improving the personality.

Learning theory of personality can be categorized as developmental approach to study personality quite separate from psychoanalytical and phenomenological theories of personality as this theory emphasize the role of learning in the development of personality. The psychologists like Watson, Pavlov, Guthrie, Thorndike, Skinner, Dollars & Miller, and Bandura & Walter are the supporter of this learning theory of personality learning theories of personality can be grouped as classical conditioning learning theories, cognitive learning the theory and social learning theory.

Classical Conditioning Learning Theory of Personality

The proponents of this classical conditioning learning theory were Evan Pavlov, E L Thorndike and Skinner. These psychologists held the view that human behaviour is shaped by response modification through practice and experience.

Pavlov highlighted learning through association of stimulus with response. B.F Skinner highlighted the role of reinforcement and punishment in the process of behaviour modification and learning though his Operant conditioning theory of learning. Details of classical learning theory may be referred in chapter-15

Cognitive Development Theory of Personality

The psychologist who proposed cognitive development theory is Jean Piaget. Piaget held the view that children develop their cognition through a sequential way passing from infancy to adulthood. Children understand their world and develop their intelligence from sensory-motor to formal operational type passing through pre-operational and concrete-operational phases and therefore his power of responding to problem and environment become modified. Along with the development of intelligence in the form of scheme to assimilation, accommodation, and equilibrium an individual become able to develop his personality. Higher is the level of intelligence or cognitive development better become the personality because one' intelligence help him to apply his response in a unique way in respect of achieving goals of life and becoming adjusted in the society.

Social Learning Theory of Personality

The proponent of social learning theory of personality is of Albert Bandura and Richard Walters (1963). According to Bandura and Walters, what an individual contribute to his world or environment is because of his personality. An individual's personality is acquired through a continuous process of structuring and restructuring experiences gathered through his social learning which may involve real or symbolic models. Therefore these psychologists highlighted the role of behavioural models resulting behavioural modification through imitation, observational and modeling. Through social learning or learning from role model, an individual gets reinforcement to become potential and improve of his personality.

ASSESSMENT OF PERSONALITY

Personality is a fascinating subject. Everybody is interested in the assessment of personality of his own and others. Personality is a complex and dynamic subject which can't be objectively measured like other physical beings. It is very difficult to assess the personality of an individual. It is indirectly measured by adopting humanistic approach and different tests.

Crude and Unscientific Methods of Assessment of Personality

Different types of crude and unreliable methods were being used in the past to assess the personality of individuals. Some of these methods are like,

- *Phrenology*: Studying personality through reading the shape of one' head.
- *Physiognomy*: Studying one's character by judging his face.
- *Graphology*: Studying one's character out of his handwriting.
- *Palmistry*: Studying one's character by judging the lines of his palms.

- *Astrology:* Studying one's character or personality by judging the position of stars and planets and their influence on him and his future events.

All of these methods applied for studying human personality were unscientific and crude. They yield no accurate and objective result in assessing personality. Therefore modern psychologists have devised and recommended some purposive and objective methods to assess the personality which are categorized as follows.

Scientific Methods of Assessment of Personality

Subjective Methods

Through subjective methods information are collected from the individual himself, from friends and relatives to assess the personality of an individual. This includes the study of Biography, study of case history of a person, interview technique, questionnaire method etc.

1. *Biography*: Biography means details about a person written in literary form or book form either in the story or some incidence, achievement of his life from birth. By reading biography, we can know about some personality characteristics of that person. But it is subjectively interpreted.

2. *Case history*: Case history or case study is another subjective method of the assessment of personality. There are some factors like heredity and environment including education, economic conditions, social conditions, family and friends' etc. act upon an influence on personality of an individual. Therefore in case history method different back grounds of an individual are studied to derive conclusion about his personality. However this method is criticized on the grounds of subjectivity.

3. *Interview method:* Interview means a face to face interaction in between the interviewer and interviewee. In this method, the interviewer interrogates the interviewee about some issue and collects information from the interviewee and records for his use. Then the interviewer analyzes the collected information by applying his judgment and interprets the personality characteristics of the subject. This method is also criticized on the grounds of subjectivity of the interpretation of data and subjectivity of the information of the interviewee.

4. *Questionnaire method*: In questionnaire technique, an inventory or questionnaire is drawn and the individual is asked to fill it up. The individual is asked to answer the questions which he feels correct. The answers then complied and interpreted by the investigator or experts to describe about the personality of an individual. Woodworth has developed a questionnaire covering 116 questions known as Woodworth Psychoneurotic Inventory which covers many phases of an individual's personality. However, this questionnaire technique also suffers from the nature of its subjectivity of interpretation of result, lack of validity and unreliability.

Objective Method

Objective methods include situational tests, observation and rating. These methods are scientific and somehow yield objective result. Objective methods include the following techniques of assessment of personality.

Situational Tests

Situational test is a device artificially created in which an individual is expected to perform his role related to personality traits under testing. The investigator systematically records the data in order to interpret the result. Situational tests are helpful to study the action and reaction of the subject in relation to a situation created for the same. For example, to test the honesty of an individual, certain situation can be created and his reaction can be tested in terms of honesty and dishonesty. A situation may be created by placing some rupees at a particular place and then watching the reaction of the individual and judging his personality trait honesty and dishonesty.

The following situational tests available may be used to test the personality traits.

1. Fernald's Test of endurance: It is used to assess the persistence of an individual taking into account the length of time or duration.
2. Maccarthur and Ryans's Numbe Series Test
3. Mac Dougall's Emotional Stability Test: This can be used to discriminate between psychotic, delinquent and normal adults
4. Sociometry method: Sociometry method helps to assess the particular trait of an individual by analyzing his position and status in a group.
5. Psycho-drama: Here an individual will have to play a role spontaneously in a specified situation and his behaviour will be observed by the observer. Out of the projection of the inner feelings in that situation in the form his role and acting, his personality traits will be assessed.

Observation Method

Observation method is a popular method which can be adopted to assess the personality of an individual in a real life situation. Planned observation yields better assessment of personality traits. Observation can be categorized as controlled and uncontrolled observation. In **controlled observation**, an artificial situation is created and the subject is allowed to display his behaviour spontaneously without being aware that he is being observed and the observer records his desired behaviour. On the other hand, in **uncontrolled observation**, the subject is allowed to display his behaviour in a natural situation and his desired behaviour is recorded systematically.

In another way, observation can be categorized as participant observation and Non-participant observation. In participant observation, the observer become a part of the group under observation and shares the situation as stranger and silent listener and observes the behaviour of the subject. In non-participant observation, the observer does not share the situation and become not a member of the group but hide himself and observe the behaviour of the subject. Non-participant observation is used to observe the behaviour of infants, abnormal persons. For better observation, the observer may use external devices like tape recorder, photographic cameras and telescope. For better observation and getting reliable result, observation may be repeated.

Questionnaire Method

Good and Hatt (1952) define questionnaire that, a device for securing answer to questions by using a form which the respondents fill in himself. A questionnaire contains a series of questions either presented in written or printed form to which the respondent will have to answer. These answers then are evaluated for personality assessment. Questionnaires may be used for quantitative and qualitative assessment of personality.

Rating Scale

James Drever defines Rating Scale as a method of recording an individual's characteristics especially traits of character and the like and the degree in which each is present, by the position of a mark on a line, the ends of which represent the two opposite or extremes." Rating is a method through which the subject's personality trait is rated by other person on some fixed scale. Rating sale reflects the impression that a subject leave upon the person who rates him. Following features are important in rating scale.

a. Traits to be rated should be specified.
b. Degree of possession or absence of the trait on the scale should be displayed.
c. There should be an appropriate person to rate the traits.

If a rater would want to rate the personality trait of students such as "sociability" then he would have to prepare the scale limiting certain points either three or five point scale. For example, he may limit the scale as Good, average and below average if it is a three point scale, Excellent, good, average, below average and poor if it is a five point scale.

Rating technique however suffer from subjectivity, halo effects and central tendency. Sometimes the rater hesitates to allot the extreme points and thus his rating tends to place at center of the scale. Rating is also biased by the subjectivity of the rater. Rating depends on the likes and dislikes of the rater and thus the result or the assessment may not be accurate. Therefore apart from appointing single rater or single judge, more rater should be assigned to rate the personality trait in order to obtain objective and accurate assessment.

Projective Methods

Projective methods help to an individual to project his wishes and feelings to some external objects. The way through which the individual projects his inner feelings provides some clue to assess his personality trait. In projective techniques, the individual is asked to write a story or to attach meaning to ink-blots. Out of his story and meaning attached to ink-blots in which the individual projects his inner feelings, his personality trait is judged. Projective techniques are useful in assessing the total personality of an individual. All the repressed and unconscious behaviour get outlet through the projection of private and inner wishes/feelings of an individual on some objects which can define his personality characteristics.

Followings are the important projective techniques used for the assessment of personality

1. Rorschach Inkblot Test: Inkblot test technique was devised by a Swiss Psychiatrist named Hermann Rorschach in 1921. This is a popular technique used to assess the personality of an individual. In this technique, an ink-blot is thrown on a piece of white paper and the paper is folded, pressed a then opened to see the resulting figure designated as an ink-blot. These ink-blots may be simple to complex and of multi coloured consisting of 10 cads on which there are ink-blots. Out of these 10 ink-blot cards, five is of black and white coloure and rest five is multi coloured. The subject then asked to see and conceive the meaning from the ink-blots one by one and expresses his feelings. The responses of the subject are recorded for interpretation of the result.

Scoring of the responses is done with reference to the following lines.

A. *Location:* Location means a part of which the subject associates his responses. It is marked by symbols as W, w, D, d and s for scoring. W stands for viewing the whole portion of the problem, w stands for a not viewing the whole problem, D stands for major details of the problem viewed, d stands for minor details of the problem viewed and s stands for viewing the white space apart from the problem.

B. *Contents*: Content means what a subject conceives out of the given ink-blots. Scoring is done on the following lines of conception like, Animal (A), Human being (H), Natural objects (N) and Inanimate objects like pot, lamp-shade (0)

C. *Originality*: Originality of the responses are tested using the scoring symbols Like O and P.O stands for original response and P stands for popular response.

D. *Determinants*: Determinant responses are judged using the symbols like F which stands for Form, C which stands for coloure, CF which stands for combination of coloure and form, FC which stands for combination of form and coloure, K which stands for shading and M which stands for movement in the progress of the cards.

In order to arrive at conclusion and for successful interpretation of the result Rorschach Ink-blot tests require training and experience on the part of a judge.

2. Thematic Apperception Test (TAT): Thematic Apperception Test was devised by Morgan and Murray (1935) at Havard University. This TAT contains 31 cards out of which 30 cards depict different scenes and one black card. Various story situations are depicted on the TAT pictures and the subject is asked to narrate or make up a story out of his observation of each picture. All pictures are presented to the subject in two sessions. Number of pictures is to be given for observation and analysis to a subject depending on his age, sex and type of the problem. Each picture is presented to the subject for one minutes and he is allowed to express his response within 3-4 minutes. TAT pictures may be administered individually or collectively on a group. Responses given by the subject are judged on the angels of Hero of the story, Needs of the hero, compelling situations to act and outcomes of the story.

TAT is clinically useful in diagnosing abnormal and mal adjusted persons. It may be used for providing guidance programme to selective normal persons such as college students and for a group having a particular attitude like racial, economic and religious prejudices.

3. Children's Apperception Test (CAT): Children's Apperception Test is suitable for measuring the behaviuoral characteristics of children of 3 to 10 years of age. The profounder of this test was Dr. Leopold Bellack. In this test, 10 cards are used to depict the picture of animals instead of human beings. These picture cards are shown to children one by one and the children associate their feelings with these pictures. The content of the picture cards deals with the life experiences, reactions and feelings of children. After showing the picture card one by one, children are asked to express their feelings in the shape of a story. Thus the story is then analyzed to reveal the problem of children and their personality characteristics.

CAT is helpful for assessing the personality characteristics of children. It provides an insight about the nature of adjustment of children with their family, school and society.

For the interpretation of the result and to derive conclusion, the following points may be kept in mind of the psychologist or the interpreter.

a. *Hero of the story narrated by children*: Personifying the hero and his personality traits
b. *Theme of the story*: Pleasant or unpleasant
c. *Climax and ending of the story*: Happy or non happy ending of the story.
d. *Attitude of Parents*: Judging the attitude of children towards their parents whether hostile or respectful.
e. *Family role*: Children may disclose their attitude towards their family members whether hostile or friendly.
f. *Other outside persons involved in the story*: Children may reveal the role and impression of outside persons leaving positive impact on them.
g. *Nature of anxiety expressed*: Children may suffer from various anxieties at their home like harassment, frustration, loss and love etc which are to be noted down.
h. *Defense and confidence*: Children might be suffering from problems for which they might be defending to protect themselves.
i. *Other factors* like language, time range to complete the story and frame work etc. are to be noted.

4. Play Techniques: Play way techniques are also mostly used devices to assess the personality traits of children. In this method, children are allowed to play with toys, dolls, blocks and other building materials and asked to draw different shapes and scenes and accordingly their mental characteristics and feelings are studied. These techniques are useful for organizing children's guidance programme. This has also therapeutic value.

5. Word Association Test: Word association test can be used to assess the personality traits of children. In this method, children are presented with a list of words one at a time and they are instructed to respond the first word that come to their mind. The examiner notes the time taken to respond the word and theme the children attach to the word they respond. This test is base on the assumption that, each word is associated with some emotional reactions. The children what they respond to a word will depict their underlying emotional feelings attached to that word uttered by them. In this test, there are 100 cards touching various aspects of life each. Word association test is one of the simple and economic ways of assessing the personality of children. In this test, there is no distinction of right or wrong responses.

6. Picture Association Test: In this test, pictures of social situations are presented as the test materials to be responded by the subjects under assessment. Rosenweing's picture-frustration study is popular one which contains 24 cartoons like drawings depicting everyday situations of frustration or stress involving his individuals, one of whom is usually shown as frustrating the other. The subject is asked to write or say in the blank caption box above the head of the frustrated individual, the first and appropriate association that comes to his mind. These associations reveal the areas of conflicts, anxieties and stress in the life of the subjects.

7. Sentence Completion Test: This technique was developed by Jullian B. Rotter and Jenet E. Rafferty. This is also called as paper pencil personality Inventory. This test has both the features of association test as well as the projection test. In this test, the subjects are asked to complete a list of incomplete sentences as he likes and any way he likes. The incomplete portion of the sentence is left for revealing the wishes, anxieties, reactions, conflicts and attitudes of the subjects. The examiner then analyses the total responses of the subjects in order to arrive at the conclusion.

Apart from these tests, there may be use of clay modeling test, drawing and painting tests for the assessment of the personality traits of the subjects.

Merits and Demerits of Projective Techniques

Merits: The following are the merits of the use of Projective Techniques used for assessment of personality:

- Proper rapport can be established in-between the examinee and examiner by the use the projective techniques.
- Projective techniques can be applied on the young children, illiterates, and handicapped children.
- Projective techniques are less expensive and economical
- Projective techniques are easily accessible and ease of administration.

Demerits: The followings are the demerits of the projective techniques,

- Projective techniques are less standardized in respect of its administration and scoring.
- There may be lack of objectivity in scoring of the test
- Projective techniques suffer from the subjectivity of the examiner/ experimenter in respect of interpretation of the result and drawing conclusion

PROBLEMS IN PERSONALITY MEASUREMENT

The followings are the problems faced in measurement of Personality.

1. It is difficult to measure a particular personality trait as it is dynamic and integrated with some other personality traits.
2. It is difficult to isolate one trait from another as traits are multi causational but not one-dimensional

3. It is difficult to identify representative sample of traits.
4. It is difficult to measure traits as because of the changeability nature of the traits. Traits change from society to society, time to time and environment to environment.
5. It is difficult to differentiate between natural and acquired traits.
6. Subjectivity of the subject under test. Sometimes the subject conceals the truth of his life and expressions.
7. Subjects find difficulties in expressing his repressed motives, emotional reactions in the fear of the possible problems and fear of his personality hamper.
8. It is difficult to find the standardized tests to measure personality of individuals
9. There is no common agreement on the subject matter of personality traits which makes it difficult to assess the personality traits properly.

APPLICATIONS OF PERSONALITY TESTS

There are the various applications of personality tests in the field of education

Selecting and Placementing: Personality tests can be applied to select individuals suitable for different jobs, courses and their placement.

Providing Training: Personality tests can be applied to identify personality traits of the individuals and thereby provide them specific training to have their adjustment.

Providing Guidance and Counseling: Personality tests give information about the interest, attitude and emotional reactions of the individuals and accordingly it becomes helpful to organize various guidance and counseling porogramme for their development and correction. It helps to organize therapeutic measures for the maladjusted individuals.

Conducting Research: Personality tests also help to conduct research activities on different dimensions of personality.

11
Mental Health and Adjustment

Everybody wants to lead a normal life without any disturbances in his body and mind. This is called as peaceful life. But it is seen that, in normal life everybody encounters some problems and become worry to get relaxed. This requires having his mental health and adjustment. Always we want to adjust with certain situations. But when we fail at that moment we feel maladjusted there develops so many mental illness like tension, frustration, abnormalities etc which requires treatment. One of the objectives of education is to develop sound mind of the learner. Aristotle defined education that it is the creation of a sound mind in the sound body. The study of mental health and adjustment is a fascinating subject in the field of psychology and education. Therefore it a need to have the detail studies of the concept of the mental health and adjustment, conditions responsible for development of mental health and defense mechanism.

MEANING OF MENTAL HEALTH

We often use the terms mental health and mental hygiene inter changeably. Mental hygiene seeks to establish conditions to promote mental health and prevent mental illness. Mental hygiene makes individuals health conscious about building good health. Crow and crow defines mental hygiene as it is science that deals with human welfare and pervades all field of human relationship. Hadfield defines mental hygiene as it is concerned with the maintenance of mental health and prevention of mental disorders.

Mental health is quite different from physical health. An individual may be seen externally and physically sound without any physical ailments but he may not be mentally happy as because of his poor mental health. He may have some mental disorders and abnormal behaviours. Health is defined as a state of physical fitness and mental soundness, social adjustment. Therefore mental health refers to the mental wellbeing of an individual free from all sorts of mental disorders and maladjustments. Physical health is precondition to have one's good mental health.

Hadfield defines that, mental health is the full and harmonious functioning of total personality of an individual. According to him, harmonious functioning means physical, mental and social aspect of an individual function with harmony to each other. Malfunctioning in one aspect will lead to deficiencies in other aspect. For example, an individual who suffer from physical handicap, face the problem to have social adjustment in a good way. Similarly, one having mental disorders also faces problems to adjust well with others. Thus, mental health can be said to have a balance feelings, desires, ambitions, and ideals to face and accept the realities of life.

CHARACTERISTICS OF MENTALLY HEALTHY PERSONS

The followings are some of the general characteristics of a mentally healthy person.

- *Self-acceptance*: Individual found mentally healthy individuals are found aware of their motives, potentialities, strength and weakness and accepts the realities of his life
- *Self-actualization*: Mentally healthy individuals are found understanding their hopes and possibilities and therefore develop their potentialities for the same. They are seen to have better adjusted with their environment and easily go along with others.
- *Personality Integration*: Mentally healthy persons maintain a variety of interests and are seen to lead a balanced life. They have an integrated personality.
- *Degree of Autonomy*: Mentally healthy persons are having decision making power of their own and have self-confidence.
- *Correct perception of reality*: A mentally healthy person is found to have his emotional maturity. He is having tolerance power and facing challenges of life.
- *Environmental Mastery*: A mentally healthy person is found to have his control over his environment. He is seen to be dynamic to adjust to varieties of situation and people.
- *Freedom from Abnormality*: Mentally healthy persons are found free from any short of abnormalities in their behaviours like phobias, psycho-somatic disorders, hysteria, and compulsions and neurosis.
- *Happiness*: Mentally healthy persons are found happy and easy going.
- *Emotionally Mature*: A mentally healthy person is found emotionally matured. He has the capacity to control his emotional reactions to different situations.
- *Intellectually Sound*: A mentally healthy person is found to be intellectually sound. He can take his own decision and solve his problems independently. He can think from different angles and judge the situation.
- *Dynamic Attitude*: A mentally healthy person is found optimistic in his outlook. He always believes in action and bears dynamic thoughts and attitude towards the situation.
- *Varied Interests*: Mentally healthy persons are found possessing variety of interests. They are never satisfied with a single act. They want to derive pleasure from different sources and they maintain different interests. They are fond of work, rest and recreation.

FACTORS AFFECTING THE MENTAL HEALTH OF PERSONS

Following factors are important in affecting the personality and mental health of a person.

Physical Factors: Physical factors are related to body style of a person. It also related to his health aspect. Poor health condition and physical deformity of the person affect his mental health and adjustment. He feels inferiority complexes among his friends and others because of his poor health conditions and physical deformities.

Hereditary Factor: Hereditary factors like body composition, size and shape of the body and level of intelligence etc also affect the mental health of a person. If somebody has poor intelligence then he is found to cope with others properly, achieve his goals satisfactorily and thus he becomes maladjusted and suffer from poor mental health. On the other hand if somebody is found to posses' extreme size of the body like extreme tallness and extreme shortness or too black or too white in his body composition, or born with blindness, deaf or dumb then these factors lead to his poor mental health. They face difficulties in adjusting with others.

Environmental Factors: Environmental factors include the home environment, school environment and social environment. Sound environment help to build sound mental health and vice versa.

Home Environment: The conditions like poor discipline, poverty, family conflicts, lack of security, large family size and disintegrated family etc. provide for development of poor mental health in the children.

School Environment: The conditions like improper organization of school activities, lack of respect for dignity, inequality, defective teaching methods, improper atmosphere of the class room arrangements lacking lights, ventilation, poor sanitary conditions, poor seating arrangements, teachers attitude and large size class room etc., rigidity of curriculum etc act for developing poor mental health in the children.

Social Environment: The conditions like poor social values, social conflicts, bad social conditions, untouchability, feeling of disparities in rich and poor etc are responsible for developing poor mental health of persons.

MENTAL HEALTH AND ADJUSTMENT

Adjustment is a psychological process. Ordinarily adjustment refers to adaptation to environment. Psychologically the meaning of adjustment is broad.

Every individual desires to satisfy his needs and motives which may be of different types. Some of these needs are inborn and some are acquired or learned. An individual strive to reach at his goals and satisfy his needs. The goals create tension in the mind of the individual and motivate him to act and reach at the goals and satisfy his motive. But sometimes the individual fails to achieve his goals due to some obstacles that obstruct the individual to easily reach at his goals. The individual tries to overcome these obstacles and reach at his goals either by directly removing the obstacle or by searching for the alternative means. When he succeeds to overcome this obstacle and reaches at his goals than he gets satisfaction of his needs and motives and thus he becomes adjusted, otherwise the individual feels maladjusted by the effect of his tension, frustration and other abnormalities.

Therefore adjustment may be defined as a process of satisfying needs or motives by reducing the tensions caused by needs or motives. If the motives will be simple, then the process of adjustment will be easy and if the motives will be complicated, then the process of adjustment will be more problematic. The continued tension will account for maladjusted behaviour in the individuals.

MALADJUSTMENT

Drever defines the term maladjustment as "a condition of an individual who is unable to adapt or adjust himself adequately to his physical, occupational, or social environment, thus affecting his emotional life and behaviour". Maladjustment is a mental state resulted out of the continued tension created in the mind of the individual in the event of his failure to satisfy his needs by overcoming or avoiding the obstructions in the way of his achievement of goals. Failure to reach at the goals may be due to two factors i.e. nature of obstacles and nature of goals. If the obstacle is simple, then it is easily tackled and if the obstacle is complicated, then it is difficult to overcome it. The obstacle may be of physical or social or psychological for the individual. Sometimes these obstacles are found within the individual in the shape of his conscience which does not allow the individual to act. The nature of goals may be of two types. i.e. simple goals and higher goals. Simple goals are easily attainable where as higher goals are not easily attainable. Higher goals need more effort and more capabilities in the individuals to be realized. When goals will be of higher in comparison to the capability of an individual, he may not be able to achieve the same and thus his tension increases and it leads to his maladjustment.

CAUSES OF MALADJUSTMENT

There are certain causes which result behavioural disorder and maladjustment in the individuals. These causes are like tension, conflicts, frustration, and complexes and theses are psychological in nature.

Tension

Tension is a psychological force arouse by needs felt by the individual. This tension compels a person to initiate actions in the direction of goals. If the goal is attained and need is satisfied then tension is released and the individual feels adjusted. But if the goal is not attained and need is not satisfied then tension is heightened and the individual feels restless and thus feels maladjusted. More is the complex of the need, there will be more tension. If the mental tension will be excessive and unbearable it will result maladjustment.

Conflicts

Conflict is a psychological factor. It is seen when there is two alternative paths to achieve the goal or two alternative goals to be achieved in front of the subject. These two alternative choices have equal or opposite driving force for the individual. Here an individual fails to take appropriate decision about which one out of the alternative options to be adopted and which one is to be omitted. This creates a conflicting situation in the mind of the individual and thus it leads to his maladjustment.

It is possible that, a several forces may be acting at the same point. The combination of several forces will develop conflicts and out of this conflict, a resultant force may come out to enable the individual to achieve his goal.

Kurt Lewin states three kinds of driving forces which drive an individual towards or away from the goal such as personal forces, Induced forces and Impersonal forces and these forces give rise to mental conflicts.

a. *Personal forces:* These forces arise in the individual himself according to his needs.
b. *Induced forces*: These forces arise from the external sources like from teachers, parents and friends.
c. *Impersonal forces*: These forces are like social laws, regulations, customs, which act as barriers to reach at the goal.

Kurt Lewin describes three types of conflicts depending on their degree of valence of motives such as approach-approach conflict, approach-avoidance conflict and avoidance-avoidance conflict.

A. *Approach-approach conflict*: This is a situation, where there are two alternate goals are kept before the individual to be achieved having equal forces or strength. Here the individual fails to discriminate which one is better and to be attained for his satisfaction. In this situation, these two alternative goals have equal approaching force that makes the individual motivated to be reached. This situation creates mental conflict in the individual.
B. *Approach-avoidance conflict*: This is a situation, where there is a same goal having both positive and negative valences. Here, the individual faces difficulties in case of attaining the goal and at the same time in avoiding the goal. Both attract the individual with same forces and thus a tension is created in the mind because of this conflicting situation.
C. *Avoidance-avoidance conflict*: This is a situation, where there are two unattractive goals having their negative valences. The individual wants to avoid both of the two optional goals but avoiding these two options will lead to a problematic situation. For example, a child wants to avoid his home assignment and at the same time he wants to avoid teacher's punishment. But at the same time these two options cannot be avoided at the same time. Thus this situation creates a mental conflict in the individual.

Frustration

Frustration is a mental state which threatens and prevents the individual in making any response to any situation. When an individual fails to reach at his goal in spite of his several attempts at that time he loses his interest to attempt any more for the same. This condition is called as frustration. Generally frustration is caused by some external sources like social restrictions, parental interferences, friends and relatives interferences in the action of the individual.

Complexes

Freud says that, unsatisfied motives are repressed in the unconscious mind of the individual and these repressed motives form a group in the unconscious mind taking similar repressed motives. Theses repressed motives coming in the form of group is called as complexes. This complex always creates tension and disturbs the mental balance of the individual and thereby makes him maladjusted. Complexes may be of two types such as superiority complexes and inferiority complexes. When someone succeeds in satisfying his needs he feels superiority complexes and when someone fails to satisfy his needs he feels inferiority complexes.

Symptoms of Maladjustment

The following symptoms give the clue to identify maladjusted individuals.

1. *Physical symptoms*: Stammering, stuttering, biting nails, rocking feats, restlessness and scratching body
2. *Emotional Symptoms*: Excessive worriness, fear, hatred, continued tension, conflicts and extreme timidity.
3. *Behavioural Symptoms*: Aggression, lying, bullying, withdrawal, negativism, sex disturbances, and poor achievement.

ADJUSTMENT MECHANISM

All individuals attempt to have their adjustment in the environment and get mental peace. But certain factors interfere in the way of their adjustment and disturb their mental peace. However the individual try to adjust himself adopting various approaches. These approaches are called as adjustment mechanism. Adjustment mechanism may be defined as any habitual method of overcoming the obstacles, reaching the goals, satisfying the motives and needs, relieving tension, conflicts and frustration and maintaining balance. Every individual is unique in adopting his adjustment mechanism. Adjustment mechanism adopted by the individual reduces tension, conflicts and frustrations and help in building mental health and his adjustment. Approaches adopted by the individual for his adjustment are of two types such as Direct Approaches and Indirect approaches.

Direct Approaches

Direct approaches include substitution of goals, removal of barriers, searching for alternative path and analyzing decision. Direct approaches are within the reach of the individual and directly help the individual to reduce the tension and making him adjusted.

Indirect Approaches

Indirect approaches are called as Defense mechanism. Indirect approaches include Attention getting, Compensation, Identification, Rationalization, Projection, Sublimation, Fantasy, Withdrawal, Regression, Reaction Formation, Displacement and Repression.

Attention Getting: When someone feels that he is not recognized by others, then he creates some peculiar behaviour like making unusual sound, by putting colourful dresses or by standing in the way of others so that he will be recognized. Different unusual activities are performed by the individual to get the attention of others about him and thus he gets satisfaction.

Compensation: Compensation means supplementing one's satisfaction in some other means. When a child fails to keep good result in Mathematics, he tries to get good result in English and thus he gets satisfaction. The physically disabled children compensate their achievement in art and craft, music and singing. Academically week students show their abilities in sports and get satisfaction.

Compensation may be of three types such as direct compensation, displaced compensation an indirect compensation.

Direct Compensation: By this method, the individual directly compensates his weakness by over emphasizing his action for getting good result. For example a stammerer attempts to become a good orator.

Displaced Compensation: By this method, an individual tries to get good result in another area in order to compensate his loss in one area. For example, an individual found week in academic areas tries to compensate it in athletics.

Indirect Compensation: By this method, Someone gets satisfaction out of some others success and compensates his loss. For example, a father who failed to become a doctor feels happy when his son becomes a doctor.

Identification: Identification is a method of adjustment where an individual gets satisfaction by identifying himself close to a successful individual. For example, an individual who fails to become a police man, he identifies himself as the relative of a policeman and gets pleasure. If a father is a great man, his son feels equally great.

Rationalization: Rationalization is a popular and mostly used method of adjustment mechanism. In this method, an individual justifies his failure by citing some other false reasons and gets pleasure. It is commonly blaming others instead of realities. For example, when a student fails in the examination, he blames the factors like questions were difficult, time was short or he suffered from headache etc.

Projection: Projection is a method of adjustment mechanism in which an individual blames others or some unfavourable factors in the environment for his own failure rather than admitting his own shortcomings. It is similar to the Rationalization method. For example, a player blames his racket when he fails to play well.

Sublimation: Sublimation is a method of adjustment mechanism in which an individual tries to channelize his unsatisfied motives by some socially approved ways. For example, when the sexual motives of a child is not satisfied by the fear of his parental control then he tries to suppress this motive and tries to involve himself in some other activity. In this method the inner urges of the individual are redirected to the benefit of the society. Freud state that, the sexual needs are not directly expressed and fulfilled; they are redirected in writing story, poetry or painting. Thus we can say that sublimation is a constructive mechanism. This method helps to convert antisocial behaviours into social behaviours.

Fantasy: Fantasy or day dreaming is a method of adjustment mechanism in which an individual gets satisfaction and reduces his tension by imaginary satisfaction of his motives which are not achieved in real life situations. In fantasy, all obstacles or obstructing elements disappear and the individual achieve his goals. It is said that, all creative things comes out of the fantasy of the individual. An individual become innovative in the field of art, music, painting etc.

Fantasy may be of three type such as conquering hero type, suffering hero type and death or destruction type. In conquering hero type of fantasy, an individual dreams as winner. He feels himself as a best singer, best painter, or best lover etc. In suffering hero type of fantasy, an individual feels defeated and dreams himself as suffering. In death and destruction type of fantasy, an individual dreams and imagine the destruction of those who were putting proems for his success.

Withdrawal: Withdrawal is a method in which an individual withdraws himself from a situation in the fear of his failure or criticism. Shy and timid children generally adopt this method and become adjusted.

Regression: Regression is a method in which an individual tends to solve problems and difficulties by adopting back tracking process either in memory or in behaviour which might have been successful in the past. It is a mechanism to adjust by adopting a type of behaviour that was satisfying in the early time.

Reaction Formation: Reaction formation is a mechanism in which an individual produces an action or attitude which is just opposite to the action that produce anxiety. For example, when an individual passes through a darken and lonely way, he blows whistles or sings or talks loudly as if he is not afraid of ghosts.

Displacement: In this method, an individual when fails to express his emotion and it is inhibited, then he transfers his emotions on some neutral objects and gets satisfaction. For example, when a child is rebuked by his father, he shows his cruel behaviour to his friends or starts to throw books, bags etc and become satisfied.

Repression: Repression is a method in which an individual pushes those of his desires or wishes into the unconscious mind which are painful and in conflict with the moral standards. For example we try to forget those experiences which are painful and unpleasant. So, repression means a process of suppressing the unfulfilled motives into the unconscious mind.

MENTAL DISORDERS AND MENTAL HEALTH

Mental health can be preserved by elimination of all sorts of mental disorders in the individuals. Mental disorder means a mental state when the individual feels tension, imbalanced emotionally, frustration, anxiety and mental conflicts which deviate him to act in different manner which is not normal in the eyes of others. In order to build good mental health and for better adjustment these mental disorders should be rectified and cured. Mental disorders may be broadly categorized as the followings.

Psycho-neurosis: Psycho-neurosis is a type of mild mental disorder which deviates an individual from normal individuals in responding to his environment in different way. It is a mild type of mental disorder which produces restlessness, distress and anxiety in the individual but it may not interfere in his day to day activities. These symptoms of psycho-neurosis may continue for some days, weeks or months. The physical symptoms of this type of disorder are like feeling of headache, excessive fatigue, and loss of sensory and motor functions, rapid respiration and heartbeat. Psycho-neurotic patients fairly know what they are doing and what difficulties they face. There are different forms of psycho-neuroses such as Hysteria, Anxiety state and Neurasthenia.

Hysteria: Both men and women suffer from hysteria. When this type of psycho-neurosis is exhibited in the individual, he shows the symptoms like loss of bodily function like paralysis of limbs, skin become insensitive, loss of memory, hard of hearing and blindness, excessive sweating and vomiting and loss of appetite. Sometimes, hysteria patients forget their identity like their names, address and family members.

Anxiety State: Anxiety state is a common symptom seen in all psycho-neurotic patients. In this state, individuals always feel hopeless, fear of death, insecurity, excitement, sleepless, depression etc.

Neurasthenia: In this type of mental disorder, an individual feels continuous exhaustion, fatigue and tiredness. He feels dull, lethargic, depressed and interests less in everything.

Obsession and Compulsion: Obsession is a state of mental disorder in which an individual is seen to be getting an idea and thought again and again but he fails to check them. Obsession means arousal of illogical thoughts in the mind of an individual. Another symptom is closely associated with this type of mental disorder i.e. compulsion. Compulsion means, a tendency to repeat an activity again and again. This obsessive and compulsive type of tendency sometimes becomes harmful to a person and to the society. Habit of stealing and habit of telling lies are examples of this type of mental disorder. Some common forms of compulsive behaviours are like follows.

- *Kleptomania*-Compulsion to steal
- *Pyromania*-compulsion to set fire
- *Poriomania*—Compulsion to move from place to place
- *Dypsomania*—Compulsion to drink reaptedly
- *Nymphomania*—Compulsion to have excessive sex
- *Phobias*—It is called as absurd or irrational fear of fire, water, darkness, open place high place, fear of lonely place, fear of crowds, fear of thunder or lightening, fear of blood and fear of closed places. Fear of fire is called as Pyrophobia, fear of water is called as Hydrophobia, fear of darkness is called as Noctophobia, fear of open place is called as Agrophobia and fear of high place is called as Acrophobia, fear of lonely places is called as Monophobia, fear of crowds is called as Ocholophobia, fear of thunder or lightening is called as Astrophobia, fear of blood is called as Hematophobia and fear of Closed places is called as Claustrophobia.

Hypochondria: This is state of mental disorder where an individual pretends to be sick in the fear of his failure in certain activity but actually he is not sick.

Psychoses: A psychosis is a condition in which an individual suffers from all sorts of delusion and hallucinations. Delusion means a subjective and false belief of something without any reality and Hallucination means a subjective and false perception of something without any reality.

Paranoia: Paranoia is a state of mental condition in which an individual is found disturbed in some aspect of his personality. His beliefs that there are enemies around him and they are planning against him but there is no reality. It is a form of delusion created in the mind of an individual.

MENTAL HEALTH IN SCHOOL

Developing mental health of learners in the schools is of important issues. Mental health of learners set a condition for their effective learning. Followings are some of the important factors which influence the mental health of the learners in their schools.

Environment of the School: School environment should be free from any short of distinction on the grounds of caste, creed and religion. A friendly environment of the schools can promote good mental health of its learners and vice versa.

Nature of Administration of the School: Authorities of the school should adopt democratic nature of administration in respect of solution of problems. Students should be given equal opportunities to share different activities conducted in the schools. Students should not be devoid of their rights and respects which may hamper their mental health.

Nature of Organization of Co-curricular Activities: A school may have different category of students like dull, average, intelligent and challenged types. Therefore varieties of co-curricular activities like drama, discussion, seminars, debate, competitions, games, sports and other cultural activities are to be organized to suit the interest of different students. Monopoly of organization of co-curricular activities in the schools will lead to disturb the interest and mental health of the students.

Teachers Personality: Teacher's personality can play the role of a model. Teacher should behave friendly with his students. He should be impartial to all of his students in caring, teaching, examining, grading and providing any short of guidance to his students.

Discipline: A school should adopt suitable disciplinary measures for its students. Rigidity in discipline may lead to abnormal tendencies in the students. Severe corporal punishment by the teachers should be avoided.

Organization of Guidance and Counseling Programme: School should organize guidance and counseling services for the benefit of those students who suffer maladjustment problems. A school may organize various types of guidance services like discussion among teachers, diagnosing maladjusted children, parental counseling, organizing human relation classes where day to day problems of the students are discussed and solutions are recommended and organizing psycho-therapy treatments etc.

Practice of Moral Education: Moral education can play a vital role for building mental health of some maladjusted students in the school. A school should organize moral and sex education classes to advise the students to solve their conflicts. It is essential for the adolescent students. A school may invite some experts to give extramural speech on moral education for the students.

Organization of Remedial Classes: Students with low intelligence and suffering from academic difficulties may develop maladjustment tendencies and their mental health is disturbed. Therefore, a school organizes remedial classes for those students who face difficulties in their reading or in any academic areas. Students who are found frustrated and disappointed in their regular classes may take benefit of these remedial classes to have their adjustment and mental health.

FACTORS EFFECTING MENTAL HEALTH OF TEACHERS

It is said that a teacher's personality has its positive impact on his student's personality. Teacher is role model for his students. So, a teacher's sound mental health can contribute to better learning of his students. Factors which are adversely affecting the mental health of a teacher are narrated below.

Inadequate Salary: It is because poor salary, teachers feel frustrated in adopting teaching profession and become maladjusted. In spite of their high devotion towards their teaching profession, when they are low paid or under paid at that moment their mental health is disturbed.

Work Load in the School: Sometimes due to inadequacy of teachers in a school, a particular teacher is given extra task and thus he doesn't get leisure time and rest. In this condition his mental health becomes hampered.

Insecurity of Service: Most of the teachers serving in private and non-government schools feel their service as insecure. Their service depends on the mercy of their boss. These teachers remain always in thoughtful conditions about their service. This leads to hamper their mental health.

Autocratic Supervision of Authorities: Sometimes the higher authorities give adverse reports about the functioning of the teachers without suggesting them for their improvement and rectification. This condition leads to create poor mental health of teachers.

Family Conditions of Teachers: The marital status, economic condition, relation with other family members of a teacher interferes in the teacher's mental health. It all these conditions are found good then a teacher's mental health will be found otherwise his mental health will be poor. He will always remain absent minded and feel maladjusted.

Rapport with other Teachers: If there will be continuous confrontation with other teachers and staff of the school and there will be no harmony among the teachers then there will develop poor mental health of teachers.

Social Restrictions: Teachers are said to be models in the society and respectable for their high morals. When a teacher is found smoking, taking alcohol and indulged in any anti-social activities then he is looked down in the society and thereby the teacher's mental health is affected.

MEASURES TO IMPROVE MENTAL HEALTH OF TEACHERS

The following measures may be taken and practiced for improving the mental health of teachers.

- Revising salary conditions as per the qualification of the teachers
- Ensuring service security of teachers
- Ensuring good rapport among the teachers
- Ensuring democratic atmosphere in the school
- Ensuring good family environment of the teachers
- Ensuring good social status to teachers
- Ensuring quality teacher training for teachers.

12
Thinking and Reasoning Ability

All of us encounter some problems in our day to day life. These problems may be of different types. But soon after facing the problem we try to solve it and get relief. Prior to solve a problem, we think of it and try to find out possible solutions. Therefore we can assume that, without thinking one cannot solve his problems. Thinking about the problem is a precondition of solution of problems. While we plan education and academic subjects, at that time we aim at developing thinking power of learners. Therefore it is a need to understand about the psychological concept of thinking, reasoning and problem solving, its nature and theories in detail.

MEANING OF THINKING

Thinking is a higher order of mental function which originates from a problematic situation. It is a mental process which enables a person to find out solution of a problem. Persons having higher thinking ability are found superior to others.

In wide sense, thinking includes perception, memory, imagination, reasoning, intuition and judgment. Thinking is always problem centered

Defining the term thinking *H.E. Garret* states, thinking is a behaviour which is often implicit or inner, in the sense not readily observable.

According to *James Drever*, thinking refers to any course or train of ideas, in its narrower and stricter sense, a course of ideas initiated by a problem.

W.M. Ryburn stated that, thinking is a cognitive process, arising from a felt dissatisfaction and proceeding by trial and errors to end-state which satisfies the conation.

Therefore, out of the above discussions about the meaning of the term thinking, it is said that, thinking is a mental activity which is directed towards the solution of a problem.

MEANING OF REASONING

Mostly thinking and reasoning is used inter changeably. But both the terms differ in their meaning. Though reasoning like thinking is also a mental activity, reasoning is something analytical. Reasoning is a stepwise thinking with a purpose of goal in the mind. It is also called as the purposeful thinking. James Drever defines reasoning that, it is a process of thinking involving inference, or of solving problems by employing general principles. But reasoning and thinking go hand in hand and both of them refer to mental abilities directed towards solution of problems. Power of reasoning differs from individual to individual in respect of degree. Power of reasoning and thinking also varies children to adults on the basis of their age. While children's reasoning is found unsystematic at that time the adult's reasoning is found to be more systematic and explorative.

Reasoning is of two types such as Inductive reasoning and Deductive reasoning. In Inductive reasoning, one has to proceed from particular fact to general conclusion. This type of reasoning helps to discover and conduct research. This reasoning helps to find out the general rule after organization of particular observations of facts and experimentations. But deductive reasoning one has to proceed from the general to particular direction. This type of reasoning helps to solve problems keeping in view of the general rules already existed.

CHARACTERISTICS OF THINKING

Followings are the characteristics of thinking.

- *Thinking is a mental activity*: Thinking is a mental activity which is internally operates in the brain on some situations.
- *Thinking is ideational*: Thinking starts with some idea or symbols. Ideas or symbols are called as the means of thinking. For example, one cannot think of the tree unless he has certain idea about the tree.
- *Thinking is acquisitive*: While some body starts thinking, at that moment he starts to acquire general information about certain objects or class of objects.
- *Thinking is abstract in nature*: Thinking is an abstract idea because one can think of ghosts, God and objects in the space to which he has not seen them in his real life situations. So we can say that thinking is imagination. All innovations and discoveries are the result of this imagination and abstract thinking.
- *Thinking is analytical and synthetical*: In thinking we can analyze a complex thought into simple form and also we can synthesize or sum up the simple thoughts into a complex thought.
- *Thinking is purposive*: All thinking is directed towards the solution of certain problem and attainment of goals. Therefore, thinking is purposive by nature. Without purpose, thinking has no meaning.
- *Thinking is expressive*: Thinking needs language or symbols for its expression. Though thinking is an internal and mental function, it requires language or any symbols for its expression. While thinking, we take the help of language or symbols in our mind.
- *Thinking is problem centric*: The origin of thinking is some problem. Whenever we face a problem, we start thinking over it for finding its solution. Therefore thinking is problem centric.

REQUISITES OF THINKING

Thinking process requires the following basic things to function.

- *Images:* When someone starts to think, he takes the image of the object in his mind in respect of its structure, characters, size, functions and coloures etc.
- *Concepts:* Concepts means a generalized idea about an object or quality. Concept is a means of thinking. Whenever we think, we think of the object in the form of its concepts.

- *Symbols and signs*: Thinking process use signs in its operation. Different signs help to think in different things. Whenever we see the sign of heavy smoke at that time we think of fire. Whenever we see the sign of red light in the traffic, at that time we think of danger and thus we make halts.
- *Percepts:* Percepts means to perceive the object. Thinking process takes the help of percepts in its operation. While some one thinks about an object, he perceives the object from different angles.
- *Language:* Thinking requires language for its operation in the mind. Thinking is expressed through language. Language adds clarity to one's thinking.

FORMS OF THINKING

Thinking can be broadly categorized into the following forms.

1. Imaginary Thinking

Imaginary thinking is a form or type of thinking which is carried out for self-gratification without any reality. Thinking about ghosts, God, and astronomical objects are imaginary thinking.

2. Realistic Thinking

Realistic thinking is a form of thinking which is carried out for actual solution of problem. Thinking about day to day problems related to actions is realistic thinking.

In another way we can classify thinking into the following types.

I. Concrete Thinking

Concrete thinking is also known as perceptual thinking. This type of thinking centers on certain object. In this type of thinking, someone perceives the object of its nature, forms, quality etc and then thinks about it. Children's thinking relates to this type of thinking.

II. Abstract Thinking

Abstract thinking is otherwise called as conceptual thinking. This type of thinking centers on certain idea or concepts. In this type of thinking, someone has to relate his thinking with his experiences. This requires the use of language for its expression. This type of thinking helps to innovate and discover new events. It helps to understand the fact in better ways.

III. Logical Thinking

Logical thinking is also called as reflective thinking. This type of thinking centers on certain purposes. This type of thinking helps the individual to solve his problem. In this type of thinking, a person reorganizes all of his mental experiences to find out the solution of the problem. Here after thinking, the individual develops an insight about the nature of the solution of the problem.

IV. Creative Thinking

Creative thinking is devoted towards innovating new ideas, new objects, and new theories that contribute for human welfare. This type of thinking is rarely found in the individuals. In this type of thinking, a person reorganizes his mental experiences to find out the new relationship, rules and interpretations keeping the fixed aim in the mind. All scientists and inventors possess this type of creativity.

According to *Charles Skinner* (1968), Creative thinking means that predictions and/or inferences for the individual are new, original, ingenious, and unusual. The creative thinker is one who explores new areas and makes new observations, new predictions, and new inferences.

M.J. Levin (1978) defined creative thinking that, it is a special form of thinking, a way of viewing the world and interacting with it in manner different from that of the general population. It is the ability to discover new solutions to problems or to produce new ideas, inventions, or works of art.

V. Critical Thinking

Critical thinking is a type of thinking which is different from ordinary thinking. It is a higher order of thinking which involves the use of cognitive skills like conceptualization, interpretation, analysis, synthesis, and evaluation for arriving at an unbiased, valid and reliable judgment of the gathered or communicated information or data as a guide to one's belief and action. Critical thinking makes an individual self-reliant, independent inquirer.

VI. Associative Thinking

Most of our thinking is directional and aim at solution of problems. But sometimes we think without any goal. This type of thinking without having any goal is called as non-directional or associative thinking. Associative thinking is reflected by day dreaming, fantasy, dreaming, delusions and hallucinations. This type of thinking may be treated as imaginary and have no reality.

FACTORS INFLUENCING THINKING

Following factors influences thinking.

Fallacy: Fallacy means arriving at conclusion by taking a particular instance which may be incorrect. The fallacious attempt will lead to vague result in thinking which will not be valid and reliable.

Wishes/Wishful Thinking: Sometimes our thinking becomes whimsical and guided by our wishes neglecting justification and reality. This type of thinking is carried out by politicians. While debating, this type of thinking becomes useful. Whatever one thinks, he expresses that.

Imperfect Insights: Drawing of conclusion by adopting trial and error thinking may not be always correct. Imperfect insight of a person about the problem leads him to improper solution of the problem. In order to have correct solution of a problem, a person should have perfect insight about that problem. Relying on faith or belief is not sufficient to the solution of problems in objective way.

Effect of Environment: Environment has a positive impact on the process of development of a person. We develop our distinct type of thought process in relation to our environment. So environment influences our thinking. We change our thinking according to the changes in the environment or situation.

Therefore one can notice the difference in the thought process of individuals residing in urban environment and individuals residing in the rural environment. Similarly there is a difference in the thought process of persons residing in industrial environment and persons residing in agricultural environment. Thinking of individuals also found different in functioning in a autocratic environment and democratic environment.

Motivation: Motivation and thinking both are closely related. One's thinking is facilitated by his motivation. If an individual become strongly motivated to act and practice, accordingly his thinking becomes superior in the direction of achievement of his goals.

Individual Differences: There is individual difference in thinking. Individual differs in their thinking process on the basis of their age, development, intelligence, environment, etc. Some individuals feel pleasure applying their thinking to his solution of problems and some individuals feel difficulties and loose interest in applying their thinking towards solution of their problems.

Adoption of Wrong Methods: Thinking will be improper followed by adoption of wrong methods. Logical thinking or correct thinking should not be carried out through assumptions, beliefs or wishes. Right approach will result in right thinking.

CONDITIONS FOR DEVELOPMENT OF THINKING

Thinking can be developed by taking the help of the following conditions.

Adequacy of Knowledge: If there would be sufficient knowledge about the phenomena or stimuli then the thinking will be of better. Adequacy of knowledge and experience result adequacy of thinking. Insufficient knowledge and experiences will lead to bad thinking and thus it will result into improper solution of problem.

Strong Motivation: All activities are done with some motive. An individual's thinking to act something also influenced by his motivation. Therefore to carry proper thinking, one must be motivated strongly and properly.

Freedom and Flexibility in Thinking: Freedom and flexibility conditions enhance the thinking power of individuals. If there will be imposition of restrictions on the individuals and the field of his thinking will be made narrow, then his thinking would be badly affected. There should be flexibility of attitude and approaches for the individual to develop right type of thinking.

Adequacy of Intelligence: Intelligence is a solid condition of thinking. Further intelligence is defined as a ability to think. Good intelligence result in good thinking and vice versa. Individuals found intelligent are also found possessing good thinking capacity.

Proper Conceptual Knowledge: Thinking about a problem requires conceptual knowledge about that problem. Therefore to have successful thinking, an individual should have adequacy of conceptual knowledge.

Efficiency in Language: Language is called as a tool of thinking. Therefore, to think properly, there should be sufficient command over the language.

Sound Reasoning Process: Thinking is influenced by the way of reasoning. Logical thinking leads to have good thinking and illogical reasoning result into illogical thinking. Therefore there should be development of the habit of logical reasoning in the individuals.

Incubation: Incubation is condition that help to develop thinking. It helps to develop thinking about the situation in the unconscious mind when someone is engaged in some other activity. If someone will fail to think about a problem, he will be advised to leave aside that problem and to be engaged in other activity, in the mean time by because of his incubation, the solution about the previous problem under taken abruptly comes to his unconscious mind.

PIAGET'S VIEWS ON DEVELOPMENT OF THINKING:

Jean Piaget (1896-1980) a Swiss Psychologist is famous for his theory of development of cognitive abilities like thinking and reasoning. Piaget has developed this theory out of his observation of development of his three children. He held the view that cognitive abilities develop in an orderly sequence following some stages. Piaget has reflected his views about the concepts like The Scheme, Assimilation, Accommodation and Equilibration in his theory. These concepts develop at different stages of development.

Stages of Development of Thinking

Following four stages were proposed by Piaget in the process of the development of thinking ability in the children.

Sensory-Motor Stage

Sensory-Motor stage covers birth to 2 years of age. According to Piaget, this is the first period of intellectual development. In this stage, all activities of children are centered on their body and basically governed by their reflex responses like sucking, grasping and movements. This is a period when children fail to differentiate their self. In this period, they develop Schemes of practical intelligence to deal with the objects. Piaget defines the concept Scheme as formation of idea about the object and dealing with them.

Pre-operational Stage

Pre-operational stage covers 2 to 7 years of age of children. According to Piaget, this is a stage of development of representational intelligence. During this period, children develop some language and images in their mind which help them to think about the objects, words, pictures and to some extent of their external world. Here in this period the power of assimilation appears in the children. Piaget defines assimilation as power of grasping the object and new experiences to the existing schemes developed in the children. During this period, sensory-motor schemes are converted into more covert and symbolic structures and the children become able to form concepts, generalize ideas and develop some principles.

Pre-operational period is marked by two stages such as Pre-conceptual stage and Perceptual or Intuitive stage. Pre-conceptual stage covers 2 to 4 years of age. During this period, symbolic and pre-conceptual thoughts develop in the mind of children. During this period, children start to deal with words by means of ideational representations through language, dreams and symbolic play. The period of Perceptual or Intuitive stage covers 4 to 7 years of age. During this period, there develops the intuitive thoughts and illogical thoughts in the mind of children. Here, children's thinking is guided by their perceptual appearances and intuition.

Concrete Operational Stage

Concrete operational stage covers 8 to 12 years of age of children. During this period, there develops logical thought in the mind of children. This is a stage where the power of accommodation develops in the children. Children shift their attention towards the transformations from the static notions. This period is also called as the period of conservation i.e. the ability to reverse internally and to focus upon the transformation from one state to another. During this period, children become able to think of conservation of quantity, volume, area and spaces.

Formal Operational Stage

Formal operational stage covers 12 years to adolescence age. During this period, there develop systematic thoughts and well integrated reasoning power. At this stage there develops abstract thinking in the individuals. At this stage, individuals become able to carry out different forms of thinking like hypothetical-deductive thinking, propositional thinking and combinatorial thinking in respect of dealing with their problems. During this stage, individuals are found to have equilibration. Piaget called equilibration as mental balance and dynamic functioning of mind.

Educational Implications of Piaget's Theory of Cognitive Development

Piaget's theory of about cognitive development has a lot of educational significances. This theory can be implied for organizing teaching learning situations in the following ways.

Organizing Acceleration Programmes: Development is a product of both heredity and environment. Therefore Piaget stressed on making environment interesting for the children which will provide a base for development of sound mentality. A Variety of enriched and accelerating programmes should be organized for the children at their schools and homes to develop their thinking power.

Study of Individual Differences: Piaget noticed individual differences in the thinking pattern of children. Some are found better and some are found poor in their thinking pattern. Therefore teachers should present suitable teaching learning materials keeping in view of the individual differences and set the ground for their development.

Organization of Curriculum: Piaget stated that curriculum should be viewed as integration of child, teacher and materials. Curriculum should be organized in such a way to suit the interest of children so that they can develop a kind of experience that will boost their thinking ability. Teaching materials to be presented should match the cognitive structure of the children.

Organizing Teaching Strategies: Cognitive development theory of Piaget has also a great educational value in respect of organizing teaching strategies in the schools. Piaget says a child is an architect of his own growth and he should be at the center of the educative process. Therefore all teaching methods to be adopted by teachers should be interesting and suiting the cognitive structure of children.

BRUNER'S VIEWS ON DEVELOPMENT OF THINKING

Jerome S. Bruner (1915) gave an eclectic approach on the development of thinking ability. Bruner's theory of cognitive development shares with the Piaget's thoughts about the development of cognitive thoughts. Bruner has suggested the following different phases of the development of thinking and concept formation.

Phases of the Development of Thinking Ability suggested by Bruner

Following phases were suggested by the Psychologist, Bruner through which human thinking ability develops.

Enactive Phase: Enactive phase covers from birth to 5 years of age. During this phase children develop their thinking associated with actions. It is through motor activities, children become able to know about the reality of objects. Enactive representation is manipulative in nature and therefore children inactively able to know how to play with balls, how to walk and how to handle toys etc.

Iconic Phase: Iconic phase covers from 5 to 7 years of age. During this phase, children develop images in their mind about objects that stands for concepts. At this stage, children fail to define the concept. Iconic representation of children is based on their internal imagery and governed by perceptual organization.

Symbolic Phase: Symbolic phase covers from 7 to adolescence age. During this phase, children develop abstract and more flexible system of thoughts. At this stage, the power of reflective thinking develops as because of development of linguistic skills in the children.

Bruner's views on the Process of Categorization

Bruner held the view that, learning centers around conceptualization and categorization. The thought processes are labeled by a "strategy" which means a sequence of mental event that is goal directed. It is through the use of strategies one's conceptualization occurs.

Bruner mentions following three important factors of categorization such as the informational situation, cognitive strain, and risk.

The Informational Situation: A person starts his activity with certain amount of information already in his possession. But a activity may need much more information to be handled. The person decides what amount of information is to be collected about certain activity for its completion so that it will be completed within stipulated time. Here a person selects the relevant and irrelevant information about the task.

Cognitive Strain: While attempting to complete a task, a person may apply a number of fallacious attempts until to gather the right information about the task which may put a strain on the cognitive structure of the person.

Risk: A person may fail to complete a task after applying all possible thoughts and thereby get unpleasant result. Therefore a person willing to deal with a task will have to take a risk. Individuals vary in their wills of taking risk and assuming tasks.

Bruner also mentions two types of categorization such as Identity and Equivalence.

A. *Identity*: Identity means to form a particular thought about certain thing among its different variations. For example, though moon passes through a series of phases, we classify each phase of moon as moon.

B. *Equivalence:* It means considering different kinds of objects quite similar to one another so are put in the same thoughts. For example, though there are differences in all planets, we put them into a same barrel as solar family.

Equivalence categories take three forms such as Active equivalence category, Functional equivalence category and Formal equivalence category form.

In active equivalence category form, objects evoke same affective responses to classify them to a same category.

In functional equivalence category form, objects having same functions are placed in the same category

In formal equivalence category form, objects are categorized in to a same category on the basis of their intrinsic properties. This requires highly abstract concepts.

EDUCATIONAL IMPLICATIONS OF THE STUDY OF THINKING AND REASONING

- Understanding the Learners and their individual differences according to their level of thinking and reasoning.
- Planning for organization of curriculum according to the level of thinking capacity of the learners.
- Organizing different co-curricular activities in the schools for development of thinking of the learners.
- Devising and applying different techniques of teaching in the class rooms suiting thinking level of the learners.
- Organizing different enrichment programme in the schools.

13
Problem Solving Ability

One of the learning objectives that are to be developed in the learners is problem solving ability. Problem solving is considered as the highest level of learning as proposed in the Gagne's hierarchy of learning. Problem solving ability requires having mastery of all lower types of learning. Every individual wants to satisfy his motive or needs by reaching at his goals set and in between he encounters some problems which block the path of the individual to reach at his goals. Therefore, the individual starts to think of different possible ways of solving this problem and reaching at his goals. So, thinking and problem solving both are closely related to each other. Problems may be of different types such as simple or complicated types by their nature and accordingly it requires the individual to apply his thought process either simple or complex types to solve his problems depending on the nature of problems. In problem solving, many mental processes like thinking, reasoning, memory, imagination, intelligence and judgment operate interactively and help the individual in solving his problems. Any problem solving requires thinking on the part an individual.

MEANING AND DEFINITIONS

Problem solving is a goal oriented activity. This may include variety of approaches. Individuals vary in their problem solving skill. Some are found easy of problem solving and some are found critical and difficulty in problem solving.

Defining problem solving, *Wood worth and Marquis* (1948) says, problem solving occurs in novel or difficult situations in which a solution is not obtainable by the habitual methods of applying concepts and principles derived from past experiences in very similar situations.

Skinner (1968) defined that, problem solving is a process of overcoming difficulties that appears to interfere with the attainment of a goal. It is procedure of making adjustment in spite of interferences.

William J. Pauli defined that, problem solving is a process of transforming the difficult into easy, complex into simple and confusing into the clear and understandable.

Thus, out of the above definitions, it can be concluded that, problem solving is a mental activity which is goal oriented and aim at overcoming the difficult situations and providing a satisfactory adjustment to that problematic situation. It requires deliberate, conscious and serious efforts on the part of a problem solver. It requires sufficient command over the environment, past experiences and conceptual knowledge in the problem solver.

APPROACHES/METHODS OF PROBLEM SOLVING

Following approaches are generally followed for problem solving.

Trial and Error Approach

This approach is also called as stimulus and response approach based on the S-R theories of learning. Thorndike stated that a problem is solved by a process of trial and error. When certain problem is faced, an individual starts to think all possible ways and tries to solve it and finally a selective thought and action become useful to solve the problem.

Cognitive Approach

Cognitive approaches of problem solving emphasize the role of perception of the whole problematic situation and find out possible relationship among its different elements/parts to arrive at the solution of the problem. This approach of problem solving was contributed by Gestalt Psychologists. According to this approach, a problem is solved all of a sudden by an insight about the problem but not through trial and error process.

Inductive-Deductive Approach

In Inductive Approach, a problem is solved by individual observation of a fact. But in Deductive Approach, a problem is solved by referring to some general principles, laws or formulas which are already existing.

Analytic-Synthetic Approach

In analytic approach, a problem is solved by examining its constituent parts. This approach helps to understand the hidden aspects of a problem and to discover the truth. All difficult situations can be understood through this analytical approach. On the other hand, in synthetic approach, a problem is solved by examining the whole aspects of it. However, both analytic and synthetic approaches go hand in hand. While analysis approach helps to collect knowledge about the problem, at that time synthetic approach helps to retain that knowledge in the memory to produce the solution.

Dewey's Problematic Situation Approach

John Dewey stated that, conflicting goal situations develop reflective thinking and helps problem solving. He suggested following three problematic situations which lead to solve the problem.

No-path Situation: In such a situation, an individual tries to reach at his goal but certain barrier or problems block the way. Then the individual starts to think of the problem and find out its solution.

Alternate Goal Situation: In this situation, the individual thinks about which one out of the two alternate and equally attractive goals is to be attained and accordingly he tries to solve his problem.

Forked-path Situation: In this situation, an individual thinks of different paths and selects one suitable path out of different paths to solve his problem and reach at his goal.

STEPS FOLLOWED FOR PROBLEM SOLVING

Effective problem solving activity follows certain steps. According John Dewey, an American philosopher the following five steps lead to problem solving.

i. Feeling difficulties
ii. Defining difficulties
iii. Searching possible solutions
iv. Considering consequences
v. Selecting a solution

Graham Wallas have suggested the following four steps for creative thinking and problem solving.

i. *Preparation:* Awareness about the problem
ii. *Incubation:* Metalizing the problem
iii. *Illumination:* Developing an insight about the problem
iv. *Verification:* Verifying the validity and truth of the result.

Rossman has suggested the following four steps involved in a problem solving activity.

i. Felt difficulties
ii. Gathering information
iii. Testing solutions and
iv. Accepting new ideas.

CONDITIONS INFLUENCING PROBLEM SOLVING BEHAVIOUR

Following conditions influence the problem solving behaviour of the individuals.

Physiological Conditions

Physiological conditions are such conditions which are seen within the individuals. These conditions include motivation, intelligence, personality characteristics, emotions, interest, habits, training, experience and thinking ability of the individuals. If these conditions favours positively, then problem solving become easy, prompt and objective otherwise, problem solving become poor, difficult, and result less.

Environmental Conditions

Environmental conditions are external conditions found outside of the individuals that include language, time, teaching methods, teaching materials, feedback and reinforcement etc. If theses environmental conditions favour positively then the problem solving ability of individual's become better and vice versa.

TECHNIQUES TO DEVELOP PROBLEM SOLVING ABILITIES IN CHILDREN

One of the major objectives of all educational endeavours is to develop problem solving ability in the children. Therefore, all educational activities are to be planned and organized to realize this objective. Teachers may adopt the following techniques to promote problem solving ability in the children.

- *Motivating the learner*: Teacher should motivate their students to take on their task independently with interest. He should moderately motivate the children using different techniques to keep on interest in task. Extreme motivation may hinder their productive thinking.
- *Presenting whole problem*: Teacher should present the whole task rather part wise to develop an insight in the children about the task leading to successful problem solving. From the whole situation, children can perceive the hidden aspects of the task.
- *Encouraging divergent thinking*: Teacher should encourage the children to attack their task in different ways. A teacher should not bind the children to adopt a single and stipulated path of solving their problems.
- *Encourage practice*: Teacher should encourage the children to practice their task again and again and gain experience and mastery. It will lead to easy of problem solving.
- *Presenting incomplete solution*: A teacher should not present the complete solution of a problem. Questions should be left unanswered by the teachers to be answered by the students so that a discovering thinking can be developed in the children
- *Promoting comprehensive power*: Teachers should encourage the children to have complete understanding about their task. Teachers are to motivate the children to develop conceptual understanding in the children which will help their problem solving skill.

14
Learning, Learning Process and Development

Every individual wants to develop. The key of his development is learning. Learning helps him to realize the needs by performing desirable acts and leads him to move towards his development. Learning is a requisite for all activities and problem solving behaviour. It is continuous and lifelong process. It is not confined to class-room rather it goes beyond the class-room. Learning is an important function of an individual which becomes a cause of his survival in the environment. All educational institutions, parents, teachers aim to facilitate the learning of their children by arranging different helpful conditions and help them to develop. Successful learning leads to successful development. Therefore, it is a need to know about the concept of learning and learning processes.

MEANING OF LEARNING

Learning is an act of through which one acquires knowledge and skills to fulfill his needs. It is an act of directing desirable response to certain stimuli and thus leads to help in adjustment. In broader sense, learning refers to modification of behaviour which is relatively permanent as a result of one's experience. Learning is not a haphazard process rather it is a continuous and systematic process which result a change in the behaviour of an individual. Thus learning brings change in the behavioural pattern.

The process through which the act of learning takes place is called as learning process. The input that helps to carry the learning process is called as learning materials. The result we get through the learning process is called as learning outcomes. The techniques or the methods that assist to carry the learning process are called as methods of learning. The situation where learning takes place is called as learning situation. The subject who performs the act of learning is called as learner. So, the cycle of learning process completes taking the elements of learner, learning situation, learning materials, learning techniques or method and learning outcomes. Coordinated and proper functioning of all these elements leads to result good learning and vice versa.

DEFINITIONS OF LEARNING

Different Psychologists have defined learning in different manners. Some of the definitions are mentioned below.

Hilgrad defines that, learning is a process by which an organism as a result of its interaction in a situation, acquires a new model of behaviour which tend to persist and affect the general behavioural pattern of the organism to some degree.

Kingsley and *Ralph Garry* defines that, learning is a process by which an organism in satisfying his motivation, adopts or adjusts to a situation in which it must modify its behaviour in order to overcome the obstacles.

Munn defines that; to learn is to modify behaviour and experience.

Gates and Others defined that, learning is the modification of behaviour through experiences and training.

Crow and Crow define learning that, learning is the acquisition of habits, knowledge and attitudes. It involves new ways of doing things as it operates in an individual's attempt to overcome obstacles or to adjust to new situations. It represents progressive change in behaviour. It enables him to satisfy interest to attain goals.

Skinner defined learning that, learning is a progressive behaviour adaptation.

To sum up, it may be said that, learning is a process through which one's behaviour is changed as a result of experience and it helps in meeting the needs, solving problems, adjusting to a new situation and overcoming obstacles. One's learning operates in his cognitive, affective and conative aspect of mind.

FUNCTIONS OF LEARNING

The followings are the functions of learning.

1. Acquisition of knowledge, attitude and skills
2. Adjustment to a new situation
3. Solution of problems
4. Establishing relationship between stimulus and response
5. Modification of behaviour

NATURE OF LEARNING

The followings are the natures of learning.

- *It is mental activity*: One's learning requires the proper functioning of his mind. His thinking, imagination, reasoning, creativity, attitude and all these mental operations goes on at the time of learning.
- *It is need based*: One's learning arises out of his need. This need stimulates him to involve in learning act. Without need, one can't proceed on for his learning. The needs motivate someone to learn and fulfill his needs.
- *It is result oriented*: Every type of learning is result oriented. The result may be fulfillment of needs, adjustment to a new situation, solution of a problem or acquisition of knowledge, principles, theories, rules etc.
- *It is problem centered:* Learning is problem catered. When someone feels the problem and tries to overcome it, then his learning starts and finally learning helps him to solve his problem.
- *It is developmental*: One's learning is seen to be developmental. According to the increase of age and potentialities, one's learning capacity also increases and perfection or development in learning takes place.
- *It is a life-long process*: Learning is a never ending process and it is therefore called as a life-long process which starts at birth and ends at death of an individual. One can learn many things through out of his life.

- *It is a systematic process*: Learning is not a haphazard process rather it is a systematic and continuous process. Any interruption in the process of learning results poor result in learning and learning becomes less effective. So all the conditions of learning should be properly arranged to have effective learning.
- *It is universal:* Learning is a universal activity found in all human beings. Learning can take place at any where, for any individual, at any time, for any purpose, of any types and by any means.
- *It is situational*: Learning doesn't take place in vaccum place. It takes place in a situation that demands for learning. Learning operates in the environment where the individual lives and survives.

TYPES OF LEARNING

Followings are the different types of learning.

- *Conceptual learning*: Acquiring knowledge about different concepts, objects, ideas, events, processes etc.
- *Skill learning*: Acquiring proficiency, ability to perform an act.
- *Perceptual learning*: Learning to perceive the relationship among the stimuli, among different elements of a situation.
- *Associative learning*: Learning to associate possible relationship among different parts and elements.
- *Verbal learning*: Learning of linguistic skills, vocabulary and speech.
- *Motor learning*: Learning to handle, do, and perform the activity employing body and hands.
- *Attitudinal learning*: Learning to change the mind set, feelings of attachment.
- *Affective learning*: Learning to acquire emotions and feelings need to complete the task
- *Cognitive learning*: Learning to change the thinking, reasoning, imagination and beliefs.

R.M. Gagne has pointed out the following 8 types of learning.

1. Signal learning
2. Stimulus-Response learning
3. Chain learning
4. Verbal learning
5. Discrimination learning
6. Concept learning
7. Principle learning
8. Problem solving

PRINCIPLES OF LEARNING

Following principles are important to be followed for making the learning effective.

- *Learning should be Active:* Learner who will carry the process of learning should be active on his cognitive, affective and conative level. Someone should pay his positive attitude, interest and motivation for making his learning active and effective.

- *Learning should be Meaningful*: Learning should be meaningful to the learner. If there will not be any meaning behind the learning, then such learning will be meaningless and less effective. Meaningless learning will yield no result for the learner.
- *Learning should be Purposive*: It is said that all learning are purposive. Without any purpose, learning is not initiated. Children learn with a purpose to earn knowledge, skills, and to become a responsible citizen of the country. Farmers learn with a purpose to yield better cultivation.
- *Learning should be Individualized*: No two individuals learn at the same rate. Therefore, learning should be individualized keeping in view of their interest, area of learning, choices etc.
- *Learning should be Interesting*: In order to make learning effective, it is need to make learning interesting so as to motivate the learner to perform the task of learning. All the conditions of learning should be organized properly.
- *Learning should be Linked with Life:* In order to make learning effective, learning should be linked to life situations. Learning should not be compartmentalized and segregated from life because life situations compel the individual to learn. Therefore, we can't learn different subjects like history, political science, economics and language in separated manner. All subjects of study should be correlated with each other.

METHODS/PROCESSES OF LEARNING

Following methods/processes help in learning of an individual.

1. Imitation Method: It is simplest method of learning. Children usually imitate their parents, elders, teachers and friends and acquire knowledge to modify their behaviour, habits and thus they learn from others by the method of imitation. It means by seeing others and to change one-self.

2. Trial and Error Method: It is also another method of learning. Psychologist, E.L. Thorndike popularized this method of learning. It means gradual diminishing of wrong attempts of doing certain activity and leading towards its perfection and complete elimination of wrong attempts. Most of our learning takes place by trial and error process. One's perfection in learning comes through this process. Children learn to speak perfectly by adopting this method. A baby learns to walk properly by adopting this process.

3. Conditioning Method: Conditioning method of learning was popularized by Ivan Pavlov. According to this method, learning takes place by a process of conditioning of responses. This method helps to modify the old habits and to form new habits in the children following the act practice or rehearsal. This method of learning is useful in learning of desirable habits and eradicating superstitions, blind notions and ugly manners in the children.

4. Insightful Method: Insightful learning method was popularized by Gestalt psychologists. By this method, an individual tries to perceive the relationship among different elements of a situation and then learn to solve a problem.

5. Transferring Method: Transferring method also help the learners to learn.

We apply this method to adjust to a new situation by applying our old/past experiences or past learning. Class-room learning helps in solving the problems of life while living in the society.

FACTORS AFFECTING LEARNING

Followings are the different factors/conditions that affect the learning.

***1. Factors within the Individual*:** Factors within the individual that affect the learning again may be categorized as physical factors and psychological factors.

Physiological Factors: The physiological factors include age, health, motive, functioning of glands, functioning of sense organs and maturation of an individual. If these conditions become conducive, then one's learning becomes better and effective otherwise they negatively affect his learning.

Psychological Factors: The psychological factors include level of intelligence, thinking, motivation, interest, attitude, attention, emotions etc which affect one's learning either in positive or negative way. If these psychological conditions are found positive in the children then their learning becomes more otherwise their learning become less.

2. Factors Outside the Individual: Factors outside the individual may be called as environmental or external factors. These factors include methods of instruction, teacher's attitude, teaching, teacher's role, teaching-learning materials, curriculum ventilation, arrangement of lights, arrangement of class-room, noises, sanitary conditions, atmospheric conditions, infrastructural facilities etc. If these conditions will be conducive, then learning will be better and vice versa.

EDUCATIONAL IMPLICATION

The study about learning and learning process has a great educational value. It has influenced the role of teachers, instructional strategies, curriculum designing, preparation of teaching aids, setting of learning objectives, organizational pattern of places of learning, infrastructural facilities and parental roles.

15
Theories of Learning

Different schools of psychology have proposed different theories of learning. Each theory attempts to explain why, when and how learning takes place. Learning theories help to understand the nature of the learner and the learning process. Therefore it is necessary to discuss the theories of learning.

CLASSIFICATION OF LEARNING THEORIES

Learning theories can be broadly classified into two main groups such as:

1. S-R Theories or Stimulus Response Theories: These are again grouped into two types:

i. S-R Theories without Reinforcement: It includes the following theories of Learning.

a. Classical Conditioning Theory of Pavlov.
b. Watson's Theory of Learning.
c. Guthrie's Theory of Learning.

ii S-R Theories with Reinforcement: It includes the following theories of Learning.

a. E.L. Thorndike's Theory of Learning.
b. Hull's Theory of Learning.
c. B.F. Skinner's theory of Learning.

2. Cognitive field Theories of learning: These include the following theories:

i. Gestalt Theory of Learning.
ii. Kurt-Lewin's Theory of Learning.
iii. Tolman's Theory of Learning

Learning Theories is depicted in diagram 15.1

DISCUSSION OF DIFFERENT THEORIES OF LEARNING

Different theories of Learning proposed by different Psychologists as shown in the above Diagram are discussed below.

Pavlov's Conditioning Theory of Learning

The Russian Psychologist named Ivan Pavlov has suggested this conditioning theory of learning on the basis of an experiment on a dog. This theory takes into account the concept of bond or connection i.e., learning as the linking of a response with a stimulus. Human organism has some innate tendencies or responses which are activated, when appropriate stimulus are presented to them. For example, fear is a natural response to a tiger and salivation is a natural response to food etc.

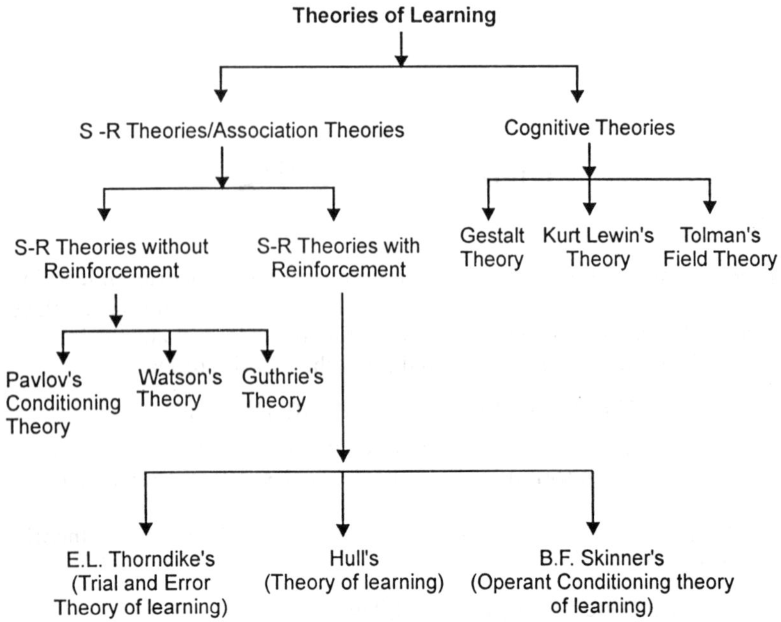

Diagram 15.1: Showing Classification of Learning Theories

Out of his experiment on a dog, Pavlov could find that, the dog salivated not only on actual eating but also when it saw the food, noticed the man who usually brought the food or even heard the foot step of its feeder. Pavlov called this phenomenon as conditioning and later on it was renamed as classical conditioning.

Meaning of Conditioning

Pavlov put forth the meaning of conditioning that every natural stimulus has the power of eliciting a natural response. For example, Food being a natural stimulus brings the response of salivation. But in the course of time, an artificial stimulus acquires the power of a natural stimulus if it is presented with it for several times and elicits the same natural response as it happens in case of the natural stimulus. A time comes, when the artificial stimulus alone is conditioned with the natural response. The organism becomes habitual to respond to an artificial stimulus, Therefore Conditioning is the linking up the original response with a secondary or substituted stimulus.

Pavlov's Experiment on Dog

Pavlov kept a dog hungry for a few days and then tied it on to the experimental table which was fitted with certain mechanically controlled devices. The experimenter kept himself hidden from the view of the dog but was able to view the experiment by means of a set mirror through a small window.

A bell was sounded and a few seconds later food was given to dog. At first the sound of the bell did not produce any saliva, but the sight of the food did elicit saliva from the mouth of the dog. After a few paring of the bell sound and food, the bell alone was sounded and food was not given. It was seen that, at the sound of the bell the dog began to salivate. Thus it was proved that the sound of the bell being an artificial stimulus which is not a biological in nature acquire the ability to elicit the natural response" Salivation" which was formally limited to the natural stimulus "Food". The dog was conditioned to salivate.

Out of the above experiment, Pavlov defined "classical conditioning as a process where an artificial stimulus being paired with natural stimulus posses the ability of a natural stimulus."

Diagrammatically, Pavlov's theory of conditioning learning can be presented in the following manner

Unconditioned Stimulus/Natural Stimulus **(Food) - S**	⟷	Unconditioned Response Natural Response **(Salivation) - R**
Artificial Stimulus/Conditioned Stimulus **(Bell Sound) - S1**	⟷	Conditioned Response Natural Response **(Salivation) - R1**

(S ≠ S1)
(R= R1)

Elements of Conditioning Process

Pavlov used the following elements in the conditioning process:

1. *Unconditioned Stimulus*: Pavlov called the "Food" as natural stimulus or the unconditioned stimulus. All unconditioned stimulus have the ability to elicit the natural response without conditioning.
2. *Unconditioned Response:* The natural response to a natural stimulus or unconditioned stimulus is called as unconditioned response. Salivation is a natural response.
3. *Conditioned Stimulus:* The artificial or a secondary stimulus is called as a conditioned stimulus. It has no independent ability of eliciting natural response. This stimulus in a process of conditioning is linked with the natural response. For e.g., Bell sound.
4. *Conditioned Response*: The response made to a conditioned stimulus is called as conditioned response. It is also called as learned response.

The theory of conditioning advocated by Pavlov states that learning as a habit formation based on the principle of Association and substitution. It is a stimulus-Response type of learning. If appropriate ground is provided then an artificial stimulus can evoke the natural response.

Principles of Classical Conditioning Learning

On the basis of the experiment, Pavlov derived certain principles of classical conditioning such as:

Extinction: Extinction means, disappearance of the connection or bond between Stimulus and Response (S and R). Delayed presentation of food followed to a sound of the bell repeatedly lead to extinction of the natural response.

Spontaneous recovery: Pavlov observed that there is no complete extinction due to time interval but there is inhibition of the conditioned response. Though there is extinction of conditioned response, it appears spontaneously but at a reduced intensity.

Stimulus generalization: Generalization is a process in which the conditioned response (C-R) to a stimulus can be generalized or induced to a similar stimulus. Pavlov observed that, any stimulus which is similar to stimulus to which the dog is conditioned can also elicit the conditioned response (CR).

Higher Order of Conditioning: Pavlov stated that, it is also possible to establish a higher order of conditioning. Pavlov first lighted the lamp, and then he sounded the bell, and then presented the food to the dog. After such joint presentation of food, he simply lighted the lamp and found that the dog began to salivate.

Diagrammatically the higher order of conditioning may be explained as:

US (Food) ⟶ UR (Salivation)

CS 1 (Bell Sound) + US (Food) ⟶ CR (Salivation)

CS 2 (Lighting the Lamp) +CS 1 (Bell Sound) +US (Food) ⟶ CR (Salivation)

Backward conditioning: If the order of presentation of CS and US will be altered, then there will be no CR. For e.g., if food (US) will be presented first and then the secondary stimulus (CS-Bell sound) will follow it repeatedly for some period of time then there will be no CR. It is called as backward conditioning.

Reinforcement: The presentation of conditioned stimulus (Bell sound) alone failed to evoke natural response (Salivation) where there is no reinforcement. When the conditioned stimulus is presented along with the natural stimulus (CS + US), the former the former is said to be reinforcement, as it could evoke natural response (Salivation).

Dimensions of Conditioning

Pavlov told, Conditioning may take two dimensions i.e., Positive conditioning (+) and Negative (-) conditioning. Positive conditioning refers to elicitation of natural response to an artificial or a secondary stimulus. For e.g. Elicitation of salivation to a Bell sound. Negative conditioning refers to the art of avoiding natural response which is expected to a stimulus. For e.g., the child avoids to drink even cold milk because, he is conditioned with hot milk which gives him pain.

Educational Implications

Followings are the educational implications of the classical conditioning theory of learning advocated by Pavlov.

Habit formation: Through conditioning good habits such as health habits, mannerisms, cleanliness, toilet habits, respect to elders, punctuality etc. can be developed in the children.

Removal of superstitions: Children may develop superstitions by conditioning. But it can be removed by de-conditioning. For example, a child develops superstition that the number nine (9) is an inauspicious number. To remove such superstition he should always be assigned with number nine.

Attitude formation: Positive and negative attitudes can be formed in the children through conditioning. Therefore a teacher should create situations for formation of positive attitudes towards learning, school and the teacher.

Love and Hatred: Fear, love and hatred towards an object or phenomena can be created through conditioning. For example, a teacher with his defective method of teaching or improper behaviour conditioned a child to develop hatred towards him, his subject and even towards the school environment. In the same way, affection, loving attitude or sympathetic treatment to a child by his parents and his teacher may develop love in the child in the process of conditioning.

Language learning: Language can be better learnt through conditioning method. The child speaks out "Elephant" when the picture of an elephant is presented to him and the word is spelt by the teacher.

Removal of fear: Conditioning method can be used to remove fears in the children and the abnormal persons. For e.g., a man expects some fear of danger after passing of a black cat on his way. But this fear can be removed by making a black cat crossing the road every day. If the man does not get any danger, then his irrational fear will be no more.

Rewards and punishment: Reward and punishment are closely related with conditioning. Rewards increase the strength of the conditioning and Punishment decreases the strength of the conditioning. Hence rewards and punishments should be judiciously applied by the teachers while dealing with the children to make them learn.

Watson's Theory of Learning

As a behaviourist, the American psychologist named J.B. Watson (1878-1958) has contributed a lot to the field of psychology. Out of his experiment on Maze learning of rats, he came into conclusion that, behaviour can be explained in terms of Stimulus-Response association.

Watson's Experiment: Watson conducted his experiment on a rabbit and a child. Initially the child did not show any fear to catch the rabbit. Later on the experimenter produced a loud sound when the child attempts to catch the rabbit. This conditioning process continued for several times and finally it was seen that the child expressed his fear to catch the rabbit. So here the stimulus (Loud sound) became associated with the response (Fear).

Laws of Learning: From his experiment, Watson proposed two important laws of learning i.e.

Law of Frequency/ Law of Exercise: The law of frequency / exercise states that, when stimulus and response occur repeatedly in close contiguity then it strengthens the bond/ connection between stimulus and response.

Law of Recency: The law of recency states that, the most recent response is strengthened more by its frequent occurrence. Therefore Watson said that learning is the shifting of old response to a new stimulus.

Educational Significance

On the basis of Watson's theory of learning, the following educational significances are drawn up that,

1. Behaviour of learners to be objectively studied by teachers.
2. Learning is a mental activity. Therefore human mind is to be studied properly to understand the learning process.
3. All types of learning can be reduced to S-R (stimulus and response) connections.
4. Teachers are to give more stress on the practice and exercise of the content matters of the study to strengthen the memory and learning.

Guthrie's Theory of Learning

Learning theory propounded by E.R. Guthrie (1886-1959) is of recent origin based on the stimulus response theories. Guthrie opposed to Watson's principles of learning i.e. Law of frequency and advocated the Principle of Effect supporting the E.L. Thorndike's theory of Trial and Error process of learning. He stated that, only the last response in the series of responses which establishes a bond/connection to the stimulus is important. The last stage of learning is more important the earlier one.

Guthrie's Experiment

Guthrie conducted his experiment on a cat in a puzzle box and arrived at the conclusion that learning is a process of association and by contiguity in the time. Learning takes place suddenly when S and R (stimulus and response) are presented at the same time and they are connected. Repetition plays an important role in the learning process.

Principles of Learning

Out of his experiment, Gutherie forwarded the following principles of learning.

1. *Principles of Conditioning:* It means learning takes place only when there is a connection between the response and the stimulus
2. *Inhibition of Conditioning:* If any other response interferes in between the original S-R then the original responses are inhibited.
3. *Principle of Practice:* It means, if the connection between the stimulus and response is practiced for more times and frequently then it is strengthened.
4. *Principle of Doing:* Principle of doing also increases the strength of S-R connection. It lays stress on more practical work than the theoretical work.
5. *Principle of identifying stimuli:* Identifying appropriate stimuli motivates more a learner respond in a right manner.

Educational Significances

Gutherie's theory of learning contributes a lot to the field of education. Principle of doing has led practical orientation to the teaching learning process. It has highlighted the role of learning by doing. It has encouraged using the external stimuli's like charts, models, pictures, in the process of teaching and learning. Guthrie's theory of learning also is useful to break the bad habits of children.

E.L. Thorndike's Trial and Error Theory of Learning

American psychologist E.L. Thorndike (1874-1949) is known for Trial and

Error theory of learning. Conducting experiments on rats, cats, and chickens Thorndike came into conclusion that all learning is the formations of bonds or connections between stimulus and responses (S-R). So the theory learning coined by Thorndike is also called as the theory of connectionism.

To Thorndike, S-R bonds are formed through a trial and error process and therefore he named this theory as Trial error theory of learning. This theory advocates that, the base of learning is trial and error. Learning occurs in the process of selecting and connecting. Trial and error theory of learning states that, learning is nothing but stamping in the correct response and stamping out of the incorrect response through a trial and error process. A person attempts to learn something or attempts to solve a problem or to reach a goal but all these made by the person may not help him to learn the thing, or to solve a problem or to reach the goal. Only a few correct attempts/responses help him in his mission. The person continues to elect the right response until he gets satisfaction. The person learns at that moment when a suitable bond is established between the response and the stimuli. Therefore, learning is the process of connecting the correct / right response to the right stimuli.

Thorndike's Experiment

Thorndike conducted his experiment on a cat putting it in a puzzle box. He kept the cat hungry and put it in the puzzle box. The puzzle box was so made that it can be opened by correctly manipulating a latch fitted to it. A fish was kept outside the box which could be seen through the wooden bars. The smell of the fish worked a strong motive for the hungry cat to come out of the box and get the fish. As a result the cat made every possible attempt to come out of the box and get the fish. In one of the random movements, the cat could open the door of the box by manipulating the latch and came out of the box and got the fish.

The same experiment was repeated for several times. It was found that in successive attempts success were more in number and gradually its incorrect attempts/responses decreased. In due course the cat learned the art of opening the door of the box.

Thorndike's the theory of trial and Error process of learning is presented in Diagram 15.2.

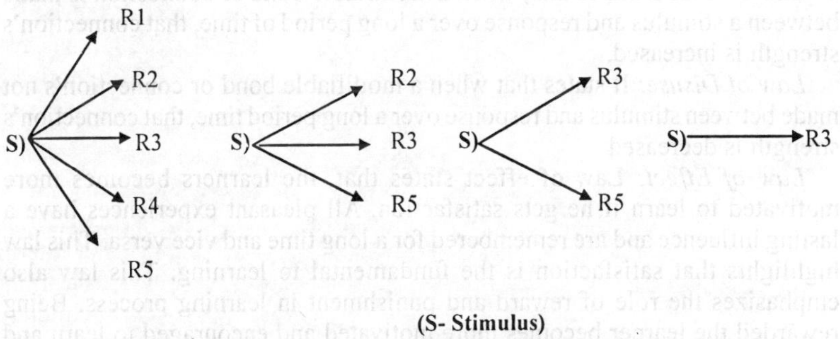

(S- Stimulus)
(R- Response)

Diagram 15.2: Gradual elimination of incorrect/ wrong responses and stamping in the right/ correct response)

Conditions of Learning Proposed by Thorndike

Out of his experiment, Thorndike summarized the following basic conditions of learning:

1. *Drive:* The subject to learn must be ready physically and mentally. (Here in the experiment, the cat was made ready/ hungry and its hungriness intensified with the sight of food—Fish)
2. *Goal:* getting of the reward (Food)/ solving the problem.
3. *Block:* Certain barrier that blocks the subject to reach the goal. (Here in the experiment, Puzzle box with its closed door was a block for the cat.)
4. *Random movements:* The subject makes a number of random trials / responses to overcome the block and to reach the goal. (The cat made a number of trials to come out of the puzzle box.)
5. *Chance success:* Out every possible random trials/ responses, by chance the subject locates a right response to solve the problem. (By chance, the cat could succeed to open the door of the box by manipulating the latch.)
6. *Selection:* The subject recognizes the right response to solve its problem. (The cat selected proper way of manipulating the latch out of its random responses.
7. *Fixation:* At last the subject learns the proper way of solving the problem and reaching its goal. (The cat finally learned the way of opening the door of the puzzle box by eliminating all the wrong responses.

Thorndike's Laws of Learning

Thorndike has recommended three important laws of learning from his experiment on cat and other animals.

Law of Readiness: To Thorndike readiness is preparation for action. This law states that a learner learns more effectively only when he is ready to learn or ready to act. Readiness implies that before learning the subject is to be physically and mentally prepared/ready to do the act or to learn.

Law of Exercise: Law of exercise has two sub laws i.e., i. Law of use and ii. Law of disuse. The law of exercise is also called as law of practice. Practicing or exercising the right action/response again and again will increase the strength of learning and memory.

Law of Use: It states that, when a modifiable bond or connection is made between a stimulus and response over a long period of time, that connection's strength is increased.

Law of Disuse: It states that when a modifiable bond or connection's not made between stimulus and response over a long period time, that connection's strength is decreased

Law of Effect: Law of effect states that, the learners becomes more motivated to learn if he gets satisfaction. All pleasant experiences have a lasting influence and are remembered for a long time and vice versa. This law highlights that satisfaction is the fundamental to learning. This law also emphasizes the role of reward and punishment in learning process. Being rewarded the learner becomes more motivated and encouraged to learn and being punished, the learner creates distaste and becomes less enthusiastic to learn.

Educational Significances of Trial and Error Theory of Learning

Trial and Error theory of learning of Thorndike has revolutionized the field of education in the following respects:

- Making the learners ready (physically and mentally) to learn before start of teaching and learning.
- Making students motivated to learn by the use of different means like, using audiovisual aids, different techniques like dramatization, storytelling, rewards, praising, and discussions etc.
- Trial and Error method is more beneficial in case of learning motor skills like dancing, singing, drawing, painting, craft learning, etc.
- Situation of learning should be made problematic keeping in view of capacity of learners.
- Teacher should encourage learners to practice the lessons more and more to strengthen the memory of learners.
- Teacher should apply reward and punishment techniques properly. Teacher should try to avoid punishment as it has negative impact on learning.

Hull's Theory of Learning

C.L. Hull is known for the learning theory called as "Drive reduction theory". Hull was a professor of psychology in USA. Out of his experiment he deduced a theory that all behaviours are the effect of biological needs which are primitive by nature.

Basic Concepts used in Hull's Theory of Learning

Following basic concepts were used in Hull's theory of Learning.

Needs: Needs instigates an organism to action in order to reduce it or to satisfy it. Needs may be of different types-biological, social, psychological etc. Without needs the organism takes no interest to act.

Drive: Drive is called as the feeling of needs. Intensity of drive depends on the nature of needs. The biological needs which are primitive by nature intensify more drive.

Reinforcement: It is a type of stimulus which has the capacity to alter the response. When one gets a stimulus, he becomes stimulated to show certain response. Then it is called as the reinforced action or reinforced response.

Hull advocated that, learning needs an association between stimulus and response (S and R). To strengthen the association between S and R, some type of reward and reinforcement is required. Reinforcement helps to maintain the desired response.

Drive reduction theory also states that, learning of an organism relates to his needs. Therefore different needs lead to different types of learning. Needs create tension in the organism and he tries to reduce the tension and fulfill his needs. In the course reducing the tension, the organism does some actions/ responses. But all responses do not establish correct bond or connection with the desired stimuli. By chance a response establishes connection with a stimuli and that S-R takes place when the organism gets reinforcement.

Educational Significances

Hull's theory of learning has enough educational significance. It has revolutionized the field of education in the area of curriculum construction. It recommends that, education should be need based and curricular and co-curricular activities meant for the students should be designed according to the need of the students. It also strengthened the support for the provision of the reward and punishment in teaching-learning process. It highlighted that teachers are to motivate the learners before start of the teaching and instruction and teachers should keep in their mind the needs and requirements f the learners.

B.F. Skinner's Operant Conditioning Theory of Learning

The professor of Harvard University in U.S. named B.F. Skinner is the chief exponent of Operant conditioning theory of learning. Operant conditioning theory of learning is an internal and special arrangement within the type of instrumental conditioning. Therefore, Skinner's operant conditioning finds its root in Thorndike's connectionism theory of learning.

In operant conditioning theory, Skinner emphasized two types of behaviour such as, Respondent behaviour and operant behaviour. Skinner said that, Respondent behaviour of an organism is spontaneous and automatic which is elicited from known stimuli. For e.g., Reflex actions like blinking of eyes to a puff of air, salivation to a sight of delicious food etc. are respondent behaviours. The respondent behaviours are controlled by autonomous nervous system and these are beyond the control of an organism. On the other hand, Operant behaviour is deliberate by nature and occurs in a situation where there are no particular instigating stimuli. For example, slipping, walking, crying etc. are operant behaviours. Operant behaviours can be controlled and manipulated by the organism. Operant behaviours are controlled by central nervous systems of an organism. Operant behaviours are observable and overt by nature.

Skinner adopted reflexes as the basic unit for analyzing the behaviour of an organism. He stressed on "Response modification" in the procedure of conditioning. According to operant conditioning, the response occurs spontaneously in the absence of any stimulus. Therefore operant conditioning is defined as learning which is based on response contingent reinforcement.

Skinner, being a practical psychologist, conducted several experiments on different reflexes in rats and pigeons. Out of his experiment he concluded that, behaviour of an organism is shaped and maintained by its consequences. Behaviour is operated by the individual and maintained by its results.

Meaning of Operant Conditioning

The process of learning helping in learning the operant behaviour is called as the operant conditioning. In operant conditioning the organism makes desired response/ behaviour and then reward is provided. The reward reinforces the response to occur again and again. In this way the response becomes instrumental in resulting reinforcement. Therefore skinner's operant conditioning is also called as "Instrumental conditioning".

Skinner's Experiment on Rat

Skinner developed his own apparatus called as Skinner box. The Skinner box or the puzzle box was so prepared that, there was a lever and a dish inside the box. The subject of the experiment is to manipulate this bar and get its reward/

food. Skinner kept a hungry cat in this puzzle box and saw that initially the rat tried to escape from the box and therefore it exhibited some random movements. Accidentally, the rat could press the bar, so that some food / reward fell into the dish. It was observed that once the rat enjoyed the reward/ food, it became conditioned to press the bar and get its reward.

Then Skinner applied higher order of conditioning in another experiment. Skinner allowed the rat to press the bar when there was light. It was found that, the rat also became conditioned to press the bar following to light and could succeed in getting its reward. Therefore skinner concluded that animals can be made to learn anything that we want. Hence skinner arrived at the conclusion that all learning is "Response modification".

Skinner's Experiment on Pigeon

Skinner also experimented on the theory of operant conditioning taking a pigeon and shaped its behaviour. In this experiment, the pigeon learned to walk in the figure of eight. Initially skinner observed the movement of the pigeon and provided the reward/ food for its turning into right direction. Again the pigeon was provided reward when it took a step into right direction. At last the pigeon learned to shape its behaviour to walk on the desired path of number eight.

Out of these experiments, skinner came into a point that complex series of responses can be learnt through the techniques of operant conditioning.

Features of Operant Conditioning

Operant conditioning states that learning is the change of responses. Skinner says, operant conditioning is a process in which response is made more probable or more frequent following reinforcement. Operant conditioning is controlled by rewards that follow it. Skinner highlighted three basic features in his operant conditioning theory of learning as displayed below.

Reinforcement and Rein-forcer: Skinner stated that, Reinforcement is a way of controlling the strength of a response. Reinforcement increases the strength of a response and its frequency. Rein-forcer may be of two types i.e. positive and negative rein forcer. Positive rein forcers facilitate the response to occur voluntarily. For e.g. rewards, praises, food, water, sexual contacts etc. are positive rein forcers. On the other hand, negative reinforcers force the desired response to occur such as punishments. Skinner stressed that reinforcement is necessary for the motivation of the organism. It requires the use of some rein forcers in the learning situation.

A positive reinforcer strengthens the desired behaviour. By contrast, negative reinforcer is one to which the organism commonly avoids and abandons which decreases the probability of the desired response.

Skinner mentions, there can be a variety of schedule of reinforcement which influences learning and motivation. Broadly, there can be two types of reinforcement schedule such as Continuous. Reinforcement schedule and Partial Reinforcement schedule.

In continuous reinforcement schedule the response produces reinforcement every time it occurs. For e.g., we can praise a child each time he gives right answer to questions. But in partial reinforcement schedule, some but not all responses are reinforced. For e.g., we can praise a child occasionally but not all time for giving correct answer to questions. Again there are following four basic schedules of partial reinforcement schedule such as:

- *Fixed Ratio Schedule (FR):* In fixed ratio schedule, the subject is required to make a fixed number of responses in order to receive reinforcement. For e.g. a child may be praised for making six correct responses.
- *Variable Ratio Schedule (VR):* In variable ratio schedule, the subject is required to respond some number f times in order t receive reinforcement. The exact number of responses required at any time changes without the knowledge of the subject to elicit the reinforcement.
- *Fixed Interval Schedule (FI):* In fixed interval schedule, the reinforcement is provided at regular time interval, say, a fixed interval of one minute. The number of responses made by the subject will have no effect on reinforcement. Suppose the rat pressed the bar fifty times in the first one minutes of the experiment and it did not result in reinforcement. Only the first response after one minute would produce reinforcement.
- *Variable Interval Schedule (VI):* In variable interval schedule, the time interval between the response and reinforcement varies from trial to trial so that, the subject never knows when a response will produce reinforcement. This type of schedule produces moderate /steady rate of responses.

Fixed Ratio schedule and Variable Ratio schedule are based on the number of responses the subject makes. But the Fixed Interval Schedule and Variable interval Schedule are based on the time intervals.

Stimulus Discrimination and Generalization: In operant conditioning the organism is trained to respond stimuli according to the desire of the experimenter. The experimenter gains complete control over the organism's behaviour in operant conditioning. The experimenter regulates the stimuli to which the organism responds and modifies the operant acts accordingly.

In operant conditioning the organism tend to discriminate and generalize. The tendency to respond differently to different stimuli is called as discrimination and tendency to act or respond in a similar manner to different stimuli is called as generalization.

Shaping: The term shaping means selective rewarding of the behaviour. When the organism is conditioned to behave r perform through proper reward in the process of conditioning then it is called as shaping. In Skinner's experiment, the pigeon got its reward when it moved in the right direction—for turning its head—for taking a step for making correct turn-until it learned to walk in right direction on the number eight. So shaping involves a chain of responses.

Difference between Classical Conditioning and Instrumental Conditioning

We can differentiate between Classical conditioning and Instrumental conditioning in the following aspects:

- *Learning:* In classical conditioning, learning takes place when a subject establishes a bond between CS and US. Therefore classical conditioning is called as S-s learning. But in Instrumental conditioning, learning takes place when a subject establishes a bond between response (R) and Stimuli (S). Therefore, instrumental conditioning is otherwise known as R-S learning.

- *Behaviour*: Classical conditioning measures the respondent behaviour which is involuntary by nature and it is fully controlled by the autonomous nervous system. But instrumental conditioning measures the operant behaviour which is deliberate and voluntary by nature and it is fully controlled by the central nervous system.
- *Environment*: In classical conditionings, the environment acts upon the organism. But in instrumental conditioning, the environment does not have any influence on the organism. The operant behaviour of the organism depends on its consequences.
- *Role of Stimulus:* In classical conditioning the unconditioned stimulus (US) is assumed as the rein forcing stimulus. But in instrumental conditioning the rein forcing stimulus is contingent upon the response. Therefore in classical conditioning the environment acts upon the response where as in instrumental conditioning the subject's response acts upon the environment affecting the reinforcemeat events.
- *Role of the Subject:* In classical conditioning the subject is a passive responder to whom events happen. For example, the subject responds in the light of occurrences of CS and UCS. Here the subject has no control over the stimuli. On the other hand, the subject is an active responder in instrumental conditioning. The subject is free to elicit any response in instrumental learning situation. The subject plays the role to control its response.
- *Law of Learning*: Classical conditioning theory is governed by the law of contiguity. But, operant conditioning theory of learning is governed by the law of effect.
- *Base:* The base of classical conditioning is stimulus substitution. So it is stimulus based. But the base of instrumental conditioning is response / behaviour modification. So it is response based.

Similarities between Classical Conditioning and Instrumental Conditioning

Whatever may be the differences between classical conditioning and instrumental conditioning, the two types of theories have many similarities. Both of them incorporate the process of discrimination and generalization, extinction, inhibition, reinforcement, and higher order of conditioning. Both the theories aim at increasing rate of responses.

Educational Implications of Instrumental/Operant Conditioning Theory of Learning

Skinner's Operant conditioning theory has a great value in the field of education. We can estimate the educational significances of operant / instrumental conditioning in the following lines:

- Operant conditioning has contributed a new approach called "Programmed Learning" to the field of teaching-learning process. Due to this now we have a variety of programmed learning materials and teaching machines which are developed on the line of skinner's Operant Conditioning.

- It has suggested using the techniques of reinforcement such as reward, praise, punishment etc. to strengthen the probability of correct responses and to increase the rate of correct responses.
- Skinner's operant conditioning can be used to eliminate negative behaviour through extinction.
- Teacher should apply immediate reinforcement for each correct response.
- It has placed the value of practicing or exercise which strengthens responses.
- It is beneficial in case learning mathematics. And learning the rules of grammar.
- It recommends that, teachers are to define the initial and terminal behaviour which he wants to install in the students and therefore he has to plan in advance to provide suitable reinforcement.

Gestalt Theory of Learning

In opposition to behaviouristic theories of learning like Trial and error theory of E.L. Thorndike, Conditioning theories of Pavlov, Watson and Skinner, Gestalt theory of learning emerged by the effort of three German Psychologists named, *Max Wertheimer*, *Kurt koffka* and *Wolfgang Kohler*. These three psychologists known as "Gestalists" have introduced the concept of organization of perception and Insightful learning.

Gestalists presumed that the whole is more important than parts. Learning occurs as a whole but not by parts. They stated that learning occurs through insight but not by trial and error or by conditioning as suggested by E.L. Thorndike and others. Learning occurs all of a sudden due to the insight of an individual. Therefore Gestalt theory of learning is popularly known as "Insightful learning theory".

Gestalt is a German word which means configuration or an organized whole. Gestalists believe that whole is more important than its constituent parts. A thing can only be better understood by the study of its whole rather to study of its parts. Learning is a process of formation of new gestalts i.e. an organized whole.

Meaning of Insight

Gestalt Psychologists used the term "Insight" in the sense that, it is the sudden perception of the relationship in a problematic situation. It is a sudden flash of idea that comes to mind and helps the individual to solve the problem. Insight refers to a total psychological attitude of an individual that enables him to learn, to solve his problem or to adjust to a situation.

Kohler defines, "Insight is the foresightful planning of behaviour in advance".

Skinner states, "Insight is the application of a single trial leading directly to the solution of the problem". Benard defines, "Insight as the sudden perception of the relationships in a total situation. The total situation consists of the organism, the goal, the environment and the obstacles

The theory of insight is closely associated with the name of Kohler who made a series of experiments on Chimpanzees and highlighted the use of three important principles in the process of learning such as:

1. The principle of Insight.
2. The principle of Whole.
3. Sudden appearance of idea leading to solution of the problem.

These three principles are applied in the learning process that, a child perceives the total/whole situation, understands the relationships and tries to get an insight b into the methods at his mental level and suddenly strikes the problem for its solution.

Kohler's Experiment on Chimpanzee

Experiment No. 1—Kohler put the chimpanzee named "Sultan" inside a cage where bananas were hung from the roof of the cage. Two boxes were placed inside the cage at different corners. At first Sultan tried to reach at the bananas by jumping, but it could not succeed. Suddenly it got an idea to place these two boxes one after another to make a jumping platform and then the sultan stood on it and reached the bananas. Thus sultan was able to display its insight to establish the relationship between the box and bananas and it became successful in solving the problem or reaching at the goal.

Experiments No. 2—In another experiment Kohler kept two sticks inside the cage i.e. one longer than the other. These two sticks were so made that the shorter stick can be fitted with the long one to become a single and long stick. Kohler kept some bananas outside of the cage in such a distance that it could not be picked up by any one of the stick unless these two sticks are tied to a single and long stick. As soon as the chimpanzee was kept inside the cage, it tried the sticks one after another to reach the bananas but it failed. Suddenly it viewed the whole situation and got a bright idea to join these sticks to make it longer and then with the help of this long stick the Chimpanzee could get its reward/ bananas. Thus the Chimpanzee performed right task through understanding the whole situation.

The experiments conducted by Kohler demonstrated the role of intelligence and cognitive abilities in higher learning i.e. problem solving. In contrast to blind trial and error mechanism adopted by E.L. Thorndike's cat and simple habit formation mechanism adopted by Pavlov's dog, the subject of Kohler (Chimpanzee named Sultan) reacted intelligently by identifying the problem, organizing its perceptual field, and using insight to reach the solution of the problem. Gestalists opined that, once the organism learns to solve the problem by insight; there is every possibility of high degree f transfer of learning to the similar problems.

Features of Insightful Learning

1. Learning takes place not by trial and error or by conditioning but by insight and understanding.
2. Learning takes place in a holistic approach and occurs all on a sudden.
3. Learning is a process of developing new insight and modifying the old one. Therefore learning is purposive, creative and explorative.
4. Individuals differ from each other in their insights. Therefore different individuals attack upon a problem differently.

5. Insightful learning is cognitive by nature and it depends on the intellectual capacity of the learner.
6. Solution of a particular problem through insight can be repeated any number of times and can be generalized or transferred to identical and similar type of problematic situations.
7. Past experiences provide the base and help in the insightful learning. A child can not solve higher mathematical problems unless he acquires the basics / fundamentals of mathematical principles.

Educational Significances of Insightful Learning Theory

1. Insightful learning theory has contributed one of the important maxim to the field of teaching-learning process i.e. "whole to part approach" A problem need to be solved should be presented as whole and then it should be solved on the part basis. While teaching geography, the presentation of globe is necessary before going to teach about a particular country.
2. Insightful learning advocates of making the learning situation interesting and problematic. Arousal of interest in the learner is the requisite in learning process leading to success in learning.
3. This theory also advocates that, teachers are to make the students understand the goals or objectives of learning.
4. It highlighted that, learning situations and learning materials are to be systematically organized so that insight of the learners can be developed.
5. Insightful learning theory stressed the value of integration in the field of curriculum construction.
6. Insightful learning is helpful in the development of imagination, thinking, reasoning, and creativity in the learners.
7. It encourages independent learning of the learners.
8. It helps to develop the problem solving skill in the learners.
9. It has prompted the heuristic and project method for the children and The Dalton plan for the grown-ups in the field of learning.

Kurt Lewin's Cognitive Field Theory of Learning

German psychologist named *Kurt Lewin* has pioneered the cognitive field theory of learning as a reaction against the gestalt theory of learning. Lewin's theory of learning came into origin by mating some aspect of Kohler's Insightful learning and some aspects of his own field theory. Thus cognitive field theory of learning emerged as relativistic way of viewing the learner and the learning process.

According to this theory learning is defined as a relativistic process by which the learner develops new insights and changes old ones.

Lewin's theory of learning places more important to behaviour in the place of experiences and makes use of motivation. Lewin states that, a person's life-space depends on his psychological forces and his life-space becomes a basis of his behaviour. The development of the insight is the outcome of changes in the cognitive structure of the life-space. A continuous reconstruction takes place in the life-space of an individual in relation to two important factors i.e., goals and barriers. An individual attempts to achieve a goal by overcoming the barriers which may be psychological or physical by nature. Any change in the psychological world leading to solve a problem or cross the barriers results in the change in the life-space of an individual and in turn there comes change in his behaviour. Lewin mentions, in order to understand learning, it is need to understand the organizational pattern of one's life-space and his psychological world.

Lewin stressed that, the level of aspirations is an important factor in learning which depends on the potentialities of an individual. Too high and too low level of aspiration have adverse impact on learning leading to low level of learning.

Concepts used in Lewin's Theory

Basic concepts used in Lewin's theory of Learning were the followings.

Life-space: the concept Life-space used in Lewin's theory connotes to one's psychological world. It includes a person and his facts, concepts, beliefs, and expectations in relation to his environment. So one's psychological world and his environment, the interaction of the both constitute his life-space.

Topology: The concept topology refers to a part—whole relationship in geometry. It is defined as a part of the geometry investigating properties of figure which remains unchanged under continuous transformation. These properties are non-quantitative. The size and shape have no significance topological geometry. For e.g., topologically the properties of a circle, a triangle, and a rectangle is same though their size and shape differs topologically. The life-space remains unchanged and equal in the following figures of circle, triangle and rectangle.

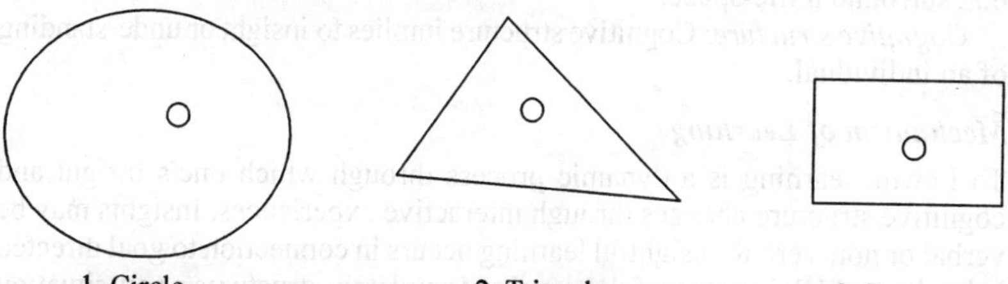

1. Circle 2. Triangle 3. Rectangle

These figures display the range of perceptions actions representing the structure of a life-space.

Vector: Vector is a scientific word which indicates magnitude and direction. Lewin states, each psychological force is a vector which influences actions of an individual in relation to his goal.

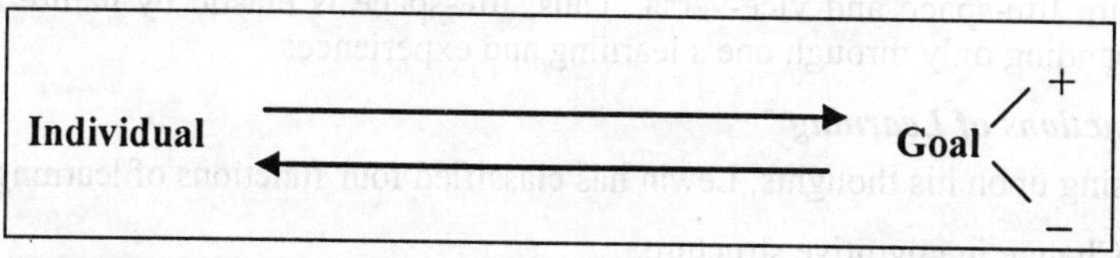

Valences: The concept valence refers to the power of attraction of a goal. Goal regions have two valences, i.e. positive and negative valence. Positive valence of a foal attracts an individual to be achieved and negative valence of a goal distracts the individual. The barriers region always posses the negative valence.

Goal: A goal represents a region of life-space to which an individual psychologically attached. Goals hold two types of valences i.e. positive and negative valence. An individual usually attempts to achieve the goal having its positive valence.

Barriers: Anything that challenges the psychological world of an individual in respect of achievement of certain goal is called as barrier. It remains in between the individual and his goal. The barriers may be of varied types such as physical, social and psychological.

Regions: The regions surround the life-space of an individual. Each part of life-space is represented by a region in which an individual can move / act freely psychologically.

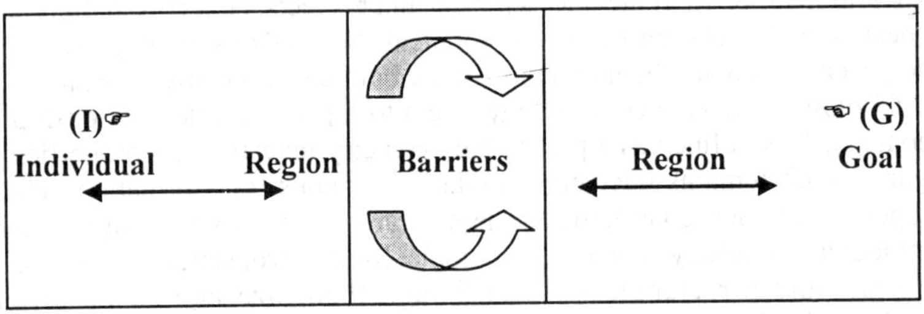

Foreign Hull: Foreign hull refers to all those non-psychological factors that surround a life-space.

Cognitive structure: Cognitive structure implies to insight or understanding of an individual.

Mechanism of Learning

To Lewin, learning is a dynamic process through which one's insight and cognitive structure changes through interactive experiences. Insights may be verbal or non-verbal. Insightful learning occurs in connection to goal directed behaviour which is purposeful. Learning completely structures a new situation for the development of the goal directed and purposeful insight. According to Lewin, learning builds psychological traces which contribute to the dynamics of future life-space and thus affect the future performance. So, there is an inherent relationship or continuity among the past, present and future life-space. Good insights into a present life-space provide good insight into the future life-space and vice-versa. Thus, life-space is elastic by nature and expanding only through one's learning and experiences.

Functions of Learning

Basing upon his thoughts, Lewin has classified four functions of learning.

1. Change in cognitive structure.
2. Change in motivation.
3. Change in group belongingness and
4. Acquisition of skills

These four functions of learning / types of learning are resulted because of differentiation, generalization and destructuralization of the regions of life-space.

Educational Significances of Lewin's Theory of Learning

Lewin's theory of learning has contributed its value to the field of education in the following lies:

1. Lewin's theory of learning has provided a n intellectual base to the field of education.
2. It has recommended t make the teaching-learning process problematic to encourage the creativeness of the learners.
3. It has emphasized to make teaching learning situation pleasant and purposeful.
4. Lewin's theory advocates enriching the past experiences of the learners so that it can support to their present and future learning.
5. It recommends that teachers are to understand the level of aspiration of the learners while planning for their education and teachers are to encourage the learners to set their aspirating and realize them.

Tolman's Sign Theory of Learning

E.C. Tolman has developed a theory of learning by conglomerating the merits of S-R theories and Cognitive field theories. Tolman's theory of learning is popularly known as "Sign theory learning "and "Purposive behaviourism".

The basis of the development of the sign theory of learning is behaviourism. Tolman viewed that the learning of a child is based on some signs and these signs lead to the goal. The organism directs his attention on sign-significant relations.

Tolman's Laws of Learning

Tolman has laid the following laws of learning:

1. The capacity of the learner plays a vital role in his learning. The amount of his learning depends upon his capacity to learn.
2. The nature of learning materials influences learning and learning depends on the learning materials.
3. Insightful learning is emphasized. Inventive ideas lead to successful learning.
4. Transfer of training takes place only when the learner perceives the essential relationship between one situation and the other.

Educational significance of sign learning

Followings are the educational significance of sign learning,

1. Teachers are to properly handle the sign learning to make it successful.
2. Sign learning is the blending of the application of insightful learning and behaviourism.
3. Teachers are to use this method of sign learning according to the need and demands of the situation and pupils.

16
Approaches to Learning and Instruction

After discussing about the theories of learning, it is essential to discuss about the theories of instruction. Teachers should be trained to apply different techniques of instruction to the learners for their effective learning. In this connection, different educationists and psychologists have suggested their theories and models of instruction which are need to be discussed.

B.S. BLOOM'S MASTERY LEARNING

Benjamin, S. Bloom and his associates have contributed a lot to the field of education. The greatest contribution of B.S. Bloom to the field of education is his model of teaching learning popularly called as "Mastery Learning". Bloom is also famous for his two books, Taxonomy of educational objectives (1956) and "Learning for Mastery" (1968).

Bloom has identified some classes of educational objectives for instructional and testing purposes called as "Task Analysis". In this process different classes of behaviour are arranged in a hierarchical order from the simple to complex which is called as Taxonomy of educational objectives.

According to Blooms, there are six classes of behaviours which are produced by two broad categories of behaviour like knowledge and intellectual abilities. The classes of behaviour identified by Bloom are:

1. Knowledge
2. Comprehension or understanding
3. Application
4. Analysis
5. Synthesis and
6. Evaluation

This Taxonomy involves two important processes such as,

1. Task description (Behavioural statement of the instructional objectives)
2. Task Analysis (ways of classification of objectives)

Domains of Behaviour

Bloom has categorized all behaviours of an individual under three major domains such as Cognitive domain which includes all the intellectual behaviours, Affective domain which includes all the emotional behaviours like interests, attitudes and Conative domain or Psycho-motor domain which includes all motor skills and abilities. Therefore Bloom stated that, education aims at the development of cognitive (Head), affective (Heart) and conation (Hand) aspect of the individual. Therefore, Bloom has developed a unique model of teaching keeping in view of these aspects for their development.

Basic Assumptions of Mastery Learning

Good and Bad Learners: It is a common agreement that the good learners can learn the more abstract and complex ideas where as the poor learners can learn only the simple and most concrete ideas. On the basis of this construct the school curriculum has been formulated in the education system.

Fast Learners and Slow Learners: The fast learners learn at an easy manner where as the slow learner learn slowly in a difficult manner. The teachers do not bother about the fast learners but they bother about these slow learners. They give extra time and efforts to make the slow learners understood the matter.

Organizational Pattern of Instructional System: Most students found similar in their ability, rate of learning and motivation when they are provided with the favourable learning conditions. This construct helps a teacher to organize his class room situation and system of education like selection procedure, grading procedure, and development of curriculum and instructional practices.

Environmental Difference of the Learner: It is admitted fact that individuals differ among themselves in different aspects. They also differ in their environment where they live and sustain their life. Studies have revealed that the learner's achievement is highly co-related with their home environment. Good home environment helps to achieve more and vice versa.

Bloom assumed that in spite of these prevailing characteristics of the learners, they can be assisted to achieve mastery over a particular area of learning provided adequate facilities and conditions can be extended to them. The poor and slow learners can be helped to have mastery over their learning if they will be allowed to learn at their own rate of learning and at their own pace of learning. The learning environment of these learners is to be reorganized. In this connection, Blooms Mastery learning is an attempt to give a new approach to curriculum and instruction.

Concept of Mastery Learning

Blooms Mastery Learning is a model of learning for independent study by the learner. Mastery learning assumes that, virtually all learners can master a good deal of what they are taught in the school if the instruction is approached systematically, learners are helped when they have learning difficulties, they are given sufficient time to achieve mastery and presenting the clear criteria of constitutional aspects of mastery.

Mastery learning advocates that, the learning tasks are to be broken into well-defined sub tasks. Then the learners are to be allowed to work through each sub task independently by employing self-instructional devices until he attains mastery or proficiency on the same task. After attaining sufficient mastery over the one task, he/ she should move to next task. Such process will eliminate fear of failure in the individuals. It will provide freedom to the learners to learn at their own rate of interest.

This approach makes use of the existing curriculum but seeks new teaching procedure, feedback and corrective techniques to ensure a high level of mastery of learning. Teachers are to guide the learners, provide the feedbacks and correct the errors of the learners in their learning process.

Requisites of Setting in Mastery Learning

There are mainly three requisites which are central to the theory of mastery learning.

A. The extent to which the learners have already learned the basic pre-requisites to the learning to be accomplished.
B. The extent to which the learner is motivated to initiate his learning.
C. The extent to which the instruction is appropriate for the learner to be given to the learner.

Basic Conditions of Mastery Learning

Entry Behaviour (EB): Entry behaviour means the previous knowledge of the learner which is necessary to acquire the new knowledge. It is also known as readiness of the learner to begin the new learning. Entry behaviour can be divided into following categories.

Cognitive Entry Behaviour (CEB): It means the pre-requisite knowledge, skills, competencies required for the learning of a new task. The cognitive entry behaviour constitutes one half of the total variance of the learning achievement in courses or in any learning tasks. Individuals vary in their cognitive entry behaviour.

Affective Entry Behaviour (AEB): Affective entry behaviour means the pre-requisite interests, attitudes, desires and enthusiasms toward the new learning. Positive affective behaviour accelerates mastery learning where as the negative affective behaviour does not help in mastery learning.

Procedure of Mastery Learning

Followings procedures are followed in Mastery Learning Scheme.

Presenting Sequential Learning Tasks: Sequential learning task means the learning materials must be divided into its sub-tasks logically and psychologically. After dividing the learning task, the sub-tasks are to be arranged in a hierarchical order in order of their difficulty level. Each learning task should be the pre-requisite condition for the next learning task.

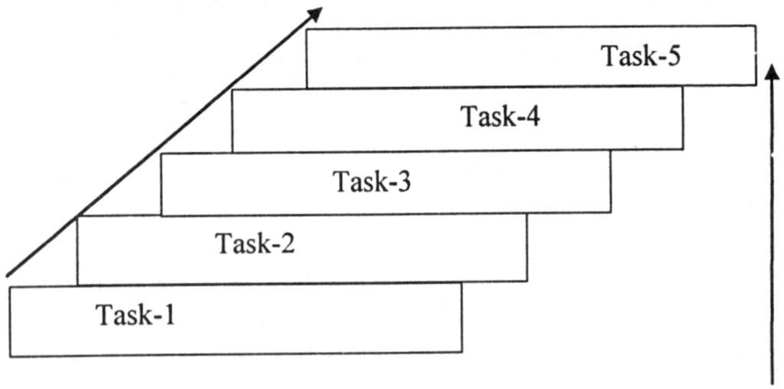

(Diagram showing the sequential learning Tasks in Mastery learning in a hierarchical order)

Allowing Self-Pacing: Mastery learning states that each learner should learn at his own pace of learning without any time restriction. Sufficient freedom is to be provided to the learner to earn his mastery over a learning task at his own pace of development. He should not be forced to complete the task within a stipulated time.

Providing Quality Instruction: The quality of instruction positively affects the learning of the learner. The materials prepared by the teacher for the purpose of the learning of the learners should be qualitative so as to motivate the learner. Mastery learning requires the quality based text books, teaching aids.

Providing Cues of Direction: Teacher should use a variety of teaching techniques like demonstration, explanation, text book method keeping in view of the interest of the learner and nature of the learning materials.

Helping Student's Participation: In Mastery learning, the pupil's participation should be active. Bothe overt and covert participation of the learner in the learning process is required.

Providing Feedback: Teacher should provide adequate feedback to the learners at the right time in the mastery learning. Teacher should take periodical tests in order to know the learning difficulties and provide feedback or corrective measures to the learners.

Stages of Mastery Learning

The followings are the stages of mastery learning,

Defining Mastery: Teacher has to select and define task objectives for each learner and select the terminal objectives expected from a learner at the end of the learning task.

Planning for Mastery: After defining the mastery, the teacher has to select the course materials keeping in view of the interest, need and capacity of the learner. Then the course is to be broken into its sub-parts and arranged in a sequence. For each unit, alternative instructional materials and corrective measures should be designed to re-teach the material or to supplement the material.

Orientation for Mastery: Before starting mastery learning the learners is to be oriented about what to learn and how to learn. They are to adopt their self-learning devices to achieve mastery over the learning task.

Teaching for Mastery: Teacher should teach each learning task in a sequence and should co-relate among them. He should allow sufficient time to the learners to have their mastery over the task.

Grading for Mastery: Teacher should administer the summative test/ final test and evaluate the terminal behaviour at the end of the course or task. He may award grades or the equivalents to the learners.

Educational Significance of Mastery Learning

Individuals differ in their learning. The pace of learning is different from one to another. Therefore we watch that there are some good learners and poor learners. Bloom states that every individual learner can obtain his mastery over certain learning task if he is allowed sufficient time and freedom to learn according to his pace of development. In this context, Bloom has suggested the concept of Mastery learning which is out come based. In order to derive the best result of this mastery learning, the teacher should try his best to prepare his instructional procedures matching to the interest of the learners. Teachers are to remain vigilant while administering the mastery learning and he should always refresh his knowledge. Teacher should proficient enough to handle this mastery learning. He should be trained to adopt the different corrective techniques.

Mastery learning has its limitations that, it cannot be applied for all courses. It is time consuming and a delayed process. However the Mastery learning of B.S. Bloom is a valuable contribution to the field of education.

GAGNE'S HIERARCHY OF LEARNING

Professor of Educational psychology, *Robert M. Gagne* (1916) of Florida University, USA has outlined a hierarchical order of learning out of his behaviouristic-eclectic approach of the educational psychology. Gagne held the view that learning occurs through certain conditions and the purpose of psychology is to observe these conditions. Gagne conceived insight narrowly and said that it has less value in the field of learning. He stressed the importance of the overt actions of an individual in his learning.

Gagne's Concept of Learning

Gagne defines learning as the change in the human dispositions or capability. It exhibits itself as a change in the overt/ observable behaviour that happens under certain observable conditions. Gagne established the fact that learning is a process comparable to other organic processes like digestion and respiration. Learning takes place in the individual's head/ brain. Gagne differentiates between the internal and external conditions of learning that the internal conditions of learning include attention, motivation, memory which is relevant to the present learning of an individual and the external conditions include all arrangements and timing of stimuli and events. These two conditions are vital to an individual's learning.

Gagne says that learning takes place through an input and output relationship process to which he called as information processing. The input is a stimulus situation (S) which includes varieties of changes in physical energy that reach the learner through his senses. These stimulus situation remains outside of the learner and can be identified and described in terms of physical sciences. The output (R) is an external and observable effect like movement of eyes, movement of hands etc.

Gagne viewed that, any new learning requires the prior learning of the sub-ordinate capabilities that are involved in the new learning. For example, the learning of a higher order rules require the learning of its simpler rules.

Outcomes of Learning

According to Gagne, there are five major human capabilities seen as the outcome of his learning:

1. Verbal Information-(Statement of mere and desired information's)
2. intellectual Skills—(Ability to compare, recognize and comprehend)
3. Cognitive Strategies—(Learning, conceptualizing, thinking and remembering)

4. Attitudes—(likes and Dislikes)
5. Motor Skills—(Muscles related functions)

Types/Conditions of Learning

Gagne distinguishes eight types of learning. Theses learning's are arranged in simple to complex order. These types of learning are also called as conditions of learning. The observable behaviour of an individual is the product of each such condition of learning.

Signal Learning: In signal learning the organism acquire a conditioned response to a given signal. In this type of learning, the response is emotional and learning is automatic and involuntary by nature. It is an automatic response to stimuli. Example of such type of learning is salivation at the sight of food, blinking of eyes in response to dusting, and withdrawing hands from the hot object etc.

Stimulus-Response Learning: In this type of learning, the organism responds specifically to a stimulus. Learning takes place in the shape of instrumental conditioning of E.L. Thorndike and operant conditioning of Skinner. It is a process of producing precise response to a discriminated stimulus. This type of learning is much beneficial in case of acquiring verbal skills and motor skills.

Chain Learning: In chain learning the individual connects a set of individual S-R bonds in a sequence. Here the individual has to apply the previously learned S-R's. Each of the S-R bonds provides a clue to the next learning in a connecting process. Learning of each complex motor skill needs a chain of simpler motor skills. For example, Learning of running requires the learning of standing, walking and then running in a sequence.

Verbal Association Learning: This type of learning is also a type of chaining in the shape of verbal units. The child first learns different verbal units and then he associates them to frame different sentences. For example, while saying "Red Pencil" the child associates the colour with the object pencil.

Discrimination Learning: The organism learns a lot of responses from his surroundings. Sometimes he becomes confused. This type of learning helps the organism to differentiate or discriminate between motor and verbal chains. When the organism produces some specificity of responses to one given stimulus to the exclusion of others, it is called as discrimination learning.

Concept Learning: In concept learning the organism responds to a class of stimuli in a generalized manner in terms of its abstract characteristics like colour, shape, position, number and volume. Concept learning, means making a common response to a class of stimulus. The organism learners to distinguish and generalize different class of stimulus

Rule Learning: In rule learning the individual relates one or more concepts. This type of learning governs the external behaviour of the individual. Learning of rules depends on the learning of concepts. For example, while stating "Round things roll" at that time the rule or the principle is learnt that all round things roll. The learning of Science and Mathematics and grammar is learnt through learning of some concepts.

Problem Solving: It is a complex type of learning. It is an extension of rule learning. It requires higher mental processes like thinking and imagination. In problem solving, the individual learns to discover a combination of previously learned rules that he can apply to achieve a solution for a novel problematic situation.

All these eight types of learning suggested by Gagne are inter-dependent on each other.

Phases of an Act of Learning

Gagne suggested eight phases of an act of learning of an individual which are a typical chaining or series. The total act of learning constitutes these series of eight phases. These are mentioned as,

1. Motivation
2. Apprehending
3. Acquisition
4. Retention
5. Recall
6. Generalization
7. Performance and
8. Feedback

Components of Instruction

Gagne suggested following four types of the components of the process of instruction to achieve the phases of learning.

Recall of previously Learned Capabilities: While teaching, a teacher should confirm that all the lower order skills are mastered before the learning of other higher order skills by the learners. Thus a teacher's first step in teaching is to get students to recall previously learned capabilities that are pre requisite to learning at hand.

Direct Presentation of Appropriate Stimuli: After making the learners to recall the previously learnt materials, the next step is to present the environmental stimuli directly to the learners. Appropriate stimuli should be used to activate the various phases of learning.

Activation of Mental Sets: For Gagne, a person's readiness for learning consists of his meeting certain pre-conditions of learning. These preconditions of learning include his attention, interest, motivation and developmental readiness. The teacher should use the manipulation of reinforcing conditions to achieve attention set.

Provision of Feedback: All learning activities require feedback if it is to be completed. To achieve feedback, teacher must communicate to students about the outcomes of their performances as accurately as possible. More cues may be used for reinforcement of student's behaviour.

AUSUBEL'S VIEWS ON LEARNING

The cognitive psychologist named David, P. Ausubel (1963) presented a related theory of Meaningful Verbal Learning. Later this meaningful verbal learning was extended to include Meaningful Discovery Learning (1969). Ausubel stated that there is an emphasis on the theoretical characteristic of the subject matter. This makes it possible that, how one kind of pre-requisite knowledge can be used to influence the acquisition of subsequent knowledge. Text books, reference books and other instructional materials are used extensively in schools to present information. When students study the materials, they try to relate the new information to what they already know.

Types of Learning

Ausubel said that there are two dimensions of learning fundamental in this theory. One dimension deals with the two ways by which knowledge to be learnt is made available to the learner. These two ways are meaningful reception learning and meaningful discovery learning.

The second dimension involves two ways by which learners incorporates new information into their existing cognitive structure. These two ways are called as meaningful learning and rote learning.

Therefore, Ausubel summarized **four types** of learning such as,

1. Meaningful reception learning,
2. Rote reception learning,
3. Meaningful Discovery learning, and
4. Rote Discovery learning.

In reception learning the entire content is presented in its final form and the process is teacher centered. On the other hand, in discovery learning not all that to be learnt is presented in final form. The learner gets some information independently. This information is thus integrated into the existing cognitive structure and recognized and transferred to produce a new or modified cognitive structure.

Reception learning emphasizes on concept assimilation, where as discovery learning stresses on concept formation. Ausubel viewed that an individual's cognitive structure seems like a pyramidal shape, with the most general propositions and concepts forming the apex, the greater number of the less general sub-concepts forming the middle level and the large number of specific information forming the base.

Ausubel's Advance Organizers

Ausubel summarized his experiments and developed his advance organizer which facilitates new learning by relating prior knowledge of the individual to the new information to be learnt. In ordinary language, advance organizer refers to the required basic knowledge which facilitates the further learning of knowledge. Advance organizers are the introductory learning materials to a lesson. It should include the concepts at a higher level of abstractness, generality and inclusiveness than those in the lesson to be learnt so that the concepts presented in the new material could be related to those in the advance organizer. When learned, these more general concepts in the advance organizer would enable the individual to relate new information to them.

Advance organizer is the components of the stimulus situation for the learning. They are the stimuli that activate recall of the previously learnt capabilities that are relevant to the new learning. The recalled elements may be knowledge, intellectual skills or cognitive strategies. These stimuli may be a variety of forms. They may be provided by pictures or symbols or statements and other situational cues.

Concept Extension and Utilization

Concepts are learned at the classificatory and formal levels and are used in generalizing to new instances, cognizing supra-ordinate and sub-ordinate relations, cognizing cause and effect and other relations among concepts and in solving problems. In this regard Ausubel formulated the constructs like cognitive structure, advance organizer; correlative subsumption and derivative subsumption to show how previously attained and newly encountered concepts are related.

According to Gagne, the relationship between and among concepts are termed as 'principles' or 'rules' whereas Ausubel called these terms as 'propositions'. Gagne stated about the internal and external conditions of rule learning, on the other hand Ausubel explained about the internal mechanisms that underline the learning of propositions and concepts.

According to Ausubel, Meaningful learning in contrast to rote learning must be related to the knowledge one already has and it must be incorporated into one's existing cognitive structure. An individual's cognitive structure is hierchically organized in the system of facts, concepts and generalizations that he holds.

The learning of propositions which are analogous to rules in Gagne's model is a function of—

1. The relevance of the anchoring (fixed) ideas in the cognitive structure to the new material to be learned.
2. The clarity and stability of the anchoring ideas within the cognitive structure and,
3. The discriminability of these learned ideas.

Proposition learning is commonly accomplished by studying definitions of terms and deducing relationships. This involves the susumption of new material under pre-existing and more inclusive ideas within the cognitive structure.

Method of Subsumption

There are three ways in which new concepts and propositions can be related to information that is already learned. Propositions, concepts that are sub-ordinate to the learned propositions are related to the more inclusive one already learned by the following ways of susumption.

Derivative Subsumption

New ideas are directly derivable from the more inclusive or supra-ordinate propositions in the Derivative subsumptions. For example, if a child already knows the propositions like cats climb trees then the specific proposition i.e., the neibhour's cat climbing the tree is subsumed under it. The planet move round the sun is a general proposition. The specific proposition, the earth moves round the sun can easily be sub summed under this general proposition.

That is the meaning of the general proposition is adequate to convey the meaning of its derivative.

In derivative subsumption specific examples are subsumed under the supra-ordinate or general proposition through deduction.

Correlative Subsumption

Correlative subsumption occurs when the new concepts or proposition extends or modifies the one already learned. If the child already has a concept of equilateral triangle as a closed plane with three sides of a triangle equal length, the three angles are also equal.

By actively correlating the new information to what he already knows, he modifies his concepts of equilateral triangle to include the new relationship involving the three equal sides and three equal angles. Ausubel indicates that a super ordinate proposition may be formed initially by inductively reasoning from already learned particulars to the more general propositions. A learner with knowledge that quadrilaterals have 360 degrees may inductively form the proposition that all quadrilaterals have 360 degrees.

Combinatorial Subsumption

A new concept or proposition may be learned when there is neither a related sub-ordinate or supra-ordinate proposition in the existing cognitive structure. This is called as combinatorial subsumption.

For example, certain background knowledge along with information obtainable from studying a model of pendulum might be combined in arriving at an understanding of the formula for the period of a pendulum.

Clarifying thinking that goes on as an individual extends his knowledge through relating concepts to one another is an important contribution of Ausubel.

17
Perspectives of Learning

Learning is a key factor for the development of human being. Learning as a universal characteristic helps an individual to reach at his goals and finally helps in his adjustment. Many theories of learning have been advocated by different psychologists describing their own principles of learning. For convenience, these theories can be grouped under certain perspectives in order to systematize our knowledge about human learning. Therefore in this chapter, attempt has been made to explain different perspective of learning.

BEHAVIOURAL PERSPECTIVES OF LEARNING

The proponents of Behaviourism are John Watson, known as the father of behaviourism, Ivan Pavlov, best known for his classical conditioning learning, B.F. Skinner, known for his Operant conditioning learning and Edward Thorndike, known for his theory of learning by trial and errors. Behaviourism is the theoretical perspective in which learning and behaviour are described in terms of an association between stimulus and response.

Behavioural perspective of learning is basically concerned with overt and measurable aspects of human behaviour. Behaviourist learning theories emphasize behavioural changes that result from stimulus-response associations made by the learner. Behaviour is directed and controlled by stimuli. An individual gives a selective response to stimuli because of his prior conditioning.

John B. Watson (1878-1958) and *B.F. Skinner* (1904-1990) are the originators of behaviourist approaches to learning. Watson viewed that human behaviour resulted from specific stimuli that elicited certain responses. He defined behaviour as sum total of activities both overt and covert activities elicited in certain situation out of the function of an individual in his environment. Watson's view of learning was based in part on the studies of *Ivan Pavlov* (1849-1936) who was studying about the digestive process and the interaction of salivation and stomach function. Out of his study, Pavlov realized that reflexes in the autonomic nervous system closely linked with phenomena. To determine whether external stimuli had an effect on this process, Pavlov sounded a bell when he presented food to the experimental dogs. He noticed that the dog salivated before they were given food. He discovered that when the bell was sounded repeatedly before feeding, the sound of the bell alone (conditioned stimulus) could cause the dog to salivate (conditioned response). Pavlov also found that the conditioned reflex was repressed if the stimulus proved "wrong" too frequently; if the bell rang and no food presented, the dog eventually ceased to salivate at the sound. Pavlov emphasized the role of reward and punishment in learning.

E.L. Thorndike being a Behaviourist carried his experiment on a cat and concluded that learning happens through a process of trial and error. The chance factor of right response elicited by the subject to stimuli makes a bond and creates learning. This learning may be strengthened and week depending upon the practice or exercise or habit of the subject. An individual's learning will be strengthened if practiced more and more and on the other hand his learning will be week if not practiced gain and again. Thorndike suggested three important principles of learning such as principle of readiness, principle of use/practice and principle of effect. These three conditions make the learning of an individual effective. He also stressed on the role of reward and punishment in the field of learning. Rewards in the learning stimulate the subject for more and developed learning. But punishment in learning stimulates for negative learning and hampers it. But in some incidence, Punishment act as positive force for learning if it is properly handled.

Behaviourist, B.F. Skinner out of his study proposed operant conditioning learning after his experiment on a pigeon. He viewed that every response can be strengthened with certain feedback. He emphasized the role of reinforcement in the process of learning and behaviour modification.

As a Behaviourist, Albert Bandura in his theory of Social learning highlighted the role of models in shaping the behaviour of the learners. He has suggested that modeling can form the basis for a variety of child behaviour. Children acquire many favourable and unfavourable responses by observing those around them. A child who kicks another child after seeing this on the playground, or a student who is always late for class because his friends are late is displaying the results of observational learning.

Behaviourists assert that the only the direct and observable behaviours are worthy of study Therefore they stressed on actions, rather than thoughts or emotions which are not directly observable. Behavioural theories of learning do not explain abnormal behaviour in terms of inner functioning of the brain. They stated that all behaviours are learned and can be modified under suitable circumstances. At the same time, the Behaviourists also held that all behaviours can also be unlearned, and replaced by new behaviours; that is, when a behaviour becomes unpleasant and unacceptable, it can be replaced by a pleasant and acceptable behaviour.

Assumptions of Behavioural Perspectives of Learning

The Behavioural perspectives of learning is based on the following assumptions.

1. *There is environmental effect on the behaviour:* Behaviourists assume that individual's behaviours are a result of their interaction with the environment. Specifically, people become conditioned, or molded, to respond in certain ways based on responses like feedback, praise and rewards.
2. *All learning occurs through an association between stimuli and responses.* Behaviourists focus on observable events rather than events that occur inside a person's head, such as thoughts, feelings and beliefs.

3. *Learning involves a behavioural change:* Theorists believe that learning has not occurred unless there is an observable change in behaviour.
4. *Learning result when stimulus and response occur close together in time:* Learners must associate their response with a stimulus. In order for that to occur, the two must happen in conjunction with each other, or, in other words, be contiguous.
5. *Learning of animals and humans happens in similar ways:* Behaviourists, unlike many other theorists, performed their experiments using animals because they believed the study of animals could explain human learning behaviour.

Educational Implications

Behavioural approach of learning can be implied in the field of education for the following purposes:

1. *Initiating learning process:* Behavioural learning approaches advocates for making learning situation interesting. It recommends organizing activity centered learning in schools.
2. *Preparing the learning background:* Behavioural learning approaches recommends for preparing the children both physically and mentally in order to start up their learning. It demands the teachers to study the motive, interest and attitude of the learners at first before making them learn.
3. *In organizing teaching learning objectives:* Behavioural learning theories stress on the selection of learning objectives like physical and motor development of the learners which require practice and exercise.
4. *Organizing and selecting curriculum:* Behavioural learning approaches recommends for organizing interesting, activity oriented and project based study materials for the learners.
5. *In organizing co-curricular activities in the school:* Behavioural learning theories implies for organization of diversified co-curricular activities to suit the interest of the learners.
6. *In motivating learners:* Behavioural learning approaches stress on proper motivation of learners for their success in learning. Therefore it emphasizes the application of different teaching learning aids by the teachers in the teaching learning process.
7. *Organizing guidance and counseling programme for the learners:* Behavioural learning approaches also recommends for the organization of guidance and counseling programme in the schools through which remedial measures may be recommended, feedback can be given and learning difficulties can be diagnosed and possible solutions can be advised for the improvement of the learning of the learners.

COGNITIVE PERSPECTIVES OF LEARNING

The proponents of cognitive perspective of learning are Jean Piaget, who developed theory of cognitive development and stages of cognitive development, Lev Vygotsky, best known for his socio-cultural development theory, Noam Chomsky, called as the father of modern linguistics, Gestalt psychologists like Max Wertheimer, Wolfgang Köhler, and Kurt Koffka who are known for their gestalt theory of learning which emphasize the role of insight and perception in learning and Jerome Bruner, who is known for his theory of Discovery learning and Representation.

Cognitive perspective of learning focuses on learning based on perception, memory thinking, and problem-solving. The cognitive perspective differs from the behaviourist perspective in two distinct ways. First, cognitive psychology laid importance on the existence of internal mental states such as belief, desire, ideas and motivation, which are disregarded by behaviourists. Secondly, cognitive psychologists claimed that memory structures determine how information is perceived, processed, stored, retrieved and forgotten which are mentally operated.

Cognitive is a school of psychology that deals with mental processes such as thinking, reasoning, problem solving, memory, and language. Cognitivism held the view that, mental processes cause for learning and development. Cognitive development and learning both are closely related to each other. Cognitive development refers to long-term changes in the mental process like intelligence, thinking and memory. Opposed to Behaviourists, the Cognitive Psychologists stressed on the covert activities of an individual contained in his mind. They stated that, all the overt activities are the reflections of their covert activities. It means, what we think, that we do. So, the observable brehaviours are the manifestation of internal behaviours guided by the mind.

Contributions of Cognitive Perspective of Learning

The following are the main contributions of the cognitive perspectives of learning.

1. *Study of Intellectual Development:* Piaget highlighted that children's mental development passes through certain stages like Sensory-Motor Stage, Pre-operational stage, concrete operational stage and finally formal operational stage. Passing all these stages, the intellectual capacity of the children develop from simple to complex order.
2. *Study of Sensation:* Cognitive psychologist held the view that learning occurs through sensation. It is called that sense are the gate way of knowledge. It is through sensation, one receives the knowledge about the stimuli with respect to its meaning and nature and accordingly someone gives his response.
3. *Study of Perception:* It is mental power to understand the meaning of the stimuli. After sensation, perception starts functioning. Here through perception an individual starts analyzing the relationships among the elements of stimuli, its nature and quality etc. which adds to the learning of an individual.
4. *Study of Memory:* Cognitive perspectives of learning highlight the study of memory in the field of psychology and learning. Memory plays a vital role in learning. Memory a mental process helps to retain the knowledge and experiences and retrieve the same at the time of need. Children having good memory power are found better in their learning.

Educational Implications

Cognitive approach of learning can be implied in the field of education for the following purposes.

1. *Setting learning objectives:* Cognitive approaches of learning have been beneficial in setting the learning objectives like development of mind of the learners. Relying on the cognitive approaches of learning, almost all the committees and commissions organized for the development of education have given importance to this learning objective.
2. *Planning for organization curriculum:* Cognitive psychologists have stressed on the study of those academic subjects which will develop the intellectual power of the learners. Therefore while planning about curriculum, subjects like literature, science and mathematics are given due place.
3. *Planning for organization of co-curricular subjects:* Cognitive psychologists advocated for organizing those co-curricular activities in the field of learning which apply the brain to function more. Such type of co-curricular activities like organization of debate, competitions, games like chess, Su-do-ku, letter arrangement, word arrangements etc, seminar and workshops etc.
4. *Applications of scientific methods:* Cognitive psychologists advocated for using scientific and heuristic methods in teaching learning process.

DEVELOPMENTAL PERSPECTIVES OF LEARNING

The proponents of Developmental perspectives of learning are Urie Bronfenbrenner who highlighted about impact of Ecological system on the development and learning, Erikson who highlighted about the Psychosocial theory development taking place in eight distinct stages, Sigmund Freud who highlighted about Psycho analytic theory of personality development where he described the role of dynamic aspects of mind i.e. Id, ego and Super ego, Piaget, who highlighted about the theory of cognitive development taking place in distinct four distinct stages like Sensory-motor, Pre-operational, Concrete operational and Formal operational stages, Lawrence Kohalberg who highlighted about the theory of moral development taking place in three distinct levels such as Pre-conventional, Conventional and Post-conventional levels taking place at different stages of life, James Maricia, who highlighted about the theory of the development of Identity status and Barbara Fredrickson who highlighted the impact of positive emotions like love, joy, gratitude, serenity, interest, hope, pride, amusement, inspiration and happiness.

Developmental psychologists have described how and why human beings develop over their life span. Originally concerned with infants and children, the field developmental psychology has extended to encompass the adolescence, adult development, aging and the entire lifespan. This developmental perspective of learning examines changes occur across a wide range of topics including motor skills, cognitive abilities, moral thoughts, language abilities social abilities, personality self-concept etc.

Developmental perspective of learning highlights the role of Nature and Nurture on the process of human development and their learning. Nature is personal factors found within the individual including his inherited traits, personality traits, intelligence, emotions; interests and thinking pattern of the individual that influence his learning over his life span. Nurture is a external factor relates to environment including the societal, family related, school related and community and culture that influence the learning and development of the individual over his life span.

The developmental perspective encompasses theories of learning that are continuous and discontinuous in nature.

Discontinuous Theories of Learning: These theories of learning are stage-like. These theories states that, the processes of learning and development involve distinct stages, which are characterized by qualitative differences in behaviour at each stage.

Continuous Theories of Learning: These theories of learning, in contrast, explains that learning and development occur in incremental processes. Learning involves gradual and ongoing changes throughout the lifespan.

Assumptions of Developmental Perspectives of Learning and Development

Developmental perspectives of learning and development believe in the following assumptions.

1. Nature and Nurture Shapes the developmental pattern and learning of human beings.
2. Learning and Development occurs continually over the life span following different stages.

Contributions of Developmental Perspectives of Learning

Developmental perspectives of learning provide the following contributions to the field of learning and development.

- It gave importance to the study of genetics as factor responsible for development of personality and learning of an individual
- It gave importance to different stages of life through which development and learning are realized.
- It gave importance to the study of environment as a factor responsible for Development of personality and learning of an individual.

Educational Implications

The followings are the educational implications of the Developmental perspectives of learning.

1. *Setting learning objectives:* Developmental perspectives of learning have helped to set the learning objectives of personality development of the learner. It placed the importance on the study of biological aspects and providing for feed backs to have development of individuality and personality of learners.
2. *Organizing individualized instructions:* Developmental perspectives of learning assume uniqueness of nature of individuals in respect of their interest, emotions, feelings, abilities, memory, intelligence, and motives

etc which grow at different stages of their life. Therefore adopting single method of instruction for all will not be justified and suitable for all. It requires the teacher to organize individualized instruction in their class room practices. And teaching.

3. *Organizing Curriculum:* Developmental perspective of learning has been helpful in organizing, planning and selecting curriculum on the principle of child centeredness.
4. *Organizing Co-curricular Activities:* Developmental perspectives of learning also guides in the sèlection and organization of different co curricular activities for the learners suitable for different stages of their academic life basing on the principle of individuality.
5. *Preparing Teaching Aids:* Teaching aids facilitates learning and development. Developmental perspectives of learning also become helpful in preparing teaching aids to be applied in the teaching and class room practices keeping in view of the nature aspect of the learner.
6. Organizing guidance and counseling programmers: All learners do not learn at the same rate. Some of the learners face difficulties in their learning and development for which guidance and counseling programme may be organized in the schools to therapy their learning difficulties. Developmental perspectives of learning also have educational significance in this respect of organizing guidance and counseling programmme for the learners.

SOCIO-CULTURAL PERSPECTIVE OF LEARNING

The main proponent of the socio-cultural perspectives of learning is *Lev S. Vygotsky*, a Russian Psychologist who highlighted the socio-cultural impact on the behaviour of learners. Vygotsky's socio-cultural theory of human learning postulates learning as a social process and human intelligence finds its origin in society or culture. The major theme of Vygotsky's theoretical framework is that social interaction plays a fundamental role in the development of cognition. Vygotsky stated that everything is learned on two levels. First is through interaction with others called as inter-psychological level and then integrated into the individual's mental structure called as intra-psychological level. Vygtosky also held the view that the potential for cognitive development is limited to a zone of proximal development (ZPD). This zone is the area of exploration for which every individual becomes cognitively ready but requires help and social interaction to fully develop. Collaborative learning, discourse, modelling, and scaffolding are strategies for supporting the intellectual knowledge and skills of learners and facilitating intentional learning.

The socio-cultural perspective approach helps to understand why humans behave the way they do. The sociocultural perspective seeks to understand human behaviour and personality development by examining the rules of the social groups and subgroups in which the individual is a member. It has highlighted the role of family, race, culture, customs, tradition, values, religion, or gender in shaping the way of interaction with the world of an individual. Socio-cultural perspectives of learning has stressed on the concept of group dynamics and its role in shaping the personality and behaviour of individuals.

Assumptions of Socio-cultural Perspectives of Learning

Socio-cultural perspectives of learning are based on the following assumptions.

1. Learning is social activity
2. Learning is contextual
3. Learning is a active process
4. Learning is motivational.

Contributions of Socio-cultural Perspectives of Learning

Socio-cultural perspective of learning has revolutionized the field of learning and development by contributing the theory of social learning. It has significantly stressed on the role of group dynamics, modelling, discourse and collaborative learning approach in resulting behaviour modification and learning. It has given due importance to the study of environmental factors which has a strong effect on the development and learning of human being.

Educational Implications

Socio-cultural perspectives of learning have the following educational implications.

- *Setting Learning objectives:* Socio-cultural perspectives of learning has helped to recognize the role of social and cultural inputs like values, gender, races, traditions, religion in shaping the learning of individuals. Therefore it has helped to set the learning objectives like development of social skills in the learners.
- *Organizing curriculum:* Socio-cultural perspectives have helped to organize, select the course materials keeping in view of the environmental factors, and socio-cultural bases. It gives importance to the study of history, philosophy and literatures in the curriculum
- *Organizing teaching strategy:* Socio cultural approaches of learning has helped the teachers to adopt novel teaching strategies like collaborative learning approach, discourse method, group discussion, debating, workshop, modelling, participatory approach etc. which has made learning an active and interactive process.
- *Dynamic process of evaluation:* Socio cultural perspectives have also contributed the innovative way of assessment and evaluation of learning potentialities. It has given the concept of qualitative assessment basing on judgment
- *Adopting new technologies in learning:* Socio cultural perspectives highlights the role of mass medias, video plays, word processors, etc which augment the learning of individuals in a social process instead of passive learning from reading of books.

CONSTRUCTIVE PERSPECTIVES OF LEARNING

Constructive perspectives of learning is the latest of all learning perspectives in the in the field of learning and education. Currently it is widely accepted and followed by the educators and curriculum developers.

Bruner was one of the founding fathers of constructivist theory of learning. Constructive perspectives of learning are based on the idea that, the learners construct knowledge for themselves. Each learner individually and socially constructs meaning as he or she learns. A major theme in constructive theory of learning of Bruner is that learning is an active process in which learners construct new ideas or concepts based upon their current/past knowledge.

Piaget formalized the theory of constructivism by articulating its mechanisms that, knowledge is internalized by learners through processes of assimilation and accommodation, and learners construct new knowledge from their experiences. Out of their environment, children acquire knowledge and assimilate them into his existing frame without changing it and then try to accommodate them in the process of reframing his mental representations of external world to fit his new knowledge.

Assumptions of Constructive Perspectives of Learning

Following assumptions were adopted by the constructive perspectives of learning.

1. The learner is in center of learning who thinks to construct meaning.
2. Knowledge is created by learners out of his experience.
3. Learning is a social process operated in the social environment.

Constructive theory of learning states that learning creates learning. An individual's learning constructs his system of meaning which again helps him to learn other similar things in a better way. Mind of the individual play a crucial role in constructing learning. Constructive learning theories also stresses on the importance of language which help the individual in carrying constructing meaning. Emphasizing the role of language, Vigotsky said that learning and language are intrinsically related.

Constructivists also said that, learning is a social process. An individual constructs his learning in his social environment by receiving different types of social inputs. Social situations help the individual to construct meaning. Teachers, peers, and parents as different social agents facilitate in constructing learning. They provide source of motivation for learning.

Constructivists also held that, learning is created contextually. Individuals construct knowledge and learn in relation to their different life situations. It is his beliefs, ideas, fears and prejudices earned at different life situations influence the process of constructing learning. Constructive perspective of learning also emphasizes the role of the state of the learner whose active involvement is required in constructing learning. It is his previous knowledge, experience, motive, intelligence, attitude, interest and ability of the learner which provide conditions for constructing learning.

Constructivism learning theory gives importance to the role of teachers as facilitators, whose role is to aid the student to learn. Teachers act like a facilitator for their students and helping them continually in creating the learning experience. It states that the role of teachers should be more than merely teaching rather teachers should act as mentor, consultant, guide, and a coach for the learners.

Types of Constructivism

Constructivism can be viewed from two angels such as cognitive constructivism and Social constructivism.

Cognitive constructivism: This perspective of learning states that, individual learners construct knowledge in terms of developmental stages and learning styles.

Social constructivism: This perspective of learning states that, individual learners construct knowledge out of his social encounters.

Contributions of Constructivism Perspectives of Learning

Constructivism perspective of learning has revolutionized the field of learning and development by contributing the value to the learner as the constructor of his knowledge out of his experience, interaction and theory of social learning. It has significantly stressed on the role of group dynamics, modeling, discourse and collaborative learning approach in resulting behaviour modification and learning. It has given due importance to the study of environmental factors which has a strong effect on the development and learning of human being.

18
Learning as Information Processing

Learning is an important mental activity of a human being. Each of us learns many things while living in the environment. We learn those things which we feel useful and interesting and store them in our memory for future use. The process our brain perform the task of learning is called as information processing. Therefore it is need to understand about information processing approach of learning which has a great value for the teachers in the field of education and learning.

INFORMATION PROCESSING APPROACH

The Information Processing approach places emphasis on how information enters into the brain and processed as learned. This approach states that, all learning items or information received through senses are encoded, stored, retrieved and utilized by the brain in a systematic and controlled process. Therefore learning becomes the process of converting our symbolic representations to memory where they are processed. According to this approach, learning is treated as a primarily approach through the study of memory. In Information Processing, memory is viewed from a *computer model* by which the mind takes in information, performs operates on it to change its form and content, stores the information, retrieves it when needed, and generates responses to it. Information processing is materialized through the following three stages.

1. **Encoding:** It means collecting, gathering and representing information through senses.
2. **Storage:** It means holding or retaining information in the memory.
3. **Retrieval**: It means obtaining the information from memory when needed.

STAGES OF INFORMATION PROCESSING

Information processing model states that information is processed and stored in three states such as Sensory Memory, Short-term Memory and Long-term Memory.

Sensory Memory

A sensory organ of a person picks up all the sensations or stimuli reaching our receptors from our environment and registers/stores them in memory. The capacity of sensory memory is quite large; however sensory information only lasts for milliseconds in the sensory register.

Short-term Memory

Short-term memory is seen as a temporary store lasting only from one to three seconds in the memory for a limited amount of information. If information is not attended to and encoded so as to pass into long-term memory, it decays. It is seen that short-term memory can handle about seven objects at once, but this can be improved by a process called chunking. Information can be retained in two distinct ways such as,

(a) Constant repetition of information in the mind, so as to keep it in short-term memory indefinitely
(b) Association of the information with the pre-existing knowledge.

Long-term Memory

Long-term memory term memory holds information in the memory for long period of time with little decay and seems to be permanent. The information reaching the long-term memory depends on the length of the information, the content, the opportunity for initial learning and the activity taking place between successive units of information. Long messages are less likely to be remembered than short ones. The level of familiarity and the language used are significant for long-term storage. Long term memory is of following three categories.

Semantic Memory: All verbal information or meaning come under this category of long term memory. These include storage of propositions, images, and schemata in the memory.

Episodic Memory: All eventual information related to a particular place and time come under this category.

Procedural Memory: All techniques, formulas and methods of doing/ performing and responding to do things come under this category. These learning items take long time to learn bur once they are learned they are stored in the memory for a long period of time or everlasting.

ROBERT GAGNE'S MODEL OF INFORMATION PROCESSING

The work of Robert Gagne has been particularly influential in the design of instructional material. Gagne's theory of learning is based on the Information Processing model. It describes a set of factors that influence learning.

Gagne identifies five major categories of learning:

1. Verbal Information—(Statement of mere and desired information's)
2. intellectual Skills—(Ability to compare, recognize and comprehend)
3. Cognitive Strategies—(Learning, conceptualizing, thinking and remembering)
4. Attitudes—(likes and Dislikes)
5. Motor Skills—(Muscles related functions)

Gagne held the view that, the factors necessary to achieve the learning outcomes are divided into two types such as internal and external factors.

The internal factors consist of the previous learning that has taken place. External factors include the stimulation provided by others (e.g. teachers) to recall, inform and guide the learner, the meaningfulness of the task and learner's motivation.

Gagne's Hierarchy of Learning

Gagne distinguishes eight types of learning. Theses learning's are arranged in simple to complex in a hierarchical order. These types of learning are also called as conditions of learning. The observable behaviour of an individual is the product of each such condition of learning.

Signal Learning: In signal learning the organism acquire a conditioned response to a given signal. In this type of learning, the response is emotional and learning is automatic and involuntary by nature. It is an automatic response to stimuli. Example of such type of learning is salivation at the sight of food, blinking of eyes in response to dusting, and withdrawing hands from the hot object etc.

Stimulus-Response Learning: In this type of learning, the organism responds specifically to a stimulus. Learning takes place in the shape of instrumental conditioning of E.L. Thorndike and operant conditioning of Skinner. It is a process of producing precise response to a discriminated stimulus. This type of learning is much beneficial in case of acquiring verbal skills and motor skills.

Chain Learning: In chain learning the individual connects a set of individual S-R bonds in a sequence. Here the individual has to apply the previously learned S-R's. Each of the S-R bonds provides a clue to the next learning in a connecting process. Learning of each complex motor skill needs a chain of simpler motor skills. For example, Learning of running requires the learning of standing, walking and then running in a sequence.

Verbal Association Learning: This type of learning is also a type of chaining in the shape of verbal units. The child first learns different verbal units and then he associates them to frame different sentences. For example, while saying "Red Pencil" the child associates the colour with the object pencil.

Discrimination Learning: The organism learns a lot of responses from his surroundings. Sometimes he becomes confused. This type of learning helps the organism to differentiate or discriminate between motor and verbal chains. When the organism produces some specificity of responses to one given stimulus to the exclusion of others, it is called as discrimination learning.

Concept Learning: In concept learning the organism responds to a class of stimuli in a generalized manner in terms of its abstract characteristics like colour, shape, position, number and volume. Concept learning, means making a common response to a class of stimulus. The organism learners to distinguish and generalize different class of stimulus

Rule Learning: In rule learning the individual relates one or more concepts. This type of learning governs the external behaviour of the individual. Learning of rules depends on the learning of concepts. For example, while stating "Round things roll" at that time the rule or the principle is learnt that all round things roll. The learning of Science and Mathematics and grammar is learnt through learning of some concepts.

Problem Solving: It is a complex type of learning. It is an extension of rule learning. It requires higher mental processes like thinking and imagination.

In problem solving, the individual learns to discover a combination of previously learned rules that he can apply to achieve a solution for a novel problematic situation.

All these eight types of learning suggested by Gagne are inter-dependent on each other.

PHASES OF AN ACT OF LEARNING

Gagne suggested eight phases of an act of learning of an individual which are a typical chaining or series. The total act of learning or information processing constitutes these following eight phases, beginning from motivation, apprehending, and acquisition, retention, recall, generalization, performance to feedback which have been discussed in chapter 16.

19
Intelligence

Man is bestowed with one of the supreme quality that is intelligence due to which he is differentiated from the lower level of creatures and animals. It is an inborn quality found in all human beings. Though genetically installed in human beings, it is nurtured and improved in the environment. All developmental possibilities in the society are dependent on the intelligence of the man. Our present condition of the society as we find to-day with the development of cybernetic age, internet, mobiles, computers application, Electronic Medias, Mass-Medias and communication processes etc. which were not in the primitive age are the result of the application of this super trait called intelligence of the human beings. Our aim of education is to develop the mind of the learners and making them leaders of the society to bring transformation, change, novelty, economic prosperity, societal harmony and peace. Therefore, it is required to know about the power of intelligence, its application, and strategies of its development.

MEANING AND DEFINITIONS OF INTELLIGENCE

The term intelligence has been derived from the Latin word "Intelligentia", "intelligere" during the middle English age, which means, to understand, to comprehend, power of discerning. It is an ability to acquire and apply knowledge and skills.

Meaning of Intelligence

All Words Dictionary (2006) defines intelligence as "The ability to use memory, knowledge, experience, understanding, reasoning, imagination and judgment in order to solve problems and adapt to new situations."

American Psychological Association defines intelligence as "Individuals differ from one another in their ability to understand complex ideas, to adapt effectively to the environment, to learn from experience, to engage in various forms of reasoning, to overcome obstacles by taking thought."

Encyclopedia Britannica (2006) defined intelligence as the ability to adapt effectively to the environment, either by making a change in oneself or by changing the environment or finding a new one. Intelligence is not a single mental process, but rather a combination of many mental processes directed toward effective adaptation to the environment."

Wikipedia (4 October, 2006) states "Intelligence is a property of mind that encompasses many related mental abilities, such as the capacities to reason, plan, solve problems, think abstractly, comprehend ideas and language, and learn."

Definitions of Intelligence

David. Wechsler defined intelligences as "a global concept that involves an individual's ability to act purposefully, think rationally, and deal effectively with the environment".

L.L. Thurstone states "Intelligence, considered as a mental trait, is the capacity to make impulses focal at their early, un?nished stage of formation. Intelligence is therefore the capacity for abstraction, which is an inhibitory process."

L.M. Terman defines intelligence as "The ability to carry on abstract thinking."

H. Gardner defines that "intelligence is the ability to solve problems, or to create products, that are valued within one or more cultural settings."

Stern defined that, "Intelligence is general capacity of an individual consciously to adjust his thinking to new situation. It is a general mental adaptability to new problems and conditions of life."

Garrett defines intelligences as "Intelligence is the ability demanded in the solution of problems which require the comprehension and use of symbols, i.e. words, numbers, diagrams, equations and formulas."

Binet defines that, Intelligence is common sense. It is the ability to give and to sustain attention to achieve certain ends."

J.P. Guilford defined that "Intelligence is an ability to perform an operation on a specific type of content to produce a particular product."

Out of the above definitions, it is understood that, intelligence is a mental faculty, a mental ability that help in carrying out abstract thinking, solving problems, adapting to environment or to a new situation, learning, producing, performing, acquiring and applying knowledge.

NATURE OF INTELLIGENCE

The followings are the different natures of intelligence which may explain the meaning of intelligence.

- It is an inborn trait found in each individual
- It is a covert action of the mind and not seen externally.
- It is manifested externally in actions and can be assessed.
- It is both genetically and environmentally influenced
- It is developmental
- It is qualitatively measured
- It varies in degree among the individuals
- It is universal characteristic found in all human beings in varying degree.

TYPES OF INTELLIGENCE

E.L. Thorndike's View

E.L. Thorndike Classified Intelligence into the following three types

1. *Concrete Intelligence:* This type of intelligence helps a person to perform his daily activities. All the performance tests reveal this type of intelligence. It is an ability of an individual to comprehend and deal with the concrete materials and situations.

2. *Abstract Intelligence:* It is an ability of an individual to deal with the symbols, signs, numbers, formulas and diagrams. It helps to comprehend and discover the relations among symbols and to solve problems accordingly. This type of intelligence is required to deal with the academic subjects in the schools. Philosophers, scientists and writers carry higher level of abstract intelligence in their thoughts.
3. *Social Intelligence:* This type of intelligence is required to deal with others and different social situations. It is an ability to react to social situations of daily life. It helps the individual in his adaptation, dealing and interacting with others. Diplomats, politicians and business persons carry such type of intelligence more in their thoughts.

Thurnstone's Classification

Thurstone classified intelligence into the following types,

1. *Spatial intelligence (S):* Ability to deal with objects imaginarily in space
2. *Perceptual intelligence (P):* Ability to perceive the situation, meaning, concepts, relationship, identify missing parts
3. *Numerical intelligence (N):* Ability to deal with numbers, quantity, figures
4. *Verbal intelligence (V):* Ability to comprehend
5. *Memory intelligence (M):* Ability to memorize quickly
6. *Word fluency (W):* Ability to think of words, deal with words
7. *Reasoning (R):* Ability to think and discover relation, rules
8. *Inductive ability (I):* Ability to generalize, arrive at conclusion
9. *Deductive ability (D):* Ability to derive principles, conclusion, rules
10. *Mechanical intelligence (MI):* Ability to deal with day to day activities, bodily and engineering acts.

THEORIES OF INTELLIGENCE

Theories of intelligence help in explaining the nature and developmental characteristics of intelligence. Some of the theories of intelligence belonging to these categories are discussed below.

Uni-factor Theory of Intelligence

The German psychologist, Wilhelm Stern introduced his unifactor theory of intelligence around the year 1911. It is called as an oldest of all intelligence theories. This theory is also known as general capacity theory. This theory advocates that, intelligence is a general or unitary ability denoted by 'G'. The amount of 'G' varies from one to another and it is highly influence by one's environment. One's intelligence is measured on the basis of his amount of 'G'. This general capacity helps an individual to deal with his day to day activities, solving his problems and dealing with concrete materials.

Two-Factor Theory of Intelligence

British psychologist, Charles Spearman was one of the earliest psychologists to propose a factor analytic approach to study intelligence. This theory states that there is one general factor (G) and one or more specific factors (S) that accounts for individual's performance on intelligence tests. Spearman conceptualized the 'G' factor as general mental ability. This factor is involved in deductive reasoning and is responsible for the "skill, speed, intensity, and extent of intellectual output. Spearman believed that general mental ability represents the inventive aspect of mental ability rather than the reproductive aspect. According to Spearman, all intellectual activities have some factors in common to which he called as general ability symbolized as 'G' factor. This 'G' factor/general ability is universally distributed in all but in varying degree. The amount of 'G' varies from one to another. A person is called as intelligent depending on his amount of this 'G' possessed by him. General mental abilities are inborn in nature but to some extent are influenced by environment.

According to Spearman, a person may have a number of 'S' factors or specific mental abilities. The 'S' factors are inquisitional and can be acquired from the environment through learning and experiences. 'S' factor may vary from activity to activity. Different performance require different amount of 'G' and different amount of 'S'. For example, mathematical performance require more of 'G' and less of 'S'. On the other hand, musical or dance performance require more of 'S' and less of 'G' factor.

Multi-Factor Theory of Intelligence

Multi factor theory of intelligence was propounded by E.L. Thorndike, an American Psychologist. This is also called as three factor theory of intelligence. Thorndike held the view that human intelligence is consisted of the mutual influence of the three different intelligences such as,

Abstract Intelligence: The ability to think rationally, apply creative thoughts, to imagine the possibilities, applies formulas to solve problems etc.

Mechanical Intelligence: Mechanical intelligence is type of intelligence that help the individual to deal with the concrete activities, mechanical deeds, carry day to day activities etc.

Social Intelligence: Social intelligence helps the individual to adjust to his society, environment, interact with others, understand others, play roles in the society, carry social functions etc.

Primary Mental Ability Theory

Psychologist Louis L. Thurstone (1887-1955) offered a different theory of intelligence called Primary Mental Ability Theory. Thurstone's theory of intelligence is also known as group factor theory of intelligence. Instead of viewing intelligence as a single, general ability, Thurstone's theory focused on ten different "primary mental abilities." The abilities that he described were:

1. *Spatial intelligence (S):* Ability to deal with objects imaginarily in space
2. *Perceptual intelligence (P):* Ability to perceive the situation, meaning, concepts, relationship, identify missing parts
3. *Numerical intelligence (N):* Ability to deal with numbers, quantity, figures
4. *Verbal intelligence (V):* Ability to comprehend verbal relations, ideas
5. *Memory intelligence (M):* Ability to memorize quickly
6. *Word fluency (W):* Ability to think of words, deal with words
7. *Reasoning (R):* Ability to think and discover relation, rules
8. *Inductive ability (I):* Ability to generalize, arrive at conclusion

9. *Deductive ability (D):* Ability to derive principles, conclusion, rules
10. *Mechanical intelligence (MI):* Ability to deal with bodily and engineering acts.

Fluid-Crystallized Intelligence Theory

Raymond Cattell and John Horn advocated a factor analytic approach to intelligence. The Cattell-Horn's Fluid-Crystallized Intelligence Theory distinguished between two types of intelligence that is fluid intelligence and crystallized intelligence.

Fluid Intelligence refers to the ability to understand and reason with nonverbal information which is culturally and educationally free. It is the mental capacity of an individual which helps him in his learning and problem solving. It is dependent upon one's neurological development. It is innate and biologically derived but not influenced by training or education. Examples of tasks that apply fluid intelligence include problem solving, identifying relationship, reasoning, comprehension and figure classifications. Fluid intelligence is thought to gradually increase during childhood and it peaks in adolescence. After peaking, fluid intelligence is thought to gradually decrease over the rest of an individual's life due to the degeneration of physiological brain structures.

Crystallized intelligence refers to the acquired skills and knowledge that an individual possess. Contrary to fluid intelligence, crystallized intelligence is not culture-free, but rather it is dependent on being exposed to culture. It does not depend on one's neurological development. It is not innate rather developed by one's training and education. This type of intelligence helps an individual to acquire general information consisting of knowledge and skills essential for performing different tasks in day to day life. Examples of tasks tapping the crystallized intelligence include vocabulary and general information. Crystallized intelligence is strongly influenced by training and education and as a result, is thought to increase at least until middle adulthood.

Again, Cattell, Horn, and Carroll proposed that there were more than two specific types of abilities that underlie learning. Further they proposed nine different broad types of intelligence by developing the Cattell-Horn-Carroll Theory of Cognitive Abilities. The nine different classifications of intelligence include the followings,

Fluid Intelligence (Gf): Refers to reasoning, sorting, and classifying abilities

Crystallized Intelligence (Gc): Refers to achievement and knowledge that results from training and experience, acculturation

Visual Processing (Gv): Refers to the ability to accurately perceive/interpret spatial information and visually and mentally manipulate figures

Auditory Processing (Ga): Refers to the ability to listen and respond appropriately to auditory information

Short-Term Memory (Gsm): Refers to immediate awareness, alertness, and retrieval of recently learned information

Long-Term Storage and Retrieval (Glr): Refers to the ability to retrieve information from long-term storage.

Processing Speed (Gs): Refers to the ability to quickly and efficiently respond to simple tasks.

Decision Speed (Gt): Refers to the ability to provide speeded responses to tasks of slight or moderate difficulty

Quantitative Knowledge (Gq): Refers to the ability to understand and apply mathematical concepts

Guilford's SI Model/Structure of Intellect theory

J.P. Guilford defined that "Intelligence is an ability to perform an operation on a specific type of content to produce a particular product." In Guilford's Structure of Intellect (SI) theory, intelligence is viewed as comprising of operations, contents, and products. There are 5 kinds of operations (cognition, memory, divergent production, convergent production, evaluation), 6 kinds of products (units, classes, relations, systems, transformations, and implications), and 5 kinds of contents (visual, auditory, symbolic, semantic, behavioural). Since each of these dimensions is independent, out of their interaction, theoretically 150 different components of intelligence (5×6×5=150 mental traits) are resulted. Guilford taking into account of the interaction of convergent and divergent operation of mind anticipated about a number of creative abilities.

J.P. Guilford's Structure of Intellect (SI)

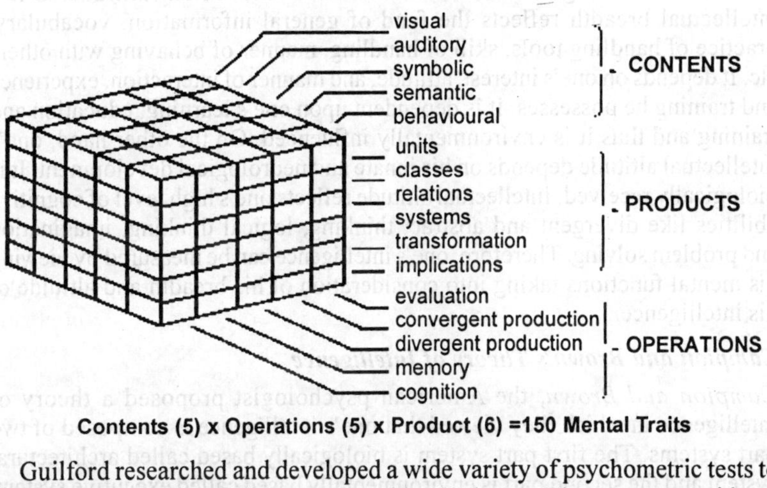

Contents (5) x Operations (5) x Product (6) =150 Mental Traits

Guilford researched and developed a wide variety of psychometric tests to measure the specific abilities predicted by SI theory. These tests provide an operational definition of the many abilities proposed by the theory.

P.F. Vernon's Hierarchical Theory of Intelligence

P.F. Vernon, a British psychologist (1950) proposed hierarchical structure of intelligence. He held the view that human mind is a kind of hierarchy in which 'G' (general ability) is the most common and prominent mental ability which is measured through an intelligence test. There are two group factors contained in 'G' termed as Ved and KM representing two kinds of mental abilities. Ved factor is concerned with the verbal, numerical and educational abilities and KM factor is concerned with practical, mechanical, spatial, and physical abilities. Again these two factors are sub divided into minor group factors and theses minor factors may further sub-divided into various specific factors related to specific mental abilities.

Mental Functioning Theory of Intelligence

This mental functioning theory of intelligence was given by Arthur Jenson (1969). This theory postulates that functioning of one's mind depends upon the types and degree of intelligence one possess. According to this theory, one's intelligence is composed of two types of abilities such as associative abilities and conceptual abilities.

Associative abilities helps an individual to memorize, remember, reproduce, identify, comprehend, classify, transfer, disseminate, discriminate and apply etc. which can be measured by intelligence tests. Conceptual abilities on the other hand help an individual to carry out higher order of thinking, reasoning, analyzing, and problem solving. Jenson viewed that, the associative abilities are innate, inborn and biological by nature but the conceptual abilities are inquisitional, and influenced by one's environment, culture, training and education.

Jenson also viewed that, attributes of intelligence in an individual is two dimensional having intellectual breadth and intellectual altitude. One's intellectual breadth reflects the fund of general information, vocabulary, practice of handling tools, skill of handling, manner of behaving with others etc. It depends on one's interest, attitude, and manner of interaction, experience and training he possesses. It is dependent upon one's learning, education and training and thus it is environmentally influenced. On the other hand, one's intellectual altitude depends on his innate and neurological development. It is biologically received. Intellectual altitude reflects one's high level of cognitive abilities like divergent and abstract thinking, logical thinking, imagination and problem solving. Therefore, one's intelligence can be measured by viewing his mental functions taking into consideration of his breadth and altitude of his intelligence.

Campion and Brown's Theory of Intelligence

Campion and Brown, the American psychologist proposed a theory of intelligence in which they viewed that one's intelligence is composed of two part systems. The first part system is biologically based called architectural system and the second part is environmentally based called executive system.

The architectural system operates as a base of one's intellectual functioning which includes memory, forgetting, and information processing. It is independent of one's education, culture and training. It is biologically influenced. On the other hand the executive system operates as a base of one's intellectual fund or store house of knowledge and information which includes cognitive abilities. The executive system of intelligence operates on a higher level and thus is responsible for highest order of mental functioning. This system is dependent upon one's training and education.

Information Processing Theories of Intelligence

The American Psychologist Robert Sternberg defined intelligence as a mental activity directed toward purposive adaptation, selection and shaping of environments relevant to onc's life. He placed this theory by adopting an information processing approach to problem solving and cognition. Information processing approach refers to a procedure to solve a problem by collecting information about the problem and then to solve it. According to Sternberg, intelligence is much broader than a single and general ability. Sternberg highlighted the following steps working in the way of one's information processing.

Steps Involved in Information Processing

Sternberg pointed out the following steps working in the ways of one's information processing.

1st. Encoding: Identifying relevant information
2nd. Inferring: Deriving necessary inferences
3rd. Mapping: Imagining relationship among the parts, previous situation with the present one
4th. Application: Applying inferred relationship
5th. Justification: Justifying the relationship, analysis
6th. Response: Solution of the problem in hand.

Studying various types of intelligence and considering the approach of information processing for executing a mental task, Sternberg developed his Triarchic Theory of Intelligence. Sternberg gave the concept of 'successful intelligence' which is comprised of three different factors. Most individuals are found to score higher in one of these three areas of intelligence.

Types of Intelligence suggested by Sternberg

Following three types of Intelligence were identified by Sternberg

Analytical intelligence: Analytical intelligence called as componential intelligence which is basic for problem-solving. It is otherwise called as problem solving ability. It helps an individual to solve academic problems and problems of his day to day life. Sternberg stated that, an individual's intellectual functioning constituted of different components like meta components, performance components and knowledge acquisition components. Through these components, one processes his information directed towards his problem solving response. According to Sternberg, Meta components involves the mental ability like planning, selecting, monitoring, regulating, executing a task etc, performance components involves the mental abilities like perception, conceptualization, and response making of a task and knowledge acquisition components involves the mental abilities like gathering information, analyzing and synthesizing information about a task

Creative intelligence: This creative intelligence which is called as experiential, involves the capacity to deal with new situations applying past experiences and current skills by using the information processing approach. Creative Intelligence reflects an individual's ability to connect their internal world to their external reality. It helps to explore new ideas, novel situations. It includes one's ability to use prior knowledge in new or innovative ways in different circumstances, such as finding a new approach to a problem. In this way, creative intelligence encompasses creative thinking.

Practical intelligence: Practical intelligence which is contextual refers to the ability to adapt to a changing environment. Practical Intelligence involves one's ability to understand, adapt, select, shape and effectively deal with everyday tasks. It is reflects, how the individual relates to the external world.

Concept of Successful Intelligence: Sternberg held the view that individuals who excel in all types intelligence as described in the Triarchic Intelligence theory may be considered to have successful intelligence, which he defines as the ability to achieve success in accordance with one's personal standards and within one's socio-cultural context. Individuals with high levels of successful intelligence tend to be better equipped for success and able to adapt well to their socio-cultural context. Sternberg's construct of successful intelligence may be applied to educational settings with the aim of increasing student learning while bridging gaps among socio-economic and ethnically diverse groups. In addition, the theory of successful intelligence offers researchers, psychologists, and educators an opportunity to redefine intelligence, and educational opportunity.

Multiple Intelligence Theory

Multiple Intelligence theory was given by *Howard Gardner* which was expressed in his book, Frame of Mind (1983). Gardner gave a broad view of intelligence opposed to 'G' factor and he viewed intelligence is set of an individual's abilities, talents and mental skills related to a multiple number of domains of knowledge in a particular cultural setting. Gardner viewed that; there are eight independent type of intelligence that develops differently in different people depending on their genetic characteristics or environmental experiences. These eight types of intelligences independently function and help an individual to perform his certain type of action or to produce certain type of response.

Types of Intelligence proposed by Gardner

The eight intelligences proposed by Gardner are,

Visual-spatial Intelligence: Spatial intelligence refers to an individual's ability to represent the spatial world in his or her own mind. It includes skill at recognizing and using patterns. Architects, urban planners, geographers, cartographers, pilots, and sailors tend to be high in spatial intelligence abilities.

Verbal-linguistic Intelligence: Linguistic intelligence is the ability to learn languages and to use one's skill in using language effectively to accomplish specific goals. Individuals found high in linguistic intelligence are often seen as writers, poets, and lawyers.

Bodily-kinesthetic Intelligence: Bodily-kinesthetic intelligence refers to an individual's ability to use mental abilities to coordinate bodily movements. According to Gardner, mental and physical abilities are related. Athletes, dancers, actors, and performers often display high levels of bodily-kinesthetic intelligence

Logical-mathematical Intelligence: Logical-mathematical intelligence is the ability to analyze problems logically. It includes skill at completing mathematical operations and solving mathematical problems as well as the ability to investigate hypotheses scientifically. Those high in logical-mathematical intelligence tend to be logical thinkers with high deductive reasoning skills.

Interpersonal Intelligence: Interpersonal intelligence is concerned with an individual's ability to understand the intentions, motivations, and desires of other people. Such skills are beneficial in working and getting along with others. Those high in interpersonal intelligence are often educators, salespeople, religious and political leaders, counsellors and social workers.

Musical Intelligence: Musical intelligence includes abilities in composing and performing music and in recognizing and composing musical pitches, tones, and rhythms. It also includes skills in recognizing and appreciating musical patterns. Individuals high in musical intelligence may have talents in vocal and/or instrumental abilities.

Intrapersonal Intelligence: Intrapersonal intelligence refers to the capacity to understand oneself—one's thoughts, feelings, fears, desires, and motivations. It includes the ability to use this knowledge toward successful outcomes. Writers and artists often demonstrate intrapersonal intelligence in their work.

Naturalistic Intelligence: Naturalist intelligence refers to an individual's ability to recognize, categorize, and draw upon certain features of the environment.

Gardner later suggested another two types of intelligence that are existential and moral intelligence. Existential Intelligence is concerned about ultimate issues and idealistic one. On the other hand the moral intelligence deals with rules, behaviours, and attitudes that govern the sanctity of human life as well as lives of other living creatures and the world they live in. Although the distinction between intelligences has been set out, Gardner opposes the idea of labeling learners to a specific intelligence. Each individual possesses a unique blend of all the intelligences. Gardner firmly maintains that his theory of multiple intelligences should "empower learners", not restrict them to one modality of learning.

EDUCATIONAL IMPLICATIONS OF INTELLIGENCE THEORIES

All theories of intelligence as described above attempt to explain the meaning and types of intelligence. An individual is seen to be a unique blend of different types of intelligence. He can't be labeled to a particular type. The individual only manifest a distinct type of intelligence in response to a particular situation. Individual only apply certain type of intelligence depending upon his need and situation and tries to accomplish his goals and solves his problem.

The discussion about theories of intelligence has a great value to education and learning. It has created awareness in the teachers, teacher educators, planners, curriculum designers about the pattern of growth and development of intelligence, types of intelligence. The study of intelligence theories has the immediate implications in the planning of the following areas like:

- Setting the learning objectives at different levels of education
- Planning and preparing curriculum/study materials for different levels of education

- Devising teaching strategies
- Preparing teaching aids
- Devising evaluation and assessment practices
- Improving problem solving practices in the learners
- Developing creativeness in the learners
- Dealing with the individual difference in class room practices and education
- Devising therapeutic measures for the slow learners/ abnormal learners/ gifted learners and idiots etc.
- Enriching educational practices
- Organizing training modules for the children with special needs having minimal IQs.

MEASUREMENT OF INTELLIGENCE

One's intelligence can't be measured directly. Only its manifestation can be assessed. It can only be observed through its manifestations in one or more tests. Intelligence as an abstract but not a substance can only be accessed through some tests. An individual's intelligence is assessed in relation to the norms set by the author of the test.

Many intelligence tests have been developed by many psychologists to assess the intelligence of human being/individuals. These tests can be grouped as Individual Intelligence test and Group Intelligence test depending upon its application. Further, depending upon the form if the test, Intelligence tests can be categorized as Verbal Intelligence Test and Non Verbal Intelligence Test.

Verbal Intelligence tests make use of language. Instructions are given in language either written or verbal. Individuals o be tested also give their response through language. The test items are loaded with verbal materials. Some of the Verbal Intelligence tests are like,

1. Vocabulary test (designed to test word power of the subjects/individual, items include, meaning, difference, antonyms, synonyms of the words etc.)
2. Memory test (designed to test LTM, includes Recognition and Recall type of test items)
3. Comprehension test (designed to test the grasping/understanding power of the subjects)
4. Information test (designed to test awareness about the things around the subjects)
5. Reasoning test (designed to test the ability to think, reason out, analytically and synthetically think the solution)
6. Association test (design to test the ability of the individuals to associate, point out the similarity, dissimilarity between two or more concepts)

Non-Verbal Tests make use of Activities and do not make use of language/ verbal materials. In this test, only oral instruction is given. Performance tests are Non-verbal intelligence tests. The type of tests like, Block building/cube construction test, To fit blocks in holes test, Tracing a Maze test, Picture arrangement/picture completion test etc. are examples of Non-Verbal Intelligence tests.

So, intelligence test may be of the following types combining their applicative and form issues like,

1. Individual Verbal Intelligence test
2. Individual non-Verbal/performance test
3. Group verbal intelligence tests and
4. Group Non-verbal/performance test

Alfred Binet (1916) a French psychologist was the first to use his Intelligence test. He is called as the father of intelligence test construction movements. Along with his associates like Simon, he had constructed first scale of verbal intelligence test including 30 items arranged in order of increasing difficulty.

A group of performance tests organized into scales or a battery is used to obtain the comprehensive idea of a person's mental ability. Some of the better known scales are like,

1. Printer-Patterson scale (designed on 1917 in USA, to test the Intelligence of the linguistically backward children and deaf children, Include tests like Puzzle test, Mare and foal picture board, the triangle test, the diagonal test, The Healy form board, Manikin test, the adaption board, the feature profile test, the cube test etc.
2. The Arthur point scale (developed by Grace Arthur by using point scale for scoring, include knox cubes, the seguine form boards, two-form figure board, Manikin test, feature profile, mare and foal picture board, Healy picture completion and koh's block design)
3. Alexander's battery of performance test (It includes passalong, block designs, and cube constructions.
4. Bhattia's battery of performance test (It include picture construction test, block design test, Alexander's passalong test, pattern drawing test)
5. Wechsler Bellevue intelligence scale (available in two forms like, for children-WISE, for adults-WAIS. It includes 11 sub tests, six of verbal and five of performance tests)
    1. Test of general information
    2. Test of general comprehension
    3. Test of arithmetic reasoning
    4. Test of distinction between similarities
    5. Test of digit span
    6. Test of vocabulary
    7. Digit symbol test
    8. Picture completion test
    9. Block design test
    10. Picture arrangement test
    11. Object assembly test

INTELLIGENT QUOTIENT (IQ)

Intelligence assessed through Intelligence tests are expressed in terms of Intelligence quotient (IQ). The German Psychologist (1914) William Stern is the first to coin and popularize this IQ, the fraction of mental age and chronological age multiplied by 100 in order to eliminate decimal points. It was Alfred Binet the French Psychologist to use the term Mental age earlier. Basing upon the Quantum of IQ range children are now grouped as gifted, intelligent, average, below average and slow learners.

There is correlation between one's IQ and his mental brightness. Merril has suggested the following groups of IQ basing upon the result of Terman-Merril Revision.

IQ Range	*Classification of Children/Brightness Level*
140-169	Very Superior/Genius/Gifted
120-139	Superior
110-119	Above Average
90-109	Normal/Average
80-89	Below average
70-79	Border line defective/ Slow learner
50-69	Moron
25-49	Imbeciles
Below 25	Idiots

There is a limitation to this formula of IQ groupings. Different psychologists have suggested different tables/groupings of IQ.

20
Creativity

Creativeness is a quality found distributive among the human beings. Not all individuals are creative. A few are found to be creative in a respective field only. Creativity is a divine gift of the God. It is a rare ability bestowed in the individual's mind by the blessing of the God. The leaders like Gandhi, Swami Vivekananda, Newton, and Shakespeare like personalities are called as creative peoples due to their creative talents. Though it is a divine quality, supreme ability rarely found, it can be developed in the children if proper education, inspiration, guidance and care are provided. Therefore is a need to know about creativity.

MEANING AND DEFINITIONS

Creativity means developing something new, innovative and unique in characteristics. Only creative mind can produce creative ideas and things.

Spearman defined that, creativity is a power of the human mind to create new content by transforming relations and thereby generating new correlates.

David Ausubel defined that, creativity is generalized constellation of intellectual abilities, personality variables and problem solving traits.

Wilson, Guilford and Christensen told that, creative process is any process by which something new is produced-an idea or an object including a new form or arrangement of old elements. The new creation must contribute to the solution of some problem.

So, it can be said that, creativity is a capacity, an ability of the individual to create some novel things or ideas even rearrangement of the old idea or event or object already known to him which proves to be a unique experience.

NATURE OF CREATIVITY

The following natures are seen in all the creative actions,

- It is universal
- It is an innate as well as acquired ability
- Novelty
- Adventures and open thinking
- It is both a means and end also
- It carries ego involvement
- Creativity and intelligence does not necessarily go hand in hand
- Creativity can't be separated from Intelligence
- Originality
- Relevancy

- Fluency
- Elaborativeness
- Flexibility

STAGES OF CREATIVITY DEVELOPMENT

Psychologist, Wallas (1926) out of his study advocated that any creative process follows the following four stages of its development.

1st. *Preparation:* (Conscious work done on the problem)
2nd. *Incubation:* (Thinking about the problem)
3rd. *Inspiration/Illumination:* (Sudden appearance of the solution of the problem)
4th. *Verification:* (Solution of the problem is checked through whether a fact)

Torrance and Myers suggested the following stages for the development of creativity:

1st. Awareness about the problem
2nd. Conjoining available information about the problem
3rd. Searching for the solution
4th. Communication of the result (Verifying on the basis of the nature of creativity)

CHARACTERISTICS OF CREATIVE THINKING

These are the following measures/characteristics which can recognize people having creative thinking,

- Receptivity:(Ability to receive and respond)
- Curiosity: (More enthusiastic to attend the problem)
- Wide range of interests: (strongly motivated with wide interests)
- Attentiveness: (Always focus on the problem)
- Connection seeking: (Seeking relationship among parts)
- Conviction: (firm faith on his own)
- Complexity: (Think divergently with complex situations)

THEORIES OF CREATIVITY

The following theories provides clue to explain the meaning and nature of creative process.

Divine Inspiration/God-Gift theory

This theory assumes that, creativity is the gift of God/almighty; it is luck to have creativity and to become creative.

Theory of Insanity

This theory assumes that, persons leading the life of insanity or living in his own world-his thinking, imagination and feelings are centered on his own interest can become creative. But it lacks logical support and empirical evidences.

Native or Inborn Theory

This theory assumes that, creative people are born creative and not made. Creativity is a born or innate ability found in the individual. It is some thong extra ordinary trait by birth seen in the individual.

Theory of Environmentally Acquired Trait

This theory assumes that, creativity is not only a divine gift got to the individual by birth or by the heredity, but it can be developed in the environment, can be acquired from the environment if proper scope is provided.

Taylore's level Theory of Creativity

This theory assumes that, creativity develops or exists in five levels arranged in a hierarchical order.

Expressive creativity: Spontaneous expression without reference to originality or quality of product

Productivity creativity: Something new is produced at this level

Inventive creativity: Novel use of old things

Innovative creativity: New ideas/thoughts/things are developed with highly developed abstract conceptualizing skills.

Emergentive creativity: It is the highest level and rarely achieved.

Hemisphere Theory of creativity

Providing a biological base, this theory assumes that, creative acts are the result of interaction in between the two hemispheres of the individual's brain. Clark, Kitano, and Kirby out their study said that creative individuals are usually right hemisphere dominant. But Logical, rational thinkers are left-hemisphere dominant.

Psychoanalytic Theory of creativity

This theory considers that, creativity is a means and product of one's emotional purging. It is an attempt for the expression of the repressed desires mostly sexual in nature. This theory tells that people become creative as a reaction to difficult circumstance and repressed emotions. Every creative action wells from the unconscious motives/drives. The root of creativity is unconscious and combined with conscious mind give planning and production of creative products.

Arieti's Theory of Creativity

This theory considers that, creative process is a magic synthesis of two modalities like the primary process and secondary process. Which is called as tertiary process? Creativity and mental illness are parallel to one another and both involve the transformation of reality.

MEASUREMENT OF CREATIVITY

Creativity is a mental ability and it is an internal function of the brain. So it can't be directly measured. Creativity only can be measured through creativity tests. Many standardized tests are now available to test the creativity of individuals. Some of the tests are mentioned below,

Western Tests

Following types of western tests are used to assess the creativity

1. Minnesota test of creative thinking
2. Guilford's divergent thinking instrument
3. Remote association test
4. Wallach and Kogan creativity instrument
5. A.C. test of creativity
6. Torrance test of creativity.

Indian Tests

Following types of Indian tests are used to assess the creativity

1. Baqer Mehdi's test of creative thinking
2. Passi's test of creativity
3. Sharma's divergent production ability test
4. Saxena's test of creativity.

EDUCATIONAL IMPLICATIONS

The study of creativity has significant educational implications. It has influences to our educational aims and objectives. Our educational endavours aims to develop the creativity and talents of the children in different fields. Both teacher and parents aspire their children should be creative. The study of creativity has influenced the design of curriculum and its preparation keeping in view of the aims and objectives of education. A school organizes different programme and co-curricular activities for its children to express their creative talents and provide opportunity to explore their creativity. It has influenced the motivational techniques, teaching-learning strategies and a teacher's teaching styles.

21
Anxiety

Every individual has his own anxiety of different forms. It stimulates him to act and fulfill his anxiety. When an individual encounters certain barriers which threatens his efforts to reach at the destination and satisfy his goals then his tension aroused and his mental peace is disturbed. As a result anxiety disorder takes the form and finally makes the individual maladjusted and abnormal. Therefore, the study of anxiety has a great value for the teachers and educationists who deal with the learners in the educational settings.

MEANING OF ANXIETY

Oxford Dictionary defines the term anxiety as a state of unease or concern. Anxiety is a type of response to a perceived threat or danger. Anxiety is a unique human experience. Every human being has his own anxiety or varieties of anxieties. Due to anxiety disorders, sometimes individuals found not able to lead their normal life.

ANXIETY DISORDERS

Anxiety disorder is common to all the neurotic patients. It results out of the faulty adaptation of stress and strain of life. People suffering from anxiety disorder are seen to be gloomy, fearful, worry, excessive thoughtful about something miss-happenings and death, sleepless and depressed. Occasional anxiety is a normal part of life. Someone feels anxious when faced with a problem at work, before taking a test, or making an important decision. Anxiety disorders involve more than temporary worry or fear.

TYPES OF ANXIETY DISORDERS

1. Generalized Anxiety Disorders (GAD)

Generalized anxiety disorder (GAD) cause constant and uncontrollable worries and fears of some situation in the individual and distracts him/her from his day-to-day activities. It ois also called as chronic anxiety neurosis. A person with such type of disorder is troubled by persistently feeling of something wrong going to happen. People with GAD are chronic worrywarts who feel anxious nearly all of the time, though they may not even know why. Anxiety related to GAD exhibits physical symptoms like insomnia, stomach upset, restlessness, depression and fatigue.

Symptoms of GAD

Following types of symptoms are seen in the people suffering from GAD

- Difficulty in concentrating

- Difficulty in sleeping
- Excessive irritability
- Fatigue/exhaustion
- Muscle tension
- Repeated stomachaches or diarrhea
- Sweating palms
- Shaking
- Rapid heartbeat
- Numbness and tingling of different parts of the body.

Causes of GAD

Following are the causes of GAD

- Family history
- Prolonged exposure to stressful situations including personal or family illnesses
- Excessive use of alcohol
- Victim of childhood abuse
- Addiction of drugs.

Treatment Measures

Following treatment measures may rehabilitate and rectify the GAD

- Psycho and cognitive therapy: Regular meeting, talks with the people with GAD and rectifying their problem by a mentally healthy person or psychologist.
- Medication: Proper diagnosis of the problem and prescribing medicines
- Counseling: Experts and experienced mentally healthy persons should counsel the patient and adopt follow up programmes.

2. Panic Disorder (PD)

A panic disorder is characterized by repeated, unexpected panic attacks and constant fear of something worse. A panic disorder may also be accompanied by certain phobias, which is the fear of being in situation/places where escape or help would be difficult in the event of a panic attack. Persons having agoraphobia, want to avoid public places such as shopping malls, or confined spaces such as an airplane. Other form of panic disorders are like hydrophobia (fear of water), pyrophobia (fear of fire), nictophobia (fear of darkness), acrophobia (fear of high place), astrophobia (fear of thunder) and hematophobia (fear of blood).

Symptoms of Panic Disorder (PD)

- Rapid respiration or a raising heart bit
- Chest pain or suffocation
- Trembling or shaking
- Choking feeling
- Feeling detached from your surroundings
- Sweating
- Nausea or upset stomach

- Feeling to be faint
- Numbness or tingling sensations
- Hot or cold flashes
- Fear of dying, losing control, or going crazy

Treatment Measures

- Cognitive and behavioural therapy: Regular talks, meeting with the people suffering from panic disorder can change their thinking pattern and rehabilitate them from fears.
- Medication and treatment
- Physical exercise and yoga practice: Panic disorder peoples should regularly practice yoga and exercise.
- Increasing coping skill: Training should be given to the Patients of panic disorder to enhance their coping skill.
- Exposures therapy: Exposing the patient with physical sensation of a panic state in a safe and controlled environment and giving the opportunity to cope.

3. Social Anxiety Disorder (Social Phobias)

Social anxiety disorder is characterized by persistence fear of being humiliated and seen negatively by others. It is otherwise known as social phobia. People having social anxiety disorder feel losing confidence in them and apprehend that he/she will be criticized, closely watched by the others. It arises out of excessive and unreasonable fear of social situations. Persons with social anxiety disorder remain afraid of committing mistakes, look bad and humiliation by others. Persons suffering from social anxiety disorder want to avoid social situations.

Symptoms of Social anxiety disorder (SAD)

Followings are the symptoms of SAD

- Fear of eating or drinking in front of others
- Fear of writing or working in front of others
- Fear of presentation of speech before audience
- Fear of interaction with others
- Fear of asking questions in the groups/class room
- Fear of reading reports in groups
- Fear of using public toilets.

Causes of SAD

Followings are the causes of SAD

- *Biological Causes:* It includes impairments in speech, vision and hearing, physical deformities/handicap, genetic problems.
- *Psychological Causes:* It includes abnormal functioning of brain, in correct perception, lack of thinking ability and less intelligence.
- *Environmental Causes:* It includes unusual behaviuor of others like laughing, making fun and ridiculing and seeing in different manner.

Treatment Measures for SAD

Following therapeutic measures may be taken for treatment of SAD

- *Cognitive-behavioural therapy:* Guiding and exposing the individual suffering from SAD to social situations in a controlled way.
- *Medical treatment:* Rectifying the physical challenges and impairments.
- *Training:* Training for improving speech practice, thinking ability and reducing shyness.
- *Counseling:* Providing counseling to develop self-esteem, confidence and social skills.

SYMPTOMS OF ANXIETY DISORDER

Each anxiety disorder has different symptoms, but all the symptoms cluster around excessive, irrational fear and dread. Anxiety disorders commonly occur along with other mental or physical illnesses, including alcohol or substance abuse, which may mask anxiety symptoms or make them worse. In some cases, these other problems need to be treated before a person can respond well to treatment for anxiety. While some symptoms, such as fear and worry, occur in all anxiety disorders, each disorder also has distinctive symptoms. The followings are some of the important symptoms of Anxiety disorders,

- Feelings of panic, fear, and uneasiness.
- Problems in sleeping.
- Cold or sweaty hands and/or feet.
- Shortness of breath.
- Heart palpitations.
- An inability to be still and calm.
- Dry mouth.
- Numbness or tingling in the hands or feet.
- Irritation feeling
- Feeling detached
- Trembling and shaking
- Sweating
- Suffocation feeling
- Chest pain
- Fearing
- Worry

DIAGNOSIS AND TREATMENT

Anxiety disorders are treatable. If someone feels having an anxiety disorder, then he/she is advised to talk to doctor and get remedial measures. Proper medication and therapy can check and benefit from the anxiety disorder and help them to lead a normal life.

EDUCATIONAL IMPLICATION

Study of anxiety has a great value to the field of teaching and learning. Level of anxiety and anxiety disorder has their direct bearing on the learning of the children. Children having anxiety disorder fail to cope in the class room and achieve good result. They fail to pay their attention towards the teaching of the teachers and complete teaching learning tasks properly. Therefore is essential for teachers to identify the children having the problem of their anxiety disorders by adopting proper diagnostic measures. Therapeutic measures should be adopted for them. Guidance and counseling measures are to be organized in the schools. If required proper medication facilities to be provided for these children in order to rectify their anxiety disorders.

CURIOSITY

Curiosity means a strong desire to know or learn something. Curiosity is an important trait of a genius. All the great personalities like Thomas Edison, Albert Einstein, Aristotle, Sachin Tendulkar, Shakespeare etc. are well known curious characters.

Importance of Curiosity

Followings are the importance of Curiosity.

- *It makes mind active instead of passive:* Curious people always seek to ask questions and search for answers. They always remain mentally active. Curiosity make mind stronger.
- *It makes mind observant of new ideas*: Curious mind always seek new ideas and never remain silent with the old ideas.
- *It opens the way of possibilities and new worlds*: Curious people only can see the new world and find different possibilities which are normally not visible.
- *It brings excitement in life:* Curious people are found not boring. Every moment the new ideas draw their attention. Curious people lead an adventurous and challenging life.
- *It makes a person optimistic:* Curios persons never feel hopeless. They remain optimistic in their attitude and outlook. They are hopeful.

Strategies to Develop Curiosity

Following strategies will help to develop curiosity in children.

Keeping open mindedness: This is essential to have a curious mind. Be open to learn, unlearn, and relearn. Some things one knows and believes might be wrong, and he/she should be prepared to accept this possibility and change his/her mind.

Trying for deep thinking and not taking things as granted: Accepting the world as it is without trying to dig deeper, someone will certainly lose the 'holy curiosity'. Never take things as granted. Try to dig deeper beneath the surface of what is around you.

Developibg habit of asking questions frequently: A sure way to dig deeper beneath the surface is asking questions: What is that? Why is it made that way? When was it made? Who invented it? Where does it come from? How does it work? What, why, when, who, where, and how are the best and close words for curious people.

Developing exploring attitude: Labeling something as boring means it is to close the door of possibilities. Curious people never call something as boring. Instead, they always explore a door to an exciting new world. Even if they don't yet find time to explore something, they leave the door open to be visited another time.

Visualizing learning as Something Fun: If someone will visualize/see learning as a burden, there's no way for him to go deeper into anything. But if someone will think of learning as something fun, he/she will naturally want to go deeper of anything. So children should visualize their learning something fun and interesting which will give them pleasure in learning and good result too.

Developing Habit of reading diverse kinds of readings: One should not be satisfied with just one world. He should take interest in other world. It will introduce someone to the possibilities and excitement of the other worlds which may spark the interest to explore them further. Therefore, one easy way to do this is through reading diverse kinds of reading. Children should be advised to read variety of books which can boost their excitement level to explore something new.

22
Attention and Learning

The word attention is frequently pronounced in our day to day conversation. In the class room, a teacher ask his learners to pay their attention towards his teaching, in the Railway platform/stations, announcer announces the passengers to pay their attention about the movement of different trains, their arrival and departure etc. So, attention is a cognitive-response on the part of an individual towards certain stimuli. Better attention produces better result and vice versa. Children who remain attentive towards the teaching, they learn better in comparison to those who remain inattentive. Attention has its positive effect on one's learning and his achievement of goals.

MEANING OF ATTENTION

The word attention means shifting of response on priority basis with interest to some situations. This response may be accompanying with our auditory sense or visual sense. Attention. It may be understood as an act, a process or a function. Attention is a process or act of listening, looking at, concentrating on a topic or on a event for attainment of desired result.

Ross defined attention that, it is a process of getting an object of thought clearly before the mind.

Morgan and Gilliland defined, Attention is being alive to some specific factor in our environment. It is a preparatory adjustment for response.

R.N. Sharma defined that, attention is a process which compels the individual to select some particular stimulus according to his interest and attitude out of the multiplicity of stimuli present in the environment.

Thus out of the above definitions it can be understood that, attention is a process but not a product, it makes us aware of the environment, It helps to have selective response, It is interest based, objective and It operates both at the cognitive, emotional and conative levels.

THEORIES OF ATTENTION

Theories of attention are categorized as two such as an early selection theory and late selection theory of Attention.

Early Selection Theory of Attention

Early selection theory is otherwise known as Filter theory of attention. Filter theory of attention was forwarded by Donald Broadbent (1957-58). This theory postulated that, there are two general systems-the sensory and perceptual remain active in attention process. This theory attributes that, many signals come to the brain from the environment at a time but only one signal is attended with our conscious attention ignoring all others which are unimportant. Thus the sensory system filters out all unimportant signals before they can reach the perceptual system. Therefore it is called as an early selection theory.

The Late selection theory of Attention

The late selection theory given by Norman (1968), Schneider and Shiffrin (1977) asserted that, ignored information are not filtered out at a sensory level but it is processed through early stages of perception and attention to one signal occur much later just before conscious awareness.

EFFECTS OF ATTENTION

It can be observed that, a person who paying his attention is seen to be turning his head, fixing his eyes or setting his year towards a stimuli/object of attention. Besides these, the biological and muscular function of the body may be seen to specifically preparing for the object of attention. A person may be seen to be adopting a specific posture and his respiration become slows down. From the facial expression of the individual, he/she may be seen to be paying his/her attention or not.

Some of the effects of attention are mentioned below.

- Attention brings mental alertness
- Attention helps in deep concentration by focusing one's conscious mind.
- Attention helps in differentiating between objects at one time.
- Attention acts as reinforcement of the sensory processes and helps in organization of perceptual field.
- Attention helps to have better understanding of the situation.
- Attention helps to continue the task sparing the obstacles.
- Attention yields better result.

TYPES OF ATTENTION

A variety of classification of attention have been given by the Psychologists. According to Ross, there are two categories of Attention. One is Volitional and another one is Non-Volitional Attention.

Volitional Attention

Volitional attention is otherwise known as voluntary attention. Volitional attention is willful and requires conscious effort on the part of the individual. It is not automatic and spontaneous. In this attention process, clear cut goal is fixed and that induces the individual to pay attention. Solving Mathematical sums, Answering questions at the time of examination, consulting the railway time table before starting our journey are the examples of such type of Volitional Attention. Volitional attention is further divided into two types such as Implicit Volitional Attention and Explicit Volitional attention.

Implicit volitional attention: It requires a single act of volition to bring about attention. For example, when a child does not remain attentive to his mathematical sum, then the teacher warns to punish the child and the child thereby pays his attention towards the mathematical problem. Here the single act of teacher's warning illicit child's will to pay his attention towards the stimuli.

Explicit volitional attention: It requires repeated act of volition to bring attention. Repeated act of will is necessary to sustain the explicit volitional attention. Here, one has to struggle hard to continue to be attentive. It needs a strong will power on the part of the individual. For example, a child is to pay attention towards his preparation for the examination irrespective of difficult situations and distractions.

Non-Volitional Attention

Non-volitional attention is otherwise known as non-voluntary attention. Non-voluntary attention means placing the attention to a thing without any desire. It is influenced by the intensity, size, novelty, mobility, repetition etc. of an object. This type of attention does not require any mental endeavour. Here there is no clear cut goal for fixing the attention.

FACTORS INFLUENCING ATTENTION

The following factors influence our attention,

External factors: External factors are also called as outside factors which relate to the environment and stimuli itself. Such factors are like, Nature of the stimuli, intensity and size of the stimuli, novelty, variety and contrast of the stimuli, repetitions of the stimuli and movement of the stimuli.

Internal factors: Internal factors are also called as inside factors which relates to the respondent/individual himself. Such factors are like, interest of the individual, goal seeking nature/will of the individual, motives, mindset of the individual.

SPAN OF ATTENTION

At a moment we pay our attention to particular stimuli we remain conscious on that. But it is sometimes seen that, we pay our attention to a more number of stimulus at a particular moment. Some people are able to grasp a number of things, or attend to a number of stimuli in one short exposure. But some fails to grasp the same in short exposure. This ability is measured in terms of span of his attention which varies from individual to individual. Span of attention may be defined as the quality, size or extent to which the perceptual field of an individual can be effectively organized in order to enable him to attend to a number of things in a given spell of short duration.

Sir William Hamilton (1859) out of his experiment on the span of attention concluded that on an average the span of the visual attention is limited to 6-7 items at a time. However, if the items are arranged in groups or units one can attend to a large number of items. Experiments to study the span of visual attention can be done with the help of an instrument called Tachistroscope and a Falling door type Tachistroscope are generally used in college laboratories. It is made up of a wooden screen having a window or hole in the middle. Digits, letters or small patterns written or printed on cards are inserted in the apparatus to be seen through the hole or window. The exposure is quite short i.e. to 1/10 seconds which is regulated by a movable falling shutter. The subject is shown the cards through the holes for the fixed exposure time and asked to record what he perceived. Number of correct responses will now help to determine his span of visual attention.

In order to measure the span of auditory attention, tapping methods may be used. In this method, the subject will be asked to record how many numbers and how many times he/she heard the taps

ATTENTION FLUCTUATION

Sometimes it is seen that attention on a certain stimuli does not remain constantly in the same intensity. The subject shifts his/her attention from one part to another. In course of time, the consciousness shifts or transferred from one stimulus to another or from one part to another of the same stimulus. This is called as attention fluctuation or attention shifting. The intensity of attention also varies from time to time and from stimulus to stimulus. Therefore we sometime pay more attention and sometimes we pay least attention depending upon the size, intensity of the stimulus. The reason for the shifting of our attention lies in the division of the field of perception or consciousness at a particular moment. Consciousness at a particular moment may be categorized as central and marginalized. When we at a particular moment focus on the wall Clock our central consciousness remain active and we ignore the rest parts inside the room which require marginalized consciousness. Therefore the attention process is a dynamic and flexible process. It is not a constant process.

DIVISION OF ATTENTION

It is seen that, our attention not only remain on a particular stimulus but also at the same time attention goes to other without leaving any negative impact on the first rather attention become more qualitative and yield better result. This is called as division of attention. For example, when we are paying attention to read a book at the same time we prefer to shift our attention to listen radios, songs etc. Here we deliberately ignore the secondary attention i.e. radio programmes or songs and remain concentrated/attentive to our reading. Division of attention means, attention is divided into two tasks at a particular moment. If more than two tasks are to be attended simultaneously then the attention will be divided among those tasks.

SUSTAINED ATTENTION

One's Sustained attention yields good result and on the other hand distracted attention will yield negative/low result. Sustained attention requires the subject to concentrate on the activity continuously. One has to pay his/her attention constantly till the end of the deed from the beginning. In case of sustained attention there is no place of wandering but the subject is to remain on the track without any distraction. For example, a hunter carries his sustained attention till the objective of hunting of the animal is completed. If desired goal is to be achieved in a reasonable period, then there is a need of one's sustained attention. The issue of having sustained attention of the learners in the class room is quite essential to have their successful learning. Many means can be used like good teaching practices using audiovisual aids, quality teaching, making teaching interesting etc can help to maintain sustained attention of the learners.

ATTENTION DISTRACTION

There are many external and internal means which interrupts in the process of our attention and exerts a negative impact on the attention process and make it less objective. These things which interfere with our attention are called as distracters.

Being a psychological term, distraction is defined by H.R. Bhatia as, any stimulus whose presence interferes with the process of attention or draws away attention from the object to which we wish to attend.

The more common external distracters, which hamper attention, are unusual environment, noises, music, sounds, improper lightings, uncomfortable temperature, uncomfortable seats, inadequate ventilation, defective teaching methods, improper teaching aids, defective voice etc. The common internal distracters are emotional disturbances, ill-health, boredom, lack of motivation, feeling of fatigue, mental worries etc which are found within the individual.

In order to make attention qualitative and objective oriented, there is need to pacify all the distracters coming on the way of attention. Effort to be made to create healthy environment with proper provision of usual/normal arrangements of required means and so also individual's physiological and emotional state should remain normal functioning.

ATTENTION AND INTEREST

Interest is an internal force of an individual closely related to attention which induces the individual to act. It is a cognitive process may be recognized as a form of curiosity that stimulates the individual to attend the selective act. Interest of the individual plays a vital role in his life in respect of achievement goals and in his success and failure analysis. The individuals found having more interest in their activity, their success amount is more and vice versa. But it is seen that, an individual may have interest in different areas at the same time. But special interest indicates the better performance in certain area and brings recognition and pleasure. Intensity of the interest varies from one to another and type of interest also varies from one to another. In teaching learning process, it is need to understand the concept of interest and strategies are to be adopted to make teaching learning process interesting in order to yield better result.

ATTENTION AND LEARNING

There is a positive correlation between attention and learning. Students who remain attentive towards their learning, their amount of learning become more and vice versa. Attention strengthens the memory and learning. A teacher may use different types of teaching aids to make his learners attentive towards his teaching.

23
Interest and Learning

Interest is an internal force of an individual closely related to attention which induces the individual to act. It is a cognitive process may be recognized as a form of curiosity that stimulates the individual to attend the selective act. Interest of the individual plays a vital role in his life in respect of achievement goals and in his success and failure analysis. The individuals found having more interest in their activity, their success amount is more and vice versa. But it is seen that, an individual may have interest in different areas at the same time. But special interest indicates the better performance in certain area and brings recognition and pleasure. Intensity of the interest varies from one to another and type of interesι also varies from one to another. In teaching learning process, it is need to understand the concept of interest and strategies are to be adopted to make teaching learning process interesting in order to yield better result.

MEANING OF INTEREST

Interest means arousal of curiosity to pay attention to something objective. It is sense of attraction or attachment to a particular object or activity. Study of interest has a special interest in teaching learning process.

Crow and Crow define Interest as the motivating force that implies us to attend to a person, a thing, or an activity or it may be an effective experience that has been stimulated by the activity itself. In other word interest can be the cause of an activity and result of participation in the activity.

J.S. Ross defined interest as a thing that interests us is just something that concerns us or matters to us.

McDougall said that, interest is a latent attention; attention is interest in action.

Drever said that, interest is an active form of some tendency.

Thus out of the discussion of the above definitions, it may be understood that interest is closely associated with attention. In fact, an individual performs most of his activities because he/she is found interested in them. When someone is found to avoid something to do that means he/she is not interested to do something.

TYPES OF INTEREST

Fields of interests are many. But in broad sense interest can be classified into two main types such as Inborn Interest and Derived Interests.

1. Inborn Interests

It is something innate and inborn tendencies found in the individuals. It is equivalent to inborn instincts. The tendency to play, eat, liking own kids, sleep, laugh and sex etc are called as inborn interests.

2. Derived interests

It is something got through experience or feelings. As a result this type of interests, individual acquires skills to perform certain activity. For example, skillful artist can immediately notice what is wrong with the art.

RELATION AND SYNTHESIS BETWEEN ATTENTION AND INTEREST

Attention and interest can't be separated from one to another. Both go hand in hand. When someone becomes interested in certain activity he/she pays his/her attention towards that activity. And when someone pays attention towards certain stimulus then he/she is found interested in that stimulus. So, it is very difficult to differentiate attention from interest and interest from attention. According to Ross, attention and interest are just two faces of a same coin. MacDougal also held the view that, interest is a latent attention and attention is interest in action. Both attention and interest lead to achieve the goal in objective manner. The learners who are interest to learn and pay more attention towards their learning, their quantum of learning become more and qualitative also. Therefore it is need to hold both for good result. Teacher should make their students interested and attentive by applying divergent techniques so that students can have better result in their learning.

SYNTHESIS BETWEEN INTEREST AND LEARNING

Leaning without interest of the learner becomes null and less effective. Learning with interest of the learners yields good and effective result. So interest is a core subject in the learning process. If the students keep interest, they pay their attention towards certain task and learn better. So learning and interest both are closely related with each other.

TECHNIQUES OF AROUSING INTEREST IN THE LEARNERS

Teachers can apply the following techniques to arouse interest in the learners,

- Introducing the relevant topic/subject to the learners.
- Adopting good methods of teaching.
- Creating peaceful and suitable class room atmosphere.
- Behaving gentle manner.
- Keeping the knowledge of individual difference in the mind.
- Presenting curriculum systematic and scientific way.
- Adopting stimulation variation techniques.
- Associating teaching with realities of life.
- Presenting teaching with examples, teaching aids and illustrations.
- Making teaching environment meaningful.

24
Emotion and Developmenmt

One's emotion plays a vital role in his life and affects his day to day affairs. Positive emotions help to develop a balanced personality and achieve desired goals but the negative emotions cause imbalanced personality and threaten the goals to be achieved. Thus emotions of an individual guides, controls, regulate and direct the behaviour of an individual. It is a biological trait found in all individuals distributed in the manner of degree but is influenced/educated/ trained by the environment. It therefore required having discussion about the emotions, their role in development of individual.

MEANING AND DEFINITIONS OF EMOTION

Emotion, a word derived from the Latin word 'emover' which means to stir up, or to excite. So, emotion is known as the excited state of the body and mind.

Crow and Crow defined emotion that, it is an affective experience that accompanies generalized linear adjustment and mental and psychological stirred-up states in the individual and that shows itself in his overt behaviour.

MacDougall defined that, Emotion is an affective experience that one undergoes during an instinctive excitement. For example, when a child perceives/knows a bull coming towards him, he experience an affective experience in the form of arousal accompanied emotion fear and consequently tries to run away.

To sum up the meaning of the term emotion, it is understood as a mental state in which a person becomes excited intensely. Emotions are related to the affective domain of the mind. Individuals who are seen to be emotional, they feel restlessness in their mind.

Sometimes we equally mean emotion and feelings. But both are different in their meaning. Both are mental conditions having both positive and negative valence. Both emotion and feelings relate to the affective aspect of the mind. But feelings are the common affective state of mind where as emotions are the complex mental conditions. Feelings either pleasant or un-pleasant are contained in emotions but emotions not necessarily contain feelings. Emotion is more intense than feelings.

DIFFERENCE BETWEEN INSTINCTS AND EMOTIONS

While instincts are biological dispositions that stimulate the individual to act, emotions are called as biological expression of actions manifested in the form of overt behaviour. Instincts are an innate and internal force that want to be fulfilled and thus engages the individual into some actions. Emotions are the biological traits reflected externally when they are expressed in some actions.

The most common form of basic instincts is hungry, sleep, sex etc. Instincts are sometimes synonyms with motives, needs, anxiety, desires etc. The common form of emotions is like fear, anger, shy, and phobias etc.

McDougall discovered 14 basic instincts with pair of associated emotions as described below.

Sl. No.	*Instincts*	*Associated Emotions*
1.	Flight/escape	Fear
2.	Pugnacity/combat	Anger
3.	Repulsion	Disgust
4.	Curiosity	Wonder
5.	Parental	Love
6.	Appeal	Distress
7.	Construction	Feeling of creativeness
8.	Acquisition	Feeling of ownership
9.	Gregariousness	Feeling of loneliness
10.	Sex/mating	Lust
11.	Self-assertion	Positive self-feeling/elation
12.	Submission	Negative self-feeling
13.	Food seeking/hunger	Appetite
14.	Laughter	Amusement

KINDS OF EMOTIONS

Emotions are of two types,

1. Positive Emotions: (All pleasant emotions like love, amusement, curiosity, happiness, affection which are helpful for normal development are positive emotions)

2. Negative Emotions: (All unpleasant emotions like fear, anger, jealousy which are not helpful for normal development are negative emotions)

EMOTIONS GENERALLY DISPLAYED

Following important emotions are generally displayed.

- *Anger:* Anger is a type of emotion which is resulted when an individual fails to achieve his objective to which he desires or it is threatened. When some external means puts barrier before the individual to act purposefully at that time his emotion in the form of anger comes out to the surface. It is a negative form of the emotion.
- *Fear:* Fear is a kind of negative emotion. It is resulted when certain incidence appears before the individual that threatens his peace and oriented with expectations of some loss to his life. Because of fear, individuals are seen to move back of some action. Sufficient control over the environment can eradicate fear.
- *Worry:* Worry is a mental condition resulted when an individual fails to decide what to do or what not to do because of the presence of many kinds of feelings.

- *Grief/Sadness:* Grief/Sadness is a mental state resulted when there is failure in succeed and feeling of helplessness. Fear, dejections and anxiety are blended together in grief.
- *Love:* Love is a positive emotion and positive state of mind resulted when there is no obstruction in the attainment of objective and gives mental peace to an individual without any threatening conditions.

NATURE OF EMOTIONS

The followings are the nature of emotions:

- Emotional experience are associated with some instincts/drives: (Drive tend to create emotions).
- Emotions are the product of perception: (Perceiving a stressful situation emotional expressions resulted).
- Core of emotional experiences are feelings: Feelings/drives remain core in all of the emotional expressions).
- Emotions breeds physiological changes: (When emotional expression resulted, physiological appearance, shape and actions become changed).
- It is seen in all: (Emotions are universal and seen in all).
- It is individualistic: (Individuals differ in their emotionality from one to another).
- Single emotion can breed similar and other emotions: (One emotion give rise to another similar emotion).
- There is negative correlation between intelligence and emotions: (Intellectuals can control the sudden upsurge of emotions).
- Emotions have the quality of displacement: (Emotion like anger aroused on account of one stimulus gets transferred to another situation).

REFLECTIONS OF EMOTION ON BODY AND BODILY CHANGES

Whenever emotional expressions come into surface, at that time following types of physiological or bodily change are reflected:

- One's heart beat increases.
- Blood circulation system is affected in case of anger, excitement but in situations of fear and shock it may reduce.
- Rate of respiration or breathing increases in case of anger and it reduces in case of fear and even it becomes nil.
- One's digestive system is also affected.
- Chemical composition of the body changes.
- Normal body temperature increases.
- Changes seen in the skin.
- Muscles of the body either become harder in case of anger or looser in case of fear.
- Functioning of the brain also affected.
- Ductless glandular secretion become over active resulting tears, sweets and saliva secretion in the individual which can be externally seen.
- Changes in facial appearance seen.
- Changes in body postures seen.
- Changes seen in the voice pattern/vocal pattern.

EMOTIONS AND EMOTIONAL MATURITY

Emotions are associated with drives/instincts of the individual. When the individual faces some strain or stressful situation at that moment, one's emotions become active. Sometimes emotions may take positive shape like love, affection and sometimes it takes the negative shape like anger, fear etc. But one's learning and maturation play an effective role in the development of his emotions. Children learn different positive and negative emotions from the environment as it is an acquired trait. Excepting some general emotions like crying and smiling, a child at the initial stage does not have the development of any specific emotions. But gradually some specific emotions grow in the individual taking the shape of positive and negative emotions. During adolescence period, emotional development is seen to be more pronounced in the young adults as at this stage, their drives become full of challenges. Necessary training and education help in developing good emotions and help in developing a stable emotions. Those who become mature, they can control their emotional expressions and vice versa. Those who attain emotional maturity, they can demonstrate a well-balanced emotional behaviour in their day-to-day life.

THEORIES OF EMOTIONS

The following theories can explain the meaning and characteristics of emotions.

James-Lange Theory

William James, the first psychologist attempted to explain the emotions. Later on, the Psychologist, Carl Lange explained the same thing about the emotions like James. Therefore this theory becomes known as James-Lange theory of emotion. Their theory explains that, emotions develop from the physiological reactions. When someone perceive certain strange stimulus that may cause harm or suit to the body of the individual at that moment, his physiological changes are seen and these changes are called his emotions.

Cannon-Bard Theory

Cannon-Bard theory of emotion proposed that, the lower brain centers specifically the thalamus and hypothalamus which are responsible for inciting emotional reactions. At the moment the individual perceives a stimulus; his sensory impulses reach the thalamic-hypothalamic regions. From there, they are carried simultaneously to the internal organs of the body and the cerebral cortex. The cerebral cortex receives and experience emotion at the same time when physical changes become evident in the body. Cannon-Bard theory holds the view that, emotion and physiological responses occur simultaneously. For example, when we perceive a bear, we become afraid and start to run away.

Schachter-Singer Theory

Schachter and Singer (1970) American Psychologists adopted an eclectic approach to both the earlier theories of emotion and developed their cognitive theory of emotions. They proposed that, both of our cognition (Perception and judgment of situation) and physiology jointly result emotions. They held the view that our emotional expressions are resulted by the interaction of the mental interpretation of the situation and physical changes. Both the cognition and physiology go hand in hand for determining emotions.

Activation Theory

Activation theory of emotion was given by Donald B. Lindsley on 1951. This theory refers that, emotion represent a state of heightened arousal rather than a qualitatively unique type of psychological, physiological or behavioural process. According to Lindsley, emotion provoking stimuli activate the recticular activating system in the brain stem, which in turn sends impulses both upward, towards the cortex and downward, towards the muscular. To produce a specific emotional behaviour the recticular system must be properly activated.

25
Emotional Intelligence

Like intelligence, one's emotional intelligence is a product of his heredity and interaction of environmental forces. The term Emotional intelligence was initially introduced in 1990 by two American University Professors, Dr. John Mayer and Dr. Peter Salovery out of their study attempting to develop a scientific measure of knowing the difference in the people's ability in the areas of emotions. But credit goes to American Psychologist Daniel Goleman (1995) who popularized the term Emotional Intelligence. Like emotions, one's emotional intelligence significantly influences his growth and development process. Sound emotional intelligence provides conditions for good development. Therefore it is need to know about Emotional Intelligence and its role in the process of development.

MEANING OF EMOTIONAL INTELLIGENCE

Emotional Intelligence is defined as the capacity to reason with emotion in four areas: to perceive emotion, to integrate it in thought, to understand it and to manage it. Emotional intelligence (EI) is the ability to recognize one's own and other people's emotions, to discriminate between different feelings and label them appropriately, and to use emotional information to guide thinking and behaviour. Emotional intelligence (EQ) is the ability to identify, use, understand, and manage emotions in positive ways to relieve stress, communicate effectively, empathize with others, overcome challenges, and defuse conflict. Emotional intelligence impacts many different aspects of daily life, such as the way behaving and the way of interacting with others. If someone possesses high emotional intelligence, he/she is able to recognize his/her own emotional state and the emotional states of others.

ATTRIBUTES OF EMOTIONAL INTELLIGENCE

Emotional intelligence consists of four attributes like,

1. *Self-Awareness*—One should recognize his/her own emotions and how they affect his/her thoughts and behaviour. One should know one's strengths and weaknesses, and have self-confidence.
2. *Self-Management*—One should able to control his/her impulsive feelings and behaviours, manage his/her emotions in healthy ways, take initiative, follow through on commitments, and adapt to changing circumstances.
3. *Social Awareness*—One should understand the emotions, needs, and concerns of other people, pick up on emotional cues, feel comfortable socially, and recognize the power dynamics in a group or organization.
4. *Relationship Management*—One should know how to develop and maintain

good relationships, communicate clearly, inspire and influence others, work well in a team, and manage conflict.

Mayer and Salovey formulated a revised model of emotional intelligence (1997), which gave more emphasis to cognitive components of EQ, and conceptualized EQ as it related to intellectual and emotional growth. This processing model contained four branches:

1. *Perceiving Emotions:* The ability to perceive emotions in oneself and others as well as in objects, art, stories, music, and other stimuli
2. *Facilitating Thought:* The ability to generate, use, and feel emotion as necessary to communicate feelings or employ them in other cognitive processes
3. *Understanding Emotions:* The ability to understand emotional information, to understand how emotions combine and progress through relationship transitions, and to appreciate such emotional meanings
4. *Managing Emotions:* The ability to be open to feelings, and to modulate them in oneself and others so as to promote personal understanding and growth

COMPONENTS OF EMOTIONAL INTELLIGENCE (EI)

Following four components of emotional intelligence are important

- Knowing Self emotion
- Managing Self-emotion
- Knowing Other's emotion and
- Managing Other's emotion

Components of emotional intelligence shown in EI Model—

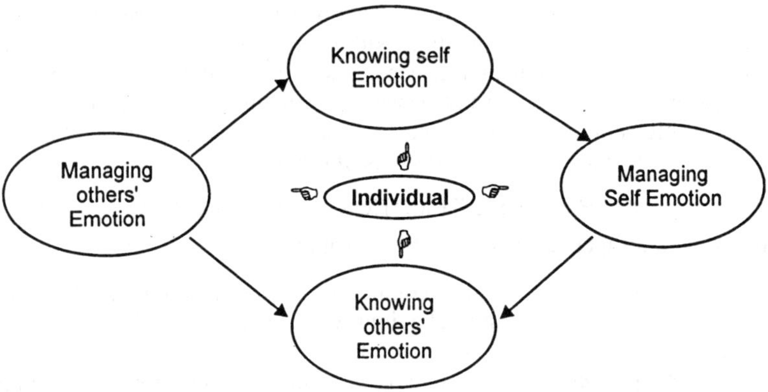

IMPACT/IMPLICATION OF EMOTIONAL INTELLIGENCE

Impact of Emotional Intelligence is felt on the following areas—

Impact on Performance at Work: Emotional intelligence can help someone navigate the social complexities of the workplace, lead and motivate others, and excel in his/her career. Many companies now view emotional intelligence as an important technical ability and require EQ testing before hiring employees.

Impact on physical health. Unable to manage stress levels can lead to serious health problems. Uncontrolled stress can raise blood pressure, suppress the immune system, increase the risk of heart attack and stroke, contribute to infertility, and speed up the aging process. The first step to improving emotional intelligence is to learn how to relieve stress.

Impact on mental health. Uncontrolled stress can also impact on mental health making vulnerable to anxiety and depression. If some one is unable to understand and manage his/her emotions, he/she will also be open to mood swings, while an inability to form strong relationships can leave you feeling lonely and isolated.

Impact on relationships. By understanding emotions and how to control them, some one better able to express how he/she will feels and understands and how others are feeling. This allows some one to communicate more effectively and forge stronger relationships, both at work and in your personal life.

STRATEGIES FOR DEVELOPING EMOTIONAL INTELLIGENCE

Emotional intelligence (EQ) is built by reducing stress, remaining focused, and staying connected to one's self and others. This can be done by learning some key skills as noted below.

- Quickly reduce stress.
- Recognize emotions and keep them.
- Connect emotionally with others.
- Use humor and play to stay connected in challenging situations
- Resolve conflicts positively and with confidence

MEASUREMENT OF EMOTIONAL INTELLIGENCE

Emotional Intelligence is measured in terms of Emotional Quotient (EQ) just like measurement of Intelligence in terms of IQ. EQ has now wide educational and social implications for the welfare of the individual and the society. Daniel Goleman stressed that, one's success necessarily not only depend on his intelligence but it is dependent on his emotional intelligence. One's emotional intelligence can be the predictor for his success and failure. Emotionally intelligent people achieve more success in their life than others.

The ideas propagated by Daniel Goleman in respect of presenting the concept of EI has brought a revolution in the fields like child care, home, school and work place management. It has also implications in the areas of guidance and counseling programmes.

In order to Measure intelligence, we use intelligence test. Like that, to measure emotional intelligence, it is need to use emotional intelligence tests or scale. No sufficient tests are available to test emotional intelligence. Some of the tests available to test emotional intelligence are like,

1. Mayer Emotional Intelligence Scale (MEIS)
2. Mayer, Salovey and Caruso emotional Intelligence test (MSCEIT)
3. Bar-On Emotional Quotient Inventory (EQ-i)

RELATIONSHIP BETWEEN INTELLIGENCE AND EMOTIONAL INTELLIGENCE

Intelligence is an ability which is innate and environmentally influenced. So also one's Emotional intelligence is innate ability and environmentally influenced. Both intelligence and Emotional intelligence can be improved by successful learning and in better environment. While intelligence helps in solving problems, adjustment, achieve goals, emotional intelligence helps in understanding one's emotion and other and thus helps in adjustment and manages his work.

One's intelligence and Emotional intelligence go hand in hand. It is seen that those who are intelligent they are able to understand them and others quickly. But in some cases, it seen that those who are intellectual, they fail to have proper social relations, interactions with others. Therefore it can be said that, intelligence is totally a cognitive process but emotional intelligence is both a cognitive, biological and social process. Emotional intelligence operates at biological, mental and social aspects of the individual. Therefore it can be said that one, who is more emotional intelligence he can be found more intelligent. But more intelligent persons may not be more emotionally intelligent one.

26
Motivation and Learning

Every action being done by the individual is purpose oriented. This purpose motivates him to act. If someone properly motivated and initiates his action then his action gets desirable result otherwise he fails to get the desirable result. Learning of children is highly correlated with their motivation. If children are properly motivated then their amount of learning become more and vice versa. Therefore it is need to understand the meaning of motivation and its related contents described as follows in this chapter.

MEANING OF MOTIVATION

The term motive is derived from the Latin word 'movere' means to move, to set in motion or to prompt to action. A motive stimulates a man to behave or act in certain way. Motivation represents the causes for an individual's actions, desires, and needs. A motive is what prompts a person to act in a certain way or at least develop an inclination for specific behaviour. For example, when someone eats food to satisfy the need of hunger, or when a student does his/her work in school because he/she wants a good grade. Motivation can also be defined as one's direction to behaviour or what causes a person to want to repeat a behaviour and vice versa. Motivation is the process that initiates, guides, and maintains goal-oriented behaviours. Motivation is what causes us to act, whether it is getting a glass of water to reduce thirst or reading a book to gain knowledge. It involves the biological, emotional, social, and cognitive forces that activate behaviour. In everyday usage, the term *motivation* is frequently used to describe why a person does something?

Motivation is a power that energizes, regulates and controls the activities of an individual. Motivation is the psychological stimulus that directs people to act in a certain way to achieve their goals.

TYPES OF MOTIVATION

Motivation is of following two types,

Intrinsic Motivation

Intrinsic motivation is the self-desire aroused in the subject itself. It is spontaneous and automatic interest expressed by an individual in certain task. It is driven by an interest or enjoyment in the task itself, and exists within the individual rather than relying on external pressures or a desire for reward. Intrinsic motivation is a natural motivational tendency and is a vital element in case of some one's cognitive, social, and physical development. Students who are intrinsically motivated are more likely to engage in the task willingly as well as work to improve their skills, which will increase their capabilities. Long lasting and long sustaining intrinsic motivation in the students' gives better result to them.

Extrinsic Motivation

Extrinsic motivation is the opposite of intrinsic motivation. Extrinsic motivation comes from influences outside of the individual. Usually extrinsic motivation is used to attain outcomes that a person wouldn't get from intrinsic motivation. Common extrinsic motivations are rewards (for example money or grades) for showing the desired behaviour, and the threat of punishment following misbehaviour. Competition is an extrinsic motivator because it encourages the performer to win and to beat others, not simply to enjoy the intrinsic rewards of the activity. A cheering crowd and the desire to win a trophy are also extrinsic incentives.

THEORIES OF MOTIVATION

The following theories may be referred to have understanding about the meaning and characteristics of motivation.

Instinct Theory of Motivation

One of the pioneers of instinct theories of Motivation is the English-born social psychologist, William McDougall, who formed the **Hormic Psychology**. 'hormic' means animal impulse or urge. The Instinct Theory of Motivation views biological or genetic programming as the cause of motivation. This theory tells that, all organisms are born with innate biological tendencies that help them survive. This theory suggests that all behaviours are driven by instincts. Instincts are goal-directed and innate patterns of behaviour that are not the result of learning or experience. According to instinct theories, people are motivated to behave in certain ways because they are evolutionarily programmed to do so. An example of this in the animal world is seasonal migration. These animals do not learn to do this; it is instead an inborn pattern of behaviour.

Psychologist William McDougall was one of the first to write about the instinct theory of motivation. He suggested that instinctive behaviour was composed of three key elements: perception, behaviour, and emotion. He also outlined 14 different instincts which are discussed in chapter no.16.

Psychiatrist Sigmund Freud used a broad view of motivation and suggested the human behaviour was driven by two key forces/instincts such as Eros and Thanatoes. Eros is the life instincts that help the individual to survive and Thanatoes is the Death instincts that threaten the survival of life. One's life is influenced by these two forces.

Psychologist William James, on the other hand, identified a number of instincts that he believed are essential for survival. These included such things as fear, anger, love, shame, and cleanliness.

Drive Theory of Motivation

According to the drive theory of motivation, people are motivated to take certain actions in order to reduce the internal tension that is caused by unmet needs. For example, you might be motivated to drink a glass of water in order to reduce the internal state of thirst. This theory is useful in explaining behaviours that have a strong biological component, such as hunger or thirst. The problem with the drive theory of motivation is that these behaviours are not always motivated purely by physiological needs. For example, people often eat even when they are not really hungry.

Arousal Theory of Motivation

The arousal theory of motivation suggests that people perform certain actions to either decrease or increase the levels of arousal. When the arousal levels get too low, at that moment a person prefer to watch an exciting movie. When the arousal levels get too high, on the other hand, a person would probably search for ways to relax by reading a book. According to this theory, individuals are motivated to maintain an optimal level of arousal, although this level can vary individually or the situational.

Humanistic Theory of Motivation given by Maslow

Humanistic theories of motivation are based on the idea that people also have strong cognitive reasons to perform various actions. This is famously illustrated in Abraham Maslow's hierarchy of needs, which presents different motivations at different levels. First, people are motivated to fulfill basic biological needs for food and shelter, as well as those of safety, love, and esteem. Once the lower level needs have been met, the primary motivator becomes the need for self-actualization, or the desire to fulfill one's individual potential.

According to humanist psychologist Abraham Maslow, our actions are motivated in order to achieve certain needs. Maslow first introduced his concept of a hierarchy of needs in his 1943 paper "A Theory of Human Motivation" and his subsequent book *Motivation and Personality*. This hierarchy suggests that people are motivated to fulfill basic needs before moving on to other and more advanced needs.

This hierarchy is most often displayed as a pyramid. The lowest levels of the pyramid are made up of the most basic needs, while the more complex needs are located at the top of the pyramid. Needs at the bottom of the pyramid are basic physical requirements including the need for food, water, sleep, warmth and sex. Once these lower-level needs have been met, people can move on to the next level of needs, which are for safety and security. As people progress up the pyramid, needs become increasingly psychological and social. Soon, the need for love, friendship, and intimacy become important. Further up the pyramid, the need for personal esteem and feelings of accomplishment take priority. After this people start to seek development of their potentialities, building confidence, becoming free from prejudices, independent to solve their problem, fulfill own interest and accept the facts which is a complex type of need called as Self-actualization.

Like Carl Rogers, Maslow also emphasized the importance of self-actualization, which is a process of growing and developing as a person in order to achieve individual potential.

Maslow's Hierarchy of Needs

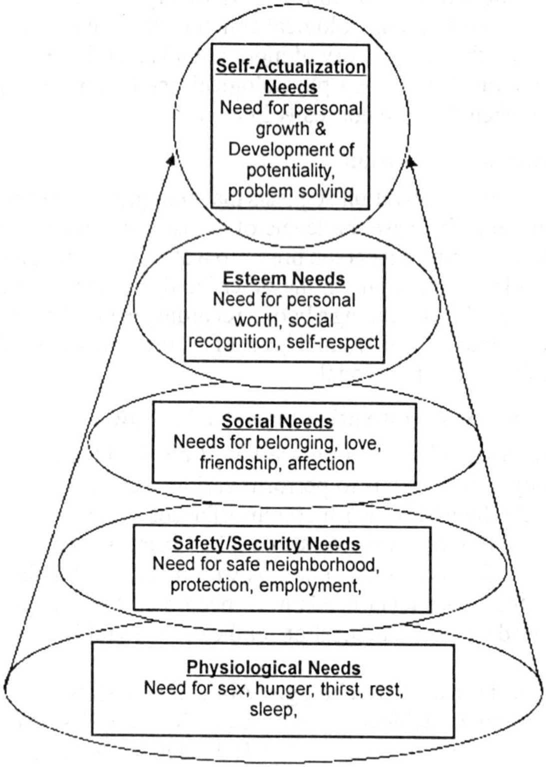

(Needs Arranged from Basic to More Complex Needs at the Top in a Pyramid Structure)

Types of Needs

Maslow believed that these needs are similar to instincts and play a major role in motivating behaviour. Physiological, security, social, and esteem needs are recognized as deficiency needs symbolized as *D-needs*, meaning that these needs arise due to deprivation. Satisfying these lower-level needs is important in order to avoid unpleasant feelings or consequences. Maslow termed the highest-level of the pyramid as growth needs recognized as being needs and it is symbolized as *B-needs*. Growth needs do not stem from a lack of something, but rather from a desire to grow as a person.

Physiological Needs: These include the most basic needs that are vital to survival, such as the need for water, air, food, Sex and sleep. Maslow believed that these needs are the most basic and instinctive needs in the hierarchy because all needs become secondary until these physiological needs are met. We need food and water to survive. We also need to breath and maintain a stable body temperature. In addition to eating, drinking, and having adequate shelter and clothing, Maslow also suggested that sexual reproduction was a basic physiological need.

Security Needs: These include the needs for safety and security. Security needs are important for survival, but they are not as demanding as the physiological needs. Examples of security needs include a desire for steady employment, health care, safe neighborhoods, and shelter from the environment. The needs become a bit more complex at this point in the hierarchy. Now that the more basic survival needs have been fulfilled, people begin to feel that they need more control and order to their lives. A safe place to live, financial security, physical safety, and staying healthy are all concerns that might come into play at this stage.

Social Needs: These include needs for belonging, love, and affection. Maslow described these needs as less basic than physiological and security needs. Relationships such as friendships, romantic attachments, and families help fulfill this need for companionship and acceptance, as doe's involvement in social, community, or religious groups.

Self Esteem Needs: After the first three needs have been satisfied, esteem needs becomes increasingly important. These include the need for things that reflect on self-esteem, personal worth, social recognition, and accomplishment.

At this point, it becomes increasingly important to gain the respect and appreciation of others. People have a need to accomplish things and then have their efforts recognized. People often engage in activities such as going to school, playing a sport, enjoying a hobby, or participating in professional activities in order to fulfill this need. Satisfying this need and gaining acceptance and esteem helps people become more confident. Failing to gain recognition for accomplishments, however, can lead to feelings of failure or inferiority.

Self-actualizing Needs: This is the highest level of Maslow's hierarchy of needs. People are self-aware, concerned with personal growth, less concerned with the opinions of others, and interested fulfilling their potential and problem solving.

Weinner's Attribution theory of Motivation

Weiner's attribution theory of motivation describes the way in which we strive to maintain our positive self-image. The basic principle of attribution theory states that a person's attributions for success or failure determine the amount of effort the individual will spend on his/her task. According to attribution theory, people tend to explain success or failure in terms of three types of characteristics such as locus of control, stability, and control.

MacCelland's Theory of Motivation

American, David Clarence McClelland (1917-98) is chiefly known for his work on achievement motivation. David McClelland pioneered work-place motivational thinking, developing achievement-based motivational theory and models, and promoted improvements in employee assessment methods, advocating competency-based assessments and tests, arguing them to be better than traditional IQ and personality-based tests.

Types of Motivational Needs

David McClelland is most noted for describing three types of motivational need, which he identified in his 1961 book "The Achieving Society"

Achievement motivation: Achievement drive motivates/induces a person to seek achievement, attainment of realistic but challenging goals and advancement in the job. There is need of feedback to have achievement and progress.

Authority/Power motivation: Authority or power drive motivates/induces a person to seek power and become influential, effective and to make an impact. It tends to increase one's personal prestige and status.

Affiliation motivation: Affiliation drive motivates/induces a person to maintain friendly relationship and a need to interact with other people. It urges to be liked by others and getting regards from others. People having affiliation motivation are found team players.

MacCelland held the view that, most people possess and exhibit a combination of these characteristics. But some people exhibit a strong bias to a particular motivational need. This mix of motivational needs consequently affect the behaviour and working style of persons.

FACTORS AFFECTING MOTIVATION

The following factors are held responsible for affecting motivation:

Self-efficacy and competence perceptions: Self-efficacy of the individual affects the motivation of the individual. Self-efficacy refers to individual's beliefs about his ability to successfully accomplish tasks he is given, and related to individuals' successful engagement and persistence in tasks.

Attributions and control beliefs: It refers to one's beliefs about the causes of his success and failure, and perceived control behaviour need to affect outcomes. Students must believe that their efforts will lead to success. This assurance enables them to manage their activities and emotions. Students who believe they are in control of their own learning and behaviours are more likely to do well and perform at high levels than students who do not feel in control.

Interest Level: High levels of both personal and situational interest are associated with more cognitive engagement, more learning, and higher levels of achievement.

Classroom Climate: Objective qualities of a classroom environment put its impact on motivation. A stronger links have been found between achievement and students' perceptions of classrooms than between achievement and objectively defined classroom qualities. Thus, it appears that teachers can influence learning processes and outcomes by structuring learning environments. They must however attend to how students perceive those environments to achieve the intended effects.

Home Climate: Home climate affect pupils' motivation in the classroom. If children come from homes where they are loved and encouraged, they will approach classroom work with eagerness and show willingness to learn. If the pupils do not have a positive home environment, they attend school with a disadvantage and a lack of motivation because of physical or emotional problems.

Teaching Style: Teaching style exercise its impact on motivation and learning. Learning can be more enjoyable and interesting to a larger degree when the pupils become part of the learning process. Students can be motivated more in their learning when teachers help them and connect to their current learning. A teacher teaching through varied styles/approaches appealing the interest of the learners and using different techniques and technologies can motivate his students more.

Interactive Actions: Interactive actions can be more motivating factors for the learners. It provides for participatory learning in the class room. Students feel free and active and take interest in the task. Teachers can organize group discussion, sports, games, seminars, workshops outside the routine tasks for the students which provide platforms for effective interaction.

Work Values: Work value also affects the level of motivation of the learners. It refers to students' perception about the utility, or how interesting and important a work/task is, that to be pursued. Students must understand how important it is to do well on the task. Parents and teachers need to provide support to the pupils' understanding of task value. Higher task value increases sense of responsibility and overall interest in the task and in turn it yield good result.

Goals: Setting goals is a key point in the motivation and learning. Encouraging students to set goals in the classroom can also provide motivation. Clearly defined goals possess more motivational force.

Locus of Control: Control can be defined as the power to determine outcomes by directly influencing actions, people and events. The word 'control' becomes even more fascinating coming close with the word locus, before it. Locus is defined as a position, point or place, or more specifically, a location where something occurs. A person's locus of control may be internal or external. Locus of control of an individual is seen to be affecting the motivation.

Locus of control may be of two types. People who attribute their success or failure on their own work and believe they control their life have an internal locus of control. Internal locus of control is guided by one's own interest, personal decision and efforts.

In contrast, people who attribute their success or failure to outside influences have an external locus of control. External locus of control is guided by extraneous factors like fate, luck, other people and other external forces.

TECHNIQUES OF MOTIVATION

Now a days, a multiple and extraneous factors have been responsible to distract the attention of the learners from their task which result in poor learning and achievement. A little percentage of students is found to have their intrinsic motivation in their learning. In the age of competition both inside the class room and outside the class room, it has become inevitable to make our learners motivated in their learning and to succeed more. A teacher has a great role to adopt different types of techniques to motivate his students in their learning. Some of the techniques are discussed below.

Presenting well defined learning objectives: It is known that every action is objective based. So learning being a great action has its own objectives. A teacher should clearly define the learning objectives before his learners so that the learners may be motivated properly.

Presenting curriculum in well organized and systematic way: Learning is facilitated with curriculum. Children find interest in learning with simple and easy curriculum and become disinterested in difficulty curriculum. Therefore a teacher will have to organize and present the curriculum in a systematic and well organized manner in order to make his learners motivated more in their learning.

Teaching with appropriate methods up to the standard of the children: Method of teaching helps in clarifying doubts and making the meaning understandable to the learners. Therefore a teacher should adopt and apply those interesting and suitable methods of teaching keeping in view of the standard of his students in respect of their intelligence, age, interest and need so that the students will be motivated more in their learning.

Teaching supplemented with adequate teaching aids: Teaching dominated by the oral and theoretical concepts kills the interest of the learners and results poor motivation in their learning. Therefore a teacher should use different types of suitable and relevant teaching aids while teaching to his students so that it will result more motivation for their learning. It will appeal to the visual sense of the learner and yield better learning facilitating their retention power.

Arranging re-creational facilities for the children during learning: Compelling students to have over learning with zero recreational activities will result boring and distract their attention from their learning. It will lead to less motivation. Therefore a teacher should allow his students to enjoy some re-creational activities during the time of their learning when they feel boring and tired so that it will help his students to be more motivated in their learning.

Avoiding mastership rather behaving in friendship and counselling manner while teaching: A teacher should not act as a master like a dictator for his students only meant for directing and teaching neglecting the interest and need of the learners. He should act like a friend, Philosopher and guide meant for guiding, helping, counselling and meeting the needs and solving the problems of his students inside the class room. This will enhance the motivation level of his students in their learning.

Providing adequate feed back to the learners: Learners feel difficulties in their learning. It is the need for a teacher to provide adequate feed back to his learners to proceed ahead. Providing feedback in due time and in proper manner will motivate the learners to learn more.

Avoiding punishment rather providing reinforcement to the learners: A teacher should avoid practicing any form of punishment for his students. Mild punishment may result in improvement and rectification in the behaviour but rigidity of punishment and heavy punishment will yield negative result in learning and motivation. Therefore a teacher should try to avoid the practice of giving punishment rather he should provide suitable reinforcements to his students so that they will be more motivated in their learning.

Making Teaching More Interactive: Passive learning makes students disinterested and less motivated. Sometimes unidirectional teaching of the teacher source makes the class room lethargic, monotonous and dull. Interactive teaching strategy involving student's participation and bi-communication and bidirectional teaching will make the class room live and active. It will make the students more motivated in their learning.

MOTIVATION AND LEARNING

Both motivation and learning are closely and positively related. Higher will be the motivation, better will be the result of learning. Whether it is extrinsic or intrinsic motivation, it leads to yield good result in learning. If the students will be motivated properly, they can learn better and can have success in their learning. A teacher should adopt varieties of techniques to motivate his students to learn.

27
Memory and Forgetting

An individual learns many things and gain variety of experiences in his life. But not all of his gained experiences stored in his mind for his future use. Some are forgotten in due course of time and some are stored in the mind for longer period of time to which he recall and utilize in different situations. This function of mind in retaining knowledge and experiences for longer period of time for its future application is known as memory. Amount of learning depends on one's memory power. If memory is found strong then one's learning become better and vice versa. It is memory which helps an individual to solve his problems effectively and facilitates his transfer of learning. Learning and memory both are closely related to each other. Therefore, it is a need to study about memory, forgetting and mechanism of memory.

MEANING OF MEMORY

Memory is a mental process of remembering information and experiences and retrieval of the same at the time of need. It is capacity of an individual to recall the past events and experiences at the conscious mind.

According to *Ryburn* (1956), memory means the power that we have to 'store' our experiences, and to bring them into the field of our consciousness some time after the experiences have occurred.

According to *Woodworth*, memory consists in remembering what has previously been learned.

According to *Good: Dictionary of Education*, Memory means 'knowledge or awareness of something previously known or experienced, accompanied by consciousness that one had the previous knowledge or experience.

According to *James Drever*, Memory is that characteristic which underlies all learning, the essential feature of which is reflection, in a narrow sense it covers recall and recognition.

Thus, out of the analysis of above definitions, we can conclude that, memory means a process of recalling and recognizing the past experiences in the conscious mind. Reflection of knowledge comes from memory. The above definitions provide the insight that, human memory involves the following four factors.

Factors of Memory

Following four factors are associated with Memory

Learning

Learning helps to human beings in acquisition of information, knowledge and experiences. It helps to register and organize the acquired experiences in the memory of the individuals for their future applications in the form of principles, events, symbols, signs, formulas and figures.

Retention

Retention means preserving the learned materials in the brain through our nervous systems for a longer period of time. Retention power varies from one to another. Some are found having more retention power and some are having less. *Ebinghaus* (1885) held the view that the degree of retention undergoes a change with lapse of time. There is no absolute loss of retention or forgetting. Rapid forgetting occurs in the first few hours of learning. Out of his experiment he concluded that, one half of the learning materials are forgotten in the first half hour, two-third of the learning materials are forgotten in 8 to 12 hours, three-fourth of learning materials are forgotten in 6 days and four-fifth of learning materials are seen to be forgotten in a month. The forgetting curve doesn't touch the base line.

Recall

Recall is a method to measure the retention or memory. Recall means simple retrieval of learning experiences in the conscious mind out of the identical observation of situations. Recall is of two types such as spontaneous recall an deliberative recall. When recall is automatic without any deliberate effort, it is called as spontaneous recall. Automatic recall freely comes to memory. For example, we recall many things at the time of our rest, sleep or working. But in deliberate recall one has to employ his efforts to recall something. For example, one has to deliberately recall something to write at the time of examination.

However, good recall results if the following conditions exist.

- *Proper association of ideas:* If the ideas are properly associated with each other, recall becomes better.
- *Proper interest:* If there is proper interest is expressed to recall something, and then recall becomes better.
- *Frequency of ideas:* If the ideas come to memory frequently, then recall becomes more and better.
- *Recency of the ideas:* Recent or new ideas are better recalled.
- *Vividness of the ideas:* If the ideas are having clarity in meaning and puts clear impression on the mind, then recall becomes better.

Recognition

Recognition is another method of measuring memory or retention. Recognition means tracing out the previously learned experiences in their original form by the conscious mind of an individual to which he wants to recall earlier. For example, an examinee recalls and then recognizes the exact answer to express at the time of examination about certain question.

Types of Memory

Broadly, Memory can be classified into following types on the basis of storage and transfer model of remembering.

Immediate Memory

Immediate memory is also called as sensory memory. After perceiving recalling something immediately is called as immediate memory. In case of immediate memory, retention time is extremely short. Immediate memory operates when something new appears and needs to be remembered for a short time and then it is forgotten. For example, we remember a telephone number immediately for a while and then we forget it after making a call.

Short-Term Memory

Short-term memory is like immediate memory but time span is little bit more in case of retention. In short-term memory the volume of information is more in comparison to immediate memory. Chunking information is better stored in short term memory.

Long-Term Memory

Unlikely short term memory, long-term memory bears limitless capacity to store with a little decay. In long-term memory, information are coded in terms of meaning, pattern, and other characteristics. It is also called as permanent memory that helps to remember things on permanent basis. It is because of this long-term memory we perform our day to day life. The incidence of remembering one's date of birth, father's name or date of marriage are examples of this long-term memory. Referring these dates we can recall many things of our life.

Personal and Impersonal Memory

Personal memory means, some mental images are formed in the memory by the individual personally. It is his own experience he wants to put in his memory. For example, an individual remembers his teachership stage of his life. But Impersonal memory means experiences or mental images are gathered from books, newspapers or some other persons and stored in the individual's memory.

Active and Passive Memory

In active memory, a child has to deliberately recall the facts to write in the examination. But in passive memory, past experiences are recalled spontaneously without any effort.

Habit and True Memory

Habit memory means, mechanically one has to remember something. Cramming is an example of this type of habit memory that helps a child when his examination nears. True memory involves mental images of past events. True memory helps to develop one's knowledge and mental make-up.

Visual and Auditory Memory

It is called as senses are the gate way of knowledge. We form mental images about something through our sight and auditory systems. Visual impressions are quick and correct and build strong memory. Therefore it is said that seeing believes. Similarly, we hear many things by our ear and store them in our memory.

Rote and Logical Memory

Rote memory means making habit to memorize something. It is also called as cramming. When the examination nears, children use this practice of rote memory and memorize many facts without understanding them. Rote memory is temporary and unreliable. But Logical memory is permanent and reliable. Logical memory bears meaning of the facts, understanding and purposive.

Factors affecting Memory

Following factors affect the memory of the learners.

Organization of learning materials: If the learning materials are well organized and associated with each other then it helps to have more memory. Here one idea can help to recall another idea. Meaningful learning materials are retained more and for longer period of time in memory than the meaningless learning materials. For example, material presented in the form of stories is bettered remembered.

Objectives of learning materials: If the objective of learning is to pass the examination then mechanical or rote learning is resulted and after examination is over the learning materials are forgotten. If the objective of learning is to earn mastery on certain things then logical learning is resulted and it is retained in memory for longer time.

Motivation of the learner: Motivation of learners affects their memory. If learners are motivated more in their learning then their learning becomes more meaningful and it adds to their memory and vice versa.

Habit or Practice of the learner: Memory depends on the amount of practice or habit. If the habit of learning will be for understanding the meaning then it will promote the memory. If the habit or practice of learning will be for casual purposes and without understanding the meaning then it will temporarily retained in the memory.

Mental capacity of the learner: Learner's mental capacity affects their memory. Learners having higher Intelligence can retain more in their memory. Learners having low intelligence fail to understand the meaning and it results less retention power.

Time of learning: Time of learning is also a factor affecting memory of the learners. If the learners feel relaxed and fresh their retention becomes more and if the learners feel bored, drowsy, and tired then their retention becomes less. Therefore the difficulty subjects in the schools like English or Mathematics are kept in the time table to be taught to the learners in the morning session in the proposition that it will help to retain more in their memory.

FORGETTING

We learn many things but forget most of them and retain less in our memory. Examinees feel ashamed of being forgotten of their learned materials for which they fail in their examination. Therefore teachers and parents try to promote good memory in their children and to minimize the forgetting. Forgetting plays a significant role in resulting low amount of learning.

Defining the term forgetting Munn (1967) says, Forgetting is the loss, permanent or temporary, of the ability to recall or recognize something learned earlier.

Drever (1952) defines that, forgetting means failure at any time to recall an experience, when attempting to do so, or to perform an action previously learned.

Summarizing the definitions about forgetting given above, it can be said that forgetting is just the reverse of remembering. It is a condition that shows inability to recall or recognize the learned experiences at the moment of requirement.

Ebbinghause's Forgetting Curve

Out of his study on forgetting, Ebbinghaouse (1885) concluded that though the forgetting starts immediately after learning and it is rapid at the initial time. Forgetting goes on increasing trend with diminishing rate proportionate with the increasing time interval.

According to Ebbinghaouse, about 47 per cent of learned things are forgotten after 20 minutes of, 66 per cent are forgotten after one day, 72 per cent are forgotten after two days, 75 per cent are forgotten after six days and 79 per cent are forgotten after thirty days of learning. He depicted the forgetting curve in the following graphical manner.

Ebbinghaouse's Forgetting Curve

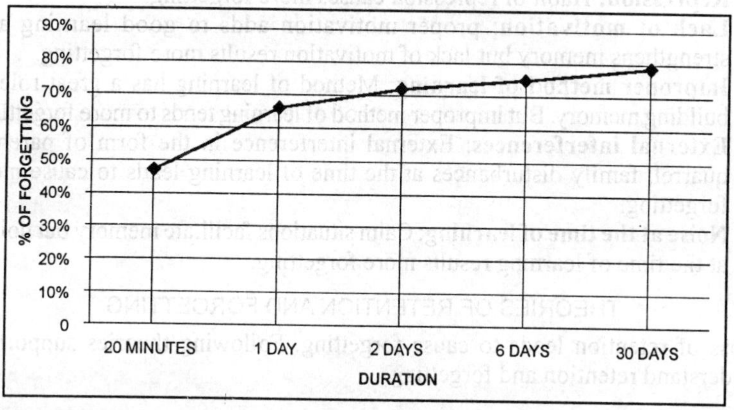

Kinds of Forgetting

Forgetting is of two kinds.

Passive forgetting: In this kind of forgetting, the individual doesn't intentionally forget something but the learned materials automatically forgotten after lapse of time. It is also called as natural forgetting.

Active forgetting: In this kind of forgetting, the individual deliberately want to forget something forcibly. The learning experiences which are painful and disturb the individual's peace, the individual try to forget them. This kind of forgetting is also called as morbid forgetting.

Factors Affecting Forgetting

Following factors affect the forgetting.

- *Nature of the learner:* If the learner is not motivated for his learning and he is forcibly made to learn, then his forgetting becomes more.
- *Nature of learning materials:* If the learning materials are not meaningful, objective oriented, purposive, organized properly, then forgetting become more.
- *Time of learning:* If the time of learning is not conducive for the learner, then amount of forgetting become more.
- *Methods of learning:* If the method of learning becomes appealing, interesting, sensory based and self-motivated then forgetting becomes less and retention become more and vice versa.

Causes of forgetting

Following causes are responsible for causing forgetting.

- **Less will to learn**: Willful learning helps cause good memory and will less learning causes more forgetting.
- **Lack of practice**: Practice strengthens memory and lack of practice weakens memory and strengthens forgetting.
- **Preference to new knowledge**: preference to learning of new knowledge in the place of old knowledge causes more forgetting.
- **Repression:** Habit of repression causes more forgetting.
- **Lack of motivation**: proper motivation adds to good learning and strengthens memory but lack of motivation results more forgetting.
- **Improper method of learning**: Method of learning has a great role in building memory. But improper method of learning tends to more forgetting.
- **External interferences**: External interference in the form of parental quarrel, family disturbances at the time of learning leads to cause more forgetting.
- **Noise at the time of learning**: Calm situations facilitate memory but noises at the time of learning results more forgetting.

THEORIES OF RETENTION AND FORGETTING

Loss of retention leads to cause forgetting. Following theories support to understand retention and forgetting.

Theory of Decay

This theory tells that loss of retention occurs with the passage of time. With the lapse of time there is gradual decrease of the degree of memory. The amount of memory tends to minimize with increasing time gap. The study conducted by Ebinghause on forgetting shows that the curve of retention tends to fall with increasing time interval with the conclusion that the speed and rate of retention decreases with more time interval.

Theory of Trace-change

Gestalt Psychologist Kuffka out of his study on perception gave this trace-change theory of memory. This theory tells that, when an individual learns through his perception, it creates a trace on his memory and it gradually becomes weak with the lapse of time. Therefore forgetting occurs with more time interval.

Theory of Motivation

Theory of motivation in memory was given by Freud. Freud stated that, pleasant learning materials have more retention power than the unpleasant learning material. Unpleasant learning materials are repressed and forgotten more. Individuals do not show interest in unpleasant learning material and they try to avoid them which cause their forgetting.

Theory of Interference

Theory of interference advocates that, forgetting results due to interfering memories. One experience is forgotten because another experience interferes or blocks it. This interference may be of two kinds such as Retroactive Inhibition and Proactive Inhibition. Retroaction means the learning of a particular task influence the learning of the similar task learned previously. If the learning of a new task negatively influences the retention of similar task learned previously it is called as retroactive inhibition. If the learning of new task positives influences the retention of similar task learned previously it is called as retroactive facilitation.

Proactive inhibition results when the subject learns a new task other than the previously decided task to be learned. Thus the learning of the new task interfere the memory of the learners in case of the learning of the previously decided learning materials to be learned. If the learning of the new task adds/helps to the retention of previously decided task to be learned then it is called as proactive facilitation. If the learning of the new task interferes the retention of the previously decided task to be learned then it is called as proactive inhibition.

MECHANISM TO BUILD GOOD MEMORY IN THE LEARNERS

A teacher can adopt the following mechanisms or strategies to promote and build goo memory power in their learners.

- Presenting the well organized learning materials.
- Presenting the meaningful learning materials
- Making the learners properly motivated and interested in their learning.
- Helping the learners to adopt proper method of memorization.
- Adopting good teaching aids to appeal the visual and auditory senses of the learners
- Providing calm and noise free learning environment.
- Making the learners emotionally attached to their learning.
- Allowing learners to take rest and change the work when they are seen bored and tired
- Providing recreational facilities to the learners in the schools.
- Making learners to have logical learning instead of rote learning.
- Making the learning objectives oriented.
- Making the learners active in learning and allowing them to participate in learning.

28
Transfer of Learning/Training

Learning is said to be a process and an act through which one acquire knowledge and experiences which in turn gives value to his life in respect of achieving goals of life. Though most of the learners show keen interest in new learning, their old knowledge and experiences have a great value for facilitating their new learning. When the past experiences help to learn some one's new learning experiences at that situation it is called as transfer of learning. For example learning of addition and subtraction helps the learners to learn about multiplication and division. Therefore it is a need to make our learners apt in their learning skill and enable them to apply their experience for their prospective functions. A teacher expects that information he imparts to his students in the class room, the students would use/apply them in other situations. Not only the learning of tricks or the knowledge acquired in a particular subject is transferred to other situation but the habits, interests and attitudes are also seen to be transferred and influence the new learning.

MEANING OF TRANSFER OF LEARNING

Dictionary of Education defines Transfer of learning that when an acquired activity is put to an actual practice in similar but distinctly different circumstances it becomes a case of transfer of training. In Education, transfer of training may also be called as transfer of learning.

Encyclopaedia of Education defines, when one practice a response to a specific stimulus situation, learning takes place. When a particular learning experience influence an individual's ability to respond effectively to stimuli different in some way from those he reacted to during learning, transfer of training is said to have taken place.

Crow and Crow define that, the carryover of habits of thinking, of working, of knowledge or skill from one learning area to another is usually referred to as the transfer of training.

Sorenson said that, Transfer refers to transfer of knowledge, training, and habits acquired in one situation to another situation.

Bigge said that, Transfer of learning occurs when a person's learning in one situation influences his learning and performances in other situations.

Gutherie and Powers defined that, transfer is a process of extending and applying behaviour.

Peterson defined that, transfer is generalization, for it is extension of ideas to a new fields.

Out of the study above definitions, it becomes clear that, transfer of learning means application of acquired knowledge to some other and similar situation. It is simply application of learning to new situation.

TYPES OF TRANSFER OF LEARNING/TRAINING

The following types of transfer of learning/training have been viewed by the psychologists,

Positive Transfer of Training: Positive transfer of training or learning occurs when the learning or training carried out in one situation proves helpful to the learner in another situation. For example, acquired mathematical knowledge of addition and subtraction become helpful in the learning of higher mathematical computations like multiplication and division.

Negative Transfer of Training: Negative transfer of training or learning occurs when the learning or training carried out in one situation proves not helpful, hinders and interferes to the learner in another situation. For example, acquired knowledge driving a Hero Honda motor cycle proves not helpful and hinders to drive the Bullet motor cycle.

Zero Transfer of Training: Zero transfer of training or learning occurs when the learning or training carried out in one situation does not have any influence on the learning of another situation. For example, acquired knowledge on playing volleyball does not have any influence in learning cricket. Similarly learning of mathematical knowledge neither become helpful nor hinders the learning of history.

Unilateral Transfer of Training: Unilateral transfer of training occurs when training of a particular limb of the body become beneficial to future performance. For example, acquired knowledge to write with the left hand become beneficial when the right hand is injured.

Bilateral Transfer of Training: Bilateral transfer of training occurs when training of a particular limb is transferred to the parallel part of the body on the other side. For example, training to write with the left hand is found to be transferred to training to write with the right hand without any extra or additional training.

Vertical Transfer of Training: Vertical transfer of training occurs when training received in lower class proves to be helpful in the higher classes. For example, acquired knowledge of simple mathematics at lower class become helpful in the learning of higher mathematical knowledge at upper classes. Similarly acquired experiences at childhood influence the individual in the performance of activities in adult life. This vertical transfer of training may be of negative and positive types.

Horizontal Transfer of Training: Horizontal transfer of training occurs when training acquired in one subject influences or helps the training of the other subject. For example, acquired knowledge on historical facts of the medieval age may also helpful to learn about the literary and cultural facts of the same medieval age.

Many experiments have been conducted by the psychologists to prove about transfer of training or learning and have given invaluable contributions in the field of transfer of training.

THEORIES OF TRANSFER OF TRAINING

Following theories may be followed for the understanding and explaining the meaning and nature of the transfer of learning.

Mental Discipline Theory

This is one of the oldest theory on transfer of training which assumes that, mind is composed of many faculties or disciplines like memory, attention, imagination, reasoning, thinking and judgment. These faculties are just like muscles of the mind like muscles of the body which can be strengthened or improved through practice and use. And these strengthened mental faculties later on become useful and applied in other situations in which they are involved. For example, some one's memory on grammatical principles strengthened by strong memorization become useful in its application at the moment of writing passages or prose that involve memory.

This mental discipline theory was firstly challenged by the Psychologist William James. Out of his experiment on strengthening of his memory on poetry of different authors, and he could conclude that, memory was not affected by training. Later on other Psychologists like Dr. Sleight and Briggs supported the view of James.

Apperception Theory

According to this theory, new ideas or mental states are associated to old and established ideas. By following this principle, an individual applies his apperceptions to new and similar situations to solve the problem. Apperception means the storage of old ideas and experiences. Successful application of this theory in the transfer of learning requires developing good memory power in the children. This theory gives importance to the study of books and role of teachers. It considers, books and teachers are the store house of knowledge to which one can refer to obtain new ideas about the solution of problem.

Identical Element Theory

Identical element theory of transfer of training states that, learning can be transferred from one situation to another if these two situations will have some identical or similar elements in common. This theory was supported by E.L. Thorndike and later on by Woodworth who gave the concept of identical components. The identity between two situations may be seen in the form of information, principles, procedures, and attitudes. This theory holds good in transferring learning from learning of mathematics to learning of physics where one can find identical elements in symbols, formulas and equations.

Generalization Theory

Theory of generalization has been forwarded by Charles Judd. This theory stresses on systematic organization of generalization of experiences to have maximum transfer of learning. Generalization is characteristic common to all situations. According to this theory, transfer can be facilitated by acquiring and learning general principles rather than learning specific principles. Judd out of his experiment conducted on dart throwing experimented on two groups called control group and experimental group on principle of refraction of light could arrive at the conclusion that, the experimental group taught about the principle of refraction of light performed better than the control group who was not taught about the same. Thus this theory implied that, generalization have positive effect on transfer of training. For acquiring generalization, human intelligence and understanding plays important role.

Transposition Theory

The theory of transposition was given by Gestalt psychologists. According to this theory, transfer of training depends on perceptual similarities between two situations. Transposition is a process of applying generalizations, principles, concepts acquired from one situation to another situation. Gestalists proposed the view that, insight developed in one situation become helpful to another similar situation to solve the problem. The process of transposition requires having consistent thinking, grouping, and structuralization and reorganization power in the individuals.

Ideals Theory

Ideals theory was forwarded by W.C. Bagley. According to this theory, transfer of training occurs when generalizations are learned as ideals or some values. According to this theory, ideals like love for wisdom, thirst for knowledge, spirit for enquiry and tolerance of differences of opinions etc are transferable from one situation to another.

FACTORS INFLUENCING TRANSFER OF LEARNING OR TRAINING

Following factors influence transfer of learning or training.

Mental Ability

Mental abilities of learner are closely related to transfer of learning. Superior mental abilities result higher amount of transfer of learning. Children found better in their mental abilities in respect of superior intelligence. Thinking, perception power and grasping power can easily find identity of relationships between similar situations and thus they can easily transfer their learning.

Teaching Strategy

It has been seen that method of teaching has a strong effect on transfer of learning. Teaching strategies which are directed towards the problem solving are helpful to create large amount of transfer. Studies of Woodworth, Overman and Salisbury revealed that there is close relationship between teaching strategies and transfer of training or learning. Therefore teaching strategies are to be so organized and systematic that can promote independent thinking, problem solving and experimentation. Which in turn will yield good result in transfer of learning?

Attitude

Attitude of learners plays a vital role in case of transfer of learning. If the students will have positive attitude towards their curricular subjects then they can learn more generalizations, principle and ideas which can help them for transfer of their learning to their life situations.

Practice/Habit

Practice or habit also provide for better transfer of training. Practice makes the storage of knowledge and memory stronger. Children having good memory are found having well in their transfer of training. Therefore in the schools, teachers should encourage their students to practice their task and make a habit in them.

Nature of Teaching Materials

Meaningful and organized teaching materials help to build sound mentality in the learners. It helps to develop a good insight and conceptualization in the learners. Meaningless teaching materials lead to lose the interest in learning and hamper the process of conceptualization. Therefore if there will be presentation of meaningful teaching materials for the learners, then it will help to accelerate their transfer.

TEACHER'S ROLE IN PROMOTING TRANSFER OF LEARNING OR TRAINING

Teachers are the main instrument to promote the transfer of learning skills in the children. Following key role a teacher can play to promote the transfer of learning in the children.

- Making his teaching interesting and meaningful
- Adopting suitable teaching strategies suiting the need to the pupils
- Encouraging students to practice their task
- Developing experimenting attitude in the children
- Presenting learning materials having positive transfer values
- Encouraging children to participate in the group activities like seminars, workshops and discussions
- Providing feedback in judicious manner
- Making children motivated to learn.

29
Culture, Learning and Development

Out of many things, culture is a significant factor influencing one's learning and development. In our earlier discussion we could learn that the biological and psychological conditions determine learning and development. But human being is himself modify his own behaviour in view of his experiences while living in his society having a cultural realm involving distinct language, custom, beliefs, rituals, values, goals and political systems which shape his experiences. Human life is culturally constituted. There is a range of variations of human behaviour observed in different societies and various ethnic groups in the same society. Therefore there is a impact of societal and cultural inputs on the perspectives of learning and development of human beings. So it is need to be discussed.

MEANING OF CULTURE

Culture can be defined in two ways. In one way culture is defined as a common characteristics shared by individuals in respect of language, common heritage and country over a period of time. Here individuals are treated as part of the culture or individuals belong to culture. In another way, culture is defined as a system of meanings and practices which act as an organizer of the experiential world of individuals. Here culture is treated as a human artifact created over a period of time.

Culture has two properties such as material and non-material properties. Material dimensions of the culture include the physical creations of the human being in his society/environment like tools, artifacts, sculptures etc. The non-material dimension of culture includes beliefs, language, attitude, norms, values, customs, notions etc. Culture is said to be bidirectional. Culture shapes individuals behaviour and in turn individuals create culture.

Different societies/countries have different cultural settings of their own. Therefore we see cultural differences in African countries and European countries and similarly in between Asian countries and American countries.

Cultural Diversity

There is cultural diversity found among peoples of different groups. Peoples differ in their values, norms, practices, languages and beliefs of their society and groups. People of one group/society assess the values, customs and practices of other groups according to their own cultural standards. This leads to development of prejudices and discriminations them.

CULTURAL SHAPING

Culture has an impact on shaping the behavioural pattern of the people of a group and their development. It influences the way of life of the people. It is through cultural transmission, individuals become a member of a culture by the help of their elders providing them social, psychological and physical environment and training. Gradually, individuals develop their distinct notions about their self and others. Today's world is shrinking with the effect of cultural diffusion and multi-culturalism temper. Electronic Medias and global interaction through mass communication process has developed pluralism of culture and influenced the life style of the people apart from their original cultural setting. Man has become more open in their behaviour tending towards universal culture.

Cultural shaping takes two ways such as Enculturation and Acculturation. Enculturation means a process through which individuals freely and automatically learn the native culture without any deliberate teaching. For example, a child belonging to Bengali family automatically learns the Bengali language and follows the Bengali customs. A child born in tribal community automatically learns the tribal dialects, languages and tribal culture. Acculturation means, a process through which individuals get changed in their culture by the contact of the culture of others.

CULTURAL TRANSMISSION

As it has been discussed, a culture develops over a long period of time. The cultural groups transmit culture to their new born members by helping them to develop appropriate behaviour. One generation transmits its culture to new generations by the process of teaching and learning. It is through the process of socialization and training cultural transmission occurs from one to another.

Socialization

Socialization refers to a process through which new born babies/children become acquainted with the culture and values of their belongings to sustain their life in a mutual context. It is by socialization, social qualities are restored in the individuals to behave as a social being. Socialization of new members of a community is materialized by the methods of imitation, learning and training. Individuals having superior knowledge and experience act as socializing agents. It is due to the nature of dependency of human babies at their initial life up to their fullest development at later stage of their life this socialization process become inevitable. Children with their gradual growth and development participate in different cultural activities in their home, schools and society and become socialized by internalizing attitudes, values, beliefs and norms of their culture.

Socialization process takes two phases such as Primary and Secondary socialization process. The Primary socialization process starts within the family and home during the infancy to childhood stage. But the Secondary Socialization Process takes place outside the family and homes during later childhood stage to adulthood stage. So socialization can be said as a lifelong process starting from birth to death of an individual.

Agencies of Socialization

Socialization activity is performed by the following agencies.

Family/Home: Family or home is called as a primary and important agency of the socialization of human child. The parents, elders, grandparents, and other relatives act as socializing agents in the family for the new born baby during his infancy and childhood period. They try to inculcate the essential values, norms and attitudes in the children and modify and shape their behaviour and development. They nurture the baby providing care, nutrition, education and training to behave according to their standards and practices. Children enculture themselves through imitation and learning by participating different occasional festivals and cultural activities try to accustom themselves and develop their sense of self. All of the elderly members of the family act as the role model for the children and shape their behaviour and socialize them.

School: School is another social agency that socializes children. It is formal educational environment where children learn different social attributes from their teachers, books and class mates. It is a place where social as well as cognitive development steers by the guidance of teachers. It develops the communication ability and promotes interaction ability to share and develop in a mutual process. Teachers teach their students different values, norms, standards, practices of the society while transacting the curriculum especially on history, music, language and literature.

Peers: Peers means a group of children of equal age range living in a common locality or attend the same school. Peers have a strong effect on the process of socialization and development of children. Children share their views and learn from each other. It helps in their learning. Peers help in performing cultural activities collectively and help them to learn.

Society: Society acts as an agency of socialization of children. It is during adolescence and adulthood stage, society plays a dominant role in shaping the behaviour of individuals. It provides certain social values, norms and practices and guides in their development. Society transmits the cultural values of its own and moulds the behaviour of individuals on certain social and cultural standards. Individuals develop according to the conformity of their social values fixed.

Community: Community is a place of living narrower than the society involving a group of people sharing common characteristics of physical, linguistic, religion and cultural background. We may refer to a tribal community or Islamic community. Children taking birth in their community inculcate their cultural practices and socialized. The elder beings of the community install the cultural values in their new members and make them adjusted and developed in the same way they belong.

Religious Places: Religious places like temple, church; Mosques etc. have also a positive impact on the socialization of human beings. These are the place of professing religion. The concept of temples differs for different religious groups. For example, for Hindus it is temple, for Muslims, it is Mosques and for Christians, it is church. But all the places are the place of professing the God of their own line. Peoples of same religion follow their distinct cultural practices and become socialized. Seniors educate their new members according to their own practices.

Mass Medias: In the age of globalization, mass Medias act as a forceful agency of the socialization of the human beings. Mass Medias include T.V., Radios, Computers, Internet, and Press and printing Medias, New papers etc. These means help in communicating the cultural values from one to another in massive process. It makes the people aware of their cultural practices of their own and others and accordingly help them in their development. Mass Medias help in acculturation of the individuals in a significant way. These means reflect the culture and values of the society and nation and make its members educated.

CULTURAL DIVERSITY AND LEARNING

School is called as a miniature society. Children belonging to all communities come to learn together. In a class room they sit together and make themselves learn from their teacher. But it is found that, children of one cultural group face difficulties, found reluctant and hesitated to interact with children of other cultural groups. This creates a aloof and separate climate in the class room for leading common teaching learning practices. There may be differences in intellectual levels in the children because of their cultural impacts and some sections of children fail to cope the common class room teaching. This leads to affect their learning and development.

Cultural Diversity in Classroom

Cultural diversity in the class room may be caused on the ground of the linguistic, religious, and socio-economic backgrounds of the children. The teacher should have to be optimistic and apply suitable teaching strategies, flexible methods and friendly approach to make them learn and developed. Proper guidance and care should be provided by the teachers to bring them to the mainstream. If required, tutorial classes should be arranged to counsel the children facing difficulties in the diversified cultural setting of the class room situations. Every short of humiliating conditions should be eradicated and the students should be encouraged to be interactive and friendly with each other in the class room environment.

Cultural Diversity and Curriculum Planning

Children in a class room may be from different cultures/groups. They may have their own language, own beliefs and own thinking pattern which interferes in their learning and development. Their cultural diversity influences their pace of learning and rate of learning. Therefore, it is need to plan for proper selection and organization of curriculum keeping in view of the cultural diversity of the learners. Curriculum should be diversified to suit the interest and choice of the learners. Linguistically the curriculum should be graded properly. Curriculum should reflect the culture of the learners. The flexibility principle should be adopted while planning and organizing curriculum.

Cultural Diversity in Class room and Teaching Strategies

It is a fact that, in a common class room, there may be children of different groups and different cultures. Their common goal is to learn and develop. A teacher should give respect to the individual differences of his students in respect of their interest, abilities, language and dialects and provide equal educational opportunity for all to prosper. Keeping in view of the cultural diversities of children in the class room, a teacher should have to apply suitable and varied types of teaching techniques so as to enable the individual learners to learn successfully and achieve their goals. Rigidity of teaching method and ignoring the student's interest will never provide good result. A teacher should be properly trained to deal with the class room having students from diverse cultures.

CLASS ROOM AS A SOCIAL GROUP

While a school is considered as a miniature society, a class room is considered as a social situation. A number of social forces operate in the class room. A class room provides a social climate to initiate the process of education. Organizational pattern of a class room provides conditions for leading the learning atmosphere for the children. Therefore, a class should not be treated as a mere collection of the learners rather it should be viewed as an organized whole. All the social forces operating and existing in a class should be understood and psychologically dealt.

A model class room should be viewed from the following angels.

Stress on individual accomplishment: The success and failure of a class depends on the individual accomplishment of its learners. Therefore, each learner should be treated as an important unit of the class and should be helped to complete his/her task satisfactorily.

Making the class room task oriented: It is important that whole class room is to be activated to accomplish the common task. The task may be of individual or group but cooperation of all the learners of a class room is essential for their completion.

Making the class room size rational: A class room size is different from other social groups. Size of the class room has a positive impact on all the teaching-learning transactions, on the role of a teacher and on the class room atmosphere. It has a stimulating effect on the learners. Therefore, a class should not either be too large or too small in its size but it should be rationally constituted. The school administration should think of the constitutional pattern of the size of the class room keeping in view of achievement of the learning objectives.

Stress on the nature of interaction in the class room: A class room provides a social situation and a place of operating the group dynamics. Members of a class room dynamically interact with their class mates. There operates three types of interactions among the members of a class room such as Individual-Individual interaction, Individual-Group interaction and Group-Group interaction.

Individual-Individual interaction: This type of interaction may be between two students or between a students and a teacher.

Individual-Group interaction: this type of interaction may be between a teacher and whole of a class or between the leader of the class and whole of the group of the students.

Group-Group interaction: This type of interaction may be between two groups of students. A class may be sub divided into different groups for meeting different purposes and at that moment such type of interaction takes place.

TYPES OF CLASS-ROOM GROUPS

Out of his study by the application of sociometric techniques, J.L. Moreno could find out the following types of class room groups on the basis of the pattern of relationship among the members of the group.

Stars: These are the students of a class-room to whom majority of the students like, prefer and select as a leader to organize the group activity.

Isolates: These are the students of a class room to whom others do not like. None of the group likes to interact with him and become reluctant to include him in the group activity. An isolated student is seen to be rejected by the whole of the group. Such isolated students should be sympathetically and psychologically handled by the teacher. A teacher should have to encourage the isolates to participate in the group activities and also motivate others to interact with the isolates.

Mutual Pairs: Some of the students of a group/class-room prefer to interact with each other with a reciprocal relationship. They don't like to interact with others except their preferred students.

Chains: There may be some small groups inside the class and the members of these small groups prefer to interact and share their views among themselves. These small groups are called as chains or cliques. These small groups try to interfere in the common activities of the class room and try to dominate. Therefore, teachers should understand them and try to minimize their influence in the class room and orient them towards the general group.

GROUP DYNAMICS

A class is viewed as a group of students constituted of a number of individual students coming from different sections of the society. Individual child is greatly influenced by the characteristics of a group. The term group dynamics means, the forces of the group. In a group, different forces become operative and active at different situations and at different times which influence the behaviour and learning of the students. The individual learners get the scope to change his behaviour by coming with contact of the group in the process of interaction.

The followings are the effects of Group dynamics on the individual learner:

- In changing the attitude of the learners
- In changing the notion and action of the learners
- In changing the learning of the learners
- In changing the feelings and emotion of the learners
- In changing the morality and ethics of the learners
- In changing the mindset of the learners
- In changing the relationship pattern of the learners
- In changing the thinking pattern of the learners (Either competitive or cooperative or leadership or friendly)

Therefore, a teacher should watch and lead the group dynamic satisfactorily in the better interest and development of the learners. He should facilitate the individual learners to derive better and socially healthy result from the group dynamics

CLASS-ROOM CLIMATE

Class room climate means organizational pattern of the class-room or simply it refers to the class-room environment. Class-room climate has its direct impact on the success or failure of the teaching-learning endavours. Conducive class-room climate helps in getting success in teaching-learning activities and thus becomes more result oriented and polluted class-room climate helps in getting failure in teaching-learning activities and thus becomes least result oriented. A class-room climate is constituted of the following conditions.

i. Kind of Teacher-Pupil relationship inside the class-room
ii. Nature of social interaction among the pupils inside the class-room
iii. Kind of relationship among the teachers of a school
iv. Size of the class-room (crowded or not crowded)
v. Arrangement of the physical facilities (Ventilation, seating arrangement, furniture, table, black board, teaching aids, light etc.)
vi. Attitude of the learners towards the teachers
vii. Previous knowledge of the learners
viii. Teacher's mindset and attitude

If the above conditions are arranged in positive direction then a better class-room climate will be seen otherwise a disturbing class-room climate will be seen.

TEACHER-LEADER IN THE CLASS-ROOM

A teacher is considered as the leaders of the class-room. He is supposed to possess higher insight, thinking, intelligence, knowledge and experience to lead the learners of a class/group. He should be trained and skilled enough to lead the class. He should have capacity to face the group boldly and demonstrate his leadership among the learners. He should also facilitate the leadership quality of the learners to develop.

As a leader, a teacher should possess the following characteristics

- Sound mind
- Optimistic in outlook
- Enough potentialities
- Cooperativeness
- Democratic in spirit and thinking
- Good intelligence
- Profound knowledge
- Skilled and trained
- Good personality
- Sympathetic outlook
- Good communication skill
- Good command over speech

Teacher as leader can be viewed in three different manners basing upon his manner of interaction he adopts in the group/class such as less effective leader, more effective leader and most effective leader. A less effective teacher-leader attempts to maintain one-way interaction process where learners are the passive listeners. But in case of more effective teacher-leader, the interaction/communication process is of two-way process. Both teacher and student influence each other and interact with each other in a reciprocal manner. In case of a most effective teacher-leader, the communication or interaction simultaneously goes on among the learners and with teacher-leader. Here the communication or interaction is controlled by the teacher-leader.

The following Diagrams shows the different types of Teacher-leader effectiveness

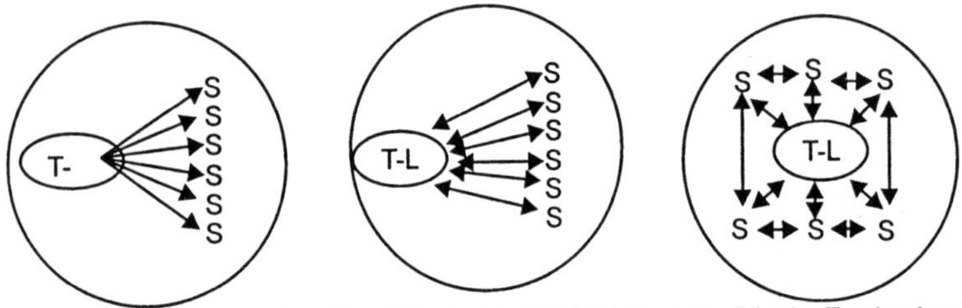

Less Effective Teacher-Leader More Effective Teacher-Leader Most Effective Teacher-Leader

(T=Teacher, L=Leader, S=Student/Learner)

TEACHER EFFECTIVENESS

Effectiveness of a teacher depends on the reaction of the learners of a group, nature of the communication he adopts, learner's achievement and personal characteristics he bears. A teacher whether effective or not effective can be assessed out of the observation of his class-room climate, his interaction style and level of achievement of the learners. An effective teacher can be viewed as an effective leader for a school and class-room. Without effective teachers, a school can't function satisfactorily. Effective teachers work dedicatedly, sincerely and intelligently to bring success of the school and its learners. Effective teachers can be viewed as friend, philosopher and guide for their students. The development of the learners, society and country totally depends upon the effective teachers.

Characteristics of an Effective Teacher

The followings are the characteristics of an effective teacher—

- Academically good.
- Bearing positive attitude
- Optimistic outlook
- Democratic approach in decision making
- Sound mind
- Motivational
- Interest in learning
- Sincere and punctual

- Encouraging
- Sound emotion and enthusiastic
- Active
- Cooperative
- Adjustable
- Confident
- Trained and skilled
- Good depth of knowledge
- Good in communication and interaction
- Adequate command over speech

Determinants of Teacher effectiveness

Determinants of the teacher effectiveness may be of following types

Inner determinants: Inner determinants include the personality characteristics of a teacher, his physique, mental condition. Intelligence, thinking, attitude, skill, training, speech pattern, communication and interaction style, motivation, knowledge, experience, emotion and confidence etc. If these conditions are found positive then a teacher can be said to be an effective teacher.

Outer determinants: Outer determinants include the conditions found externally influencing the work of a teacher in his school or class-room. These conditions include, distance of the school, working hour of the school, nature of the administration of a school, nature of attitude and interaction of other teachers, parents and head of the institution, physical facilities available in a school and class-room, reinforcement, feedback, remuneration or salary of the teacher, opportunities for professional growth, influence of community etc. If these conditions are found positive and conducive, then a teacher can be effective for a school otherwise if these conditions will not be conducive, then there is a least hope for a teacher to be effective.

However, both inner and outer determinant's combine help develop an effective teacher.

Assessment of Teacher Effectiveness

Teacher effectiveness can be assessed on the basis of the following three methods.

Viewing as a Process: On this basis, teacher effectiveness is assessed taking into view of the learning process that takes place inside the class-room situation. By observing the teacher-learner's interaction, discipline and learner's rapport with the teacher while carrying the teaching learning activities in the class-room.

Viewing as a Product: On this basic, teacher effectiveness is assessed taking into view of the learning outcomes of the learners. The quality of learner's performance in their examinations and co-curricular activities conducted in the school provides a base for the parents, administrators, headmaster/principal and supervisors to assess the effectiveness of teachers.

Viewing as a Presage: On this basis, teacher effectiveness is assessed taking into view of teacher's personal characteristics which include teacher's academic qualification, training, skill, knowledge, intelligence, social skills and their professional competency. Teacher's participation in workshops, seminars and conferences and their publications etc. also contribute to enhance the teacher effectiveness.

In order to judge the teacher effectiveness, collectively all of these three methods/criterions described above are to be taken into consideration.

TEACHING SKILLS

A teacher to be effective should have sufficient mastery over the teaching skills along with possessing the requisites of positive personal characteristics. An effective teacher should be apt in executing different teaching skills in the class-room and adequately motivate the students to obtain maximum learning.

An effective teacher should have the mastery over the following teaching skills.

Skill of introducing the topic: An effective teacher finds easy in introducing difficult and new topics in the class in an interesting manner by using different techniques such as by using teaching aids, using examples and narrations, by questioning and by demonstration. It helps a teacher to make the students mentally ready to learn.

Skill of Explanation or illustration: It is an important teaching skill. After introducing the topic in the class, the actual teaching starts. In order to make the students understand the lesson or content satisfactorily, an effective teacher should have mastery over the skill of explanation or illustration. A skilled and effective teacher finds easy to explain the difficult, abstract and complex concepts by citing concrete examples from life situations, by demonstrations, by verbal explanations, diagrams and figures and thus helps the students to clarify their doubts.

Skill of Questioning: An effective teacher should have the mastery over the questioning skill. It is a best tool in the hand of a teacher to make the students ready, attentive and alert about their teaching learning activity inside the class-room. It can motivate and stimulate the students in their learning. It helps to establish two-way communication between teacher and students. An effective teacher should be apt in asking varieties of questions like probing questions, divergent questions, evaluative questions, knowledge/information seeking questions, comprehension test questions and application test questions using proper approach and perfection in language.

Skill of Black Board using: Use of Black-Board inside the class room is said to be an important teaching skill in the part of an effective teacher. An effective teacher can use the space of black board in highlighting teaching points, drawing charts, diagrams, and figures and make his teaching effective and helping the students to see and note down them for their memory and learning. In order to attain this skill, a teacher should have to acquire good writing skills and good hand writing to make his writing effective.

Skill of providing reinforcement to the learners: An effective teacher should have adequate command over providing reinforcement to his students while teaching inside the class room. Providing reinforcement help to lead participatory teaching learning process in the class-room. An effective teacher is found apt in providing verbal reinforcement like okay, thank you, very good, good, excellent, etc. and encourage the students to be involved in the teaching learning process. Though sometimes, negative reinforcement like corporal punishment and blaming yield better result and become effective, a teacher should try to avoid these. This skill of reinforcement goes hand in hand with the skill of questioning.

Skill of providing feedback to the learners: An effective teacher should have mastery over the skill of providing feed back to the students. It is true that not all students learn at equal rate. There may be some slow learners in the same class sitting with the gifted and average learners. They fail to cope with the normal class-room teaching. For these students a teacher should provide adequate feed backs for their improvement. An effective teacher finds easy and pleasure to provide feed backs to the needy students.

Skill of teaching with teaching aids: In order to make teaching-learning activity interesting, memorable and facilitating for learning, an effective teacher should be skilled in using different types of teaching aids in the class-room context. Teaching aids helps the student to understand the concept in a clear way.

TEACHER'S ROLE PERCEPTION IN THE CLASS-ROOM

Teacher is looked as a source of knowledge for the learners. Apart from performing the role of teaching, a teacher is perceived as a distinguished personality projected in the class room playing dynamic role to change the behaviour of the learners. A teacher with his power of knowledge and interaction with the learners in the school and class room tries to motivate and change the behavioural pattern of his students and making them good citizens. A teacher's role is determined in the context of a school and community with relation to the expectation of students, administrators, supervisors, teachers and parents. Along with, the personal characteristics of a teacher and external surroundings of a school play a significant role in determining the role of a teacher. Generally students and parents perceive the role of a teacher in the following manners.

As a Leader: A teacher plays a significant role in his class-room as a leader. By virtue of his superior knowledge and experience, he leads the group of students. As a leader he directs, guides and controls the teaching-learning activities of the class-room, organization of the co-curricular activities in the school. As a leader he gives noble ideas to his students.

As a Model: A teacher also plays a significant role as a model for the students inside the class-room. Because of his better ideas, attitudes, moral values, inspiring nature, sound personality characteristics, a teacher is perceived as a model for his students and become effective in changing the behaviour of his students.

As a Facilitator: A teacher is also looked as a facilitator in the eyes of the parents and teachers. An effective teacher facilitates the learners to learn more and solve their problems. A teacher as a facilitator acts like a friend for his students in meeting the requirements of their learning and problem solving.

As a Negotiator: A teacher is also looked as a negotiator in the class room. He will have to negotiate with the students about the smooth management of the class room activities. Some times he will have to negotiate between the students when some confronting situation arrives in the class room among the students relating to some teaching learning activities. As a negotiator, teachers also have to deal with the parents of the students and school administration relating to teaching learning problem of his students.

As a Manager: As a manager, an effective teacher plays a very important role in the school in general and in the class room in particular. As a manager the activities an effective teacher performs include planning, organizing, coordinating, leading, supervising, directing, controlling and evaluating the entire class room activities including curriculum, co-curriculum, time table and examination activities.

As a Guide: As a guide an effective teacher always tries to help his students in solving their academic as well as personal problems in the class room. He pays individual attention towards his students, shares the views of his students, discusses with his students and provides feed backs for improvement of his students, assists in fulfilling study needs of his students with enthusiastic manner.

As a Motivator: As a motivator, an effective teacher always encourage his students, recognize the talents and limitations of his students and accordingly provide help and assistances, inspires students to do good in their teaching learning activities. He makes his students hopeful and encouraging.

30
Exceptional Children: Their Learning and Development

Education is key factor for the development of all human beings. Realizing this objective, we have now expanded our insight towards education for all with the approach of inclusive education by fulfilling the motive behind the act of right to education of children where all children without any discrimination will get equal scope of learning and development. While practicing teaching-learning process inside a class-room, a teacher often finds some special categories of children apart from the normal children requiring special attention for their care and education. This has demanded individualized attention and adjusting instruction strategies to make the special children able to cope with the normal class-room practices. This needs to know about the exceptional children, understand their psychology and teaching-learning practices and accordingly providing them opportunity for their learning and development.

MEANING OF EXCEPTIONAL CHILDREN

Exceptional children refers to those children who feel difficulties to cope with the normal children and develop normally due to their certain disability conditions or extreme functioning of traits either in their body or mind and therefore they need special help/assistance for their development. These children have their special type of needs. The other terminologies may be used as handicapped children, disable children and Children with special needs. These children feel difficulties and fail to derive satisfactory result out of the normal treatment inside the class-room. Therefore their needs are to be addressed properly and accordingly special provisions should be made for them.

Kirk defined exceptional children that, 'an exceptional children is he who deviates from the normal or average child in mental, physical, and social characteristics to such an extent that he requires a modification of school practices or special educational services or supplementary instruction in order to develop to his maximum capacity'.

TYPES OF EXCEPTIONAL CHILDREN

The followings are the types of exceptional children that draw the attention of a teacher inside a normal class-room.

Physically Exceptional Children: Physically challenged children include visually impaired children, hearing impaired children, speech impaired children, and health impaired children and orthopedically impaired children.

Mentally Exceptional Children: Mentally challenged children include learning disabled children, slow learners and mentally retarded children.

Emotionally Exceptional Children: This category of children includes children with behavioural disorders, Problem children, and psycho-neurotic children.

Socially Exceptional Children: This category of children includes juveniles and socially backward children.

IDENTIFICATION OF EXCEPTIONAL CHILDREN

It is a need to identify the exceptional children at an early before initiating them for their learning and providing instruction. The following methods may be adopted to identify the nature, types and degree of exceptionality of the children.

- *Medical Test:* It is one of the important procedures to identify the exceptional children. It is useful in detecting physically challenged children.
- *Observation:* Observation of day to day activities can help to identify the physically challenged children, socially challenged children,
- *Tests/Examination:* Achievement and intelligence tests can help to detect the mentally challenged children and help to detect the slow learners, mentally retarded children and gifted children.
- *Psycho-test:* This type of method is useful for detecting emotionally and mentally challenged children.

DEALING WITH EXCEPTIONAL CHILDREN IN THE CLASS-ROOM AND HELPING THEM TO LEARN

There may be some exceptional children in a class-room having their specific problems due to their distinct type of impairments or improper functioning of their brain which interferes in the teaching of a teacher inside the class-room and they demand some special help for their learning and development. It requires a teacher to understand and deal with them differently in order to make them adjusted.

Dealing with Physically Exceptional children

Physically exceptional children are those who possess impairment in their musculoskeletal conditions of their body involving the joints, limbs, and associated muscles and/or neurological conditions involving the central nervous system i.e. brain, spinal cord or peripheral nerves and impairment in visual, auditory and speech organs which affect the ability to move or coordinate the control movement. A physical impairment may be present from birth (congenital) or acquired later through an accident or illness. There are different types of physically challenged children like visually impaired children, hearing impaired children, speech impaired children, and orthopedically handicapped children.

Visually Impaired Children

Visually impaired children are those who possess problems in their vision ability. In educational terms, it refers to any diagnosed condition of the eye or visual system that impact on access to learning. Disease, damage or injury causing vision impairment can occur to any part of the visual system i.e. the eye, the visual pathway to the brain or visual center of the brain. Vision impairment can be present at birth or can occur at anytime from disease or accident or can be part of a medical condition or syndrome.

Most visual condition in children is stable and vision remains relatively unchanged. Some conditions however are progressive, resulting in reduced vision over varying periods.

The symptoms like feeling headache, covering one eye and thrusting the hands forward, rubbing eyes excessively, holding objects close to eyes, blinking eyes frequently, asking others to read and listen them, having smaller eyelids or red-rimmed eyelids, becoming sensitive to light, watering of eyes, putting false steps while walking etc. are helpful to identify visually impaired children.

Visually impaired children usually face the problems like academic retardation, poor intelligence, inadequate speech development, socially adjustment problem and personality disorder.

For making the visually impaired children learn, educated and developed, educational provisions like arrangement of special classes, medical care, co-curricular activities, minimum visual task, special equipments, residential schools etc. can be made available to them. Parents and teachers are to develop positive and sympathetic attitude towards the visually impaired/handicapped children.

Hearing Impaired Children

Hearing impaired children are those having full or partial loss of the ability to detect or discriminate sounds due to an abnormality associated with the physiology, anatomy or function of their ear. A hearing impairment can be described in terms of the degree of a hearing impairment, ranging from a mild hearing impairment to a profound hearing impairment.

A hearing impaired child may use speech and/or sign to communicate. Some children who use sign prefer to be referred as Deaf.

Hearing impairment in children can be identified through Developmental scale, Neuropsychological tests, Medical examinations, Case study and systematic observation. Hearing impaired children may face the problems like socially adjustment problem, linguistic problems, social and personal development problems, learning problems, personality problem, emotional disorders etc.

For making the hearing impaired children learn, educated and developed, the educational provisions like use of hearing aids, vocational training, auditory training, speech reading, and special class room facilities should be made available to them. Parents and teachers are to take special care for these hearing impaired children while talking with them and they should sympathetically deal with them.

Speech Impaired Children

Speech impaired children are those who face difficulties of communication through speech due to malfunctioning of their speech organs or defective speech organs. Communication disorder or speech disorder in children may be of organic or functional based on etiology. Organic speech disorder consists of speech handicap due to palatal anomalies, dental irregularities, paralysis and tumours of the larynx, brain damage etc. The functional speech disorder represents failure to learn speech due to general personality and emotional disturbances. Some classify speech disorders as articulation disorder, voice disorder, delayed speech, stammering and rhythm disturbances.

Children having speech impairments face a lot of problems in their day-to-day life. They develop inferiority complex in them. The normal children sometimes tease/fun at them. Speech disorder children also are found slow in their learning and suffer from maladjustment problems and problems in their personality development.

For making the speech impaired children learn, educated and developed, the educational provisions like speech therapy, articulation correction, speech training activities, organization of extra-curricular activities etc. should be made available to them. Parents and teachers are to sympathetically deal with these children and encourage them to learn and developed.

Orthopedically Handicapped Children

Orthopedically handicapped children are those who have impairments or peculiarities in their skeletal structure of the body involving defects in muscles or bones or joints which affects their ability to feel or move or both the categories. It may include disabilities of the upper extremities like amputation or congenital absence of one or both arms, loss of one or more fingers or a part below wrist, elbow or shoulders and disabilities of the lower extremities like impairments of one or both the legs. It is easy to detect the orthopedically handicapped children as their disabilities either in the upper extremities or lower extremities are externally visible and from their walking, movement of the body and hands it can easily be detected.

Orthopedically handicapped children may face problems in social adjustment, personal problem and problems in personality development, development of self esteem, problem in performing tasks, academic problems, adjustment problems, emotional problem. Other may tease/fun at these children due to their irregular formation of the body and disability in the body functioning resulting to put harm to the sentiment and personality of these children leading further to their poor academic achievement in the class.

For making the orthopedically handicapped children learn, educated and developed the educational provisions like hospital school for those who need extensive care and treatment in the hospital, special schools with medical and health facilities, therapy rooms, rest areas, and a lunchroom., special classes with equipment as standing tables, special chairs, parallel bars, and reading devices, home instruction for those who need more rest, use of school-home telephone services and education through television etc. should be made available to them. It is recommended to provide vocational education and training to make these orthopedically handicapped children empowered and developed. School should provide artificial limbs and appliances to the needy orthopedically handicapped children. Transportation facilities may be arranges for them to bring them school and help them learn. Parents and teachers should be trained in dealing with this category of handicapped children.

Mentally Exceptional Children

Mentally exceptional/challenged children refer to those children having malfunctioning of their mind and suffer from intellectual disabilities. Mentally challenged children include slow learners, mentally retarded children and learning disables. Gifted children also come under this category as their needs are different from those of normal children which need special treatment for their adjustment and development.

Slow Learners

Slow learners are those who possess below average intelligence and their thinking skills have developed significantly more slowly than the norm with respect to their age. These children develop at the same age similar to the normal children but slowly.

Slow learners can be detected by observing their characteristics like, immature language pattern and speech problem, immature social behaviour, poor judgment, prefer to mix with younger children, suffering from anxiety, aggression and frustration, poor memory, proficiency in particular area out of total academic subjects, poor understanding, dislike to read, word confusion, committing spelling mistakes and repeating words while reading, difficulty in understanding mathematical concepts, visual difficulties, perceptual difficulties, poor hearing, attention deficit, low self-concept, emotionally instable, socially hyperactive, nervous, quite, constant movements and low tolerance capacity.

In order to help these slow learners learn and developed, the educational provisions like providing intensive/tutorial classes, extra classes, remedial classes, reinforcement and feedback programme, avoiding traditional pattern of home task and providing alternate home tasks, motivating and encouraging them and teaching them the reading techniques etc. should be made available to them. Apart from these programmes, teachers and parents should personally supervise and chat with these children for their better learning.

Mentally Retarded Children

In the place of mentally retarded, other terminologies like, feeble minded, mentally handicapped, mentally deficient, and mentally subnormal or mentally sub-average are used.

The WHO (1954) referred mental retardation as incomplete or insufficient general development of mental capacities. The American Psychiatric Association (1968) has defined mental retardation as subnormal intellectual functioning which originates during the developmental period and is associated with impairment of either learning or social adjustment or maturation or both. The American Association on Mental Deficiency (AAMD), (1983) refers to mental retardation as significantly sub-average in general intellectual functioning existing currently with deficit in adaptive behaviour and manifested during the developmental period. British Mental Deficiency Act (1981) defines that, mental retardation is a condition of arrest or incomplete development of mind existing before the age of 18 years whether arising from inherent causes or induced by disease or injury. Taking into reference of all these definition of mental retardation, it can be said that, mental retardation or mental deficiency is the state of poor functioning of mind due to incomplete development of mind.

Previously the level of Intelligence Quotient (IQ), the ratio to mental age and chronological age, mathematically expressed as IQ=(M.A/C.A x 100) determined the mental retardation. Persons possessing IQ of 110 and more are treated as Superior, IQ of 90 to 110 are treated as average/normal, IQ of 80 to 90 are treated as feeble minded, IQ of 70 to 80 are treated as Borderline, IQ of 50 to 70 are treated as morons, IQ of 25 to 50 are treated as Imbeciles and IQ of below 25 are treated as Idiots. But in recent days referring to the Binet test of intelligence test, mental retardation has been classified into the following groups.

1. *Mild Mental Retardation:* Mild mental retardation category displays the IQ range of 68 to 52. About 90 per cent of mentally retarded individuals fall to this category. Children having mild mental retardation are educable. They require little supervision, parental assistance and special training. They can be taught to be self-supporting.
2. *Moderate Mental Retardation:* Moderate mental retardation category displays the IQ range of 51 to 36. Children having moderately mental retardation are called as trainable retarded. About six percent of mentally retarded come under this category. The rate of learning of these children is very slow. Though some of these children require institutionalization, they can manage to live safely under protection of their family members.
3. *Severe Mental Retardation:* Severe mental retardation category displays IQ range of 35 to 20. About three percent of mentally retarded individuals are found to belong to this category. These categories of children suffer from severe retardation in their motor and speech development. These children can be called as dependent retarded who need permanent institutionalization and constant care. Under supervision they can perform simple occupational task.
4. *Profound Mental Retardation:* Profound mental retardation category displays the IQ range of fewer than 20. About one percent of mentally retarded individuals fall into this category. Profoundly mentally retarded children are also called as life support mentally retardates. These children are unable to master simple tasks and deficient in adaptive behaviour. They fail to attend their basic physical needs. These children require constant and permanent supervision throughout their life for their survival.

Mentally retarded children suffer from inferiority complex, adjustment problems, emotional problems and poor achievements. Others sometimes ignore and ill treat them.

Defects in sense organs in the aspect of vision, hearing, speech lead to develop mental retardation in children. Apart from this, other conditions like improper care of parents, nervous disorders, psychosocial problems, malnutrition, diseases, illness and mental injuries cause mental retardation in children. Mental retardation may arise at thc time of birth through genetic problems or after birth through environmental and psycho-social problems.

General characteristics like slow in rate of learning, lack of abstract thinking, lacking interests in acts/learning, poor attention power, poor intelligence, poor adjustment skill, inability to solve problems and attend tasks, dependability nature, care seeking, distorted shape of the ears, nose, hand, feet, head etc. and lack of muscular coordination are evident in the mentally retarded children.

In order to help the mentally retarded children learn and developed, educational provisions like, delayed school practices, adjusted curriculum with skill training, vocational training, simple learning task with less abstraction, grouping and classifying the MRs, orienting school and class room practices to individual needs, organizing co-curricular activities, providing special trained teachers etc should be made available to them. Parents, teachers and community members are to look at these children sympathetically and provide necessary care and assistance for their learning and development.

Learning Disabled Children

Learning disabled children are those who have specific learning disability. These children's level of intelligence is found to be average or above average. Learning disability is present in at least 10 percent of the population. Learning disability are problems that affects the brains ability to receive processes, analyze or store information. The problems that make the learner to learn as quickly as someone who isn't affected by learning disability. Learning disabled children are those who suffer from serious learning disabilities exhibiting exceptionally inferior qualities/capacities in terms of learning and understanding in comparison to the normal children of their age. The Association for Children with Learning Disabilities USA (1967) states that, a child with learning disability is one with adequate mental ability, sensory processes, and emotional stability who has a limited number of specific deficit in perceptual, integrative, or expressive processes which severely impair learning efficiency. This includes children who have central nervous system dysfunction which is expressed primarily in impaired learning efficiency. National Joint Committee on Learning Disability, USA say, that "learning disability as a generic term refers to a heterogeneous group of disorders manifested in significant difficulties in the acquisition and use of listening, speaking, reading, writing, reasoning, and mathematical abilities. These disorders are intrinsic to the individual presumed to be due to their central nervous system dysfunction and may occur across the life span. Problems in self-regulatory behaviours, social perception and social interaction may exist with learning disabilities but do not by themselves constitute a learning disability. Although learning disability may occur concomitantly with other handicapping conditions (for example, sensory impairments, mental retardation, serious emotional disturbances or social maladjustment) or with extrinsic influences (such as cultural differences or lack of opportunity to learn), they are not the result of those conditions or influences,"

Learning disabled children suffer from poor academic achievement and uneven pattern of language development, physical development, academic development, and perceptual development.

The factors causing learning disability in children accounts like genetic or hereditary, organic or physiological and environmental factors.

For improving the standard of these learning disabled children and helping them to learn and developed, the educational provisions liked provision of specialized classes or schools, special remedial and educational programme, restructuring and improving the environmental set-ups etc, should be in use. Along with parents and teachers should take special care for education and learning of their learning disabled children.

Gifted Children

Gifted children are those who possess higher level of intelligence and higher intellectual ability. According to Terman and Merill, gifted children's IQ is above 140. But some other psychologis classify thir IQ range as above 130. It is very difficult to say about the actual range of IQ of the gifted children. But it is commonly accepted that, gifted children have their superior and sharp brain and higher and outstanding intelligence. Children showing interest in difficult areas of knowledge can be recognized as gifted. They take interest in social, economic, and educational field and prove their leadership and talents.

Terman and Oden defined that, gifted children are far above the average in physique, social adjustment, personality traits, school achievement, play information and versatility of interests.

James and Drever stated that, Children possessing high intellectual ability, generally or in a particular field are called as gifted.

Havighurst stated that, the talented or gifted child is one who shows consistently remarkable performance in any worthwhile line of endavour.

Kolesnik defined that, the term gifted has been applied to every, who in his age group is superior in same ability which may make him an outstanding contributor to the welfare and quality of living in our society.

Summarizing all the definitions, it can be said that, gifted children are those who have better intellectual capacity having wide range of interests in any difficulty task resulting outstanding and remarkable performance in any area comparable to their average age groups.

Gifted children may be identified by observing the characteristics like high IQ, early talking, walking and other activities, better study habit and ability, higher working capacity, attentiveness, having of abstract thinking, better reasoning and thinking power, good imagination. Better problem solving skill, good attitude, less dependent, independent in thinking and working, possessing varied interests, good understanding power, emotionally stable, courageous and enthusiastic, disciplined and perfection in functioning of sense organs. Giftedness of children arises due to their good genetic or hereditary factors or better environmental factors.

Problems faced by Gifted Children: Because of their superior brain, gifted children face problems in coping with the normal class-room practices. They fail to adjust with the normal pace of teaching and learning activities as they quickly understand the concepts and teachings of the teachers and thus get irritated and instability with normal class room teaching. Ordinary class-room teaching does not satisfy them. They have their special needs and seek to satisfy them for their adjustment. Gifted children also face adjust problems in their homes because of their better insight and better intelligence and need more attention of family members to fulfill their needs.

Identification Method: In order to identify the gifted children, the techniques of observation, intelligence test, achievement tests, test of special abilities, psychological tests etc. can be undertaken by the teachers.

Educational Provisions: In order to make these gifted children adjusted, learn and developed, the educational provisions like provision of accelerating programme, double promotional facility, special tutorial classes, special classes and special schools, making curriculum comprehensive, good library and laboratory in the schools, organization of group activities, better method of teaching and enrichment programme should be made available to the gifted children. Teachers are to be trained to teach and deal with the gifted children. Parents are to understand their gifted children and accordingly provide further facilities for their development.

Emotionally Exceptional Children

Emotionally exceptional children are those who are having emotional instability, irritation, behavioural disorders. These children include the children with behavioural disorders and problem children.

Children with Behavioural Disorders

Children are generally found naughty, defiant and impulsive from time to time which is perfectly normal. However some children have extremely difficult and challenging behaviour that are outside the norm for their age. The most common behavioural disorders include Oppositional Defiant Disorder (ODD), Conduct Disorder (CD) and Attention Deficit Hyperactive Disorder (ADHD). These three behavioural disorders share some common symptoms. Hence, diagnosis of behavioural disorder can be difficult and time consuming. A child may have two types of disorders at the same time. Other exacerbating factors can include emotional problems, mood disorders, family difficulties and substance abuse.

Oppositional Defiant Disorder: Around one in ten children under the age of 12 years are found to have oppositional defiant disorder (ODD), with boys out numbering girls by two to one. Some of the typical behaviours of a child with ODD include the easily angered, annoyed and irritated, frequently temper tantrum, frequently arguing with others, refusing to obey rules, deliberately trying to annoy or aggravate others, low self-esteem, low frustration threshold and blaming others for any misfortunes or misdeeds.

Conduct Disorders: Children with conduct disorder (CD) are often judged as 'bad kids' because of their delinquent behaviour and refusal to accept rules. Around five percent of ten years old children are thought to have CD, with boys out numbering girls by four to one. Around one third of children with CD also have attention deficit hyperactive disorder (ADHD). Some of the typical behaviours of a child with CD may include, frequent refusal to obey their parents and authorities, repeated truancy, tendency to use drugs, cigarettes or alcohols at their early age, lack of empathy for others, found aggressive to animals and other people or showing sadistic behaviour including bullying and physical or sexual abuse, keenness to start physical fights, using weapons in physical fights, frequent lying, criminal behaviour such as stealing, deliberately lighting fires, breaking into houses and vandalism, tendency to run away from home and suicidal tendencies etc.

Attention Deficit Hyperactive Disorder: Around two to five percent of children are thought to have attention deficit hyperactive disorder (ADHD), with boys out numbering girls by three to one. The characteristics of ADHD can include, difficulty in concentrating, forgetting instructions, moving from one task to another without completing anything, taking over the top of the others, having a short fuse, being accident prone, constant restlessness and fidgeting tendency.

Behavioural disorder may grow up to be dysfunctional adults if such children suffering from behavioural disorders will be left untreated. Treatment for these children may be multifaceted depending on the particular type of disorder and factors contributing to it. In order to rectify the behavioural disorders of children following treatments methods may be undertaken like, parental education—for example teaching parents how to communicate with and manage their children, functional family therapy–entire family is helped to improve communication and problem-solving skills, cognitive behavioural therapy—to help the child to control their thoughts and behaviour, social training—the child is to be taught important social skills such as how to have conversation or play cooperatively with others, Anger management—the child is to be taught how to recognize the sign of their growing frustration and given a range of coping skills designed to defuse their anger and aggressive behaviour, Relaxation techniques and stress management skills are also to be taught to children with behavioural disorders, Support for associated problems—a child with a learning difficulty will benefit from professional support, Encouragement—Many children with behavioural disorder experience repeated failures at school and in their interaction with others. Encouraging the child to excel in their particular talent Such as sports) can help to build their self-esteem and Medication—to help control impulsive behaviours. Parents and teachers are to deal with their children suffering from behavioural disorders sympathetically with communication practices. Co-curricular activities like games, sports and yoga classes should be organized in the schools to harness the talents of behavioural disorders and make them adjusted and relaxed.

Problem Children

Problem children are those who lack normal behaviour and face problems in adjustment in one way or other. Valentine define that, problem children are those whose behaviour or personality in some way is found seriously abnormal. It is necessary to detect such children in the class room and make them adjusted in a normal class room setting. Problematic child may be seen exhibiting their characteristics like, prone to sexuality towards opposite sex, thievery, fleeing from class, making vandalism, masturbation, non-reliable, talking non-sense, and indiscipline, cruel and threat to others, shameful, restlessness, murmuring etc. If these characteristics hinder the child in his normal adjustment process, then he/she become problematic.

Cyril Burt has classified problem children into two categories such as Threatening and excited children and Suppressed or Impatient children. Threatening and excited children are those who fight and quarrel with others over small things and get excited. They suddenly adopt the threatening activity. On the other hand, Suppressed or impatient children are those who are found fearful and anxious due to some reason.

The problem children should be detected at an early and provided adequate therapy otherwise they will be developed as disturbed adults into the society. The problem children are to be separated from common/normal children before treatment. The common problems the parents and teachers face about the problem children include thievery tendency, lying habit, late coming to the classes and non-compliances of their home task.

The causes that develop problematic tendency in children may be hereditary and environmental by nature. Hereditary caused that lead to develop mal adjustment in children include defects in sense organs, physical and emotional abnormalities. But environmental causes include evil company of children, improper family atmosphere, hard discipline, sexual problems, imitation, non-fulfillment of needs, and improper care of parents, adventure etc.

In order to help the problem children learn, adjusted and developed the educational programmes likes, developing good family atmosphere, parental education, advising to have good company, establishing high ideals by the teachers, arranging attractive and affective educational system, developing a balanced curriculum, arrangement of suitable co-curricular activities, developing the habit of self-discipline and arrangement of guidance and counseling services should be made available to them.

Socially Exceptional Children

Socially Exceptional children include backward children and Delinquent children.

Backward Children

Backward children are those who fall at the lower extreme of the normal distribution of the educational attainment trait. Backward children may be categorized as of mentally retardation and educational retardation. Taking intelligence test and achievement test, the degree of backwardness of children can be assessed. Backward children are found to deviate from their classmates in their school achievement. Backward children do not get benefit from the normal class-room teaching. They are treated as a liability for the society and nation.

Burt defined backward child as "one who in mid school career is unable to do the work of the class next below that which is normal for his age". Burton Hall defined that, backwardness in general is applied to cases where other educational achievement falls below the level of their natural abilities. Schonell defined that; backward pupil is one who compared with other pupils of his chronological age shows marked educational deficiency. According to Burt, backward children's educational quotient (EQ) falls below 85, (EQ=M.A (mental age)/C.A (chronological age) x100). Backward children can be identified by observing the characteristics like, slow learning and poor academic achievement.

The causes that lead to develop backwardness may be attributed as, physical causes like poor health, malnutrition, weakness, defects in sense organs, improper functioning of glands etc, mental causes like poor intelligence, poor attitude and understanding ability, social causes like poor economic condition of the family, domestic violence and dispute, illiteracy of parents, poor social standard etc, and school related causes like lack of facilities in the schools, absence of guidance facilities in the schools and regular absence of the child in the school. Like other types of the exceptional children, the backward children also find problems in adjustment in the class-room and schools due to their poor academic achievement and slow learning, emotional problems, and social problems.

In order to help the backward children learn, and developed the educational provisions such as providing suitable curriculum, professional education and training, adjusting teaching methods, moral education, special classes, incentives for learning, providing individual attention, their parental counseling, adopting suitable method of motivation for the backward children should be made available. Teachers are to sympathetically deal with these children and have proper communication with their guardians.

Delinquent Children

Delinquent children are those who are porn to anti-social behaviours or crimes tendencies. Juvenile delinquents are those minor children committing major criminal activities. These children violate the law and commit offences like theft, gambling, cheating, pick-pocketing, murder, robbery, loss of property, assault and violence, intoxicating, begging, kidnapping, abduction and other sexual offences etc. Therefore juvenile delinquency should be considered as a serious challenge to the wellbeing of the society. The young delinquents if not treated properly at an early, they will become detrimental for the society.

Valentine stated that, broadly speaking, the term delinquency refers to breaking of some law.

Cyrill Burt defined the term delinquency that, a child is technically delinquent when his anti-social tendencies become so grave that he becomes or ought to become the subject of official action.

Hadfield defined that, delinquency is an anti-social behaviour.

Klausmeier and Goodwin stated that, a delinquent is a child or youth who repeatedly commits acts which are punishable as crime.

So, after summarizing the definitions, we may conclude that, delinquency is a type tendency of the children or youths to commit anti-social activities in the society. It is considered as a social problem found in the children. They are found exceptional because, they deviate from the normal children in their social behaviours and prefer to commit anti-social activities. The act of delinquency is always intentional and the delinquents intentionally found involved in certain crimes. Delinquency is a form of mal-adjustment in the children and a type of disorder development. Delinquents put problems for others and break their peace.

Causes of Delinquency: The cause of the development of the delinquency tendency is fulfillment of the desire against restrictions. When the needs or desires of a child gets threatened, then his rebellion attitude develops and he wants to expresses his aggression in destroying, damaging or changing the environment to realize his needs. Thus there develops a delinquency tendency in the child. Certain hereditary factors like physical defects in the children, mental retardation, emotional instability, mal-adjustment genes of the children received from their parents also contribute to their delinquency nature. Environmental factors like poor socio-economic status of the family, poverty, hunger and starvation, unemployment, domestic violence, illiteracy of parents, favouratism in the family, quarrel among parents, step father and step mother attitudes, over and under parental protection, extreme and hard discipline, bad companions, sexual and bad film programme, lack of cultural education and value education, class-conflict in the society, lack of parental and teacher's guidance, improper behaviour of teachers in the schools, lack of co-curricular activities in the schools, defective curriculum and over loaded home task etc lead to develop the delinquency nature in the children.

Type of Delinquents: There are two types of delinquents. There are some delinquents are found active, energetic, restless and having strong spirit of adventure. They commit crimes for their progress in the eyes of their companions and are generous, thoughtful and trustworthy.

The other type of delinquents is found shy, quiet, selfish and vindictive in nature and they are least thoughtful of others. They commit crimes but remain silent and foolish before the parents and teachers just like unknown of anything and keep themselves smiling.

Identification Characteristics: In order to identify the delinquents, the characteristics like anti-social behaviour, indiscipline, habit of breaking law, disobedience, aggressive and hostile behaviour, immoral activities, higher anxiety level, mal-adjustment symptoms, poor economic background may be observed.

Therapeutic Measures and provisions

In order to help the delinquents to learn and developed, the educational provisions like, reforming the home environment by proper parental education and their literacy, mitigating family conflicts, enhancing parental love and affection, good relationship, caring to satisfy the basic needs of the children and displaying ideal behaviour in the family, reforming social environment in respect of providing good and ideal schools, maintaining public library, enforcing healthy laws, opening children's garden, juvenile courts etc, reforming schools in respect of its curriculum, co-curricular activities, teacher's attitude, organizing scouts and guide programme, NCC and NSS programme, organizing guidance and counseling services, moral and value education classes, and providing medication and curative measures to check mal-adjustment problems, emotional problems, mental retardation, mental disorders in the children should be made available to the delinquent children. Parents are to be given education and training to deal with their delinquent children. Teachers in the schools are to deal with these children with positive attitudes.

References

Agrawal, J.C., *Psychology of Learning and Development*, Delhi: Shipra Publications, 2011.

Baron, R.A. and Misra, Girish, *Psychology* (5th Ed.), Delhi, India: Pearson, 2014.

Baron, R.A., Psychology (5th Ed.), New Delhi: Prentice Hall of India, 2001.

Bhatia and Bhatia, *A Text book of Educational Psychology*, Delhi: Doaba House, Naisarak, 2007.

Bhatnagar, S. *et al.*, *Advanced Educational Psychology*, Meerut, India: R. Lall Book Depot, 2008.

Chand, Tara., *Modern Child Psychology*, New Delhi: Modern Publications Pvt. Ltd., 2006.

Chand, Tara, *Educational Psychology*, New Delhi: Anmol Publication Pvt. Ltd., 2010.

Chaube, S.P., *Educational Psychology*, Agra: L.N. Agrawal, 1983.

Chauhan, S.S., *Advanced Educational Psychology*, New Delhi: Vikas Publishing House Pvt. Ltd., 2007.

Dash, M., *Educational Psychology*, New Delhi: Deep & Deep Publications Pvt. Ltd., 2004.

Gupta, Manju, *Special Education*, New Delhi: KSK Publisher and Distributers Ansari Road, Darya Ganj, 2007.

Hurlock, E.B., (Rev. Ed)., *Adolescence Development*, New York: Mc Graw Hill Book Co, 1981.

Kupuswami, B., *Advance Educational Psychology*, New Delhi: Sterling Publishers Pvt. Ltd., 2006.

Kundu, C.L. *et al.*, *Educational Psychology*, New Delhi: Sterling Publishers Pvt. Ltd., 2006.

Mangal, S.K., *Advanced Educational Psychology*, New Delhi: PHI Learning Pvt. Ltd., 2010.

Mathur, S.S., *Educational Psychology*, Agra, India: Vonod Pustak Mandir. 1981.

Morse, William. C, and Wingo, G. Max., *Psychology and Teaching* (3rd Ed.), Bombay: D.B. Taraporevala Sons & Co. Pvt. Ltd., 1970.

Panda, B.B., *Foundations of Educational Psychology*, Cuttack: Vidyapuri, Balubazar, Cuttack, India, 1991.

Panda, K.C., *Elements of Child Development*, New Delhi, India: Kalyani Publisher, 1981.

Penthoi, A.K., Special Education, New Delhi, India: APH Publishing Corporation, 2011.

Penthoi, A.K. and Dash, S., Teaching English Language in India, Agra, India: Radha Prakashan Mandir, 2009.

Prasad, S.B., *Special Education*, Jaipur, India: Pointer Publishers, 2011

Singh, K.P., *Advance Educational Psychology*, Meerut: R. Lall Book Depot, 2011

Skinner, C., *Educational Psychology*, New Delhi: Prentice Hall of India Pvt. Ltd., 2006

Thagard, Paul. *Mind: Introduction to Cognitive Science* (2nd Ed.), New Delhi: Prentice Hall of India, 2006.

Woolfolk, A., *Educational Psychology*, Delhi: Dorling Kindersley (India) Pvt. Ltd., 2006.

Online References

www. Google.co.in

Possible Questions

CHAPTER-1

Long Answer type

1. Define educational Psychology and write its natures.
2. Describe the relationship between education and psychology
3. Narrate, how a teacher can apply the knowledge of educational psychology in the field of education
4. Describe the scope of educational psychology.

Short Answer type

1. What is educational Psychology?
2. How educational psychology is a positive science?
3. How educational psychology can apply psychology?
4. How educational psychology helps a teacher?

Objective Type

1. **Mark the statement as right or wrong putting tick (✓) mark and cross (X) mark against the same.**
   a) Psychology means the study of mind. ( )
   b) Psychology is the study of behaviour. ( )
   c) Educational psychology in an applied science. ( )
   d) Educational psychology helps to improve teaching learning practice. ( )
   e) Educational psychology is a normative science. ( )
2. Choose the correct answer out of the four alternatives.
   a) Educational psychology is called an applied science because,
      i) Principles of psychology are applied in the field of education.
      ii) Psychology and education are related each other.
      iii) Educational psychology is applied in the field of science.
      iv) No one is correct.
   b) Educational psychology is a,
      i) Normative science. ii) Positive science.
      iii) Natural science. iv) Physical science.
   c) Who said that psychology is the study of human behaviour and human relationship
      i) Woodworth ii) Crow and Crow
      iii) Watson iv) N.L. Munn

Answer Key

Q. 1 a-X, b-✓, c- ✓, d-✓, e-X Q.2 a-i, b-ii, c-ii

CHAPTER-2

Long Answer type

1. What is the use of the methods of educational psychology?

2. Describe different methods used in the field of educational psychology.
3. What is observation method? Write its advantages and disadvantages:

Short Answer Type

1. What is introspection Method?
2. What is observation Method?
3. What is an Interview?
4. What is experimental method?

Objective type

Choose the correct answer out of the given four alternative answers

1. In which method more number of people can be studied at a time?
   a) Experimental method b) Interview method
   c) Questionnaire Method d) Case history method.
2. Which method is helpful in diagnosing the problem of child?
   a) Questionnaire method b) Experimental method
   c) Case history method d) introspection method.
3. Which method helps examining one's own self?
   a) Introspection method b) Experimental method
   c) Questionnaire Method d) Interview method.
4. Participant observation means?
   a) Child participate in the observation
   b) Observer participate in the observation
   c) Both children and observer participate in the process of observation
   d) None of these
5. Interview method is helpful because
   a) It help disclosing the personal feelings of the interviewee
   b) It helps in disclosing the intention of the interviewer
   c) It helps in collecting varied information's from the interviewee
   d) None of these
6. Natural observation means—
   a) Observation of nature b) Observation in natural setting
   c) Observation of natural things d) No one is correct.
7. Verifying the result is possible in case of
   a) Observation method b) Interview method
   c) Experimental method d) Questionnaire Method
8. Which method is also known as clinical method-?
   a) Anecdotal method b) Observation method
   c) Interview method d) Case study method
9. In which method interaction of the two individuals operates.
   a) Case study method b) Observation method
   c) Interview method d) Experimental method
10. Methods of educational psychology are used to—
    a) Study the educational problems of the learners
    b) Introduce the new method in the field of education
    c) Apply various techniques to motivate the learners.
    d) Study the behavioural problems of the learners.

Answer Key

Q.1-c, Q.2-c, Q.3-a, Q.4-b, Q.5-a, Q.6-b, Q.7-c, Q.8-d, Q.9-c, Q.10-d

CHAPTER-3

Long Answer Type

1. Discuss that Behaviourism was a revolt against Introspectionism.
2. Describe, how Gestalists interpreted learning?
3. Distinguish between structuralism and functionalism.
4. Differentiate between behaviouristic and gestalt theory of learning.
5. Describe the contributions of psychoanalysis school to the field of psychology.
6. What is Hormic School of psychology? Write its significance in the field of education and psychology.

Short Answer Type

1. What is Libido?
2. What is life and Death instincts?
3. What are the dynamic aspects of mind?
4. What is perception?
5. What is insightful learning?
6. What do you mean by sentiments?
7. What is behaviour?
8. Compare the subject matter of structuralism and functionalism.
9. Write different aspects of instincts.
10. What are the different zones of sexuality according to Freud?

Objective Type

Choose the correct answer out of the given four alternatives.

1. The father of Hormic School.
   a. Sigmund freud b. James R. angel
   c. Carl Jung d. Mc Dougall
2. Who is the founder of Behaviourism?
   a. Sigmund freud b. J.B. Watson
   c. Wertheimer d. Woodworth
3. Dream analysis is the contribution of—
   a. Gestalt School b. Functionalism
   c. Behaviourism School d. Psychoanalysis School
4. Which school stated that whole is more important than part in the process of learning?
   a. Structuralism b. Functionalism
   c. Gestalt School d. Psychoanalysis School
5. Who did give the concept of motives?
   a. Alfred Adler b. Carl Jung
   c. Mc Dougall d. Benet
6. What is social and moral in nature?
   a. Id b. Ego
   c. Id and Ego d. Super Ego
7. The meaning of Gestalt is.
   a. An aspect b. Organized whole
   c. Organization of parts d. Relation between whole and part
8. The word Gestalt is an
   a. An American Word b. German Word
   c. Italian Word d. Greek Word
9. Who propounded the school of functionalism?
   a. Word worth b. J.B. Watson
   c. Mc Dougall d. James R. Angel

10. Who is not a supporter of the school of behaviourism?
    a. B.F. Skinner b. J.B. Watson
    c. E.L. Thorndike d. Mc Dougall

Answer key

1-d, 2-b, 3-d, 4-c 5-c, 6-d, 7-b, 8-b, 9-d, and 10-c

CHAPTER-4

Long Answer Type

1. Describe, how, body and mind is closely related.
2. What is a nervous system? Write its importance in human body.
3. What are the roles of Ductless glands in human body?

Short Answer Type

1. What is brain?
2. What is spinal Cord?
3. What are Duct glands?
4. Write the importance of gonads in human body?
5. What is the function of thyroid glands?
6. What is the composition of central nervous system?
7. What so you mean by cognitive aspect of mind?

Objective Type

Choose the right answer out of the given four alternatives.

1. How many of aspects of mind exists
   i) Two ii) Three
   iii) Four iv) Five
2. Thyroid glands helps in—
   i) Physical Development ii) Emotional Development
   iii) Sexual Development iv) Moral Development
3. Nervous System links to—
   i) Spinal Cord and brain ii) Brain Only
   iii) Spinal Cord Only iv) Pituitary Glands
4. Who did say that sound mind exists in sound body—
   i) J.B. Watson ii) Aristotle
   iii) Gandhi iv) Allport
5. Which is a growth gland?
   i) Gonads ii) Pituitary Gland
   iii) Adrenal Glands iv) Thyroid Gland

Answer Key

Q. 1-ii, Q. 2-i, Q.3-i, Q.4-ii, Q. 5-ii

CHAPTER-5

Long Answer Type

1. What is growth and Development? Distinguish between the two.
2. Explain the principles of development with suitable examples.
3. Explain the factors that determine the growth and development of the child.
4. What is the role of Heredity and Environment in growth and development of an individual?

Short Answer Type

1. What is Heredity?

2. What is Environment?
3. What is Growth?
4. What is the law of variation?
5. What is the law of resemblance?

Objective type

Recognize the statement whether true or false.

1. Growth denotes to the physical change of the body. (True/False)
2. Development is a process (True/False)
3. Growth and development are complementary to each other (True/False)
4. Growth is a continuous process (True/False)
5. Maturation does not have any role to development (True/False)
6. Sex can't be regarded as a factor of development (True/False)
7. Heredity plays an important role in growth and development (True/False)
8. Environment means the situations where we live. (True/False)
9. Psycho-environment relates to one's mind. (True/False)
10. Non-Transmission of acquired traits is of a law of heredity (True/False)

Answer Key

1. True, 2. True, 3. True, 4. False, 5. False, 6. False, 7. True, 8. True, 9. True and 10. False

CHAPTER-6

Long Answer Type

1. Differentiate between Growth and Development. Write the major dimensions of the growth and Development.
2. Describe the characteristics of Physical Growth and Development taking place in different stages of life.
3. What is Mental Development? Narrate the process of Mental Development taking the reference of Piaget's Views.
4. Write with example about social development during different stages of life.
5. What is Emotion? How Emotional development takes place at different stages of life?
6. What is Moral Development? Write the theories suggested by different Psychologists on Moral Development.
7. Describe the characteristics of Moral Development during Adolescence stage.
8. Describe how language development occurs from Infancy period to Adolescence Period.
9. Narrate different theories about language development of children.
10. Compare between the Transactional Theory and Rational Frame theory of Language Development.

Short Answer Type

1. Write the Characteristics of Physical growth and Development.
2. Write the characteristics of Mental Development.
3. Briefly write about the phages of Mental Development suggested by Piaget.
4. Write the characteristics of Social Development.
5. Write the characteristics of Emotional Development.
6. Write the natures of the Emotional Development.
7. Write the factors influencing the Moral Development of Children.
8. Write the factors influencing the Emotional Development of Children.

9. Write the different components of the Language Development of Children.
10. Briefly discuss about the nature of Language Development of children.

Objective Types

Choose the right answer out of the following given four alternatives.

1. Which is a characteristic of Physical Growth and Development?
   (a) Changes in Nervous System
   (b) Changes on Language pattern
   (c) Changes in Emotions
   (d) Changes in Friendship pattern
2. Which one is a characteristic of Emotional Development?
   (a) Changes in Nervous System
   (b) Changes on speaking habit
   (c) Development of Anger
   (d) Development of Intelligence
3. Which one indicates the characteristics of the Social Development?
   (a) Development of Fear
   (b) Development of Thinking
   (c) Development of Height
   (d) Development of the sense of sharing
4. Concrete Operational Stage of Cognitive Development was given by,
   (a) Skinner (b) Piaget
   (c) Brunner (d) Noam Chomsky
5. Noam Chomsky's theory is famous in the field of,
   (a) Cognitive Development (b) Social Development
   (c) Emotional Development (d) Language Development
6. Transactional theory of language development was given by,
   (a) Noam Chomsky (b) Brunner
   (c) Piaget (d) Vygotsky
7. Which age range indicates the Childhood stage?
   (a) 6-12 Years (b) 5-11 Years
   (c) 13-19 Years (d) 7-14 Years
8. Which age range indicates the Adolescence period?
   (a) 11-19 Years (b) 13-19 Years
   (c) 10-?0 Years (d) 12-18 Years
9. Lawrence Kohlberg is known for his theory of,
   (a) Cognitive Deployment (b) Social Development
   (c) Emotional Development (d) Moral Development
10. Jean Piaget is known for his theory of,
   (a) Cognitive Deployment (b) Social Development
   (c) Emotional Development (d) Moral Development

Answer Key

Q.1-a, Q.2-c, Q.3-d, Q.4-b, Q.5-d, Q.6-d, Q.7-a, Q.8-b, Q.9-d and Q.10-a

CHAPTER-7

Long Answer Type

1. Why the period of Adolescence is called as the period of stress and strain? Justify your views with reference to the characteristics of Physical growth and Development during adolescence Period.
2. Describe the characteristics of the cognitive development during the Adolescence Stage.

3. Describe the Characteristics of Emotional Development of Adolescents.
4. Narrate the characteristics of the Social and Moral Development of adolescents.
5. Describe the different needs and problems of the Adolescents.

Short Answer Type

1. What is self-identity?
2. What is Self-concept?
3. What is identity diffusion?
4. What is social-identity?
5. What is moral development?

Objective Types

Select correct answer out of the given four alternatives:

1. Teen agers mean,
   (a) Children (b) Infants
   (c) Adolescents (d) Adults
2. Adolescence period is called as a period of stress and strain because,
   (a) Adolescents fail to develop (b) Adolescents fail to decide
   (c) Adolescents fail to succeed (d) Adolescents fail to achieve
3. Age range of Adolescence stage is,
   (a) 12-18 (b) 11-19
   (c) 13-19 (d) 9-19
4. Identity diffusion is evident in,
   (a) Childhood (b) Infancy
   (c) Adulthood (d) Adolescence
5. Who said that adolescents face the problem of self-identity?
   (a) Skinner (b) Brunner
   (c) Erikson (d) Piaget

Answer Key

Q.1-c, Q.2-b, Q.3-c, Q.4-d, and Q.5-c

CHAPTER-8

Long Answer Type

1. Describe the Psychoanalytical theory of human development.
2. Write about the Erikson's theory of psychosocial development.
3. State about the learning theories of development.
4. Compare between Bronfenbrenner's Ecological system theory of development and Albert Bandura's social learning theory of development.
5. Explain the Epigenetic Psychobiological system theory of development.
6. Explain the humanistic theory of personality development of Carl Rogers

Short Answer Type

1. What is Super Ego according to Freud?
2. What is the role of Ego in human mind?
3. Write the stages of psychosocial development suggested by Erikson.
4. Write the importance of role-model in social development?
5. What are the levels of the environment that affect the development of an individual according to Bronfenbrenner?
6. What is natural selection according to Darwin?
7. State the elements of the phenomenal field pointed by Carl Rogers?
8. State the role of conditioning in learning and development
9. Write the role of reinforcement in learning.
10. State the stages of cognitive development suggested by Piaget.

Objective Type

Choose the correct answer out of the given alternatives.

1. Who was the contributor of Evolutionary theory of human development?
   (a) Piaget (b) Bandura (c) Darwin (d) Thorndike
2. Who was the pioneer of Operant conditioning theory of learning?
   (a) Piaget (b) Pavlov (c) Thorndike (d) Skinner
3. Who was the profounder of Psychoanalytic Theory of development?
   (a) Kohler (b) Freud (c) Piaget (d) Kurt Lewin
4. Social cognitive development theory was given by,
   (a) Koffka (b) Albert Bandura (c) Piaget (d) Kurt Lewin
5. Who stated about five levels of environment that affect the human development?
   (a) Urie Bronfenbrenner (b) Darwin
   (c) Skinner (d) Erikson
6. Who stated about the phenomenal field?
   (a) Erikson (b) Terman (c) Binet (d) Carl Rogers
7. Who gave the concept 'good life'
   (a) Urie Bronfenbrenner (b) Carl Rogers
   (c) Piaget (d) Pavlov

Answer Key

Q.1-c, Q.2-d, Q.3-b, Q.4-b. Q.5-a, Q.6-d and Q.7-b

CHAPTER-9

Long Answer Type

1. What is Individual difference? Discuss the areas of individual difference.
2. Education should be child centered. Discuss the statement in the light of the study of individual difference.
3. Discuss the causes of individual difference with examples.
4. Discuss the impact of the study of individual difference on the field of teaching and learning.

Short answer Type

Answer the following questions briefly.

1. Discuss how heredity plays for making individual difference?
2. Individualized instruction is the contribution of the study of individual difference.
3. Write on normality and variability in individual difference.
4. Explain how environment is responsible for individual difference.
5. Distinguish between longitudinal and cross-sectional tests in individual difference.

Objective Type

Find out the correct answer out of the four given alternatives.

1. Which factor makes physiological differences in individuals?
   a) Environment b) Heredity c) Education d) Maturation
2. Which source helps the individual to avail his acquired traits?
   a) Environment b) Heredity c) Education d) Maturation
3. Which type of cause operates in individual differences of boy and girls?
   a) Sex b) Heredity c) Education d) Maturation
4. If someone is better in cricket and other one is better in singing. Then which type of individual difference is marked
   a) Attitude b) Interest c) Intelligence d) Aptitude

5. If someone is better in learning and other one is not better in learning. Then what may be the cause of their individual difference?
   a) Sex b) Culture c) Intelligence d) Education

ANSWERS KEY

Q.1-b, Q.2-a, Q.3-a, Q.4-d, and Q.5-c

CHAPTER-10

Long Answer types

1. What do you mean by the term personality? Explain different types of personality with examples.
2. Write different trait theories of personality?
3. Compare between typological and trait approaches of personality.
4. Describe the factors that influence personality of individuals.
5. Write about different techniques of personality assessment.

Short Answer types

1. Write about Soma types of personality.
2. Write the personality types of E. Krestchmer.
3. Write about Cattel's classification of personality traits.
4. Briefly write about Gordon Allport's classification of personality traits.
5. Write about the techniques of Rorschach's Inkblot test of personality.
6. What is TAT in personality test?
7. Write about projective techniques of personality assessment.
8. What is word association test in personality assessment?
9. Write different applications of personality tests.
10. Write the merits and demerits of projective techniques of personality test.

Objective Types

Find out the correct one out of the given four alternatives.

1. Whose contribution is the Soma types of Personality
   (a) spranger (b) Scheldon (c) Cattel (d) None of these
2. Who classified personality according to their field of interest?
   (a) Spranger (b) Cattel (c) Allport (d) Freud
3. Whose classification of personality types tells about Introvert type of personality?
   (a) Krestchmer (b) Eysenk (c) Cattel (d) Allport
4. Inkblot test was devised by,
   (a) Gordon Allport (b) Rorschach (c) Freud (d) None of these
5. Social learning theory of personality was given by,
   (a) Thorndike (b) Cattel (c) Piaget (d) Bandura
6. Psycho-analytical approach to study personality was given by, Freud
   (a) Maslow (b) Bandura (c) Freud (d) Cattel
7. Who gave importance to the motivation in the personality development?
   (a) Carl Rogers (b) Piaget (c) Maslow (d) Skinner
8. Cognitive theory of personality development was given by,
   (a) Maslow (b) Piaget (c) Freud (d) Pavlov
9. Need theory of personality development was highlighted by,
   (a) Maslow (b) Skinner (c) Bandura (d) None of these
10. Hierarchy of personality traits was the contribution of,
    (a) Piaget (b) Maslow (c) Cattel (d) Allport

Answer Key

Q.1-b, Q2-a, Q.3-d, Q.4-b, Q.5-d, Q.6.-c, Q.7-a, Q.8-b, Q.9-a, and Q.10-c

CHAPTER-11

Long Answer Type

1. Define mental health. Discuss about the factors that affect the mental health and adjustment of an individual.
2. What is adjustment? Describe the methods of adjustment with suitable examples.
3. What is mental disorder? Discuss about different types of mental disorders and their treatment mechanism.
4. Describe the conditions that affect the mental health of teachers. Discuss the remedial measures that can improve the mental health of teachers.
5. Describe about the factors influencing the mental health of learners in the schools. Write about the steps that can be taken to improve the mental health of learners in their schools.

Short Answer Type

1. Differentiate between mental hygiene and mental health.
2. What is adjustment mechanism?
3. Briefly write about mental disorders
4. Briefly write about symptoms of maladjustment
5. Write about environmental conditions that contribute to mental health of individuals.

Objective Type

Choose the right answer out of the given alternatives.

1. What is true about mental hygiene?
   (a) It tells about techniques to maintain mental health
   (b) It tells about factors affecting mental health
   (c) It tells about adjustment mechanism
   (d) It tells about mental processes
2. Which one is a symptom of good mental health?
   (a) Feeling irritation (b) Feeling restlessness
   (c) Feeling satisfaction (d) Feeling happy
3. What symptom is associated with frustration?
   (a) Feeling not well (b) Feeling drowsy
   (c) Feeling interested in action (d) Feeling disinterested in action
4. Which one is not a characteristic of adjustment mechanism?
   (a) Having self actualization (b) Having self respect
   (c) Having self confidence (d) Having emotional stability
5. Which one is a cause of maladjustment?
   (a) Being tension free (b) Being satisfied
   (c) Being physically fit (d) Being frustrated

Answer Keys

Q.1-a, Q.2-d, Q.3-d, Q.4-b, and Q. 5-d

CHAPTER-12

Long Answer type

1. Differentiate between thinking and reasoning. Write the characteristics of thinking.
2. Discuss about different forms of thinking.
3. What is thinking? Describe the factors influencing thinking.
4. Describe the conditions that help in development of thinking of children.
5. Compare between the Piaget's and Brunner's views about thinking.

Short answer type

1. What is thinking?
2. What is Reasoning?
3. What is concrete thinking?
4. What is abstract thinking?
5. What is Iconic Phase according to Brunner's views about thinking?
6. What is the process of categorization according to Brunner?
7. Write the requisites/tools of thinking.

Objective Types

Choose the correct answer out of the given alternatives.

1. Whose classification of tells about Iconic phases of the development of thinking process?
   (a) Skinner (b) Brunner (c) Erikson (d) Piaget
2. Who told about the process of categorization in the development of thinking?
   (a) Skinner (b) Cattel (c) Brunner (d) Piaget
3. Sensory-motor phase of cognitive development was highlighted by,
   (a) Skinner (b) Brunner (c) Erikson (d) Piaget

Answer Key

Q1-b, Q2-c, Q3-d

CHAPTER-13

Long Answer Type

1. What is problem solving? Write the different approaches of problem solving.
2. Describe the conditions affecting problem solving ability of children. How can a teacher promote problem solving ability in his students?

Short Answer Type

1. Write the techniques of developing problem solving ability in children
2. Write short notes on environmental factors influencing the problem solving ability of children.
3. Write the steps followed in problem solving.

Objective Type

Choose the correct answer out of the given alternatives.

1. Trial and error approach of problem solving was suggested by,
   (a) Pavlov (b) Brunner (c) E.L. Thorndike (d) Piaget
2. Cognitive approach of problem solving was suggested by,
   (a) Pavlov (b) Brunner (c) E.L. Thorndike (d) Piaget

Answer Keys

Q.1. (c), Q.2. (d)

CHAPTER-14

Long Answer Type

1. Define learning. Write the nature of learning.
2. Describe the different types of learning with suitable example.
3. What is learning? Narrate the different methods of learning.
4. Describe the factors affecting learning with examples.

Short Answer Type

1. What is learning?
2. What is trial and error method of learning?

3. What is conditioning method of learning?
4. What is insightful method of learning?
5. What is imitation method of learning?

Objective Type

Select the correct answer out of the given alternatives.

1. Seeing others and to learn is called as
   (A) Conditioning learning (B) Insightful learning
   (C) Imitation (D) None of these
2. Committing mistakes at initial stage and to learn is called as
   (A) Imitation method (B) Conditioning method
   (C) Trial and error method (D) Insightful method
3. Understanding relationship and to learn means following
   (A) Insightful method (B) Conditioning method
   (B) Trial and error method (D) None of theses

Answer Key

Q.1-C, Q.2-C, and Q.3-A

CHAPTER-15

Long Answer Type

1. Distinguish between classical conditioning theories of learning with reinforcement and conditioning theories of learning without reinforcement.
2. Explain the theory of learning given by Ivan Pavlov. Write the principles of conditioning theory of learning and its contribution to the field of education.
3. Compare the learning theory of Watson and Pavlov with respect to their principle of learning.
4. Explain the educational significance of the learning theory pioneered by Guthrie.
5. What is trial and error method of learning? Explain the principle of trial and error theory of learning.
6. Describe about the Hull's theory of learning. Write its educational value.
7. Compare between the learning theory of Pavlov and Skinner. Write their educational significance.
8. What is operant conditioning in learning? State the role of reinforcement in the field of learning.
9. What is Gestalt theory of learning? State the features of insightful learning.
10. Explain the cognitive field theory of Kurt Lewin. Write its principles and educational value.

Short Answer Type

1. What is conditioning?
2. What do you mean by operant conditioning?
3. What is the role of reinforcement in learning?
4. Write the principles of trial and error process of learning.
5. Write the principles of conditioning theory of learning.
6. Write the principles of insightful learning.
7. What do you mean by sign learning?
8. Write the significance of cognitive field theory of leraning.

Objective Type

Select the correct answer out the given alternatives.

1. On which animal, Watson conducted his experiment to prove his theory of learning?
   (a) Cat (b) Rat (c) Dog (d) Rabbit

2. Who contributed the concept of insightful learning?
   (a) Skinner (b) Kohler (c) Thorndike (d) Watson
3. Who is the psychologist offered the Drive reduction theory?
   (a) Hull (b) Piaget (c) Tolman (d) Freud
4. Operant conditioning theory of learning is given by
   (a) Gutherie (b) Pavlov (c) Skinner (d) Thorndike
5. The main profounder of cognitive field theory is
   (a) Pavlov (b) Piaget (c) Skinner (d) Kurt Lewin
6. Law of effect as a principle of leårning was given by,
   (a) Thorndike (b) Skinner (c) Tolman (d) Hull
7. Gestalists had conducted their experiment on,
   (a) Chimpanji (b) Rat (c) Dog (d) Rabbit
8. Which theory of learning recommends the Law of readiness as a principle of learning?
   (a) Conditioning learning theory
   (b) Operant Conditioning learning theory
   (c) Trial and error theory of learning
   (d) Theory of insightful learning
9. Who is the psychologist giving the theory of Sign learning?
   (a) Thorndike (b) Skinner (c) Tolman (d) Hull
10. Principle of extinction relates to which theory of learning?
    (a) Trial and error theory of learning
    (b) Gestalt theory of learning
    (c) Sign theory of learning
    (d) Conditioning theory of learning

Answer Key

Q.1-d, Q.2-b, Q.3-a, Q.4-c, Q.5-d, Q.6-a, Q.7-a, Q.8-c, Q.9-c, Q.10-d

CHAPTER-16

Long answer Type

1. What is Mastery Learning? Describe about the basic Assumptions of Mastery Learning.
2. Describe the salient features of Gagne's Hierarchy of Learning.
3. State the basic principles of the learning theory postulated by Ausubel and write the educational value of Ausubel's types of learning.

Short Answer Type

1. Briefly state the stages of Mastery learning.
2. What is entry behaviour according to Mastery Learning?
3. What is Gagne's Concept Learning?
4. What are the components of the Instruction as suggested by Gagne?
5. What is rote Discovery Learning?
6. What are different methods of Subsumption?

Objective Types

Select the correct answer out the given alternatives.

1 Whose contribution is the Mastery Learning?
  (a) Piaget (b) Bloom (c) Ausubel (d) Gagne
2. How many types of learning arranged in the Gagne's Hierarchy of Learning?
   (a) 2 (b) 4 (c) 6 (d) 8

3. Who propagated the concept of Advance organizer?
   (a) Ausubel (b) Piaget (c) Bloom (d) Thorndike
4. Who contributed the concept of Meaningful learning?
   (a) Skinner (b) Bloom (c) Ausubel (d) Piaget
5. How many phases of an act of learning mentioned by Gagne?
   (a) 10 (b) 12 (c) 8 (d) 6

Answer Key

Q.1-b, Q.2-c, Q.3-a, Q.4-c, and Q.5-c

CHAPTER-17

Long Answer Type

1. Write about the assumptions and contributions of behavioural perspectives of learning.
2. Describe the assumption and educational contributions of cognitive perspectives of learning.
3. Narrate the features of developmental perspectives of learning.
4. Describe the assumptions and educational contributions of socio-cultural theory of learning
5. Describe about the constructive perspectives of learning and its educational implications.

Short Answer type

1. Write about the contributions of behavioural perspective s of learning.
2. Describe the educational contributions of cognitive perspectives of learning.
3. Write the educational contribution of the developmental perspectives of learning.
4. Describe the assumptions of socio-cultural theory of learning.
5. Describe about the constructive perspectives of learning and its educational implications.

Objective Type

Choose correct answer out of the given four alternatives

1. The main proponent of behavioural perspectives of learning is
   (a) Watson (b) Skinner (c) Thorndike (d) Pavlov
2. Social learning theory was developed by.
   (a) Bandura (b) Piaget (c) Skinner (d) Thorndike
3. Who is a member of the Cognitive perspectives of learning?
   (a) Bandura (b) Vygotosky (c) Skinner (d) Thorndike
4. Who was the psychologist to tell about the role of model for shaping behaviour?
   (a) Skinner (b) Noam Chomsky (c) Albert Bandura (d) Carl Rogers
5. Who is called as the father of modern linguistics?
   (a) Vygotosky (b) Piaget (c) Skinner (d) Noam Chomsky
6. Who gave the psychosocial theory of Development?
   (a) Bandura (b) Erikson (c) Skinner (d) Kohler
7. Who is the founder of constructive perspectives of learning?
   (a) Bruner (b) Piaget (c) Skinner (d) Thorndike

Answer Key

Q.1-a, Q.2-a, Q.3-b, Q.4-c, Q.5-d, Q.6-b and Q.7-a

CHAPTER-18

Long Answer Type

1. What do you understand by information processing? Justify how learning is an act of information processing.
2. Describe about the information processing model of Robert Gagne and implication to the field of learning.

Short Answer Type

1. What is shot-term memory?
2. What is long-term Memory?
3. Write the different categories of learning suggested by Gagne.
4. Write the conditions of learning suggested by Gagne.
5. Write the different phases of an act of learning mentioned by Gagne.

CHAPTER-19

Long Answer Type

1. Define Intelligence. Write the natures of intelligence.
2. Describe different types of intelligence.
3. Narrate about different theories of intelligence.
4. What is intelligence? Describe the theory of intelligence proposed by Guilford.
5. Describe about the information processing theory of intelligence.
6. Compare between factor analytic and information processing theory of intelligence.
7. Write the Educational implications of the study of different theories of intelligence.

Short Answer Type

1. What is Intelligence?
2. Write the nature of intelligence.
3. What is uni-factor theory of intelligence?
4. What is Two-factor theory of intelligence?
5. State the multifactor theory of intelligence.
6. What is theory of fluid-crystallized intelligence?
7. What is SI model of Guilford in intelligence?
8. Write about the multiple intelligence theory of Gardner?
9. Distinguish between Verbal and Non verbal test of intelligence.
10. What is IQ?
11. What is abstract intelligence?
12. Distinguish between concrete and abstract intelligence.

Objective Type

Select correct answer out of the given four alternatives.

1. Who is the Psychologist, stated about multifactor theory of intelligence?
   (a) Watson (b) Thorndike (c) Piaget (d) Cattell
2. Who gave the concept of Uni-factor theory of intelligence?
   (a) Cattell (b) Horn (c) Piaget (d) Stern
3. Who gave the multiple intelligence theory?
   (a) P.F. Vernon (b) Guilford (c) Howard Gardner (d) Stern
4. Hierarchical theory of intelligence was given by,
   (a) Guilford (b) cattell (c) Thorndike (d) P.F. Vernon
5. Mental functioning theory of intelligence was given by,
   (a) Arther Jenson (b) Vernon (c) Guilford (d) Skinner

6. Which theory of intelligence is given by Cattell and Horn,
   (a) Two-factor theory (b) Uni-factor theory
   (c) Fluid-crystalized theory (d) Hierarchical theory
7. Who gave the concept of IQ for measuring intelligence?
   (a) William Stern (b) J.B. Watson (c) Charles spearman (d) R.B. Cattell
8. Idiots possess their IQ level of,
   (a) 25-49 (b) Below 25 (c) 50-69 (d) 70-79
9. Normal individuals possess IQ level of,
   (a) 90-109 (b) 70-79 (c) 110-119 (d) 120-139
10. Gifted individuals possess IQ level of,
   (a) 120-139 (b) 110-119 (c) 140-169 (d) Above 170

Answer Key

Q.1-b, Q.2-d, Q.3-c, Q.4-d, Q.5-a, Q.6-c, Q.7-a, Q.8-b, Q.9-a, and Q.10-c

CHAPTER-20

Long Answer Type

1. Define creativity. Describe about different theories of creativity.
2. Write different characteristics of creativity.

Short Answer Type

1. What do you mean by creativity?
2. What are the steps of creativity development?

Objective Type

Select the correct answer out of the given alternatives.

1. Psychoanalytic theory of creativity has been given by
   (a) Galton (b) Skinner (c) Freud (d) Pavlov
2. According to whom, awareness about the problem is a step of creative process?
   (a) Piaget (b) Torrance and Mayer (c) Wallas (d) Taylor
3. According to whom, incubation is a step of creative process?
   (a) Wallas (b) Tylore (c) Freud (d) Torrance

Answer Key

Q.1-c, Q.2-b, and Q.3-a

CHAPTER-21

Long Answer Type

1. What do you mean by anxiety? Describe different types of anxiety disorders.
2. What is anxiety disorder? What are the symptoms of anxiety disorder?
3. What is curiosity? What are strategies a teacher can apply to develop the curiosity of his students?

Short Answer Type

1. What is anxiety disorder?
2. Write the symptoms of anxiety disorder.
3. What is curiosity?
4. Write the importance of curiosity in life.

Objective Type

Select the correct answer out of the four alternatives given.

1. Pyrophobia means,
   (a) Fire (b) Water (c) Food (d) High place

2. Hydrophobia means,
   (a) Water (b) Fire (c) Loneliness (d) Darkness
3. Agrophobia means,
   (a) Water (b) Agriculture (c) Open place (d) Fire
4. Noctophobia means
   (a) Open place (b) Darkness (c) High place (d) Water
5. Astrophobia means,
   (a) Thunder (b) Fire (c) Water (d) Air

Answer Key

Q.1-a, Q.2-a, Q.3-c, Q.4-b, and Q.5-a

CHAPTER-22

Long Answer Type

1. Define attention. Write different types of attention.
2. Describe the factors influencing attention in learning.
3. Write the effect of attention in learning.
4. Describe the theories of attention.

Short Answer Type

1. What is attention?
2. What is sustained attention?
3. What is attention distraction?
4. What is volitional attention?
5. What is non-volitional attention?
6. What is the relation between attention and interest?
7. What do you mean by span of attention?

Objective Type

Select correct answer out of the given four alternatives.

1. Who is the pioneer of filter theory of attention?
   (a) Skinner (b) McCelland (c) Donald Broadbent (d) Norman
2. Who is the pioneer of Late Selection theory of attention?
   (a) Skinner (b) McCelland (c) Donald Broadbent (d) Norman

Answer Key

Q.1-c, Q.2-d

CHAPTER-23

Long Answer Type

1. What do you mean by interest? Justify your statement about any relationship between learning and interest of the learners.
2. Write about the relationship between attention and interest.
3. Write the techniques of arousing interest in the learners.

Short Answer type

1. What is interest in learning?
2. What is attention in Learning?
3. What is inborn interest?
4. What is derived interest?

CHAPTER-24

Long Answer Type

1. What is emotion? Write different types of emotions with suitable examples.
2. Write the natures of emotion and kinds of emotional expressions on body.
3. Describe different theories of emotion.

Short Answer type

1. What is emotion?
2. What do you mean by emotional maturity?

Objective Types

Choose correct answer out of the given four alternatives.

1. What is not a positive emotion?
   a) Love (b) Gregariousness (c) Fear (d) Amusement
2. What is not a negative emotion?
   a) Anger (b) Fear (c) Disgust (d) Love
3. What is a reflection of emotional expression?
   (a) Change in facial appearance (b) Change in eating habit
   (c) Change in Playing habit (d) Change in writing habit
4. Who said that emotions develop from physiological reaction?
   (a) Cannon-Bard (b) James-Lange
   (c) Schachter-Singer (d) none of these
5. Whose theory of emotion stressed on thalamus and hypothalamus for causing emotional reactions?
   (a) Cannon-Bard (b) James-Lange
   (c) Schachter-Singer (d) none of these

Answer Key

Q.1-c, Q.2-d, Q.3-a, Q.4-b, and Q.5-a

CHAPTER-25

Long Answer Type

1. What is emotional intelligence? How it is related to one's emotion?
2. Write the attributes of emotional intelligence.

Short Answer type

1. What are the attributes of emotional intelligence?
2. What do you mean by emotional maturity?
3. How can you measure emotional intelligence?

CHAPTER-26

Long Answer Type

1. What is Motivation? Describe how motivation is related to learning?
2. Write different types of Motivation.
3. Narrate about different theories of motivation and their contribution.
4. Write the factors affecting motivation.
5. Write the techniques to arouse motivation of the learners.

Short Answer Type

1. What do you mean by motive?
2. What is intrinsic motivation?

3. What is extrinsic motivation?
4. What is Locus of control?
5. What is Self-actualization?
6. What is a esteem need according to Maslow?
7. What is safety and security need?

Objective Type

Select correct answer out of the given four alternatives.

1. How many types of needs are reflected in the Maslow's hierarchy of needs?
   (a) Five (b) Four (c) Seven (d) Six
2. Who has contributed the instinct theory of motivation?
   (a) Freud (b) Maslow (c) MacCelland (d) McDougall
3. Who is the profounder of attribution theory of motivation?
   (a) Freud (b) Weinner (c) MacCelland (d) McDougall
4. Which kind of motivation results when followed by reward?
   (a) Extrinsic motivation
   (b) Intrinsic motivation
   (c) Partly Extrinsic motivation
   (d) Both extrinsic and intrinsic motivation
5. Punishment act as a condition for,
   (a) Partly intrinsic motivation (b) both intrinsic and extrinsic
   (c) Intrinsic motivation (d) extrinsic motivation

Answer Key

Q.1-a, Q.2-d, Q.3-b, Q.4-a, and Q.5-d.

CHAPTER-27

Long Answer Type

1. Define memory. Write about the different factors of memory.
2. Describe the factors affecting human memory. Write the measures to promote the memory of children.
3. Discuss about different kinds of memory.
4. What is forgetting?. What factors cause forgetting in the children?
5. Discuss different theories of retention and forgetting.

Short Answer Type

1. What do you mean by recognition?
2. What is trace-change theory about the retention and forgetting?
3. What is forgetting?
4. Write how motivation relates to memory?
5. Distinguish between retention and forgetting.

Objective Type

Choose the right answer out of the given alternatives.

1. Which one is a condition for good learning?
   (a) Climatic condition (b) Personal condition
   (c) Good memory (d) good forgetting
2. Which one is a measuring instrument of memory?
   (a) Learning (b) Motivation (c) Recall (d) Training
3. Which one is helpful for building memory?
   (a) Action (b) practice (c) knowledge (d) forgetting

4. Who is the Psychologist studied and gave the Curve of forgetting?
   (a) Thorndike (b) Gestalt (c) Munn (d) Ebbinghause
5. Which is not good for building permanent memory?
   (a) Casual learning (b) Logical learning
   (c) Rote learning (d) impersonate learning

Answer Key

Q.1. (c), Q.2. (c), Q.3. (b), Q.4. (d), Q.5. (c)

CHAPTER-28

Long Answer Type

1. What do you mean about transfer of training? Describe the factors that affect transfer of training.
2. Describe about different theories of transfer of learning.
3. Define transfer of learning. Write about different types of transfer of learning.
4. Describe about the techniques to be adopted by a teacher to promote transfer of learning for his students.

Short Answer type

1. What is positive transfer of training?
2. What is Zero transfer of training?
3. Write briefly on the theory of identical elements supporting transfer of training.
4. What is the theory of transposition in Transfer of training?
5. What is the theory of generalization in transfer of training?

Objective Type

Choose the correct answer out of the given four alternatives.

1. Who coined the theory of identical elements in transfer of training?
   (a) Woodworth, (b) Skinner (c) Herbert (d) E.L. Thorndike
2. Who said that transfer of training holds good by the theory of identical components?
   (a) Piaget (b) Woodworh (c) E.L. Thorndike (d) None of these
3. What is right for negative transfer of learning?
   (a) Learning of one field helps to learn in another field
   (b) Learning of one field interferes in learning of another field
   (c) Learning of one field neither helps nor interferes in the learning of another field
   (d) None of these
4. Theory of transposition in transfer of learning was the contributed by,
   (a) Cognitive psychologists (b) Behaviourists
   (c) Gestalt psychologists (d) None of these

Answer Keys

Q.1-(d), Q.2-(b), Q.3-(b), Q.4-(c)

CHAPTER-29

Long Answer Type

1. What is cultural shaping? Write how cultural shaping takes place?
2. What do you mean by cultural transmission? Write about the role different social agencies in cultural transmission.
3. What is group dynamics? Describe the role of a teacher in a group dynamics.
4. Describe the conditions of a class room climate. Write the techniques to improve the quality of a class room.

5. Write the characteristics of teacher effectiveness. Write the different criterions of assessing teacher effectiveness.
6. Describe the different types of teaching skills an effective teacher should possess.

Short Answer Type

1. What is acculturation?
2. What is Enculturation?
3. Briefly write the role of Mass Medias in cultural transmission.
4. What do you mean about cultural diversity in the classroom?
5. What is skill of explanation?
6. What is product based assessment techniques of teacher effectiveness?
7. What is process based techniques of teacher effectiveness?
8. What is presage based assessment techniques of teacher effectiveness?

Objective Type

Choose the correct answer out of the given alternatives.

1. What is the primary social agency in the process of Socialization?
   (a) Religious Places (b) Mass Medias (c) Home (d) School
2. What is called as a miniature Society?
   (a) Family (b) Church (c) Press (d) School
3. Socialization process is a,
   (a) Narrower Process (b) Long term process
   (c) Life long process (d) none of these
4. Judging teacher effectiveness through learning outcomes is called as
   (a) Process based evaluation
   (b) Product based evaluation
   (c) Presage based evaluation
   (d) none of these
5. Judging teacher effectiveness through personal characteristics is called as
   (a) Product based (b) Process based
   (c) Presage based (d) none of these

Answer keys

Q.1-c, Q.2-d, Q.3.c, Q.4-b, and Q.5-c

CHAPTER-30

Long Answer Type

1. What do you mean by exceptional children? Write about the techniques of identification of exceptional children.
2. What are the different types of exceptional children? Write about the educational provisions for physically exceptional children for their development.
3. What do you understand about hearing impaired children? Write different educational provisions for their learning and development.
4. What is an emotionally exceptional child? How can you recognize these children and rehabilitate them?
5. What is delinquency? What factors lead to develop delinquency in the children? Write the educational provisions for the delinquents.

Short Answer Type

1. Write the characteristics of physically impaired children.
2. Write the characteristics of mentally retarded children?
3. Write the methods of identification and characteristics of the slow learners.

4. Who are the backward children?
5. Who are the visually impaired children? Write the characteristics of these children.
6. Write the educational provisions for the delinquents to make them adjusted and developed.
7. Who are the gifted children? Write the characteristics of the gifted children.
8. What educational programmes are suitable for the gifted children for their adjustment and development?
9. What is behavioural disorder? Write the techniques to detect the children suffering from behavioural disorders.
10. What is the difference between IQ and EQ. write the techniques to determine IQ and EQ

Objective Type

Select correct answer out of the given alternatives..

1. What is the EQ range of backward children?
   (a) Above 85 (b) below 85 (c) Above 75 (d) Below 75
2. What is Chronological age?
   (a) Actual mental age (b) Actual age
   (c) Approximate age (d) Middle age
3. What is the IQ range of gifted children?
   (a) Above 140 (b) Below 120 (c) 90-110 (d) 110-120
4. Delinquency is a
   (a) Mental problem (b) Political problem
   (c) Social problem (d) Economic problem
5. Behavioural disorder is seen in the
   (a) Normal children (b) Socially adjusted children
   (c) Emotionally exceptional children (d) Visually impaired children

Answer Key

Q.1-b, Q.2-b, Q.3-a, Q.4-c and Q.5-c